AF681985

Tightening the Reins of Justice in America

Contributions in Legal Studies
Series Editor: *Paul L. Murphy*

The American Codification Movement: A Study of Antebellum Legal Reform
Charles M. Cook

Crime and Punishment in Revolutionary Paris
Antoinette Wills

American Legal Culture, 1908-1940
John W. Johnson

Governmental Secrecy and the Founding Fathers: A Study in Constitutional Controls
Daniel N. Hoffman

Torture and English Law: An Administrative and Legal History from the Plantagenets to the Stuarts
James Heath

Essays on New York Colonial Legal History
Herbert S. Johnson

The Origins of the American Business Corporation, 1784-1855: Broadening the Concept of Public Service During Industrialization
Ronald E. Seavoy

Prologue to Nuremberg: The Politics and Diplomacy of Punishing War Criminals of the First World War
James F. Willis

The Network of Control: State Supreme Courts and State Security Statutes, 1920-1970
Carol E. Jenson

Drugs and Information Control: The Role of Men and Manipulation in the Control of Drug Trafficking
Jerald W. Cloyd

State Supreme Courts: Policymakers in the Federal System
Mary Cornelia Porter and G. Alan Tarr, editors

The Future of Our Liberties: Perspectives on the Bill of Rights
Stephen C. Halpern, editor

Tightening the Reins of Justice in America

A Comparative Analysis of the Criminal Jury Trial in England and the United States

MICHAEL H. GRAHAM

CONTRIBUTIONS IN LEGAL STUDIES, NUMBER 26

GREENWOOD PRESS
WESTPORT, CONNECTICUT • LONDON, ENGLAND

Library of Congress Cataloging in Publication Data

Graham, Michael H.
Tightening the reins of justice in America.

(Contributions in legal studies, ISSN 0147-1074 ; no. 26)
Bibliography: p.
Includes index.
1. Criminal procedure—Great Britain. 2. Trials (Robbery)—England—Birmingham. 3. Criminal procedure—United States. I. Title. II. Series.
KD8329.G7 1983 345.42'05 82-12029
ISBN 0-313-23598-8 (lib. bdg.) 344.2055

Copyright © 1983 by Michael H. Graham

All rights reserved. No portion of this book may be reproduced, by any process or technique, without the express written consent of the publisher.

Library of Congress Catalog Card Number: 82-12029
ISBN: 0-313-23598-8
ISSN: 0147-1074

First published in 1983

Greenwood Press
A division of Congressional Information Service, Inc.
88 Post Road West, Westport, Connecticut 06881

Printed in the United States of America

10 9 8 7 6 5 4 3 2 1

Copyright Acknowledgment

Excerpts have been reprinted from Thomas A. Mauet, *Fundamentals of Trial Techniques* (Little, Brown & Co., 1980) with permission of Little, Brown & Co. and Thomas A. Mauet.

To my children Laura, Lisa, and Lee.

CONTENTS

FIGURES AND TABLES

FIGURES

TABLES

PREFACE

Beginning December 1980, I spent several months at the Institute of Judicial Administration, University of Birmingham, Birmingham, England, as a Hays-Fulbright Research Fellow. After seven years of practice as a litigator, principally in New York City, and seven years as a law professor concentrating on trial practice, evidence, and procedure at the University of Illinois, I intended to spend my sabbatical in England observing the criminal jury trial process in action. I wanted to pay particular attention to the relationship between the division of the bar into solicitor and barrister and the operation of rules of trial procedure, practice, and evidence. In addition, I planned to compare the English criminal jury trial process with the procedures employed in the United States and to observe the effect such variations in practice had upon the outcome of the trial. I also intended to note the fairness of the English process as a whole. Most importantly, I was hopeful that an in-depth study of the English criminal jury trial process would suggest reforms for a more effective and efficient criminal jury trial in America. In sum, I hoped the English criminal jury trial would provide an awareness of procedures for use in the United States to tighten the reins of justice. In the course of the project, I discovered that several American practices merited consideration for incorporation into the English criminal jury trial. This book is the result of my observations.

It was my desire to isolate, with the cooperation and assistance of those involved in the day-to-day operations of the criminal justice system in Birmingham, a representative case file (to the extent any case can be termed representative) and to study the case from arrest through verdict. I began the process in December 1980, spending many hours in the public gallery of the Victoria Law Courts, the Crown Court for Birmingham. During the same period, I thoroughly digested the few, and there are only a few, general works describing the jury trial system in England. I also carefully reviewed both *Cross on Evidence* and Archbold, *Pleading, Evidence and Practice in Criminal Cases* (1979). In mid-January, with the cooperation of Mr. Ian Manson, Chief Prosecuting Solicitor of Birmingham, I spent several days with various members of his staff discussing and observing pretrial procedures in the Magistrates' Court and trial procedures in the Crown Court. For most of the time I consulted Robert Dean, the assistant in charge of the Crown Court Division. After completing my view of the practice of the prosecuting solicitor's office in Birmingham, I spent considerable time in the company of Mr. George Jonas, a prominent solicitor specializing in the defense of criminal cases, and his legal executive, Graham Wharton. I not only had the opportunity to discuss various matters with these gentlemen, I also accompanied them at the Magistrates' Court.

Following this two-month period of observation, questioning, and study, with the assistance of Messrs. Dean and Jonas, I selected the case of *Regina v. David Fisher* in late January 1981 for in-depth study. Mr. Fisher was accused of robbing a bank during March of 1980. His trial was scheduled to begin February 9, 1981. We made immediate arrangements, through Mr. Norman Jones, Clerk of 3rd set of Chambers in Birmingham (hereinafter referred to as Chamber 3), for me to meet counsel for both sides prior to trial. All three counsel, Mr. Escott Cox, Q.C., Mr. Coleman Treacy, acting as his Junior, representing Mr. Fisher, and Mr. David Jones, representing the Crown, are members of Chamber 3. At the same time, we made arrangements with the Courts Administrator for the Midland and Oxford Circuit, Mr. Clive Pratley, and with Mr. David Warner, Courts Administrator for the Victoria Law Courts, to make a transcript of all proceedings conducted at the trial of David Fisher. The court reporter transcribed all statements at trial, including matters not normally recorded in England, such as the jury selection process and speeches of counsel.

During the remaining months of my stay in Birmingham, and during the many months spent completing the manuscript upon my return, each and every one of the aforementioned individuals continued to display exceptional cooperation in all aspects of the project. Robert Dean of the Crown and Graham Wharton for the defense provided copies of files. Mr. David Warner provided copies of exhibits. In addition, numerous inquiries concerning both the case of *Regina v. David Fisher* and the general nature of criminal trials in England received prompt attention from Messrs. Cox, Dean, Jones, Treacy, and Wharton.

Three words of special thanks. First, to all three barristers, who not only cooperated with me fully, but went beyond expectation in agreeing to perform a mock examination of David Fisher, with Coleman Treacy portraying Mr. Fisher, at the conclusion of the trial. We did this for the sake of completeness after it was decided for tactical reasons that Mr. Fisher would not testify at trial. Second, to Professor Ian Scott, Director of the Institute of Judicial Administration, University of Birmingham, whose support was instrumental throughout this research project. Finally, to Dr. Michael McConville of the Faculty of Law, University of Birmingham, whose knowledge and guidance with respect to the criminal justice system in England proved invaluable.

Tightening the Reins of Justice in America

1 INTRODUCTION

With increasing frequency during the last twenty years, elected officials, lawyers, and judges in the United States have all spoken out concerning the rise in crime on the streets and the need for society to respond by creating a more effective and cost-efficient criminal justice system. However, having once assumed this stance, potential reformers have generally been at a loss to suggest meaningful remedial action. Proposals almost invariably involve altering sentencing procedures, redefining crimes, creating new categories of custodial care, providing more money to hire policemen, providing job training in prison, and so on. One also finds jurisdictions previously favoring indeterminate sentences moving to fixed sentences, while other jurisdictions previously favoring fixed sentences move toward indeterminate sentences. Legislation to amend the federal criminal code has been before Congress for much of the period. None of these responses is new. Each has been tried over and over again. In addition to these traditional methods of supposedly tightening up on crime, occasional proposals are heard to eliminate the exclusionary rule barring introduction of illegally seized evidence.

Concern with the rising tide of crime has led many advocates of reform to look to the system of criminal justice in England for guidance. English visitors to America bring with them a great respect, and an even greater desire to communicate a great respect, for the quality of British justice and its effectiveness in punishing the guilty. They express the British belief that their system of justice is the best in the world, their policemen are the best, their barristers are the best, and, most fervently espoused, their judges are the best. The British discuss judges such as Denning and Devlin with a degree of admiration no current U.S. Supreme Court justice comes close to commanding in America. In addition, English visitors perceive America as a violent country, where the police cannot control crime in the cities and where the court system, for reasons most often unknown and of little concern, often permits the guilty to be set free. Public media in England highlight American problems in dealing with crime at every opportunity. Since many Americans share the same feelings, citizens of both countries, whether lawyers or laymen, come to any discussion of the American response to crime on similar footing.

Of course, many of the Americans discussing comparative criminal procedure have traveled to London. They have asked directions of the London "Bobby" and have received a polite response in an appealing accent. One of the places to which American lawyers and judges frequently ask directions is the Old Bailey, the Central Criminal Court in London. Every year, hundreds of American lawyers and judges spend from five minutes to a couple of hours watching a criminal jury trial from the gallery of the Old Bailey in London. These lawyers, many if not most of whom are not trial lawyers and certainly not criminal trial lawyers by trade, are duly impressed by the majesty, dignity, and gentlemanliness of the proceedings they observe. They see the high court judge in a red robe and white wig high above several black-robed and white-wigged gentlemen taking turns eloquently addressing questions to witnesses in deep rich tones. They observe the defendant in the dock located at the far rear of the chamber. They are quite impressed. They ask, "Wouldn't it be nice if we in America could practice law, even criminal law, in such a grand manner?" These lawyers know that redesigning courtrooms and attiring participants in wigs and robes cannot be the whole difference. In light of these casual observations, they seize on an obvious difference in the practice of law between the two countries—division of the legal profession in England into solicitors and barristers. "Ah ha," they tell their friends upon their return, "we should consider adopting the division of the profession as a means of. . . . Well, ah, that is the way law was meant to be practiced."

This comparative study explores in detail the criminal jury trial process in England, including the role of the police, the functioning of the divided profession, and the operation of specific aspects of procedure, trial practice, and evidence. On the basis of the comparative analysis, specific suggestions are made for tightening the reins of justice in America. The vehicle chosen for this task is the case of *Regina v. David Fisher*, a trial which occurred in the Victoria Law Courts, Birmingham, on February 9, 10, and 11, 1981. Chapter 2 presents the basic facts surrounding the commission of a bank robbery on February 25, 1980. The subsequent arrest and interrogation of David Fisher, the search of his premises, and the denial of bail by the police are outlined for the convenience of the reader in Chapter 3. Chapter 4 sets forth the initial appearance by David Fisher in the Magistrates' Court, his remand, the selection of a place for trial, and the committal proceeding. Preparation for trial initially by solicitors for the Crown and the accused, and later by barristers briefed by both sides, is discussed in Chapter 5. Chapter 6 outlines generally the structure of the Crown Court trial, while Chapter 7 contains the transcript of the trial of David Fisher. The next two chapters, 8 and 9, provide, respectively, comments on the English criminal jury trial, followed by observations and recommendations for reform of the American criminal justice system based upon the foregoing comparative analysis. Last, Chapter 10 summarizes the overall conclusions reached.

An actual trial transcript is incorporated for several reasons. Use of a transcript presents an actual trial for examination, not only by the author, but by the reader as well. From the transcript, together with accompanying pre-trial information in the possession of the solicitor and barrister set forth in the appendices, experienced trial lawyers and judges in America can evaluate the author's comments as well as draw their own conclusions. Full transcripts in England are rare. Records on appeal usually consist of the transcript of the judge's summation, sometimes accompanied by selected segments of witness testimony; the record rarely includes a transcript of the testimony of every witness. Moreover, in England the reporter does not record either jury selection, known as jury vetting, or the opening or closing speeches of counsel. Thus, even when a full transcript is prepared for appeal, such items are not included. Special arrangements were made for the recording and transcription of these matters in the trial of David Fisher. In addition, the flavor of the trial, its civility, and its effectiveness in convicting the guilty can best be appreciated by means of a transcript; the best way to judge how something works is to observe it at work. Finally, use of a transcript of an actual trial helps focus on what is important—the overall thrust of the English criminal justice system and the jury trial in particular.

The case of *Regina v. David Fisher* was selected with various criteria in mind. First and foremost, the trial had to be representative in the broad perspective of a typical English criminal jury trial, to the extent any single trial may be said to be either typical or representative. In addition, the trial had to be relatively short by American standards, approaching the average trial time of 8.5 hours consumed for jury trials in England. Any longer trial would make presentation of the full trial transcript unmanageable. The project also required the cooperation of the solicitor and barrister of both the prosecution and defense. Cooperation had to extend not only to providing copies of pre-trial and trial documents, but also to the opportunity to discuss the case with the solicitor and barrister for the defense before and during trial and with the barristers for both sides at its conclusion. Finally, a case that contained a statement of the accused was sought to highlight the operation of the Judges' Rules compared to *Miranda* warnings. As an extra bonus, the case selected also contained a search of the accused's room without a warrant leading to the seizure of relevant items. During the trial of David Fisher, counsel, in consultation with Mr. Fisher, decided the accused would not testify. In this respect the trial cannot be said to be representative because the accused testifies in an overwhelming majority of cases in England. In order to remedy this situation to the extent possible, counsel conducted a mock examination of David Fisher at the conclusion of the trial.

At several points in this book, reference is made to statistics relating to English criminal justice. Unless otherwise indicated, the statistical information was derived from one of three sources: *Criminal Statistics*, England and Wales 1977; *Judicial Statistics*, 1978; or *Report of the Royal Commission on Criminal Procedure*, its *Law and Procedure Supplement*; and *Research Studies* 1981.

2 THE CRIME

On Monday, February 25, 1980, at approximately 3:00 P.M., David Fisher robbed £3,800 from the Midland Bank located on the A41 at the junction of Great Hampton Street and Wells Street in Hockley, Birmingham.

The Midland Bank is situated in a mainly manufacturing district on the fringe of Birmingham's jewelry quarter, from which it draws most of its customers. The bank's interior is modern and well lit, with security glass and grills at each of its three tills. At about 3:00 P.M. on Monday, February 25, 1980, Miss Yvonne Gardener, a twenty-year-old bank clerk, was alone at the counter, serving at the center till, when she saw a man enter the bank. There were no other customers present in the bank. After about a minute the man approached the center till. After Miss Gardener spoke to the man, he promptly produced a gun from his pocket and said, "Money, money," indicating Miss Gardener's till. She then took from a drawer a bundle of bank notes, later ascertained to be £3,800, and handed them to the man. He placed the money in a white plastic bag with red letters and ran out of the bank into Wells Street. As he escaped, the man passed Mr. Norman Witham, the bank manager, who was walking along Wells Street in the opposite direction. Miss Gardener and Mr. Witham were the only persons located by the police who saw the robber.

On the afternoon of the bank robbery, Yvonne Gardener accompanied the police to the police station, where an identikit picture, sometimes referred to as a photofit, was compiled from her description of the robber. She also gave a written statement describing the incident and the perpetrator. Figure 1 shows the identikit picture of the robber produced from the description of Yvonne Gardener, referred to as Exhibit 11 at trial.

In her statement, Miss Gardener first described the robber as a "coloured man." She later stated:

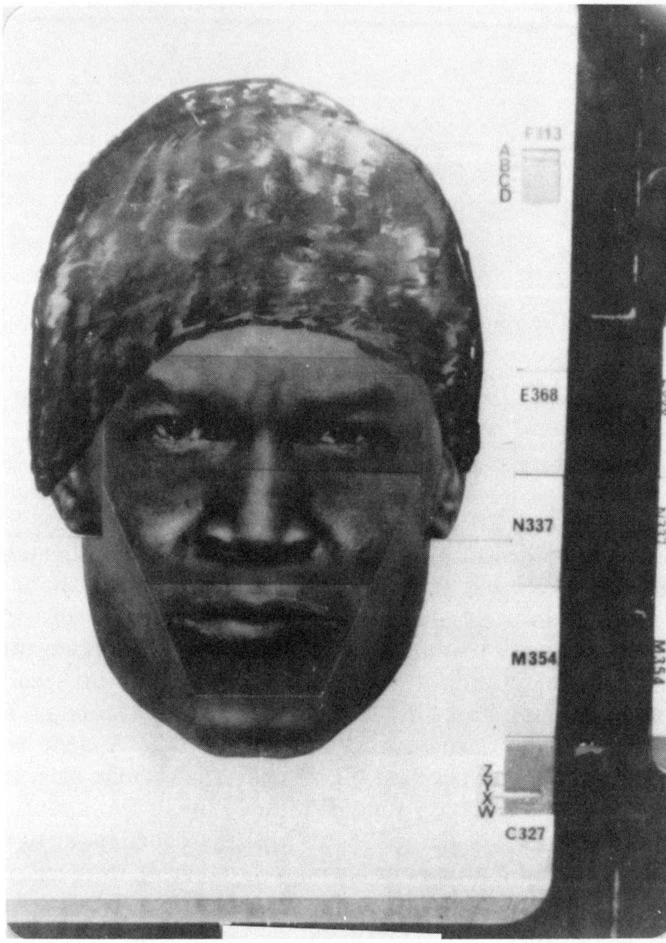

Figure 1
Identikit Picture of the Robber

I describe him as about 25 years old, 5′10″ tall, he was either Asian or a very light skinned West Indian. He had a dark green woolen hat over his head, covering his hair and his ears. He had dark brown eyes, a long wide mouth, but not thick lips.
He was wearing a dark khaki jacket, plain in style. I think I could recognize him again.

On the same day, Mr. Norman Witham described his recollection of the events in a written statement to the police:

At about a few minutes to 3 o'clock Monday, 25th February, 1980, I parked my vehicle in the car park of my bank, having returned from Wolverhampton. I then had to walk from my car along Wells Street to the bank. It was raining and I was carrying my umbrella. I was walking along Wells Street on the same side of the bank, I was about 20 yards from the front door of the bank. At this stage my attention was centered on the telephone engineers who were working on electrical equipment housed on the outside wall of the bank. As I was watching the engineers I saw a man run past them towards me on the same pavement as myself.

I would describe this man as late teens or early twenties, about 5 '5 " to 5 '6 ", slim build. He struck me as being dark skinned, possibly coloured. He was wearing a dark green woolen hat pulled down over his ears, the hat was close to his head, suggesting he had short hair. He had a khaki coloured short jacket similar to an anorak or combat type jacket. It had smooth material and possibly two pockets at the hips. He was wearing dark trousers, gave me the impression they were short possibly just above his ankles. They appeared to be trouser material as opposed to jeans or corduroy. The style was parallel, not particularly tight fitting. His shoe wear gave me the impression they were dark soft soled boots. As this man ran past me his arms were crossed just below his chest level as though he was cradling something.

As a result of these descriptions and the identikit picture, the police commenced searching for an Asian or light-skinned West Indian as the perpetrator of the bank robbery.

David Fisher was born on January 3, 1947, in Birmingham. He is single with no fixed address. He was educated at a secondary modern school until leaving at the age of fifteen.[1] After leaving school, interspersed with custodial sentences, David Fisher had occasional odd jobs as a guilder's laborer or casual worker. He also worked occasionally as a shop assistant in his father's iron mongery business. For much of his adult life, however, David Fisher had been unemployed. At the time of his arrest, he was receiving £25.10 unemployment benefit per week. David Fisher had a number of previous convictions, including a conviction for robbery in August 1976, for which he received a five-year custodial sentence. Upon his release in December 1979 until his arrest in March 1980, Fisher resided in an ex-offenders hostel at 155 Warwick Road in the Olton area of Birmingham.

David Fisher is white with a swarthy complexion. The pictures taken of David Fisher upon his arrest, referred to as Exhibit 12 at trial, appear in Figure 2.

NOTE

1. Generally speaking the education system in England may be described as follows: Children attend primary school through age eleven. In the last year of primary school, children take what is called the 11+ examination. Those passing the examination proceed to what is called grammar school, those not passing go to

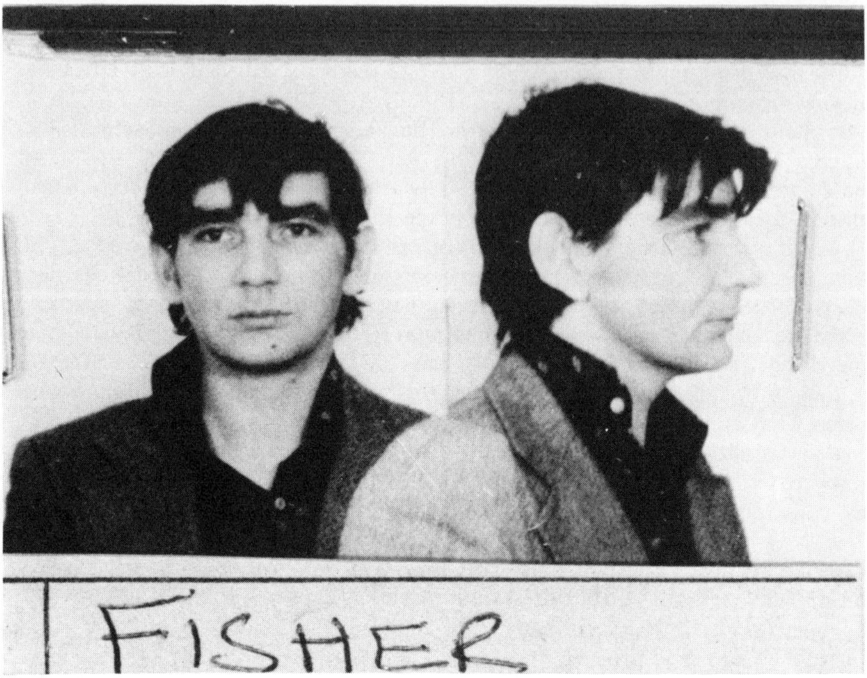

Figure 2
Pictures Taken of David Fisher upon His Arrest

secondary modern school. In some areas all students over the age of eleven attend what is called a comprehensive school. Students in all these categories of educational institution may take examinations for the General Certificate of Education, referred to as ordinary or "O" levels.

Students may drop out of school at age fifteen. Students complete their education at grammar school, secondary modern school, or comprehensive school at age sixteen.

Students desiring education beyond age sixteen may continue in a two-year program culminating in another set of examinations referred to as advanced or "A" levels. Students discontinuing their education at either age sixteen or before or after completing "A" levels are referred to as school leavers. In England, only about 12 percent of the population goes on to higher education. See Central Statistics Office, *Annual Abstract of Statistics* (1980), Table 5.7 at p. 127.

3 THE INVESTIGATION BY THE POLICE

The apprehension of David Fisher approximately one month after the robbery of the Midland Bank in Hockley provides the starting point for this comparative analysis. The discussion proceeds by setting forth in a chronological fashion the facts uninterrupted by commentary as they relate to the apprehension and subsequent charging of David Fisher with robbery. The flavor of the flow of events, the speed with which things progress, and the simplicity of procedure can best be appreciated in this manner. At the conclusion of this description, each of the three important aspects for comparative analysis, that is, the arrest, the interrogation, and the search and seizure, will be examined. Finally, the discussion turns to the availability of bail being granted by the police.

APPREHENSION

On Wednesday, March 19, 1980, at approximately 11:00 A.M., David Fisher arrived at the Birmingham International Airport on a flight from Dublin, Ireland. As part of the security check for suspected terrorists, airport security police detained him when they determined he had £1,358.07 in his possession and was unemployed. In response to a radio message, at 11:25 A.M., Police Constable (PC) Abolins, then assigned to the airport police unit, proceeded to the International Arrivals Lounge to question David Fisher. Detective Constable (DC) Sutcliffe joined PC Abolins shortly thereafter. In response to questions, Fisher told the officers that he had won the money gambling. DC Sutcliffe fold Fisher, "I am arresting you on suspicion of having stolen the money." DC Sutcliffe then cautioned Fisher by advising him that he was not obliged to say anything unless he wished to do so, but that whatever he did say may be put in writing and given in evidence.

Fisher was then taken to the Airport Police Station for questioning. After a series of questions seeking the names of persons from whom Fisher won the money and the location of the games, DC Sutcliffe advised Fisher that he was going to search his room and make inquiries at other addresses found in his possession. Fisher asked whether DC Sutcliffe was going to "turn over" all his friends and make life difficult for him. DC Sutcliffe responded that he was going to do his duty. After a few minutes for thought, Fisher admitted to the two police officers that he had acquired the money by robbing the Midland Bank in Hockley. Fisher then dictated a statement to DC Sutcliffe detailing the events concerning the bank robbery and signed the statement in the presence of two police officers. A typewritten version of the written statement, introduced at trial as Exhibit 6, is reproduced below.

WEST MIDLANDS POLICE

'L' Division, Birmingham Airport
19th March, 1980

STATEMENT OF DAVID FISHER B. 5.1.47
155 WARWICK ROAD, OLTON
UNEMPLOYED

I David Fisher wish to make a statement. I want someone to write down what I say. I have been told I need not say anything unless I wish to do so and that whatever I do say may be given in evidence.

(Signed) D. Fisher

I had been out drinking at a pub in the town. I'd got no money I hadn't paid any rent at the hostel because I'd blown it on beer. I'd got a starting pistol on me. I bought it from Bates's in the town. I was three parts drunk. First of all I looked in the Midland Bank in Hockley opposite Cannings there was a young girl talking to another bloke a cashier like but there was no customers. I walked in pointed the pistol at the girl and said, "Give us the money." She just handed over some money to me. I just ran round a few corners. I tried a telephone box to get a taxi but it was broke. I managed to get a taxi later and went to the hostel and then went and got something to eat. I stayed in and around Birmingham for a week or so and then last Tuesday I went across to Ireland and I have been there ever since. Just spending the money like a fool. I'm not absolutely positive but I think there was £4,300 I had in tenners and fivers apart from three brand new £1 notes. I know I've been stupid, what more can I say. I'm sorry.

(Signed) D. Fisher

I have read the above statement and I have been told that I can correct alter or add anything I wish. This statement is true. I have made it of my own free will.

(Signed) D. Fisher

Statement taken down by me at Birmingham Airport Police Station on Wednesday 19.3.80 commenced at 12.55 p.m. ended at 1.15 p.m.

(Signed) Thomas Sutcliffe DC 6455

(Witnessed By) D.S. Abolins PC 'L' 3398

After signing the statement, Fisher advised the police officers that the gun used in the robbery was in his room.

At the conclusion of the interrogation, David Fisher was placed in a holding cell. In the early afternoon, PC Abolins recovered from Fisher's room at 155 Warwick Road a "38" Chief Starting Pistol, containing six live and two used starting blanks, and one box of 6mm blank cartridges. David Fisher, the confiscated money, the items in David Fisher's possession at the time of his arrest, and the starting pistol with cartridges were all then taken to Steelhouse Lane Police Station, where the officer in charge of the investigation of the bank robbery, Detective Constable (DC) Pyke, was stationed.

Upon being informed of David Fisher's arrest and subsequent statement, DC Pyke, accompanied by Detective Constable (DC) Butler, also went to David Fisher's room at 155 Warwick Road. They removed several items, including a red woolen hat, a blue anorak, and two plastic bags. At 4:20 P.M. on the afternoon of March 19, 1980, DC Pyke, in the presence of DC Butler, cautioned David Fisher that he was not obliged to say anything unless he wished to do so, but whatever he did say would be taken down in writing and given in evidence. DC Pyke then asked, and David Fisher responded to, questions concerning the starting pistol, his route taken in fleeing the scene of the robbery, and his handling of the money. Fisher was asked to identify whether items in his possession at the time of his arrest, and items found in his room, were purchased with proceeds from the robbery. Fisher admitted wearing the blue anorak and red woolen hat during the robbery and placing the stolen money in one of the two plastic bags recovered from his room. Fisher then dictated and signed a statement detailing the foregoing. A typewritten version of the handwritten statement of David Fisher, introduced at trial as Exhibit 10, is reproduced below.

WEST MIDLANDS POLICE

Criminal Investigation Department,
'F' Division, Steelhouse Lane,
19th March, 1980

STATEMENT OF DAVID FISHER B. 5.1.1947
155 WARWICK ROAD, OLTON
UNEMPLOYED

4:35 p.m. I David FISHER wish to make a statement. I want someone to write down what I say. I have been told that I need not say anything unless I wish to do so and that anything I say may be given in evidence.

(Signed) D. Fisher

I've been spending like mad since I had the money from the Bank. I've spent a lot on booze and hotel bills. I bought the airline ticket to Dublin and back. Also train tickets and taxis. I bought the 2 rings you showed me with part of the money. I think they were £68 each. The watch was £53, the radio about £8. The doll was £9.99, the after shave £4.95. The fawn jacket was £10.99 I think. The brown suit was £39 I think it was and also the brown bag I bought. Also I bought the watcha-macallit was a couple of quid. These were all bought with the stolen money. The starting pistol you showed me is the one I used. The lucky seven bags you've got, it was one of them I put the money in. I was wearing the woolen hat you found. 4.50 p.m.

(Signed) D. Fisher

I have read the above statement and I have been told that I can correct alter or add anything I wish. This statement is true. I have made it of my own free will.

(Signed) D. Fisher

Statement taken down by me the undersigned at SHL Police Station at the dictation of the maker and signed by him in my presence after being invited to make any additions or alterations thereto.

(Signed) Christopher Butler DC 2253
(Witnessed By) John Pyke DC 7086

The officers then charged and cautioned Fisher, to which he made no reply.

On the basis of the gravity of the charge and the accused's bad record, the charging officer refused to grant bail. He set the initial appearance at the Magistrates' Court for March 20, 1980.

ARREST

When DC Sutcliffe arrested David Fisher at the airport on March 19, he did so under Section 2 of the Criminal Law Act 1969 which provides that, "Where a constable, with reasonable cause, suspects that an arrestable offense has been committed, he may arrest without warrant anyone whom he, with reasonable cause, suspects to be guilty of the offense." Theft, for which Fisher was originally arrested, and robbery, for which he was indicted, are both arrestable offenses.

Fisher was arrested by two police officers for theft based solely upon the knowledge that Fisher, an unemployed person, possessed a large sum of money and that Fisher claimed he had won the money gambling. The police officers making the arrest had no current knowledge of a robbery of the Midland Bank in Hockley and no facts with which to connect Fisher with any particular offense. Nevertheless, the police officers probably had reasonable cause to suspect that an arrestable offense had been committed and reasonable cause to suspect that David Fisher committed the offense as required by Section 2 of the Criminal Law Act 1969.

Reasonable cause to suspect an individual sufficient to justify an arrest is satisfied by evidence which might fall far short of that needed to justify subsequently charging the accused with a crime. Thus, the police in England apply two distinct standards. The first is reasonable cause to suspect justifying an arrest. The second is the acquisition of evidence which justifies charging the accused, consisting of evidence admissible at trial, if offered in the proper form with the proper foundation, sufficient to permit a reasonable jury to properly find the accused guilty beyond a reasonable doubt of the crime charged. Accordingly, a person can be charged by the police only if the police possess information which, when introduced in evidence in proper form with a proper foundation, would constitute a prima facie case. Lord Devlin, in the case of *Sharbin Bin Hussien v. Chong Fook Kam*,[1] explains that reasonable cause is a lower standard than information sufficient to prove a prima facie case. Reasonable cause may take into account matters that could not be put into evidence at all or matters that, although admissible, would not on their own prove the case. The circumstances of the case should be such that a reasonable man acting without passion or prejudice would fairly have suspected the person of having committed the offense. It is important that hasty or ill-advised police action should be avoided. If on the other hand the police hesitate too long to arrest a person when they have proper and sufficient ground for suspicion against him, they may lose the opportunity of arresting him or may enable him to destroy evidence. Suspicion arises at or near the starting point of an investigation of which the obtaining of prima facie proof is the end.

During the period between arrest and charge, the police interrogate the accused, seeking a confession. The police discharge between 10 to 20 percent of all individuals arrested for various reasons without charging them.[2] Unlike the United States, once the English police charge the accused, neither the police, the prosecuting solicitor, nor the barrister briefed in the case may terminate the matter without judicial action.

In the United States, a police officer could properly arrest David Fisher without a warrant if the police officer had probable cause, that is, possessed reasonable grounds to believe that a felony had been committed and that the person arrested committed the felony. Generally speaking, this standard is satisfied by information in the possession of a police officer sufficient "to warrant a man of prudence and caution in believing that the offense has been committed."[3] Information justifying a "reasonable ground to believe" that the accused committed a felony possesses greater probative value than information merely giving rise to a reasonable cause to "suspect" the same event.[4] No post-arrest procedure generally exists in the United States comparable to the "charging" decision made by the police in England. In most states, the court at the preliminary hearing judges whether there is sufficient evidence to proceed to trial against the foregoing reasonable grounds to believe standard. Thus, in the United States, in most instances, at no time prior to the presentation of evidence at trial is the prosecution's case judged against the standard for a prima facie case, that is, evidence sufficient to justify a reasonable jury in finding the accused guilty beyond a reasonable doubt. This contrasts with the dual standards of reasonable suspicion for arrest and prima facie evidence for charge employed in England. In short, law enforcement officials need less evidence to arrest but more evidence to introduce the matter into the court system in England than in the United States.

The practical result of the different standards applied in the two countries for arrest and charge is difficult to assess on a general basis. However, with respect to David Fisher, it is certainly clear that, while reasonable cause to suspect was present at the time of his arrest, an American court would find mere possession of money by an unemployed worker insufficient evidence to support a reasonable belief that a crime had been committed and that the defendant had committed the crime.

At the time of the arrest, DC Sutcliffe told David Fisher, "I am arresting you on suspicion of having stolen that money," referring to the £1,358.07 in Fisher's possession. Fisher was thus informed at the time of arrest of the grounds of the arrest; the advice failed in any respect to identify the particular incident involved because the police did not know of this fact at the time. Unless excused by reason of the arrested person making disclosure impossible, such as by fleeing the scene or resisting arrest, failure to advise an accused of the grounds for arrest renders the arrest unlawful.[5] An officer may correct a failure to inform an accused by subsequently informing him, making the arrest lawful.[6] The unlawfulness of the arrest for any reason has no effect, however, upon the introduction of evidence derived from the accused at his subsequent trial. The English do not employ concepts like the exclusionary rule[7] or the "fruit of the poisonous tree."[8] As stated by the House of Lords in *Regina v. Sang and Mangan*,[9] "The court is not concerned with how [such evidence] was obtained." Reliance in monitoring police compliance with law is placed upon a right, in theory, to bring a civil suit for false arrest and a right to complain to the Police Complaint Board. Complaints filed against individual police officers may lead to disciplinary action. The lack of practical effect such theoretical constraints have upon improper police action needs no elaboration.[10] As will be seen in later discussion involving confessions and search and seizure, the practice of permitting introduction of evidence derived from unlawful conduct of the police pervades the English criminal justice system.

CONFESSION

The Facts

In the course of interrogation on March 19, 1980, David Fisher made four separate confessions to the police. During the interviews conducted by PC Abolins and DC Sutcliffe at the airport, Fisher first confessed verbally to robbing the Midland Bank in Hockley and then signed his detailed statement, Exhibit 6. Similarly, during questioning by DC Butler and DC Pyke at Steelhouse Lane Police Station later the same day, Fisher once again made damaging admissions followed by a signed statement, Exhibit 10.

At a very early stage of the initial interview at the airport, Fisher maintained that he had won the money found in his possession by gambling. DC Sutcliffe, on the basis of reasonable cause to suspect that Fisher had committed an arrestable offense, immediately arrested Fisher and advised him that he was being arrested on suspicion of having stolen the money. DC Sutcliffe then cautioned Fisher, as required by the Judges' Rules:

> You are not obliged to say anything unless you wish to do so but what you say may be put into writing and given in evidence.

DC Sutcliffe continued to question Fisher, who at one point, according to Sutcliffe, responded, "I want to see a solicitor and I'm saying no more to you until you let me see one." DC Sutcliffe, in testimony at trial, stated that he replied: "Yes, you will be able to have a solicitor if that is what you want." DC Sutcliffe continued to question Fisher, who after a few minutes admitted the bank robbery. David Fisher contended that he told the officers he wanted to see his solicitor on many occasions and told them further he would not answer any questions until they let him see his solicitor. Fisher contended that the police laughed in response to his statement, advising him he would have to answer their questions first. Fisher described the attitude of the police to his request to see his solicitor as one of not wanting a "brief interfering" until he had confessed. The police did not charge David Fisher until the conclusion of the interview with DC Butler and DC Pyke. He was then once again cautioned in accordance with the Judges' Rules:

> Do you wish to say anything? You are not obliged to say anything unless you wish to do so but whatever you say will be taken down in writing and may be given in evidence.

Fisher made no reply.

In the recreated examination of David Fisher, based upon the Proofs of Evidence, Appendix VII,[11] counsel inquired into the reasons behind his signing two statements, both of which he asserted were false. Fisher maintained:

> Well it was hopeless. I mean, they wouldn't let me see my brief or anything. They said, you know, I'd got to answer their questions and they said they'd turn over all my mates and make life difficult for people I knew, and I didn't want that to happen so I thought, well, I'll tell them what they want to know because I knew a bit about it from this Paki, and I thought I'll tell them what they want to know and I can prove my innocence later in court, so I thought it wouldn't do any harm to sign it. I know it sounds stupid, now but that is what I thought at the time. I thought they'd keep me there forever and not let me see anyone.

Thus, Fisher maintained his confession was the direct result of intimidation threatened to his friends, his fear of being denied bail by the police and being kept in custody for a long time without appearing before the court, and denial by the police of his repeated request to see a solicitor.

The Law

The law and practice with respect to confessions is an area of great complexity, and more than a little confusion, in both the United States and England. In both countries, the general requirement of admissibility based upon "voluntariness" governs confessions. Moreover, the companion notion that rules of practice are needed to protect the accused's privilege against self-incrimination, as referred to in the United States, and right of silence, as referred to in England, against intrusion by the police during the interrogation process also controls admissibility of confessions.

AMERICAN APPROACH

In the United States, to be admissible as evidence, a confession must be both voluntary and taken in compliance with *Miranda*. The concept of voluntariness incorporates three protected interests, the violation of any one of which results in the confession being inadmissible. Confessions are considered involuntary if they

> (a) [are] of doubtful reliability because of the practices used to obtain them; (b) were obtained by offensive police practices even if reliability was not in question (e.g., where there is strong corroborating evidence); or (c) were obtained under circumstances in which the defendant's free choice was significantly impaired even if the police did not resort to offensive practices.[12]

Regarding the reliability of a confession, application of the voluntariness test requires examination of the "totality of the circumstances" surrounding each confession. If, upon examination of the totality of the circumstances, the court concludes that the accused's will was overborne and his capacity for self-determination critically impaired, it will prohibit introduction of the confession at trial.[13] Factors deemed most important are physical abuse,[14] threats,[15] extensive questioning,[16] incommunicado detention,[17] and denial of the right to consult with counsel.[18] Courts also examine the characteristics and status of the suspect, such as his lack of education,[19] emotional instability,[20] youth,[21] or sickness.[22] Also considered is whether the statement was extracted by any direct or implicit promises or by the exertion of any improper influence.[23] Application of the foregoing factors in any particular case obviously leads to imprecise rulings on whether the accused's capacity for self-determination has been critically impaired.

With respect to employment of the voluntariness concept to deter improper police conduct, in *Rogers v. Richmond*[24] the defendant's confession was obtained after the police pretended to order that his ailing wife be arrested for questioning. The state court ruled that the statement need not be excluded if the artifice or deception was not calculated to procure an untrue statement. The Supreme Court disagreed, emphasizing that convictions based upon coerced confessions must be overturned "not because such confessions are unlikely to be true but because the methods used to extract them offend an underlying principle in the enforcement of our criminal law: that ours is an accusatorial and not an inquisitorial system."[25] Of course, decisions such as *Rogers* provide little guidance to lower courts and the police in determining the parameters of proper and improper police conduct regarding the accused's privilege against self-incrimination.

Finally, *Townsend v. Sain*[26] highlights the objective of requiring the confession be the result of the accused's "free and rational choice," even in the absence of offensive police practices. In *Townsend*, the ailing defendant had received a drug with the properties of a truth serum, after which he gave a confession in response to questioning by police unaware of the drug's effect. Although the police did not obtain the confession by conscious wrongdoing, and although the confession apparently was reliable, the Court held its use impermissible: "Any questioning by police officers which in fact produces a confession which is not the product of free intellect renders that confession inadmissible."[27]

As is obvious from even this cursory exploration, the concept of "voluntariness," as applied to confessions analyzed on a case-by-case basis, fails to provide an effective means of ensuring the admissibility of only reliable confessions resulting from the free and rational choice of an accused whose capacity for self-determination was not critically impaired by improper police conduct or otherwise. In recognition of this fact, in 1966 the Supreme Court in *Miranda v. Arizona*[28] shifted its emphasis for achieving the interests protected by the voluntariness test from case-by-case analysis to specific guidelines for the police. The Court designed these guidelines to advise the accused of his privilege against self-incrimination as enforced by on-the-scene counsel in place of after-the-fact judicial scrutiny. In practice, *Miranda* warnings also serve to enhance the likelihood that any purported confession or admission of the defendant was actually made.

The operation of the rules of conduct set forth for police interrogation in *Miranda* have been summarized in Israel and LaFave, *Criminal Procedure: Constitutional Limitations* as follows:

(1) These rules are required to safeguard the privilege against self-incrimination, and thus must be followed in the absence of "other procedures which are at least as effective in apprising accused persons of their right of silence and in assuring a continuous opportunity to exercise it."

(2) These rules apply "when the individual is first subjected to police interrogation while in custody at the station or otherwise deprived of his freedom of action in any significant way," and not to "general on-the-scene questioning as to facts surrounding a crime or other general questioning of citizens in the fact-finding process" or to "volunteered statements of any kind."

(3) Without regard to his prior awareness of his rights, if a person in custody is to be subjected to questioning, "he must first be informed in clear and unequivocal terms that he has the right to remain silent," so that the ignorant may learn of this right and so that the pressures of the interrogation atmosphere will be overcome for those previously aware of the right.

(4) The above warning "must be accompanied by the explanation that anything said can and will be used against the individual in court," so as to ensure that the suspect fully understands the consequences of forgoing the privilege.

(5) Because this is indispensable to protection of the privilege, the individual also "must be clearly informed that he has the right to consult with a lawyer and to have the lawyer with him during interrogation," without regard to whether it appears that he is already aware of this right.

(6) The individual must also be warned "that if he is indigent a lawyer will be appointed to represent him," for otherwise, the above warning would be understood as meaning only that an individual may consult a lawyer if he has the funds to obtain one.

(7) The individual is always free to exercise the privilege, and thus if he "indicates in any manner, at any time prior to or during questioning, that he wishes to remain silent, the interrogation must cease"; and likewise, if he "states that he wants an attorney, the interrogation must cease until an attorney is present."

(8) If a statement is obtained without the presence of an attorney, "a heavy burden rests on the Government to demonstrate that the defendant knowingly and intelligently waived his privilege against self-incrimination and his right to retained or appointed counsel," and such waiver may not be presumed from the individual's silence after the warnings or from the fact that a confession was eventually obtained.

(9) Any statement obtained in violation of these rules may not be admitted into evidence, without regard to whether it is a confession or only an admission of part of an offense or whether it is inculpatory or allegedly exculpatory.

(10) Likewise, exercise of the privilege may not be penalized, and thus the prosecution may not "use at trial the fact that [the defendant] stood mute or claimed his privilege in the face of accusation."

The Supreme Court has more recently asserted that *Miranda* "recognized that these procedural safeguards were not themselves rights protected by the Constitution but were instead measures to insure that the right against compulsory self-incrimination was protected. * * * The suggested safeguards were not intended to 'create a constitutional straightjacket,' but rather to provide practical reinforcement for the right against compulsory self-incrimination." *Mich. v. Tucker*, 417 U.S. 433, 444 (1974).[29]

The *Miranda* enunciation of police procedures designed to provide practical reinforcement for the right against self-incrimination has itself given rise to litigation interpreting the numerous concepts set forth above. For example, questions concerning the meaning of "custody," of "otherwise deprived of his freedom of action in any significant way," of what constitutes an effective waiver of *Miranda* rights, and of how multiple interrogation sessions should be handled, have all been considered by reviewing courts.

ENGLISH APPROACH

The law with respect to admissibility in England in several respects parallels that of the United States. Only voluntary confessions are admissible in evidence. As stated in the Preamble to the Judges' Rules:

(e) That it is a fundamental condition of the admissibility in evidence against any person, equally of any oral answer given by that person to a question put by a police officer and of any statement made by that person, that it shall have been voluntary, in the sense that it has not been obtained from him by fear of prejudice or hope of advantage, exercised or held out by a person in authority, or by oppression.

Director of Public Prosecutions v. Ping Lin,[30] a decision of the House of Lords, mandates a totality of circumstances approach:

> The trial judge should approach his task by applying the test enunciated by Lord Sumner [in the Judges' Rules] in a common sense way to all the facts in the case in their context much as a jury would approach it if the task had fallen to them. In the light of all the facts in their context, he should ask himself this question and no other: have the prosecution proved that the contested statement was voluntary in the sense that it was not obtained by fear of prejudice or hope of advantage exercised or held out by a person in authority, or . . . by oppression.

Ping Lin dealt with the question of "hope of advantage." Ping Lin and others were convicted of conspiracy to contravene the Misuse of Drugs Act 1971. He had been taken into custody after the police found him smoking Chinese heroin with friends in his flat, where further significant quantities of the drug were discovered. Two police officers subsequently interviewed him under caution. When Ping Lin endeavored to make a bargain under which he would disclose the name of his supplier if released, the police told him this was not possible. He then admitted to being a dealer, though only in a small way. He persisted in his efforts to obtain immunity or lenience saying, "If I help police, can you help me?" After reiterating his inability to do a deal, the superintendent conducting the interview added, "If you show the judge that you have helped the police to trace bigger drug people, I am sure he will bear it in mind when he sentences you." Ping Lin subsequently suggested a means of entrapping his supplier and made further incriminating remarks about his own activities. These activities, however, amounted to little more than an amplification of what had already been said. The House of Lords held the judge entitled to find that the accused's self-incrimination was not caused by the superintendent's remark, although that may have contributed to the betrayal of the supplier. The House of Lords was also of the opinion that the case would have been very different if the remark had preceded the confession. To quote Lord Salmon:

> It would then, in my view, have been very difficult, if not impossible, for a judge properly to hold that he was satisfied that the accused's confession had not been obtained by the hope held out to him by Mr. O'Brien [the interviewing officer] that if he "helped the police" he was likely to receive a lighter sentence than if he refused to do so.[31]

The totality of circumstances approach also governs a determination by the court as to whether the prosecution has established that the statement was not obtained by oppression. Thus in *Regina v. Prager*,[32] an espionage trial, the Court of Appeal held a confession of a sergeant in the Royal Air Force, made after a prolonged though interrupted interrogation, not to have resulted from oppression. The Court of Appeal adopted a statement made by Sachs, J., in *Regina v. Priestley*:

> Whether or not there is oppression in an individual case depends upon many elements. . . . They include such things as the length of time of any individual period of questioning, whether the accused person had been given proper refreshment or not, and the characteristics of the person who makes the statement. What may be oppressive as regards a child, an invalid or an old man or somebody inexperienced in the ways of this world may turn out not to be oppressive when one finds that the accused person is of a tough character and an experienced man of the world.[33]

In addition to the general requirement that a confession be voluntary, the Judges of the Queen's Bench Division have established certain rules, known as the Judges' Rules, which the police are required to follow in the course of their investigations. The current Judges' Rules, issued to the police in 1964 following a review by the court, still closely parallel the original Judges' Rules issued by the Kings Bench Division in 1912 and 1918. An important Preamble, stating certain principles not affected by the Rules, prefaces the Judges' Rules. A set of Administrative Directions to the Police, drawn up by the Home Office and approved by the judges accompany the Rules. These Directions concern particular detailed points arising from the Judges' Rules, including the keeping of records, the provision of refreshment, and the circumstances permitting interviews of juveniles and mentally handicapped persons. A reissue of the document in June 1978 incorporated some minor changes in the Administrative Directions. The Introductory Note to the Rules, largely historical in nature, the Preamble, the Rules themselves, and the Administrative Directions are usually included together in any reference to the Judges' Rules. The Judges' Rules are set forth in full in Appendix I.

The Judges' Rules provide as follows. A police officer may question any person whether in custody or not (Rule I). He need not caution the person unless and until the officer has enough evidence to afford reasonable grounds for suspecting that the person has committed an offense (Rule II). As soon as a police officer has evidence which would afford reasonable cause for suspecting that the person has committed an offense, he must caution that person, or cause him to be cautioned, before putting to him any questions, or asking further questions, relating to that offense. The caution must be in the following terms:

> You are not obliged to say anything unless you wish to do so but what you say may be put into writing and given in evidence.[34]

The caution has a number of effects. In addition to advising the suspect of his "right of silence," that is, that he is not obligated to answer questions put to him by the police, it indicates to the suspect that he may be in peril of prosecution. The caution also tends to show the voluntariness of any statement subsequently made. Neither the Judges' Rules nor any common law principle requires that questioning must cease if the suspect indicates that he wishes to remain silent (see Rule I). The Judges' Rules place no limit on the number of questions put to a suspect before charge. Furthermore, in England, contrary to American practice, evidence of the questions posed and the fact that the suspect did not answer or gave an evasive answer is admissible evidence, forming a part of the case considered by the trier of the fact. The prosecution may, of course, also introduce in evidence anything the accused actually says.

As soon as a police officer possesses enough evidence to charge the suspect, that is, evidence sufficient to establish a prima facie case, the police officer must cause the suspect to be charged or be informed that he may be prosecuted for the offense without delay (paragraph (*d*) of the Preamble). An officer may not thereafter question the accused about the offense charged (Rule III (*b*)). The police again caution the suspect after charging him, or informing him that he may be prosecuted. The caution mirrors that given on arrest except that the suspect is told that anything he says "will," as opposed to "may," be taken down in writing (Rule III(*a*)).

If at any stage the suspect wishes to make a written statement, the Judges' Rules prescribe the form it should take (Rule IV). The person himself or a police officer may write the statement. The Judges' Rules state that, in either event, the statement should be in the suspect's own words, without prompting or questioning. The suspect is required to write and sign a declaration indicating that he has been cautioned and makes the statement of his own free will.

Rules governing the admissibility of statements which are voluntary but taken in violation of the Judges' Rules are both complex and confusing. As I hope will become clear, confusion arises not simply as a result of complexity, but also from the fact that the relationship among the Judges' Rules, voluntariness, and admissibility has yet to be satisfactorily resolved by the courts.

The Note and Preamble to the Judges' Rules together provide that:

1. A statement which is involuntary is inadmissible.
2. A court may properly consider the fact of violation of guidelines for conduct laid down in the Judges' Rules for police interrogation in determining whether the statement is involuntary.
3. A statement made in nonconformity with the Judges' Rules, however, is not by reason of this fact alone rendered inadmissible at trial.
4. Nonconformity with the Judges' Rules may render voluntary answers and statements liable to be excluded from evidence in subsequent criminal proceedings.

To illustrate operation of the Note and Preamble, consider principle (*c*) of the Preamble:

> (*c*) [E]very person at any stage of an investigation should be able to communicate and to consult privately with a solicitor. This is so even if he is in custody provided that in such a case no unreasonable delay or hindrance is caused to the processes of investigation or the administration of justice by his doing so.

The Administrative Directions to the Judges' Rules, set out in full in Part B to Appendix I, provide that the person arrested must be informed on arrival at the police station of this right, and that "in most cases a person in custody will name a member of his family or solicitor as the person whom he wishes to be informed of his detention, and such a person should normally be considered 'reasonably named.'" In addition, a person arrested has the right under Section 62 of the Criminal Law Act 1977 to have the news of his arrest and the address of the place where he is held "sent to one person reasonably named by him, without delay or, where some delay is necessary in the interests of the investigation or prevention of crime or the apprehension of offenders, with no more delay than is necessary." Thus, under both the Judges' Rules and Section 62 of the Criminal Law Act 1977, an arrested person has the right to contact and consult a solicitor prior to any questioning by the police.

Both principle (*c*) of the Preamble and Section 62 contain provisos that access to a solicitor may be refused when "hindrance would be caused to the process of investigation" (*c*), or "where some delay is necessary in the interests of the investigation" (Section 62). The text of a circular issued by the Home Office regarding Section 62, set forth in full in Appendix II, in part states:

> 6. When a request is made consideration will also need to be given to the possible application of that part of Section 62 which provides that intimation may be delayed in the interest of the investigation or prevention of crime or the apprehension of offenders for so long as this is necessary (but no longer). It will be for the station officer and/or duty officer, in consultation with the officer in charge of the case, to decide when this qualification applies. . . . The qualification will no doubt be particularly relevant where the arrested person is, or may be, associated with others involved in crime, or where the family of the arrested person, or a person living at the same address, may be aware of his criminal activities and there is a risk, for example, that stolen property will be disposed of, or evidence destroyed. In such cases immediate intimation may lead to the escape of other offenders, the destruction of evidence or the commission of other offences. It will therefore be appropriate to delay the intimation until such considerations have ceased to apply. Where the police decide that the qualification is to apply the arrested person should be informed that his request for an intimation to be conveyed is being delayed.

7. The following are some examples of situations when it may be considered necessary to delay an intimation—

(i) The police have arrested one member of a terrorist gang, and consider that immediate intimation of his arrest carries the risk that other members will escape and be able to continue their activities.

(ii) They have arrested a man in the act of conveying stolen goods to a receiver, and wish to conduct a search of the area for the receiver; immediate notification may lead to his escape.

(iii) A person suspected of being a persistent shoplifter is arrested and there is reason to believe that the family, if notified, will move or destroy the proceeds of previous thefts.

(iv) The police have arrested a member of a bank robbery gang and immediate intimation may lead to the destruction of evidence or threats to witnesses.

The Secretary of State recognizes however that no list of possible situations in which the qualification may be appropriately exercised can be comprehensive. Equally, however serious the offence under investigation, the qualification set out in the latter part of Section 62 should never be applied as a matter of routine, but only after a careful review of the considerations which apply in that particular case.

In spite of the statement in the Home Office circular that the proviso should not be applied routinely, research has shown that police officers, knowledgeable that a solicitor will frequently advise the accused to exercise his right to remain silent, usually refuse to permit access to a solicitor. The two most thorough studies indicate that three-quarters of all defendants asking to see a solicitor had their requests refused by the police.[35] "It has become almost standard practice to refuse access to a solicitor in any serious case."[36]

Breach of the Judges' Rules by improper denial of access to a solicitor results in the inadmissibility of a subsequent statement, as a matter of law, only if the resulting statement is involuntary. Mere denial of access to counsel, however, will rarely, if ever, result in the declaration of a subsequent statement as involuntary, when voluntary is defined as in (*e*) to the Preamble as a statement which "has not been obtained from him by fear of prejudice or hope of advantage, exercised or held out by a person in authority, or by oppression."

The common law concerning whether a voluntary statement obtained in breach of the Judges' Rules could be excluded in the discretion of the court, and if so under what circumstances, was never either easy or straightforward. The decision by the House of Lords in *Regina v. Sang and Magnan*[37] has made the question all the more complex. The narrow question at issue in *Sang* concerned the ambit of judicial discretion to exclude evidence of a crime when instigated by an agent provocateur. The Court of Appeal certified the following question as fit for consideration by the House of Lords:

Does a trial judge have a discretion to refuse to allow evidence—being evidence other than evidence of admissions—to be given in any circumstances in which such evidence is relevant and of more than minimal probative value?[38]

Four out of five members of the House gave the following answer:[39]

(1) A trial judge in a criminal trial has always a discretion to refuse to admit evidence if in his opinion its prejudicial effect outweighs its probative value.[40]

(2) Save with regard to admissions and confessions and generally with regard to evidence obtained from the accused after his commission of the offence, he has no discretion to refuse to admit relevant admissible evidence on the ground that it was obtained by improper or unfair means. The court is not concerned with how it was obtained.

The House of Lords thus concluded that other than with regard to admissions, confessions, and "evidence obtained from the accused after his commission of the offence," encompassing evidence resulting from a search of the accused or premises he occupied, the court lacks discretion to exclude evidence on the ground that it was obtained improperly or unfairly. "The court is not concerned with how [such evidence] was obtained." With regard to evidence of admissions, confessions, and evidence resulting from an illegal search and seizure, the terms of the certified question and the disagreement expressed in the speeches of authority leave open whether discretion to exclude such evidence ever rests in the court, and if so under what circumstances. As stated in *Cross on Evidence*, the court's discretion to exclude evidence, referred to in the Preamble of the Judges' Rules, on the grounds that a statement was obtained in nonconformity with the Judges' Rules "does not appear to have been affected by the decisions of the Court of Appeal and House of Lords in *Regina v. Sang and Mangan*."[41]

In spite of the lack of a clear holding by the House of Lords concerning whether the trial court possesses discretion to exclude voluntary confessions or admissions taken in violation of the Judges' Rules along with illegally seized evidence, and if so under what circumstances, the speech of Lord Diplock in *Sang* may very well portend things to come. To appreciate the thrust of the speech of Lord Diplock, it is first necessary to explore briefly the two leading cases highlighting the broader question addressed in *Sang*. The opinions in *Kurama Son of Kaniu v. Reginam*[42] and *Jeffrey v. Black*[43] both commence discussion of judicial discretion with a statement that admissibility as a matter of law does not depend upon how the evidence was obtained. As stated in *Jeffrey v. Black*:

It is firmly established according to English law that the mere fact that evidence is obtained in an irregular fashion does not of itself prevent that evidence from being relevant and acceptable to a court. The authority for that is *Kurama Son of Kaniu v.*

Reginam and I need only refer to one passage to make good the proposition which I have already put forward:

> In their Lordships' opinion, the test to be applied in considering whether evidence is admissible is whether it is relevant to the matters in issue. If it is, it is admissible and the court is not concerned with how the evidence was obtained. While this proposition may not have been stated in so many words in any English case, there are decisions which support it and, in their Lordships' opinion, it is plainly right in principle.

There one has that pronouncement from the Privy Council, and I have not the least doubt that we must firmly accept the proposition that an irregularity in obtaining evidence does not render the evidence inadmissible. Whether or not the evidence is admissible depends on whether or not it is relevant to the issues in respect of which it is called.[44]

With respect to discretion, Lord Goddard, C.J., delivering the advice of the Privy Council in *Kurama*, a case involving unlawful possession of ammunition by the accused obtained by the police as a result of an illegal search of his person, went on to say:

> No doubt in a criminal case the judge always has a discretion to disallow evidence if the strict rules of admissibility would operate unfairly against the accused. This was emphasised in the case before this Board of *Noor Mohamed v. Regem*, and in the recent case in the House of Lords of *Harris v. Director of Public Prosecutions*. If, for instance, some admission of some piece of evidence, e.g., a document, had been obtained from a defendant by a trick, no doubt the judge might properly rule it out.[45]

In *Jeffrey v. Black*, Lord Widgery, C.J., later opined:

> If the case is exceptional, if the case is such that not only have the police officers entered without authority, but they have been guilty of trickery or they have misled someone, or they have been oppressive or they have been unfair, or in other respects they have behaved in a manner which is morally reprehensible, then it is open to the justices to apply their discretion and decline to allow the particular evidence to be let in as part of the trial.
>
> I cannot stress the point too strongly that this is a very exceptional situation, and the simple, unvarnished fact that evidence was obtained by police officers who had gone in without bothering to get a search warrant is not enough to justify the magistrates in exercising their discretion to keep the evidence out.[46]

Thus both Lord Goddard and Lord Widgery indicate that if the illegality of the police goes beyond a mere violation of a rule, such as failure to obtain a search warrant, give a caution, or permit access to a solicitor, so as to involve trickery or other morally reprehensible conduct, the court has discretion to exclude the resulting evidence.

Certain of the considerations mentioned by Lord Goddard and Lord

Widgery, such as oppression, would result in exclusion of a statement of an accused as a matter of law because involuntary and thus unreliable. Other considerations may best be viewed as aspects of unfairness against the accused excludable under the concept accepted by four out of five members of the House of Lords in *Sang*, including Lord Diplock, that a "trial judge at a criminal trial has always a discretion to refuse to admit evidence if in his opinion its prejudicial effect outweighs its probative value." However, still other considerations neither affect reliability of the evidence nor result in evidence whose prejudicial effect outweighs its probative value. These considerations, such as trickery and other morally reprehensible conduct of the police, relate solely to the discretion of the court to exclude reliable and probative evidence capable of proper appreciation by the jury as a means of discouraging illegal conduct by the police. Lord Diplock disagrees with this concept of discretion:

> The function of the judge at a criminal trial as respects the admission of evidence is to ensure that the accused has a fair trial according to law. It is no part of a judge's function to exercise disciplinary powers over the police or prosecution as respects the way in which evidence to be used at the trial is obtained by them. If it was obtained illegally there will be a remedy in civil law; if it was obtained legally but in breach of the rules of conduct for the police, this is a matter for the appropriate disciplinary authority to deal with. What the judge at the trial is concerned with is not how the evidence sought to be adduced by the prosecution has been obtained but with how it is used by the prosecution at the trial.
>
> A fair trial according to law involves, in the case of a trial on indictment, that it should take place before a judge and a jury; that the case against the accused should be proved to the satisfaction of the jury beyond all reasonable doubt on evidence that is admissible in law; and, as a corollary to this, that there should be excluded from the jury information about the accused which is likely to have an influence on their minds prejudicial to the accused which is out of proportion to the true probative value of admissible evidence conveying that information.
>
> If these conditions are fulfilled and the jury receive correct instructions from the judge as to the law applicable to the case, the requirements that the accused should have a fair trial according to law is, in my view, satisfied; for the fairness of a trial according to law is not all one sided: it requires that those who are undoubtedly guilty should be convicted as well as that those about whose guilt there is any reasonable doubt should be acquitted. However much the judge may dislike the way in which a particular piece of evidence was obtained before proceedings were commenced, if it is admissible evidence probative of the accused's guilt it is no part of his judicial function to exclude it for this reason.[47]

As previously noted, the terms of the certified question coupled with the fact that a majority of the five members of the House of Lords in *Sang* did not expressly share Lord Diplock's position deprive Lord Diplock's assertion that the court is not concerned with the exercise of disciplinary powers over the police of the force of law. Knowledgeable observers predict, however, that subsequent case law on the subject will move slowly but steadily toward the position advocated by Lord Diplock.

As a practical matter, the foregoing discussion is of more academic interest than day-to-day importance. First, most illegal police conduct, such as denial of a solicitor, does not involve morally reprehensible conduct. As Lord Widgery took great pains to stress, mere illegal conduct by the police does not provide a ground for the exercise of discretion to exclude an admission, a confession, or evidence resulting from an illegal search. Second, even with respect to the "very exceptional situation" envisaged by Lord Widgery for the exercise of discretion, trial judges very rarely exercise such discretion, assuming it exists, to exclude otherwise admissible evidence for the purpose of curbing abuses by the police. Thus, the exclusionary rule as applied in the United States, whether or not available in theory, does not operate in practice in England. Moreover, in comparison to the United States, courts very rarely exclude admissible evidence through the exercise of discretion that everyone acknowledges, that is, the court's power to exclude evidence on the ground that its prejudicial effect outweighs its probative value.

In summary, merely because the police illegally deny an accused access to his solicitor does not render, as a matter of law, a voluntary confession or admission inadmissible, nor may a court exclude the statement in its discretion on the basis of such conduct alone. Moreover, even assuming the presence of discretionary authority to exclude evidence based upon trickery or other morally reprehensible conduct by the police, such conduct rarely accompanies denial of access to a solicitor. Defendants in England are relegated to attempting to ameliorate the effect of introduction by arguing to the jury that either the confession was involuntary, and thus inaccurate, or that they never made the confession. Naturally enough, defendants more often attack written confessions and admissions on the grounds of voluntariness, while disputing whether oral statements were ever made. Table 1 represents the actual frequency with which accused individuals dispute written and oral statements in contested trials in the Magistrates' Court. When an accused asserts that the police fabricated an oral confession or admission, the defendant charges that the officers "verballed" him.[48]

SEARCH AND SEIZURE

Following David Fisher's interrogation and confession, the police searched Fisher's room at 155 Warwick Road the same day on two separate occasions. The first search by PC Abolins resulted in the seizure of the starting pistol and cartridges. The second search by DC Pyke and DC Butler resulted in the seizure of various items purchased with proceeds of the robbery, including a doll and a "watchamacallit,"[49] as well as a blue anorak and a red woolen hat worn by Fisher during the robbery. In addition, the officers discovered the plastic bag used by Fisher to carry the money taken at the robbery. The police did not obtain a warrant for either search. After the trial, when the author inquired of the police seeking the authority relied upon to conduct the search, the response received was that after the conclusion of each of the two interrogation sessions, David Fisher orally consented to a search of his room. Whether or not David Fisher in fact so consented is a question which will forever go unanswered.

If David Fisher in fact consented, the police conducted both searches lawfully. If the police officers had sought a search warrant from a magistrate as provided by Section 26(1) of the Theft Act 1968, the warrant would have rendered a subsequent search lawful. Moreover, if the police simply went to David Fisher's room without either first obtaining his consent or obtaining a search warrant, the search of David Fisher's room would nevertheless still be lawful even though Fisher was arrested hours before at the airport. As stated in the Law and Procedure Supplement to the 1981 Report of the Royal Commission on Criminal Procedure, there "seem[s] to be a right on arrest to search the premises of the arrested person even if the arrest took place elsewhere."[50] The common law authority frequently cited includes *Ghani v. Jones*[51] and *Jeffrey v. Black*.[52]

In the United States, a search of David Fisher's room absent either consent or the issuance of a search warrant would have been illegal, and the fruits of the illegal search would have been excluded from evidence at trial.[53] In England, the same principles applicable to the admissibility of admissions or confessions obtained in nonconformity with the Judges' Rules govern the position with respect to evidence that results from an

TABLE 1
Frequency With Which Defendants Dispute Statements in Contested Trials in the Magistrates' Court

	Written Statement		**Oral Statement**		**Total**	
	No.	*%*	*No.*	*%*	*No.*	*%*
Denied	3	8.3	40	50.6	43	37.4
Statement involuntary	14	38.8	2	2.5	16	13.9
Not disputed	19	52.7	37	46.8	56	48.7
Total	36	100.0	79	100.0	115	100.0

Source: J. Vennard, *Contested Trials in Magistrates' Court: The Case for the Prosecution*, Royal Commission on Criminal Procedure, Research Study No. 6 (London, 1980). Reproduced with the permission of the Controller of Her Majesty's Stationery Office.

illegal search and seizure by the police. Thus, the mere fact that police obtain the evidence illegally does not require exclusion of the evidence as a matter of law. Moreover, the mere fact that the seizure of evidence was illegal by reason, for example, of the police not bothering to procure a warrant does not convey upon the court discretion to exclude the illegally obtained evidence. Whether conduct which is not only illegal but can be characterized as morally reprehensible conveys upon the trial court discretion to exclude relevant evidence, to discourage the police from engaging in such conduct in the future, was left unresolved in *Regina v. Sang and Mangan*. Even if such discretion exists in law, a doubtful premise, trial judges in practice permit the introduction of the illegally seized evidence. Trial judges apparently agree with Lord Diplock's statement in *Regina v. Sang and Mangan*: "It is no part of a judge's function to exercise disciplinary powers over the police or prosecution as respects the way in which evidence to be used at the trial is obtained by them."

The accused following an illegal search may pursue a civil action against the police officer for trespass to land or chattels. Like the potential remedy for false imprisonment following an illegal arrest, the theoretical possibility of a civil judgment for trespass does little to dissuade illegal police conduct, if for no other reason than the risk of a civil action "is not much risk."[54] In addition, a defendant may also complain to the Police Complaint Board. In 1979, less than 5 percent of such complaints were determined to have been substantiated—a figure unlikely to deter illegal police conduct.[55]

AVAILABILITY OF BAIL

On March 19, 1980, at the conclusion of questioning at the Steelhouse Lane Police Station, David Fisher was formally charged with having robbed the Midland Bank in Hockley on February 25, 1980, contrary to Section 8 of the Theft Act 1968.

As provided in Section 38 of the Magistrates' Court Act 1952, as amended by the Bail Act 1976, when a person is in custody at a police station after arrest without a warrant, a police officer not below the rank of inspector or the officer in charge of the station (1) may inquire into the offense in respect of which the arrest was made and (2) must inquire into that offense if it will not be practicable to bring the arrested person before a Magistrates' Court within twenty-four hours. As provided in Section 4(1) of the Bail Act 1976, the basic tenet is that an accused awaiting trial shall normally be granted bail. In order for bail to be denied, the police must show substantial grounds for believing either that he will fail to surrender to custody, commit further offenses, or obstruct the course of justice. The police, and later the court if the police deny bail and the defendant seeks bail in court, must, pursuant to Section 9 of Schedule 1 to the Bail Act 1976, consider the following matters: (1) the nature of the charge; (2) the strength of the prosecution case; (3) the defendant's character and antecedents, associations, and community ties; (4) the failure to surrender to bail on previous occasions; and (5) any other matter which appears relevant. The latter category includes the likelihood of the defendant interfering with prosecution witnesses or committing further offenses while awaiting trial.

A person released on bail by the police or the court must appear before the Magistrates' Court at such time and place as is specified. Section 21 of the Criminal Justice Act 1967 provides that the conditions on which bail is granted may include conditions likely to result in the appearance of the accused at the time and place required, such as reporting to the police station at stated intervals, or conditions necessary in the interests of justice or for the prevention of crime. Pursuant to Section 21, the police or the court frequently grants bail subject to the accused providing one or more sureties satisfactory to the police. A surety is a person who enters into a recognizance at a stated sum of money, which may be forfeited if the defendant does not appear. Section 21 requires no actual deposit of money or security.

The police refused to grant David Fisher bail on the basis of his bad record and the seriousness of the charge. He remained in custody pending appearance before the Magistrates' Court on March 20, 1980.

NOTES

1. [1969] 3 ALL E.R. 1626.
2. Report of the Royal Commission on Criminal Procedure 43 (1981).
3. Carroll v. United States, 267 U.S. 132, 161 (1925).
4. Brinegar v. United States, 338 U.S. 160, 175 (1949):

   "The substance of all the definitions" of probable cause "is a reasonable ground for belief of guilt." McCarthy v. De Armit, 99 Pa. St. 63, 69, quoted with approval in the Carroll opinion. 267 U.S. at 161. And this "means less than evidence which would justify condemnation" or conviction, as Marshall, C.J., said for the Court more than a century ago in Locke v. United States, 7 Cranch 339, 348. Since Marshall's time, at any rate, it has come to mean more than bare suspicion: . . .
5. Christie v. Leachinsky [1947] 1 ALL E.R. 567.
6. Regina v. Kulynycz [1970] 3 ALL E.R. 881.
7. Alderman v. United States, 394 U.S. 165 (1969).
8. Nardone v. United States, 308 U.S. 338 (1939).
9. [1979] 2 ALL E.R. 1222.
10. In 1979, less than 5 percent of all complaints were declared substantiated by the Police Complaint Board. Appendix 17 to Investigation and Prosecution of Criminal Offences in England and Wales: The Law and Procedure (1981).
11. For a discussion of Proofs of Evidence, see p. 65 infra.
12. Israel and LaFave, *Criminal Procedure: Constitutional Limitations* 218 (1980).

13. Culombe v. Connecticut, 367 U.S. 568 (1961).
14. Lee v. Mississippi, 322 U.S. 742 (1948).
15. Payne v. Arkansas, 356 U.S. 560 (1958).
16. Turner v. Pennsylvania, 388 U.S. 62 (1949).
17. Davis v. North Carolina, 384 U.S. 737 (1966).
18. Fay v. Noia, 372 U.S. 391 (1963).
19. Culombe v. Connecticut, 367 U.S. 568 (1961).
20. Spano v. New York, 360 U.S. 315 (1959).
21. Gallegos v. Cole, 370 U.S. 49 (1962).
22. Jackson v. Denno, 378 U.S. 368 (1964).
23. Mallory v. Hogan, 378 U.S. 1 (1964).
24. 365 U.S. 534 (1961).
25. Id. at 540-41.
26. 372 U.S. 293 (1963).
27. Id. at 308.
28. 384 U.S. 436 (1966).
29. At 229-31 (1980).
30. [1975] 3 ALL E.R. 175, 182-83, per Lord Hailsham.
31. Id. at 189.
32. [1972] 1 ALL E.R. 1114, 1119.
33. [1966] 50 CR. App. R. 183.
34. Evidence refers to information that would be admissible in court. Regina v. Osborne [1973] 1 ALL E.R. 649.
35. Royal Commission on Criminal Procedure, Report 97 (1981).
36. Barnard, *The Criminal Court in Action* 55 (1979).
37. [1979] 2 ALL E.R. 1222.
38. Id. at 1225.
39. Id. at 1231.
40. Part (1) is a statement of those considerations involving concern over misapplication of evidence by the jury incorporated into the Federal Rules of Evidence by Rule 403:

> Exclusion of Relevant Evidence on Grounds
> of Prejudice, Confusion, or Waste of Time
>
> Although relevant, evidence may be excluded if its probative value is substantially outweighed by the danger of unfair prejudice, confusion of the issues, or misleading the jury, or by considerations of undue delay, waste of time, or needless presentation of cumulative evidence.

41. At 548 (1979).
42. [1955] 1 ALL E.R. 236.
43. [1978] 1 ALL E.R. 555.
44. Id. at 558-59.
45. [1955] 1 ALL E.R. at 299.
46. [1978] 1 ALL E.R. at 559.
47. [1979] 2 ALL E.R. at 1230.
48. While the question of "verballing" also arises in the United States, the giving of *Miranda* warnings, access to counsel, the use of written waiver forms to be signed by an accused before making any statement, taken together with an untrusting

attitude displayed by many courts with respect to oral admission made following the giving of *Miranda* warnings unaccompanied by a subsequent signed statement or at least a signed waiver form, undoubtedly reduces the frequency of "verballing" after arrest.

49. A "watchamacallit," in this instance, refers to an inexpensive plastic sculptured head of an odd-looking person having the word "watchamacallit" written on its base.

50. At 11.

51. [1969] 3 ALL E.R. 1700.

52. [1978] 1 ALL E.R. 555.

53. Moreover, if at a preliminary hearing it was determined that the police officer making the arrest lacked probable cause, thus making the arrest illegal, evidence discovered in David Fisher's room would be excluded as illegally seized. The evidence is tainted by the illegal arrest, it being the fruit of the illegal arrest. The fact that Fisher may later have consented to the search or that a warrant was subsequently obtained under the facts at hand would not have altered the result.

54. Ghani v. Jones [1969] 3 ALL E.R. 1700, 1702, per Lord Denning. See also text accompanying note 9 supra.

55. Appendix 17 to Investigation and Prosecution of Criminal Offences in England and Wales: The Law and Procedure (1981).

4 THE MAGISTRATES' COURT

AN OVERVIEW

On March 20, 1980, David Fisher appeared for the first time at Birmingham Magistrates' Court. A Magistrates' Court consists of a tribunal of either justices of the peace, unpaid laymen without legal qualification, or a stipendiary magistrate, a qualified lawyer paid a fixed salary for his work. Stipendiary magistrates sit in the very busy Magistrates' Courts in London and large cities such as Birmingham. Where the court consists of lay justices of the peace, the panel will usually consist of three persons, with two being the minimum acceptable number. The Lord Chancellor appoints justices of the peace under Section 1 of the Administration of Justice Act 1973. Committees of magistrates advise the Lord Chancellor's Department in the various commission areas regarding suitable persons for appointment as justices of the peace. In practice, the people who become magistrates are those who through work for the various political parties or through volunteer social service have shown an interest in the welfare of the community.

Every justice is appointed to one of the commission areas in England and Wales and has jurisdiction solely for that area. These areas are the various counties in England and Wales, the five commission areas of the Metropolis (Inner London, Middlesex, South West, South East, North East), and the City of London. Each Magistrates' Court has attached to it a clerk who usually is, but need not be, legally qualified. The clerk advises the court on points of procedure and law and arranges for the day-to-day administration of the court. While justices of the peace themselves receive basic instruction on the law, they tend to rely on their clerk when facing any complex matter.

The prosecution commences all proceedings at the Magistrates' Court by presenting to the lay magistrates or stipendiary magistrate an information alleging that the person named therein has committed some specified offense. The information is usually, but not necessarily, in writing and may be substantiated on oath. When the police have arrested and charged the defendant, they hand in the charge sheet at court, making it the information. The Magistrates' Courts Rules 1968 regulate the contents of the statement of the offense: the information must allege only one offense or it will be bad for duplicity; the offense must be described in ordinary language avoiding technical terms; the information must refer to the act or other enactment which creates the offense, if any; and it need not negative any exemption, proviso, or excuse contained in the definition of the offense. With respect to David Fisher, the charge sheet which became the information stated that David Fisher:

In the City of Birmingham did rob Yvonne Gardener of £4300 cash the property of The Midland Bank Ltd., Great Hampton St., Hockley, Birmingham at about 3 p.m. on Monday 25th, February 1980. (Contrary to Section 8 Theft Act 1968)

A Magistrates' Court has jurisdiction to hear an information against any person who has been arrested with or without warrant and brought before it or who has answered to a summons issued by the court. The powers of the court upon hearing the information are either (1) to consider the issue of whether the accused is guilty or not guilty of the charge contained in the information, sometimes referred to as a summary trial or (2) to sit as examining justices either to determine whether sufficient evidence exists to warrant committing the defendant for trial to the Crown Court on indictment or, if that issue is not disputed, to make a formal committal to the Crown Court under Section 1 of the Criminal Justice Act 1967. The gravity of the offense determines whether the matter must be tried in the Magistrates' Court, in the Crown Court by judge and jury on indictment, or in either court. To illustrate, most traffic offenses, drunk and disorderly charges, being a suspected person, and assault upon a policeman may only be tried summarily by the Magistrates' Court, while committal, indictment, and Crown Court trial before judge and jury are mandated for murder, treason, causing death by reckless driving, and, most important for the matter at hand, robbery. Offenses which may be tried either way include taking vehicles, burglary without involving violence, and theft.

If the offense is a summary offense, that is, one that can be tried only in a Magistrates' Court, the judge asks the defendant how he pleads to the information and, depending on his answer, proceeds either to trial or an immediate sentencing. The trial may be conducted forthwith or scheduled for the future at a time certain. If the offense is triable either way, the court, pursuant to Sections 19-22 of the Criminal Law Act 1977, must decide whether to sit as examining justices and hold a committal proceeding to determine whether the case may be sent to the Crown Court or to proceed as if the case were summary, disposing of the matter entirely. In reaching this determination, the court will consider both the seriousness of the alleged offense and the court's powers of sentence. The court is unaware of any previous conviction of the accused when making this decision. If the magistrates decide the case is appropriate for summary trial, the court must then explain to the defendant that he has the right to be tried by judge and jury at the Crown Court. The court also informs the defendant that if he is tried summarily by the magistrates, they can nevertheless commit him for sentence to the Crown Court if they convict him and then, learning of his character and prior criminal activity, come to the conclusion that greater punishment should be imposed than the court has the power to inflict.

If the Attorney General or the Director of Public Prosecutions conducts the prosecution, the court must sit as examining justices if the prosecution so applies. As a practical matter, if a local prosecuting solicitor conducts the prosecution, when the prosecution requests that the case be tried in the Crown Court, the magistrates deciding the matter almost invariably find the case not appropriate for summary trial and thus conform to the prosecution's request.

Since the information presented on March 20, 1980, charged David Fisher with robbery, the function of the stipendiary magistrate to whom the information was presented was to set the matter for a committal proceeding when the prosecution was ready to proceed.

APPLICATION FOR LEGAL AID

David Fisher, like all persons accused of a crime in England, was entitled to representation by a solicitor at the proceedings conducted before the Magistrates' Court. Fisher could, of course, hire privately a solicitor or even a barrister to appear on his behalf. Fisher knew of a solicitor whom he wanted to represent him. As is frequently the case, however, Fisher lacked the resources needed to retain counsel himself.

Had David Fisher not known of a solicitor he desired to have represent him, if requested, a solicitor would have been assigned to him through the operation of one of the duty solicitor schemes operating in the Birmingham area. Similar schemes exist throughout much of England. In its most basic form, duty solicitor schemes provide that a solicitor engaged in private practice, drawn from a list of such solicitors participating in the scheme, is assigned each working day to represent defendants scheduled to appear in the Magistrates' Court for the first time. The solicitor is given an opportunity that morning to discuss the case with the accused prior to the accused being asked to respond in any way in open court. The accused in fact appears with privately retained counsel or seeks appointment of the duty solicitor in only about 40 percent of all matters heard by the Magistrates' Court. An extremely high percentage of those appearing without counsel plead guilty.

Whether privately contacted, as in the case of David Fisher, or appointed pursuant to a duty solicitor scheme, the solicitor usually assists the defendant forthwith in preparing an application for legal aid. The application is submitted to the court for its consideration and approval providing that legal fees be paid from public funds. Frequently this process occurs in its entirety on the date of the defendant's first appearance in court. The only cases in which a court must grant legal aid involve those where a person is committed for trial on a charge of murder or in which the prosecutor appeals, or applies for leave to appeal, from the Court of Appeal or the Courts Martial Appeal Court to the House of Lords. In all other cases, the decision lies within the discretion of the court to which application is made, provided that if any doubt exists about whether legal aid should be granted the court must resolve the doubt in favor of the accused.

In exercising its discretion, the court must consider both the means of the defendant and the nature of the charge to determine if it warrants legal aid. With respect to the nature of the charge, the Widgery Committee[1] recommended granting legal aid in the following cases: (1) where the charge is a grave one in the sense that the accused is in real jeopardy of losing his liberty or livelihood or of suffering serious damage to his reputation; (2) where the charge raises a substantial question of law; (3) where the accused is unable to follow the proceedings and state his own case because of his inadequate knowledge of English, his mental illness, or his other mental or physical disability; (4) where the nature of the defense involves the tracing and interviewing of witnesses or expert cross-examination of a witness for the prosecution; or (5) where legal representation is desirable in the interests of someone other than the accused as, for example, in the case of sexual offenses against young children, when it is undesirable for the accused to cross-examine the witness in person. The application form used in Birmingham sets forth these criteria as "Reasons for Wanting Legal Aid."

Regarding the financial condition of the accused, the applicant must satisfy the court of his need for assistance in meeting the cost of the proceedings. If he has some means, the court may require him to make a contribution toward the cost. The court can require the applicant to furnish a written statement of his means and, if it appears that he is likely to be required to make a contribution, it can refuse to enter an order providing for legal fees to be paid to the solicitor until he makes payment on account of the contribution. In 1979, approximately 9 percent of all legal aid orders provided for contribution.[2]

Legal aid is granted in nearly every case applied for where committal proceedings are required prior to trial at the Crown Court, in about 90 percent of cases tried in the Magistrates' Court that could have been tried either way, and in about 60 percent of the very few applications made for legal aid in summary offenses cases triable only in the Magistrates' Court.

Legal aid provides payment for representation at both the Magistrates'

Court and Crown Court, applying to preparation as well as court appearances. A person granted legal aid in a Magistrates' Court, whether for a summary trial or for committal proceedings, normally has a solicitor only. A person granted legal aid for a trial in the Crown Court will normally have a solicitor and a barrister. If the accused is convicted, he may also have counsel's advice on potential grounds for an appeal and, if grounds exist, the assistance of counsel in the preparation of an application for leave to appeal, or assistance in giving notice of appeal. In the case of David Fisher, following the committal proceeding, an additional application for legal aid for assistance of Queen's Counsel as well as a junior barrister was submitted and approved by the Crown Court on July 18, 1980. The ground stated in the application was that David Fisher faced by reason of the charge and his past record a significant custodial sentence if convicted.

REQUEST FOR BAIL

When David Fisher appeared before the Magistrates' Court on March 20, 1980, the only matter of consequence that occurred was the submission and approval of the legal aid application. The prosecution was not yet prepared to proceed to the committal proceeding. The court remanded David Fisher in the custody of the local prison to await trial. An accused in custody may be remanded for no more than eight clear days,[3] at the conclusion of which he must be brought physically before the court once again. The court may then remand him for another eight clear days, with the process continuing until the prosecution is ready to proceed with the committal proceeding and, if committed, until the commencement of the trial.

David Fisher's solicitor did not make an application for bail on March 20, 1980, preferring to await his next apperance by which time the solicitor would stand in a better position to put forth the best case for bail possible on Fisher's behalf. On March 26, 1980, David Fisher's bail application was denied by the court on grounds that there was reason to believe that Fisher would fail to surrender to custody because of the serious nature of the charge. Renewed applications for bail made on each of four subsequent appearances, concluding the day of the committal proceeding, April 24, 1980, were denied on similar grounds.

COMMITTAL PROCEEDINGS

On April 24, 1980, the Birmingham Magistrates' Court committed David Fisher for trial to the Crown Court at Birmingham, charging him as follows:

On 24th February 1980 in Birmingham, robbed Yvonne Gardener of £3,800 cash. (Part recovered) (Contrary to Section 8(1) Theft Act 1968)

On 25th February 1980 in Birmingham at the time of robbing Yvonne Gardener of £3,800 cash, you had with you a certain imitation firearm, namely a .38 "Chief" blank firing gun. (Contrary to Section 17(2) Firearms Act 1968)

A Magistrates' Court faces a particular task whenever a person appears charged either with an offense triable only by judge and jury, such as robbery, or with an offense triable either way where the magistrates have either declined to deal with the offense summarily or the accused has exercised his right to elect trial by judge and jury. Pursuant to Section 7(1) of the Magistrates' Courts Act 1952, the Magistrates' Court must decide at a committal proceeding whether "there is sufficient evidence to put the accused upon trial by jury for any indictable offense." Like the preliminary hearing in the United States, the Magistrates' Court at the committal proceeding does not decide whether the accused is guilty of the offense charged; the court simply decides whether the evidence is sufficient to justify committing the accused to stand trial before judge and jury at the Crown Court. Evidence is sufficient to justify committal for trial only when the facts presented to the Magistrates' Court, if properly introduced at trial, would constitute a prima facie case, that is, there must be evidence upon which a reasonable jury could properly find the accused guilty beyond a reasonable doubt. While both the committal proceeding in England and the preliminary hearing in the United States act as a filtering process to safeguard persons from being held for trial on serious offenses with insufficient evidence, evidence sufficient to meet the probable cause test of the preliminary hearing may very well fail to meet the prima facie test of the committal proceeding. Evidence upon which the court finds reasonable grounds to believe that it is more probably true than not true that the accused committed the offense charged meets the probable cause test of a preliminary hearing. Such evidence may fall short of constituting evidence upon which a reasonable jury could find the accused guilty of the crime charged beyond a reasonable doubt.

The sole purpose of a committal proceeding is to ensure that no person shall stand trial at the Crown Court unless a prima facie case exists against him.[4] It is not a purpose of the committal proceeding that the defense hear all the prosecution witnesses, that any particular witness or witnesses give their evidence in chief, or that such witnesses be made available for cross-examination. The prosecution is not required to call all their witnesses at committal proceedings; if it can make out a prima facie case without calling any particular witness or witnesses, even an important witness, the prosecution may do so. Neither the defense nor the court can require any witness to be called. Thus, in theory, committal proceedings do not provide a means by which the defense may obtain full disclosure of the prosecution's case before trial. However, in practice, in most cases the prosecution does present all its evidence at the committal proceeding.

Moreover, if it does not, the prosecution must later give notice before trial, including a copy of the statement of each new witness with respect to any additional evidence it proposes to call.

Committal proceedings may take the form of either a hearing under Section 7 of the Magistrates' Courts Act 1952 or a committal for trial without consideration of the evidence by the magistrates under Section 1 of the Criminal Justice Act 1967. All stages of all committal proceedings normally take place in the presence and hearing of the accused. There are limited exceptions specified in Section 45 of the Criminal Justice Act 1967, when the accused is so disorderly as to make it impractical for evidence to be introduced in his presence or when he is absent for reasons of health but is legally represented and has consented to the introduction of evidence in his absence.

The traditional form of committal proceedings under Section 7 of the Magistrates' Courts Act 1952 requires the Magistrates' Court to consider the evidence. A full committal proceeding usually begins with a short address by the advocate for the prosecution explaining the nature of the evidence against the accused and how this evidence establishes the offense charged. The evidence then submitted to the Magistrates' Court may be either oral or written. With respect to oral evidence, witnesses are called by the prosecutor and examined orally by him, cross-examined by the defense advocate, and then reexamined by the prosecutor. The clerk of the court records the evidence of the witnesses in the form of reported speech. The clerk reads the record over to the witness at the end of his evidence. The witness is then asked to make any needed corrections and sign it. This written record of the evidence of a witness is known as a deposition. The presiding magistrate must either sign each deposition or, at the end of the proceedings, sign a certificate authenticating all the depositions and written statements tendered at the committal proceeding.

The procedure involving the recording of the oral evidence of each witness as a deposition may be modified by allowing for the admission in evidence of a written statement of a witness prepared by the police in accordance with Section 2 of the Criminal Justice Act 1967. An advantage of this modification of the procedure is that a witness whom the defense does not wish to cross-examine at the committal proceeding need not be called to give evidence at those proceedings. Section 2 provides that the written statement shall be admissible in a committal proceeding as evidence to the like extent as oral evidence provided that:

1. the statement purports to be signed by the person who made it;
2. the statement contains a declaration by that person to the effect that it is true to the best of his knowledge and belief and that he made the statement knowing

that, if it were tendered in evidence, he would be liable to prosecution if he willingly stated in it anything which he knew to be false, or did not believe to be true;

3. before the statement is tendered in evidence, a copy of the statement is given, by or on behalf of the party proposing to tender it, to each of the other parties to the proceedings; and
4. none of the other parties, before the statement is tendered in evidence at the committal proceedings, objects to the statement being so tendered under this section.

Section 2(5) provides that either the whole statement should be read aloud to the court or else the statement should be summarized and then handed in. It must be noted that such a statement can only be used when the defense has not objected before the statement is read. Even after it has been read, the Magistrates' Court, on application by either side or on its own motion, may require the maker to attend and give oral evidence.

At the conclusion of the prosecution evidence, the defense can submit that the evidence produced by the prosecution does not carry sufficient weight to warrant committing the accused for trial. Such a submission is appropriate either when the prosecution has failed to produce any evidence to establish an essential element of the offense or when the prosecution's evidence is so weak, or has been so discredited by cross-examination, that no reasonable jury could find each element of the offense proven beyond a reasonable doubt. The magistrates decide by a majority vote whether to uphold the defense submission. If they uphold the submission, the accused is discharged; if not, the committal proceeding continues.

If the proceeding continues, the clerk of the court next reads over the charge to the accused. The clerk informs the accused of his right to remain silent, to make an unsworn statement to the court from the dock, or to give evidence from the witness box, in which case the accused will be liable to cross-examination. In many cases the defendant, fully knowledgeable that nothing he could say would destroy the prima facie case, will decide to say nothing at all and thereby "reserve his defense" until he appears at the Crown Court. When, however, the accused has a strong case, he may decide to give evidence at the committal proceeding, in the hope that his evidence may satisfy the Magistrates' Court that the prosecution's case is too weak to warrant committal. The defendant's advocate may address the court in an opening speech if he intends to call witnesses to the events apart from the defendant. In practice, defense counsel rarely exercises this right to make an opening speech because it gives the prosecution a right to address the court on the facts at the conclusion of the defense evidence—a right the prosecution does not otherwise have.

The defendant and his witnesses give evidence in exactly the same manner as the prosecution witnesses. Their evidence is recorded as depositions, which are read over to them and signed with any corrections they wish to make. Once the defense completes its evidence; the accused's advocate may address the court regarding whether there is sufficient evidence to warrant committal. The magistrates still refrain from considering the question whether the defendant is guilty or innocent: they only consider whether there is a prima facie case. This time, however, they do so on the totality of the evidence, bearing in mind the defendant's explanations of matters alleged by the prosecution witnesses. If the magistrates decide not to commit the accused for trial, he is discharged.

Section 1 of the Criminal Justice Act 1967 specifies an alternative form of committal. The act provides that when all the evidence before the court, whether for the prosecution or defense, consists of written statements, tendered with or without exhibits, the Magistrates' Court may commit the accused for trial at the Crown Court without consideration of the contents of those statements. The act excludes situations where (1) the accused, or one of them, is not legally represented; or (2) counsel, or a solicitor for the accused or one of them, has asked the court to consider a submission that the statements disclose insufficient evidence to put that person upon trial by jury for the offense. The written statements are prepared by the police in the same manner as those submitted in accordance with Section 2 of the Criminal Justice Act 1967 described above.

Before submitting the written statements, the solicitor representing the Crown has the responsibility of deleting all inadmissible portions, such as hearsay statements. Copies of the edited statements are provided prior to the hearing to the defense solicitor, who must satisfy himself that there is in fact a case to answer, before agreeing to a Section 1 committal. While there is no information kept nationally concerning the use of committals under Section 1 of the Criminal Justice Act 1967, as opposed to those under Section 7 of the Magistrates' Courts Act 1952, it is generally thought that the proportion of the latter to the former is extremely small. The limited research available bears out this impression. In a study of cases committed for trial by Sheffield Magistrates' Court during 1972, only 1 case out of a total of 356 had a full committal proceeding. Of 2,406 cases set for trial in the Crown Court at Birmingham during 1975 and 1976, only 4 had full committals, while in 18 others some of the evidence was given orally.

NOTICE OF ALIBI

"Alibi evidence" is evidence tending to show that by reason of the presence of the defendant at a particular place, or in a particular area, at a particular time, he was not, or was not likely to have been, at the place where the offense is alleged to have been committed at the time of its alleged commission. By virtue of Section 11(1) of the Criminal Justice Act 1967, the accused may not adduce evidence in support of an alibi at his trial on indictment without leave of the court, unless he gives notice of the particulars of the alibi within seven days from the end of the committal proceeding. This provision includes alibi evidence given only by the accused. The defendant may give notice either at the Magistrates' Court during, or at the end of, the committal proceeding, or thereafter in writing to the solicitor for the prosecution. Notice given by the accused's solicitor is deemed to be notice authorized by the accused. Notice of Alibi was in fact given on behalf of David Fisher on July 5, 1980, and revised on January 27, 1981. At no point in the proceedings was an issue raised that David Fisher's Notice of Alibi was served late.

ASSIGNMENT TO CROWN COURT

Once the magistrates have decided to commit the accused to stand trial, whether as a result of a traditional hearing on the evidence or because the accused's advocate has agreed to a Section 1 committal, they then have to decide to which sitting of the Crown Court the accused should be sent for trial. Unlike the ancient criminal courts of Assize and Quarter Sessions, now abolished, the Crown Court has jurisdiction to try all offenses wherever they may have occurred in England or Wales. In committing the accused for trial, the magistrates must specify the place at which he is to be tried. When selecting the place, magistrates must consider the convenience of the defense, the prosecution, and the witnesses, expediting the trial, and questions relating to the class of judge for assignment of the case. Three different classes of judges sit at the Crown Court: (1) high court judges, who also sit in the Court of Appeal and Queen's Bench Division; (2) circuit judges, full-time criminal judges or judges who divide their time between criminal work and the civil and divorce jurisdiction of the county courts; and (3) recorders, that is, barristers and solicitors, in practice but sitting for a number of weeks every year as temporary judges trying criminal cases.

The Crown Court sits in many towns throughout the country. All three classes of judges sit in the larger towns, like Birmingham. In the smaller towns, only circuit judges or recorders sit. The work of the Crown Court is assigned between the various judges on the principle that the high court judge should try the more serious or difficult cases. Section 7(1) of the Courts Act establishes directions, which in effect provide for four classes of offenses:

Class 1: cases which must be tried by the high court judge (e.g., murder, treason, spying),

Class 2: cases which should normally be tried by the high court judge, but which the high court judge in charge of the circuit may assign to a circuit judge or recorder (e.g., manslaughter, infanticide, rape, incest),

Class 3: cases which may be tried by either the high court judge, a circuit judge, or a recorder (e.g., arson, robbery, wounding or causing grievous bodily harm with intent, unlawful intercourse with a girl under thirteen, perjury, corruption of government or local government officers), and

Class 4: cases which will normally be tried by a circuit judge or recorder (e.g., causing death by reckless driving, burglary, and all cases triable either way).

The Magistrates' Court serves an order to attend trial at the selected Crown Court on each witness whose personal appearance at trial will be required. After taking into account any representation made by the accused or the prosecution, the Magistrates' Court may decide that the presence at trial of a witness is unnecessary on the ground that his evidence is unlikely to be required or disputed. In such a case, the witness is conditionally ordered to attend the trial, meaning that the witness is not obliged to attend unless either the prosecution or the defense subsequently requires his attendance. The Magistrates' Court must inform the accused of his right to require the attendance of a witness conditionally ordered to attend. The statements or depositions of witnesses conditionally ordered to attend and not subsequently required to attend in person may be read as evidence at the trial of the defendant.

The clerk of the Magistrates' Court which commits the accused for trial promptly sends the following documents to the proper trial court officer:

1. the information, if in writing;
2. the depositions and written statements with the certificate authenticating them and any formal admissions made;
3. all statements made by the accused before the magistrates;
4. a list of the witnesses subject to conditional witness orders;
5. the recognizance of the surety, if any;
6. a list of exhibits;
7. the accused's Notice of Alibi, if any;
8. a statement that it was a Section 1 committal, if it was;
9. any order made authorizing full press reporting;
10. a certificate of the costs of the prosecution.

The Magistrates' Court also issues a certificate of the committal to the Crown Court.

Copies of the information, if in writing, the depositions, written statements, and of the list of witnesses are provided automatically to the accused. The solicitor for the accused also receives access to all exhibits prior to trial, along with the accused's record of prior convictions, referred to as his form. In addition, if prosecuting counsel knows of a credible witness who can speak to material facts which tend to show the accused's innocence, he must either call that witness himself at trial or make his statement available to the defense in advance of trial. The prosecuting counsel must also inform the defense, in advance, of the bad character or criminal record of any prosecution witnesses and inform the defense of any statement made by a prosecution witness which substantially conflicts with what it is anticipated he will now testify to at trial.

On April 24, 1980, David Fisher was committed for trial to the Crown Court under Section 1. Copies of the written witness statements submitted at the committal proceeding are annexed as Appendix III. The trial was assigned for trial by a circuit court judge.

Upon receipt of the committal papers at the Crown Court, the clerk of the Crown Court draws up the indictment. In the case of David Fisher, the indictment, drawn on May 16, 1980, charges David Fisher with:

Count 1

Statement of Offense: Robbery, contrary to Section 8 of the Theft Act 1968.
Particulars of Offense:
David Fisher, on the 25th day of February 1980, robbed Yvonne Gardener of £3,800.

Count 2

Statement of Offense: Possessing firearm whilst committing an offense, contrary to Section 17(2) of the Firearms Act 1968.
Particulars of Offense:
David Fisher, on the 25th day of February 1980 at the time of robbing Yvonne Gardener of £3,800 cash had in his possession an imitation firearm, namely, a .38 "Chief" blank firing gun.

A different solicitor was retained by David Fisher during May 1980. On June 16, 1980, the Crown Court so amended the order granting legal aid. On July 18, 1980, the legal aid order was once again amended on the basis of the probable serious penalty facing the defendant in the event of a conviction. The amendment provided for two counsel, a Queen's Counsel and a Junior Barrister. On July 23, 1980, the Crown Court granted an application for bail made by junior counsel, subject to the provision of a surety in the sum of £1,000 acceptable to the police, and the condition that David Fisher reside at a specified address in Birmingham, reporting at 7:30 P.M. daily to the Shard End Police Station. The surety was obtained and David Fisher was released on bail.

SUMMARY TRIAL IN THE MAGISTRATES' COURT

With respect to those crimes only triable in the Magistrates' Court, or triable summarily upon election, if the accused pleads not guilty the Magistrates' Court will determine guilt or innocence.

In all but the simplest cases, the prosecuting solicitor opens his case on the trial of the information with a summary of the evidence the Crown intends to introduce and of the effect of that evidence. The prosecution then calls its witnesses one by one. Each is examined on direct and subjected to cross-examination by the solicitor for the accused. In the process of cross-examination, defense counsel must challenge the witness by putting to the witness in question form evidence the accused intends to introduce later in the trial that disputes the testimony given by the witness during direct examination in order that the witness have the opportunity to deny or explain.[5] The witness is then reexamined by the prosecution. The evidentiary rules at summary trial are the same as in any other criminal proceeding, though in practice the rules are sometimes relaxed, particularly when the accused is not legally represented.

When the case for the prosecution has been closed, the defendant has two alternatives. He may submit that there is no case for him to answer, or he may proceed to present his own case. If the evidence introduced by the prosecution fails to establish every element of a prima facie case, if the defense badly upsets the prosecution witnesses during cross-examination, or if the witnesses have contradicted each other, the defendant may submit to the court that there is no case for him to answer. He may support his submission by a speech drawing the attention of the court to the omissions and inconsistencies in the case for the prosecution. The court will then consider the submission and may retire in order to do so. If the court accepts the submission, the case is dismissed. If they find that there is a case to answer, the trial proceeds. Alternatively, the court in its discretion may allow the prosecution to reopen its case in order to supply missing evidence.

If the court finds the existence of a prima facie case, or if the accused does not challenge the existence of a prima facie case, the defense solicitor, if he chooses, may address the court. The defendant may next remain silent, make an unsworn statement from the dock, or give his own evidence, in addition to calling witnesses on his behalf. If the accused gives sworn evidence, he must do so before calling other witnesses. Witnesses called by the defense will in turn be challenged by the prosecution on cross-examination. The prosecutor may next introduce evidence in rebuttal. Because little advance preparation is possible, and the accused may appear without counsel, defense evidence will frequently reveal unexpected facts. Accordingly, the prosecution may introduce evidence in rebuttal without first obtaining leave of the court.[6] The rebuttal evidence must, however, relate to unanticipated evidence, and not merely reinforce the prosecution's case.

The rules governing closing speeches are complicated in theory, if not in practice. The Magistrates' Court Rules 1968 at Rule 13 provides:

Order of evidence and speeches: information (b)—

(1) On the summary trial of an information, where the accused does not plead guilty, the prosecutor shall call the evidence for the prosecution, and before doing so may address the court.

(2) At the conclusion of the evidence for the prosecution, the accused may address the court, whether or not he afterwards makes an unsworn statement or calls evidence.

(3) At the conclusion of the evidence, if any, for the defence, the prosecutor may call evidence to rebut that evidence.

(4) At the conclusion of the evidence for the defence and any unsworn statement which the accused may make and the evidence, if any, in rebuttal, the accused may address the court if he has not already done so.

(5) Either party may, with the leave of the court, address the court a second time, but where the court grants leave to one party it shall not refuse leave to the other.

(6) Where both parties address the court twice the prosecutor shall address the court for the second time before the accused does so.

Thus, if counsel for the accused makes an opening speech, his right to make a closing speech rests in the court's discretion. Failure to permit a second address under some circumstances is considered a denial of justice, resulting in a vitiated conviction. In England, a person whose conviction is set aside on appeal may not normally be retried; he goes free. The prosecution may also apply for the right to make a closing speech. If both sides apply, when the court grants one party's request it may not refuse the other's. If both sides are to address the court, the prosecution proceeds first; the defense has the last word. As a practical matter, in most summary trials the defendant guarantees his right to make a closing speech simply by not making an opening speech. When the defense only makes a closing speech, the prosecutor usually does not ask for leave to make a closing speech. Thus, in practice, only the prosecution opens, and only the defense closes. This procedure is facilitated by the right and obligation of counsel on cross-examination to challenge testimony of opposing witnesses and in the process make his position clear to the magistrates.

The trial of an information before the Magistrates' Court differs from the trial of an indictment in the Crown Court in all of the ways that a bench trial differs from a jury trial. In addition, the Magistrates' Court makes no provision for discovery by the accused, although in practice many prosecuting solicitors provide defense solicitors with access to witness statements in advance of trial. When such voluntary disclosure does not take place, the defense solicitor is at a substantial tactical disadvantage.

After hearing the evidence and the parties' speeches, the Magistrates' Court reaches its decision as to the guilt or innocence of the accused. If not in immediate agreement, the magistrates may retire to discuss the case. The court decides by a majority; there is no need for unanimity. If the magistrates are equally divided, they will order a new trial. Magistrates may ask their clerk for private advice on points of law, but they must not seek or listen to his views on issues of fact. It is improper for them to request the clerk to retire with them when no issues of law arise in the case. Lord Goddard explains as follows:

5 PREPARATION FOR TRIAL

Previous chapters followed David Fisher from the moment of his detention under suspicious circumstances through his arrest, his subsequent confessions, the search of his room, and court proceedings leading in April 1980 to committal for trial in the Crown Court and release on bail in July 1980. With this background, it is now possible to turn to a more detailed examination of the respective roles played by the police, solicitors, and barristers concerning pre-trial procedures and final preparation for trial.

THE PROSECUTION

The Role of the Police

While private individuals may bring criminal prosecutions in England, the police bring the vast majority of prosecutions. This power to institute and control criminal prosecutions arose in the nineteenth century as a gradual historical development rather than a deliberate decision to convey such power to the police. A description of the critical role the police play in deciding to prosecute must precede a discussion of the role of solicitors and barristers representing the Crown.

The police make a number of decisions in bringing a person before a court to face a criminal charge. These decisions are affected by the seriousness of the offense, the circumstances in which it first comes to light, whether there is a power of arrest, whether the suspect is an adult or a juvenile, and the evidentiary complexity of the case. The first decision concerns whether to follow up an incident which may amount to a criminal offense. Clearly, following up all such incidents would be impossible. The officer on the street, therefore, makes decisions about which incidents to pursue. An officer will more likely exercise his discretion to take no formal action when more minor conduct is involved. Assuming further action is necessary, the way in which other early decisions as to prosecution are made depends on whether the offense carries a power of arrest. If the offense does not carry a power of arrest, the officer may report the matter to a senior officer. The choice then lies between administering a formal caution, prosecution, and no further proceedings. Formal cautions are used almost exclusively with juvenile offenders willing to acknowledge guilt. The decision whether or not to prosecute is normally ratified within the police at the chief inspector level or above. If the police decide to prosecute, a summons commences the proceedings. The police exclusively decide whether to prosecute: the prosecuting solicitor must proceed if the police desire to push forward.

When the offense carries a power of arrest, the officer concerned may choose either to arrest the person or to report the matter with a view toward prosecution. If the latter course is adopted, the procedure mirrors that described above regarding a nonarrestable offense. When an arrest is made, the person is taken to the police station.

Four possible outcomes await a person arrested without a warrant. First, he may be released without charge if the police, after making the arrest, discover evidence which exculpates the suspect or decide there is insufficient evidence to justify his prosecution. This occurs in up to 20 percent of all arrests. Second, the police may release the accused while considering prosecution, retaining the option to initiate prosecution by way of summons. Third, if the officers cannot complete inquiries into the offense forthwith, they may release the accused on bail to attend at a specified police station. Fourth, the accused may be charged with the offense and cautioned as provided under the Judges' Rules. An accused who has been charged may be released on bail to appear before a Magistrates' Court or may be retained in custody and brought before a Magistrates' Court as soon as practicable. The person arrested under warrant on a criminal charge must be taken before the court issuing the warrant immediately unless the warrant is endorsed for bail.

The police conduct all investigation leading to the arrest and make all decisions to charge suspects. Prosecuting solicitors do not employ investigators. The police interview every witness and obtain a signed statement from each witness for presentation at the Section 1 committal proceeding. The police also prepare a short statement of facts for use by the solicitor at the initial appearance of the accused and a more detailed factual summary of witness statements, sometimes referred to as a police report, for use by the solicitor at the committal proceeding. The operative segments of the police report in the case of David Fisher are annexed as Appendix IV. The police prepare diagrams and take photographs where believed helpful at the committal or trial. An Antecedent Report, prepared by the police, attached as Appendix V, contains the prior convictions of the accused, together with a statement of the accused's background. The Antecedent Report functions much the same as the Pre-sentence Report does in the United States. However, since the Antecedent Report is made available to the court and opposing counsel well in advance of trial, sentencing of a convicted defendant usually follows immediately upon return of the guilty verdict.

The police not only obtain written statements of witnesses but must also assure the presence of witnesses at court. The officer placed in charge of the case performs this task. If a witness needs to have his recollection refreshed before trial, the policeman in charge of the case must show the witness his statement. If unexpected contingencies arise, as occurred at the trial of David Fisher when a witness not originally intended to be called turned out to be eight months pregnant and in need of transportation to the Crown Court, the officer in charge of the case for trial makes appropriate arrangements, in this case, sending a police car to drive the woman to court. The officer in charge of the case, usually but not necessarily the officer in charge of the investigation, is present in court throughout the trial to assist counsel in any way possible. It is very important to keep in mind that no one on the prosecution side, other than a police officer, will have interviewed occurrence witnesses called at trial on behalf of the prosecution at the Magistrates' or Crown Court. Preparation of occurrence witnesses by the attorney for the prosecution, as it occurs in the United States, simply does not take place in England; the solicitor in the Magistrates' Court summary trial or committal proceeding, or the barrister at the Crown Court jury trial, will first hear the voice of his occurrence witness when he states his name on the stand. Expert witnesses are prepared by prosecution attorneys prior to trial.

The Prosecuting Solicitor

RELATIONSHIP TO POLICE

Control over the prosecution of a person charged by the police rests in the hands of the local police force itself. Apart from the role of the Director of Public Prosecutions, which is comparatively limited in the number of cases that come his way though they are usually significant in substance, arrangements for police prosecutions are at the discretion and control of the local chief constable and the police authority for each of the forty-three separate police force areas. Within these forty-three separate police force areas, arrangements for obtaining legal advice vary from force to force. The basis for the practice in most forces is the recommendation made by the Royal Commission on the Police 1962 that consideration be given to the appointment of a prosecuting solicitor for every force to give legal advice in deciding upon prosecutions and presenting cases at trial. As of June 1980, thirty-one police forces had prosecuting solicitors' departments of some kind. In addition, the Metropolitan force had its own solicitors, and the legal staff of the Common Council assisted the City of London force. In several of the ten forces without a department of any kind, the chief constable has, in the past, requested a department. Those forces without a prosecuting solicitor most often employ private firms on an ad hoc basis when legal advice is perceived as necessary. With respect to those police force areas having prosecuting solicitors' departments, there is great variation in structure, administration, and function.

The exact relationship between the solicitor and the police is not precisely defined, and much depends on the cooperation and understanding of the individuals concerned. Clearly, however, the basic relationship between the chief constable and his prosecuting solicitor is one of client and solicitor. The solicitor acts upon the instructions of the police; the solicitor may advise, but the chief constable is not bound by that advice. Thus, while the solicitor may offer advice, the final decision on who shall be prosecuted and for what offense rests with the police. This is equally true if any question arises whether a prosecution should be withdrawn with the consent of the court at any stage, for example, if further evidence comes to light.

Practice varies from force to force as to representation of the police in the Magistrates' Court. Generally, whether the police are legally represented in cases tried summarily depends on the complexity and importance of the case, as well as on such other factors as whether the defense is also represented and whether a plea of not guilty is expected. The Royal Commission on the Police 1962 regarded as "undesirable" police officers appearing as prosecutors, except for minor cases. A member of the prosecuting solicitor's office, a private solicitor, or a barrister may legally represent the police in the Magistrates' Court.

In proceedings conducted at the Crown Court there is, of course, no question of police or even solicitor advocacy—only barristers may appear in Crown Court. In practice, the choice of barrister in cases heard on indictment at Crown Court rests either with the prosecuting solicitor, as is the case in Birmingham, with the police, or, in cases which he has taken over, with the Director of Public Prosecutions. In response to the fact that slightly more than 25 percent of serious crime committed in England and Wales each year occurs in London, a permanent group of prosecuting barristers—the only one in the country—has been established. They are called Treasury Counsel, numbering at present seven senior and ten junior counsel appointed by the Attorney General at London's Central Criminal Court.

THE PROSECUTING SOLICITOR'S OFFICE IN BIRMINGHAM

There are no nationally prescribed standards for the organization of prosecuting solicitors' offices. The prosecuting solicitor and his staff may be employed by the police authority itself, or they may be on the staff of the local authority, perhaps with other duties to perform on behalf of that authority. There is little uniformity of terms and conditions of a solicitor's service, and no unified career structure throughout the country. Similarly, there are wide variations in the type and amount of work performed by prosecuting solicitor's offices and the way the work is handled. Offices range in size from less than half a dozen legally qualified staff to more than fifty attorneys in the large metropolitan areas. Some are highly centralized, with solicitors going daily from one office to the various courts; others are decentralized, with one or two solicitors permanently attached to a particular court. In some cases, the prosecuting solicitor is employed full time on police work; in others he may also occasionally prosecute on behalf of the local authority or agencies such as the British Transport Police.

The Solicitors

The office of the prosecuting solicitor in Birmingham is divided into two principal departments. The first department consists of over fifty legally qualified solicitors[1] and the occasional barrister who represent the Crown in all contested proceedings in the Magistrates' Court. In Birmingham, with the exception of very few extremely minor uncontested matters, a legally qualified solicitor or a barrister from the prosecuting solicitor's office, and not a policeman, makes all appearances on behalf of the Crown.

To assist the solicitor at the initial court appearance of the defendant, whether following an arrest or following the issuance of a summons, the police complete a one-page form highlighting the nature of the offense charged. The form provides a short statement summarizing the prima facie case against the accused, taking a position with respect to the granting of unconditional bail, and giving the relevant background of the defendant. Copies of the charge sheet, the record of convictions where applicable, written statements of the defendant, and written witness statements to date are annexed to the form. Armed with this form and appendices, the prosecuting solicitor is prepared to represent the Crown before the Magistrates' Court in connection with a plea of guilty, an application for bail, a remand for either a summary trial or committal proceedings, or to conduct a summary trial held either forthwith or at a date certain fixed for the future. If, as is usually the case, all necessary witness statements have not been obtained at the time of the initial appearance of an accused who intends to plead not guilty, the solicitor will request a remand to permit the police to obtain the required witness statements for the summary trial or committal proceeding to follow.

With respect to both the summary trial and the contested committal proceeding, advocacy on behalf of the Crown seems more routine in nature than in a trial upon a similar offense in the United States. The factors are many and varied. To begin with, the prosecuting solicitor does not interview the witnesses. The police present the solicitor with a report summarizing the evidence and outlining the thrust of the case, together with written statements of each witness detailing his knowledge of relevant facts. Direct examination of each witness called by the Crown consists of inquiries by the solicitor based upon the witness's statement designed to elicit answers in conformance with the witness's statement. In addition, in about 29 percent of all contested cases at the Magistrates' Court, the accused will have made a confession or damaging admission. Motions by the defendant to bar introduction of confessions, admissions, or physical evidence are naturally rare, given the state of the law governing the admissibility of evidence obtained in violation of the law.

The law governing criminal trials is itself extremely sparse and simple to find in England in contrast to similar laws operating in the United States. Both the prosecution and defense solicitor often ascertain the applicable law by looking in Archbold. Archbold's *Pleading, Evidence and Practice in Criminal Cases* is a 2,135-page book in its fortieth edition covering, as the title indicates, pleading, evidence, and practice in criminal cases. This is not to suggest by any means that all the answers are clear and simple or even clearer and simpler in Archbold than in the United States. In fact, the contrary is probably true. Nevertheless, since everyone relies on Archbold almost exclusively, research is simplified even if the conclusion reached is less than perfectly clear. Moreover, solicitors often choose not to object to inadmissible evidence actually offered at trial out of concern that objection may only serve to highlight evidence in the mind of the lay panel even if the evidence objected to is ultimately excluded at trial. To this reluctance to object to evidence actually heard by the magistrates can be added various assumptions relating to the ability of the trial court to evaluate evidence which result in an overall less rigid enforcement of rules of evidence by the court where objection is made in bench as compared to jury trials.

The approach of the attorney representing the prosecution also differs in the two countries. In the United States, young aggressive lawyers frequently begin their careers in the office of the local prosecutor or public defender. They handle minor matters at first, moving on later to more serious matters tried to the bench alone or to a jury, and finally to major felony jury trials. Misdemeanor bench trials are learning experiences, vehicles for the development of skills needed later on. Most of these young lawyers, after a few years performing felony jury trials, will move on to other jobs, whether in civil practice, the judiciary, or more administratively oriented positions within the office of the prosecutor or the public defender.

In England, the career pattern of the prosecuting solicitor is different. The prosecuting solicitor's office is a career-oriented position, not a vehicle to obtain experience qualifying the attorney for future positions. Moreover, the prosecuting solicitor never will try major cases before a jury because Crown Court jury trials are the exclusive province of the barrister. It is also worth noting that prosecuting solicitors in England present evidence on behalf of the Crown to a panel of lay magistrates drawn from the middle class. Thus, the panel would be expected to be extremely responsive to a low-key, matter-of-fact presentation on behalf of the Crown. Recent disclosures by the Home Office now indicate that 75 percent of all summary trials result in a conviction.[2] If one adds to this that approximately 40 percent of the acquittals result from some collapse in the prosecution's case, the percentage of guilty verdicts in cases in which the Crown presents a prima facie case approaches 85 percent.

In summary, the prosecuting solicitor in the Magistrates' Court represents the Crown concerning the disposition of a vast number of minor offenses. Each day he responds to bail applications, schedules cases on remand, and advises the court on guilty pleas as to facts underlying the offense and as to the background of the defendant, including prior convictions relevant to sentencing. The prosecuting solicitor submits papers prepared by the police in connection with Section 1 committal proceedings and occasionally presents witnesses in a contested committal proceeding. Finally, he tries summary cases from witness statements prepared by the police, without talking to a witness in advance, in front of lay magistrates very likely to convict if a prima facie case is presented. The prosecuting solicitor faces each new day knowing that tomorrow he will be back in Magistrates' Court doing the same things once again. The job is important because society needs to be protected. Yet everything about the role of the prosecuting solicitor—career development, preparation of cases, trial before middle-class magistrates ready to convict, and lack of complexity as to the law in practice, if not in theory—tends to make the occupation more routine in nature than the job of prosecuting similar offenses in the United States.

The Crown Court Assistants

Following committal of the defendant for trial at the Crown Court, the legally qualified solicitor who appeared at the Magistrates' Court transfers the entire file to the Crown Court assistant's department of the prosecuting solicitor's office. Crown Court assistants are not legally qualified lawyers. For the most part, the assistants are grammar or comprehensive school graduates who may be characterized as coming from the academically most qualified group of individuals who did not go on to college.[3] While some in-service training courses are available, most of the assistant's knowledge is gained from on-the-job experience. There are over twenty Crown Court assistants in the prosecuting solicitor's office in Birmingham.

The Crown Court assistant assists in any way possible the preparation and prosecution of the action, from committal to sentence. He reviews the witness statements contained in the committal papers and strikes those portions which are inadmissible, for example, by reason of the rule against hearsay. This procedure serves as a second review, because the prosecuting solicitor handling the committal is also responsible for deleting inadmissible material from witness statements furnished in a Section 1 committal. The assistant also reviews the exhibits to ensure that a proper foundation for admissibility has been prepared for the introduction of the exhibits at trial. If legal questions arise from a reivew of the file, the Crown Court assistant first researches the question, which usually involves research in Archbold. If the matter is of particular difficulty, the Crown Court assistant may request legal advice from a barrister.

In the case of David Fisher, the diagram and both sets of photographs of the scene were accompanied by witness statements of the preparer of the diagram and photograph, respectively. The identikit picture resulting from a description given by Yvonne Gardener was accompanied by a witness statement from the identikit compiler, Detective Sergeant Taylor. The Crown Court assistant perceived no evidence or other legal problems worthy of special attention. That part of bank manager Norman Witham's witness statement relating to perceiving a light-colored Negro driving a car near the scene of the bank robbery was, however, deleted as irrelevant.

Like the legally qualified prosecuting solicitor at the Magistrates' Court, the Crown Court assistant never interviews an occurrence witness. If additional witness statements are needed to establish or clarify a point, the assistant asks the police officer in charge of the case to obtain the additional statements. Since the police are the client of the prosecuting solicitor's office, the Crown Court assistant merely asks the police to perform their tasks rather than ordering them to do so. The police, not the Crown Court assistants, have responsibility for assuring the attendance of witnesses at all court proceedings and of refreshing their recollection in advance of trial by means of their written statement, where appropriate.

Several weeks before the trial of David Fisher, the Crown Court assistant prepared a Brief to Counsel. Enclosed with it were copies of all the committal papers, the police report summarizing witness statements prepared in connection with the committal, the Notice of Alibi, the Antecedent Report containing a short background description of the accused with an attached record of prior convictions, copies of the two sets of photographs of the scene, and the identikit composit picture. The Brief for the prosecution submitted to counsel stated:

Brief for the Prosecution

This defendant appeared before the Learned Stipendiary Magistrate for the City of Birmingham on the 24th April 1980 charged with offences of robbery and possessing an imitation firearm. Proceedings were taken under the provisions of Section 1, Criminal Justice Act 1967 and the accused was committed to Birmingham Crown Court in custody. Witnesses were conditionally bound to attend and a guilty plea is anticipated.

The facts of the case are summarized in the enclosed copy police report and your instructing solicitor feels there is no need for repetition.

Counsel will see that the evidence concerning the identification of the accused is far from satisfactory but the offences are admitted verbally and in two written statements.

Counsel will see that the accused has many previous convictions and in 1976 at Birmingham Crown Court he was sentenced to five years' imprisonment for offences of robbery and carrying a firearm.

If Counsel requires further instructions relating to any aspect of this case he is requested to draw such matters to his instructing solicitor's attention as soon as possible.

Counsel is requested to appear at the Birmingham Crown Court on behalf of the Prosecution and to return the brief to the prosecuting solicitor's representative at the conclusion of the case.

The head of the Crown Court assistants' department selects the chambers where the Brief will be sent and may request that a particular barrister be instructed (retained) to handle the matter. The Brief for the prosecution was forwarded to Norman Jones, Clerk to Chamber 3 in Birmingham. Chamber 3 has thirty-two barristers sharing the services of Norman Jones and his assistant clerks. The clerk attempts to arrange with the court administrator's staff an organization of cases which permits the barristers requested to be instructed to be available for trial on the date set. When this is not possible, or when a specific barrister has not been requested, the clerk selects counsel of suitable experience to be instructed. This requires obtaining the agreement of the barrister and the Crown's representative, who in the case of David Fisher was the head of the Crown Court assistants' department representing the prosecuting solicitor, who represents the police and the Crown. Mr. David Jones was instructed to appear on behalf of the Crown. Mr. Jones reviewed the Brief with enclosures over the weekend before the trial. If the case had been scheduled for a day other than Monday, the barrister would generally examine the Brief with enclosures for the first time the evening before trial.

At the trial itself, the Crown Court assistant takes a seat behind counsel for the Crown usually alongside the police officer in charge of the case. Together they assist counsel, for example, with the handling of exhibits or locating an original statement for the purpose of impeachment. The responsibility for the producton of witnesses and their preparation remains, however, solely with the policeman in charge of the case.

The Crown Court assistant spends a tremendous amount of time in court observing trials. He draws on this experience in determining whether a particular file necessitates seeking the advice of counsel in advance of trial or obtaining additional information from the police. Since counsel will probably not examine the file before the night preceding trial, these decisions made by the Crown Court assistant may significantly affect the outcome of the litigation.

THE DEFENSE

The Role of the Solicitor and Legal Executive

The accused, unless he intends to plead guilty to a very minor charge, will almost always be represented by a solicitor. At the time of his arrest, the accused may know of a solicitor he desires to represent him. On other occasions, relatives or friends suggest a solicitor. Still other times, the police recommend a good solicitor to handle the accused's case. Finally, the defendant may acquire a solicitor pursuant to one of the many duty solicitor schemes operating throughout England. The method of selection of a solicitor has no effect upon the eligibility of the defendant to have legal aid pay the solicitor from public funds. All solicitors representing criminal defendants are privately employed. There is nothing in England equivalent to the public defender system existing in the United States. Most solicitors representing criminal defendants also engage in a wide range of general practice. Other solicitors specialize solely in crime. There are approximately 34,000 solicitors in England and Wales.

Before proceeding to explore the activities of the solicitor in representing a person accused of a crime, it is important at this initial stage to keep in mind what is obvious from earlier discussion: solicitors do appear in court in contested matters. Solicitors representing criminal defendants argue summary trials and contested committal proceedings in the Magistrates' Court. Solicitors representing clients in civil matters may appear before a judge sitting in the county court. The jurisdictional limit of the county court is currently £2,000 or about $3,500. Thus, the image of the solicitor as the office lawyer preparing contracts and wills and giving legal advice to clients, although correct, is incomplete. Many solicitors are also trial lawyers. Certainly all solicitors handling crime are trial lawyers. Moreover, as will be developed more fully, the image many Americans have concerning the solicitor-barrister relationship with respect to jury trials of the solicitor preparing the cases for trial by the barrister, while not incorrect, is certainly misleading when it comes to representation of the criminal defendant in an ordinary matter.

The role of the solicitor may commence with a telephone call from a person held in custody by the police requesting his presence and legal advice. In most cases, however, the accused does not ask to see a solicitor when under interrogation. Moreover, the police usually deny such a request when made. Thus, the first contact the solicitor has with the defendant normally occurs after the defendant has been either charged or issued a summons to appear in court. If the accused was arrested and charged, depending on his bail status, the solicitor may see the accused either in custody or in his office.

The solicitor normally, but not always, conducts the initial interview with the accused. One of the solicitor's staff of legal executives normally conducts further interviews with the accused, interviews witnesses for the defense, and prepares statements to be signed by these witnesses regarding matters destined for the Crown Court. Sometimes the initial interview with the accused is also conducted solely by the legal executive. Solicitors do not normally employ investigators. Neither the defense solicitor nor his legal executive usually conducts interviews with witnesses for the Crown. When such interviews do occur, they normally take place prior to the committal proceeding after notification has been given to the prosecuting solicitor of the intention to interview, thereby facilitating the presence of a representative of the Crown. With respect to matters at the Magistrates' Court, in addition to interviewing the accused and defense witnesses, the legal executive assists the solicitor in coping with the problem of having several clients appearing before different panels of magistrates during the same morning. This includes ensuring that all defendants, witnesses, and sureties, if necessary, are present at the right place at the right time. In addition, legal executives research legal questions, usually from Archbold, concerning matters arising both at the Magistrates' Court, where the solicitor represents the accused, and at the Crown Court, where a barrister has been instructed.

The position of legal executive, like the position of Crown Court assistant, tends to be held by those among the most highly qualified individuals leaving secondary education and not going on to college. In order to progress in the career of legal executive in a solicitor's office, the person so employed usually pursues the requirements of the Institute of Legal Executive leading to the position of Fellow of the Institute. The program leading to the position of Fellow requires successful completion of prescribed courses of instructions given at various colleges throughout England, passing various examinations given by the institute, and employment by a solicitor for a specified duration.

With respect to David Fisher, on March 19, 1980, his solicitor did not see him prior to his being charged and refused bail by the police. The police ignored requests by Fisher to see his solicitor. His solicitor first saw David Fisher on March 20, 1980, sometime before his initial appearance at the Magistrates' Court. The solicitor soon discovered that Fisher was charged with robbery, a crime which only the Crown Court may try, and that Fisher claimed innocence. The only action taken at the Magistrates' Court on March 20 was an application for legal aid. During Fisher's remand until March 26, the solicitor conducted an initial interview with Fisher at the jail to ascertain information needed to apply for bail and to begin to develop from David Fisher his version of relevant facts. This included his whereabouts on February 25, 1980, when the robbery of the Midland Bank occurred, and how he acquired knowledge of the bank robbery if he was not involved. With this information in hand, the solicitor could ask his legal executives to begin to locate witnesses who might be needed at trial. Full-scale preparation for trial often commences in earnest only after the defense learns of the factual support for the prosecution case. This occurs when the defense is provided by the prosecuting solicitor's office with a copy of the committal papers prior to the committal proceeding. If the defense solicitor could raise a serious question whether a prima facie case is made out by the committal papers, the solicitor and the solicitor's legal executives, where necessary, would immediately set out to gather factual support for such an attack and to research potential legal issues. Since a serious question of the existence of a prima facie case being made out by the witness statements furnished in connection with the committal proceeding could not be raised regarding David Fisher, his solicitor agreed to a Section 1 committal.

At the moment when the case of *Regina v. David Fisher* moved from the Magistrates' Court to the Crown Court, as a practical matter, the responsibility for Fisher's defense moved from the solicitor, assisted by the legal executive, to the legal executive. Thus, while the solicitor himself continues in law to represent the accused after committal and is thus ultimately responsible for preparation of his defense, in all but the most unusual case the job of preparing the case for trial in fact falls on the legal executive. Preparation includes obtaining signed statements from defense witnesses, researching the law including, where appropriate, seeking the advice of counsel, preparing the brief to counsel on behalf of the accused, attending conferences with counsel, if any, securing the attendance of the defendant, if on bail, and other witnesses in court, and assisting counsel in court in any way. The solicitor acts in a supervisory capacity, ensuring that everything proceeds smoothly and intervening where his expertise is of particular assistance.

There are thus three stages of representation in most cases tried in the Crown Court. First, the solicitor represents the accused at proceedings in the Magistrates' Court assisted by the legal executive. Second, the legal executive, acting under the supervision of the solicitor, prepares the case for trial and instructs the barrister. Third, the barrister tries the case, assisted by the legal executive.

Preparation for Crown Court Trial

The defense of David Fisher began to take shape in mid-June, about two months after receipt of the committal papers and one month after retention of a new solicitor. On June 26, the legal executive interviewed David Fisher in jail. He saw Fisher again on June 30, July 4, July 7, and July 11. As a result of these interviews the legal executive prepared two written statements. The first, dated July 7, 1980, outlined the background of the accused. The second, dated July 11, 1980, detailed his version of the events relating to his knowledge of the existence of the bank robbery and his arrest. In addition, on July 4 David Fisher gave his comments concerning the accuracy of the witness statements submitted at the committal proceeding. The comments were later reduced to writing and entitled "Comments Upon Deposition." On July 5, defendant's solicitor served a Notice of Alibi on the prosecuting solicitor's office:

> We act on behalf of the above-named client who faces a charge alleging that he robbed Yvonne Gardener of £3,800 at 3:00 P.M. Monday 25th February 1980.
>
> In accordance with Section 11 of the Criminal Justice Act 1967, our client wishes to raise the following Notice of Alibi.
>
> At 2:40 P.M. on that day our client left the Gothic pub, Great Hampton Street, Hockley and then went to a Mr. James' flat at 47 Martineu Tower arriving there at 2:50-2:55 P.M.
>
> Our client remained there until 3:30-3:45 P.M. and went to a hostel on the Warwick Road.

On July 11, the legal executive requested counsel to consider whether in his opinion the gravity of the offense, the substantial sentence likely to be imposed, and the disquieting features of the Crown's case concerning identification together warranted the addition to the legal aid order of a Queen's Counsel, a senior barrister of distinction. Application for leading and junior counsel was made and approved on July 18, 1980. On July 23, 1980, junior counsel moved for bail, which was granted subject to certain conditions.

The legal executive held a meeting with David Fisher on August 7 in the solicitor's office to obtain a detailed account of David Fisher's whereabouts on the date of the bank robbery. Several other meetings were held later in the year to discuss the inability of the legal executive to locate the alibi witness at the Highcroft Hospital, the address provided by David Fisher. On January 27, 1981, the prosecuting solicitor was advised by letter that the correct name of the alibi witness referred to as Mr. James in the notice of July 5, 1980, is James Jackson.

In mid-August, the prosecuting solicitor on request provided a copy of the identikit picture. On October 21, 1980, the court announced that the trial had been set for February 9, 1981. In mid-November, the solicitor representing David Fisher contacted Chamber 3 to arrange for leading counsel to be instructed along with junior counsel, Mr. Coleman Treacy. Mr. Treacy was the counsel for Mr. Fisher who had rendered the advice regarding the propriety of the appointment of a Queen's Counsel in early July and who had represented Mr. Fisher in obtaining an order on July 23, 1980, by the Crown Court providing for bail. Mr. B. R. Escott Cox, Q.C., undertook leading counsel.

In early January 1981, the legal executive prepared and forwarded to both leading and junior counsel, a Brief to Counsel on behalf of the accused. The Brief read as follows:

Regina
v.
David Fisher

Counsel has herewith:

1. Indictment,
2. Depositions,
3. Comments upon Depositions,
4. Proofs of Evidence of the Accused,
5. Copy of Photofit [Identikit] picture supplied by the Prosecution,
6. Copy of Notice of Alibi.

Instructing Solicitors act on behalf of David Fisher who is due to appear before the Birmingham Crown Court charged with offences of robbery and possessing a firearm whilst committing an offence.

To both the above charges our client intends to plead Not Guilty.

Fisher, who is a single man aged 33, was last released from a custodial sentence in December 1979. This was a 5 year sentence of imprisonment for robbery.

He is now charged that, on the 25th February 1980 at 3:30 P.M., he robbed Yvonne Gardener, a cashier at the Midland Bank, Great Hampton Street, Hockley of £3,800.

In the course of this robbery an imitation firearm was used, which now forms the basis of Count 2 on the Indictment.

Miss Gardener, in her statement to the Police, describes the man responsible for the robbery as being coloured. Our client is most definitely white and could no way be mistaken as being of negroid appearance.

Our client has supplied details of his movements during this particular time and a Notice of Alibi was served on the 5th July 1980, a copy of which is enclosed in Counsel's papers.

Instructing solicitors are at present making arrangements to see Mr. Jackson but we have discovered that he is an alcoholic and has been admitted to Highcroft Hospital for treatment. We can only hope that he will have some recollection of this incident but on the face of it, it must remain unlikely.

Fisher was arrested on the 15th March 1980 in the International Arrivals lounge of Birmingham Airport. He had been for a short holiday to Ireland to visit friends.

On his arrest our client had over £1,400 in his possession. He had been initially apprehended by Airport Security Officers who searched his property. Upon finding the money the Police were called for.

His explanations at this stage were far from convincing and the Police, not surprisingly, wanted to know how a man who had been unemployed could afford to go to Dublin with so much money in his possession.

Counsel is asked to refer to the evidence of P.C. Abolins and D.C. Sutcliffe, starting at Page 16 of the depositions.

Fisher stated that the money had been won gambling and this indeed forms the basis of our client's case. He will state that during the course of approximately one week he played cards with various acquaintances and won a total of approximately £2,000.

He met these people in local pubs and played cards in a cafe on the Alum Rock Road.

Our client will state that one of the fellow gamblers admitted as to having been responsible for the robbery and Fisher's proceeds from the card game were from this robbery.

He also instructs us that this same person had also been given a gun, belonging to our client, on approval.

The gun was not sold and so was returned to our client and was eventually found by the Police. Clearly this is not the strongest part of our client's case.

Fisher's winnings from the gambling spree were neatly clipped together and can be said to be in a similar fashion to the way the Midland Bank uses paper clips to bundle its notes together.

The Police, clearly, did not believe our client's account of receiving the money and told him they would be going to search his flat at 155 Warwick Road.

The Police will state that, at this, our client's attitude completely changed and he asked the officers to leave him to sort matters out in his own mind.

He then made a voluntary statement under caution, admitting his involvement in the robbery at the Midland Bank.

He was then taken to Steelhouse Lane and was further interviewed by D. C. Butler and D.C. Pyke. He is then alleged to have elected to make a further voluntary statement, basically setting out his disposal of the money.

Not surprisingly, our client's recollection of the events is slightly different.

The mention of our client's flat was made in order to threaten him. He states that the Police threatened to "turn over" the flats of various friends and let them know who had caused the aggravation.

This must have had an effect on Fisher who instructs us that it was for this reason that he made a false statement.

He has mentioned that his life would have been severely disrupted if the Police had indeed carried out their threats.

Unfortunately for our client we are now having to face the difficulty of challenging two statements of admission.

Instructing Solicitors feel that our client's account will provide him with problems when he is questioned in Court but the overriding factor remains that the Main Prosecution Witnesses appear to be sure that it was a coloured man who was responsible for the robbery and there is no admissible evidence on the papers to suggest that more than one man was involved.

We have also been supplied with a photocopy of a photofit picture by the Prosecution and although being a very poor copy it will give Counsel some idea of this aspect of the evidence.

Our client was also given bail by His Honour Judge Ross on the 23rd July 1980 after Junior Counsel Mr. Treacy informed the Court of the difficulties the Prosecution may have with their evidence.

Clearly further information will have to be taken but Instructing Solicitors would be grateful if a conference could be arranged to gain Counsel's opinion.

The case has been fixed for trial on the 9th February 1981 and Counsel is asked to appear.

The depositions referred to in the Brief are in fact a full set of documents submitted at the Section 1 committal proceedings. The set includes copies of signed witness statements along with copies of the two written confessions made by David Fisher. The Comments upon Depositions is the document bearing the same title prepared on July 4, 1980, from an interview by the legal executive with Fisher while he was still in custody. The Proofs of Evidence are the summaries of interviews with Fisher prepared on July 7 dealing with background, on July 11 dealing with Fisher's knowledge of the bank robbery and events leading to his arrest, and on August 7 concerning his whereabouts on the date of the robbery itself. Copies of the Comments upon Depositions and Proofs of Evidence are annexed as Appendices VI and VII, respectively. Junior counsel at the bail hearing in July had been provided with a copy of the Antecedent Report, Appendix V, annexed to which is David Fisher's record of prior convictions.

The conference requested by the legal executive was held on January 26, 1981. Present were David Fisher, the legal executive, leading counsel Escott Cox, and junior counsel Coleman Treacy. Various matters were discussed. David Fisher's version of all relevant events reflected in the Brief and accompanying documents were confirmed with him. It was also confirmed that Fisher was never placed in a lineup, referred to in England as an identification parade, and that the alibi witness, Mr. James Jackson, still could not be located. In the usual case, a conference is not held in advance of trial. Instead, counsel on the morning of the trial, at court, one half-hour before court commences, speaks to the accused and confirms his understanding of the accused's version of the relevant facts. Where necessary, counsel also clarifies ambiguous matters raised in the Brief and accompanying documents. Having confirmed his version of the relevant facts personally with the defendant, counsel feels justified in challenging the testimony of prosecution witnesses.[4] In addition, at the January 26, 1981, conference, counsel discussed with David Fisher whether he should testify at trial if the prosecution is able to present a prima facie case. It was tentatively agreed that, since it would be difficult to persuade a jury that the two signed confessions resulted from his concern with having the police disrupt his friends and blame David Fisher for causing the aggravation, Fisher would not testify.

Fisher appeared at the conference with long hair and a beard. Counsel suggested that he should alter his appearance to conform with that depicted in the photograph taken of him upon his arrest. Finally, counsel and accused discussed trial strategy. Considering that the description of the robber given by the bank teller, Yvonne Gardener, to the police was "Asian or a very light-skinned West Indian," that the identikit composite picture made from Gardener's description looked nothing like Fisher, and that an identification parade was not held, the question was raised whether counsel should go for broke and ask Yvonne Gardener at trial to confirm that the man in the dock, David Fisher, was not the man who robbed the Midland Bank in Hockley on February 25, 1980. It was decided that, given the strength of the prosecution's case built around Fisher's confession, the physical evidence seized from his room, and the inability to locate the alibi witness, counsel might have no choice but to ask Yvonne Gardener whether Fisher was the man.

At the conclusion of the conference, counsel told Fisher to proceed to the solicitor's office on the morning of February 9, to be escorted by the legal executive to the appropriate courtroom.

THE BARRISTERS

The barrister is a trial lawyer.[5] While he may appear in Magistrates' and County Courts, his main occupation is the conduct of civil trials before the court alone,[6] and criminal trials before judge and jury, in the Crown Court. There are approximately 4,500 barristers in England and Wales.

Barristers engaged to represent the Crown or the accused on occasion become involved following committal, but well before trial, to the extent of arguing preliminary matters at the Crown Court or giving advice. This occurred to a limited extent with David Fisher's counsel, Mr. Treacy, when he moved the court for the appointment of leading counsel and appeared on behalf of Fisher's application for bail. Normally, however, counsel for Crown and accused each reads his Brief the night before the trial. He proceeds to court in the morning without ever having talked to any occurrence witness or otherwise assisting in the preparation of the case. An exception is normally made if an expert witness will be called at trial. In that case, arrangements are made to have the barrister consult with the expert in advance of trial. In most cases, however, everything the barrister knows about the facts of a case comes solely from the Brief to Counsel with Appendices. The barrister obviously has little time for legal research. The little research he may perform often involves picking up Archbold. When the matter at hand is concluded, it is time to read the Brief for tomorrow, consider the appropriate position to take with respect to a plea in mitigation following a guilty plea, prepare a motion in a civil matter, or otherwise do what is necessary to perform the upcoming day's work.

As previously mentioned, the three counsel involved in the trial of David

Fisher were all from Chamber 3 in Birmingham. Each barrister is an individual entrepreneur who employs the same clerk and shares the expenses of chambers. The law perceives no conflict of interest in having counsel for both parties in one set of chambers. Counsel frequently meet in the late afternoon in chambers to discuss nonprivileged matters occurring that day. This process serves to pass the wisdom of senior barristers on to those less experienced. With respect to the trial of David Fisher, in no way could it be said that such conversation compromised either side's interests.

Some barristers describe the atmosphere of chambers as that of an officer's club. There is a silent respect for each other's talents and an understanding of the need for all to comply with the rules of custom if the trial process is to continue to function well. This understanding has over the years resulted in the development of practices concerning both pre-trial preparation and trial which make it possible for a barrister to prepare for a trial the night before and try a case solely from a Brief and accompanying documents. The operation of the pre-trial system in England leading to the Brief to Counsel with accompanying documents has already been explored. The structure of the Crown Court trial will be examined in Chapter 6.

NOTES

1. To become a solicitor the aspirant usually completes an undergraduate three-year college course in law. This is followed by an academic year-long course similar to a bar review course in America, leading to an examination conducted by the Law Society. Upon successful completion of the examination, the aspirant completes the process of becoming a solicitor by serving a two-year apprenticeship, referred to as articles, in the office of a practicing solicitor.

2. *Times*, January 14, 1981.

3. With respect to the educational system in England, see Chapter 2 at note 1 supra.

4. With respect to challenging a witness, see page 82 infra.

5. To become a barrister the usual course is for the aspirant to complete an undergraduate three-year college course in law. This is followed by an academic year-long law course, similar to a bar review course in America, leading to an examination conducted by the Counsel of Legal Education. Upon successful completion of the examination, the aspirant must undergo six months of apprenticeship, referred to as pupilage, in the chambers of a barrister. In addition, during the period of education the aspirant must eat a prescribed number of dinners at one of the four Inns of Court in London, upon which occasions the aspirant meets barristers and absorbs from them the traditions of the profession. In America this is sometimes referred to as learning how to separate prune from pit.

6. There are jury trials in some civil cases. However, no more than 3 percent of civil cases are tried to judge and jury. See Jackson, *The Machinery of Justice in England* 92 (1972).

6 THE STRUCTURE OF THE CROWN COURT TRIAL

As is true of each of the various procedural steps up to trial, the structure of the trial itself may have a profound influence on its outcome. Each of the various stages of the Crown Court trial of David Fisher are examined in turn. The object is to provide the reader with a framework against which to appreciate the transcript of the proceedings. This will help the reader analyze the trial transcript and begin to form conclusions regarding how pre-trial preparation and the structure of the trial in England influence the result in contrast to the manner in which such subjects are approached in the United States. In addition, the reader is asked to begin to consider whether the English approach or its American counterpart to various aspects of the criminal jury trial, taken alone or together, best achieves a fair trial for the accused, while at the same time serving the legitimate concern of society to convict the guilty, and doing both without incurring needless expense.

The various aspects of the trial are approached in the order that events normally occur in the English Crown Court criminal jury trial:

1. Setting the Scene
2. Arraignment and Plea
3. Empaneling the Jury
4. Prosecution Counsel's Opening Speech
5. The Case for the Prosecution
6. Submission of No Case to Answer
7. Defense Counsel's Opening Speech
8. The Case for the Defense
9. Prosecution Evidence in Rebuttal
10. Closing Speeches

11. The Judge's Summation
12. The Verdict
13. Sentence
14. Appeal

SETTING THE SCENE

It is almost 10:30 A.M. on February 9, 1981, in Courtroom 13 of the Victoria Law Courts, Birmingham. Counsel have completed pre-trial preparation. The trial of David Fisher is about to begin. The three barristers, David Jones representing the Crown and Escott Cox and Coleman Treacy representing David Fisher, have left their chambers together at about 10:20 A.M. to proceed to the cloaking room to put on their robes, wigs, and bands (collars). The defendant is in the dock. The jury in waiting is seated in the right rear of the courtroom. The legal executive and the Crown Court assistant have arrived and taken their customary seats. The officer in charge of the case is seated behind the jury in waiting rather than next to the Crown Court assistant. The occurrence witnesses are outside the courtroom, having been advised by the police that they could not be present in the court prior to giving their testimony. The barristers arrive. Everyone stands as the judge enters. On February 9, 1981, at 10:30 A.M., Courtroom 13 appears as shown in Figure 3.

The bench, witness stand, jury box and dock all are raised. Items taken from the accused when arrested and those recovered from his room are in open view on the clerk's table. Notice that the defendant is not seated near counsel. The tactic employed in the United States by defense counsel of appearing to consult and converse with the defendant to personalize him before the jury, while conveying a sense of caring, is unavailable in England.

ARRAIGNMENT AND PLEA

Proceedings at the Crown Court commence with the clerk calling the accused to the bar by name. The bar, which is the traditional barrier separating the court and its officers from the parties and gallery, is in fact the front of the dock. The accused stands in the dock. The clerk reads the indictment one count at a time to the accused, who with respect to each count may plead guilty, not guilty, stand silent, or make objection on legal grounds to the trial proceeding, such as that he is unfit to stand trial. David Fisher pleaded not guilty to each count.

EMPANELING THE JURY

Once the defendant has pleaded not guilty to any count of the indictment, a jury must be empaneled to try him. The jury panel will normally wait outside the court during the arraignment, because if the defendant pleads

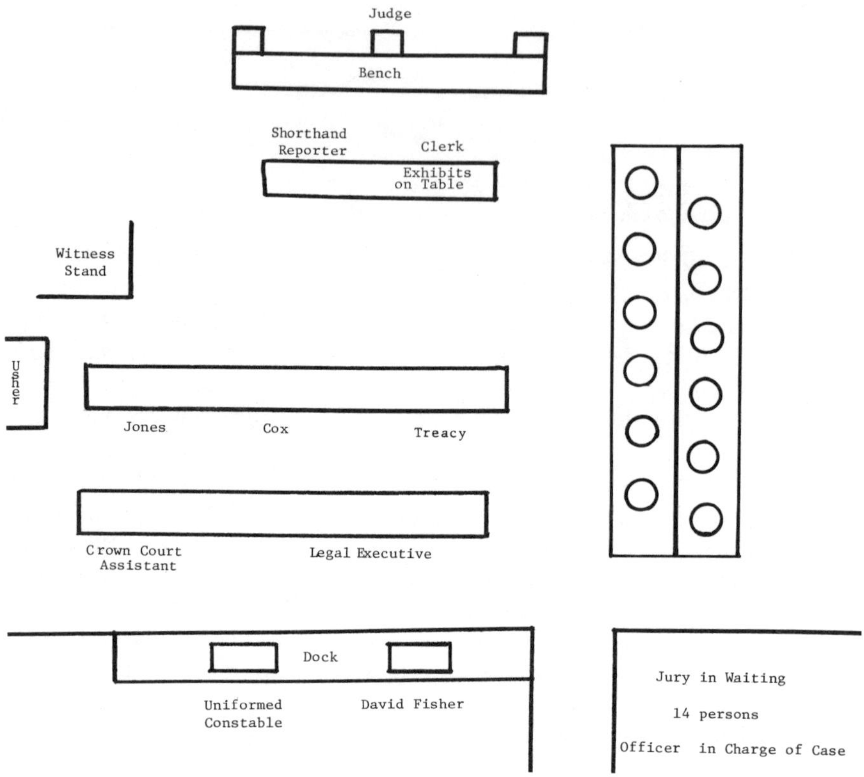

Figure 3
Appearance of Courtroom 13 on February 9, 1981

guilty to some charges and not guilty to others the jury must not normally hear that he has admitted his guilt of such offenses. In the case of David Fisher, the jury panel was in fact seated in the right rear of the courtroom during the arraignment.

A jury consists of twelve people, male and female, aged between eighteen and sixty-five, who are qualified to serve as jurors because they are registered parliamentary or local government electors and have been resident in the United Kingdom for any period of five years since reaching the age of thirteen and who are not disqualified or ineligible. Any person is disqualified who has been sentenced to imprisonment for three months or more in the last ten years or who has ever been sentenced to imprisonment for life or for five years or more. If such a person serves on a jury, however, the jury's verdict is not thereby void. Four groups of people are ineligible for jury service: (1) those who have at any time held judicial office, including justices of the peace and chairmen of tribunals; (2) those who have held certain occupations in the last ten years, such as barristers and solicitors, whether or not in actual practice, their clerks and legal executives, court staff, the police, probation officers, and forensic scientists; (3) clergy and vowed members of religious orders; and (4) the mentally ill. All but the mentally ill are ineligible because of the undue weight that might be given to their opinions by lay members of the jury.

Three groups of people may claim excusal as of right: (1) members and officers of Parliament and peers and peeresses; (2) full-time serving members of the armed services; and (3) practicing members of professions relating to medicine, including veterinary surgeons and pharmacists. Three categories of discretionary excusal also exist: (1) a person who has served on a jury within the last two years or longer period allowed by the court in a particular case; (2) a person who shows good reason to be excused, such as being personally concerned in the facts of or with the parties or witnesses to a case, personal hardship, or conscientious objection; and (3) a person who appears to the appropriate officer of the court to be incapable of acting effectively as a juror because of a physical disability or an insufficient understanding of English.

A panel of more than twelve jurors usually is brought into court, and the clerk selects twelve jurors by ballot. In the case of David Fisher, a panel of only fourteen was already seated. The clerk tells the defendant that the jurors whose names are called out will form the jury to try him but that he has the right to challenge the jurors before they take the oath. The prosecution also has certain rights of challenge. Either side may challenge the array, that is, challenge the whole body of jurors on the ground that the official responsible for summoning the jurors in question is biased or has acted improperly. Either side may challenge an individual juror for cause because the juror is disqualified, is ineligible, is partial, or might be partial. The defendant, but not the prosecution, has the right to make three peremptory challenges , which are challenges for which no reason need be given. The prosecution may require that individual jurors should stand by, that is, be excluded unless it is impossible to form a jury from the panel of prospective jurors without calling on them. Jury selection is referred to in England as jury vetting.

If it appears to the court that the jury is likely to be incomplete, it may require persons in, or in the vicinity of, the court to be summoned without written notice up to the number needed to make a full jury after allowing for disqualifications, ineligibility, excusals, and challenges. This procedure is called praying a tales.

The right to exercise challenges for cause and peremptorily or to ask jurors to stand by is a right in name only in England because counsel is barred from asking any questions at all to prospective jurors. The court does not question jurors either. Jury questionnaire forms, used in many jurisdictions in the United States, are not employed in England. While counsel may request, prior to trial, to see a list of all jurors summoned for the two-week jury term, the list contains only the citizen's name and address. For obvious reasons, this right is rarely exercised. For equally obvious reasons, prospective jurors are rarely challenged. None were challenged in the case against David Fisher. The jury selection in the case of David Fisher took no more than five minutes.

Once the clerk of the court has duly sworn a jury of twelve, he reads the indictment to them, tells them that the defendant has pleaded not guilty to the indictment, and states that it is their charge to say, having heard the evidence, whether he is guilty or not guilty. Alternative jurors are not selected. If a juror or jurors cannot continue to serve, the trial will usually continue, provided the jury does not fall below nine members.

In the United States, during jury selection, or "voir dire," counsel is usually permitted to propound questions to prospective jurors, although it is becoming more common for all questioning to be conducted by the trial judge, assisted by the submission of written questions from counsel. Whichever method of questioning is employed, the sole legitimate objective of voir dire is inquiry of the prospective jurors to obtain information leading to challenges for cause and the intelligent employment of peremptory challenges. The process seeks an unbiased jury by permitting each party to challenge jurors unsympathetic toward him.

When the attorney himself asks questions of prospective jurors, he frequently seeks to accomplish two other objectives while at least appearing to inquire regarding matters relevant to the intended exercise of challenges. The first is ingratiation, which refers to an attorney's attempt to present himself and his client in a favorable light and in the process establish rapport with the jury, thus creating a relationship with them that will enhance his prospects for persuasion later in the trial. Ingratiation is sometimes colloquially referred to as visiting with the jury or crawling into the jury box. The second is indoctrination, or familiarizing the jury with certain factual or legal concepts, often accompanied by the securing of a commitment from the juror to act in a specified manner if a given situation results at trial. Indoctrination, especially concerning legal questions, is tolerated in only some jurisdictions. Where permitted, attorneys employ the following types of questions.

Q. As my client sits here, he's presumed innocent. You understand that, don't you?

Q. It would be unfair to consider him guilty just because the prosecution charged him with a crime, wouldn't it?

Q. Do you have any difficulty in presuming him to be innocent now?

Q. The prosecution is required to prove any defendant guilty beyond a reasonable doubt. You understand that, don't you?

Q. If they fail to meet their burden, you must find the defendant not guilty. Do you have any difficulty in accepting that proposition?

Q. The defendant has a constitutional right not to present any evidence or testify himself. If my client stands on his rights, you wouldn't hold that against him, would you?

Q. Do you have any relatives or friends who are police officers or work in law enforcement?

Q. A police officer's testimony should be judged by the same standards as any other witness, shouldn't it?

Q. You wouldn't believe a police officer merely because he's a police officer, would you? You'd have to see if his testimony made sense, wouldn't you?

Q. Will you follow the law the judge gives you and base your verdict on the law and the evidence you hear?

Q. If the prosecution fails to prove my client guilty beyond a reasonable doubt, you wouldn't have any reluctance in signing a "not guilty" verdict, would you?[1]

Voir dire in the United States represents the initial opportunity for the attorney for each side to sell himself and his cause to the jury. It also provides defense counsel with his first of many opportunities to educate the jury regarding the burden upon the prosecution to establish the case beyond a reasonable doubt and the presumption of innocence. The more successful defense counsel is in conveying these concepts to the jury, the more likely an acquittal. The more times the jury hears of such concepts, the more likely it will understand the concepts and apply them during its deliberation.

One of the potential consequences of the lack of inquiry of prospective jurors in England is many hung juries, given the inability of the prosecution to identify those jurors predisposed to acquit all defendants. In fact, substantial numbers of hung juries never materialized in England. The possibility of a significant number of hung juries has now been all but eliminated by Section 13 of the Criminal Justice Act 1967. Section 13 enables the court to accept a majority verdict, provided that the jury have had not less than two hours for deliberation, or such longer period as the court deems reasonable considering the nature and complexity of the case, and at least ten of the jurors, or nine if there are only ten jurors, agree on the verdict.

Jurors in England are permitted to take notes. It did not appear that any jurors chose to do so during the trial of David Fisher.

PROSECUTION COUNSEL'S OPENING SPEECH

The actual trial commences in England with the opening speech of prosecution counsel. In his opening address, counsel for the prosecution outlines the facts the prosecution intends to prove in support of the charges laid in the indictment and shows how such facts amount to the offense charged. Thus, counsel in his opening speech is expected to argue his case by drawing the attention of the jury to inferences which support guilt arising from the evidence to be presented. The opening speech of the prosecution must also advise the jury of the obligation of the Crown to prove the defendant guilty beyond a reasonable doubt. Over recent years, courts have interpreted this obligation to mean, alternatively, that the jury must be "completely satisfied," be "sure of the defendant's guilt," or be "satisfied that you are sure of the defendant's guilt." Courts usually use the latter interpretation when instructing the jury.

Counsel for the Crown in his opening speech may refer to exhibits if defense counsel has agreed before trial that the introduction of the exhibits will not be opposed at trial. Unlike defense counsel in the United States, who frequently assume the stance of not agreeing to anything, thus putting the prosecution to its full proof, counsel for the accused in England will readily agree in advance of trial to the introduction of exhibits where no ground of objection is anticipated. Conversely, where defense counsel has stated in advance that particular evidence, whether testimonial or in the form of an exhibit, will be contested as inadmissible at trial, counsel for the Crown may not make reference to such matters in his opening speech. Questions of admissibility of evidence in England are decided when the evidence is offered rather than, as is becoming more frequent in the United States, on a motion in limine before trial.

In his opening speech, prosecution counsel should also outline evidence he will present during the Crown's case in chief to refute anticipated defense allegations, subject to defense counsel's courtesy in telling him whether such matters will be put forward. He might, for instance, refer to similar fact evidence, that is, other crimes, wrongs, or acts, to rebut a defense of accident or advise the jury of evidence that meets an attack on the character of a prosecution witness. Presentation of evidence in the nature of rebuttal during the prosecution's case in chief reduces the frequency with which evidence is offered on rebuttal in England. In the case of David Fisher, for example, the prosecution learned through the cross-examination of its principal witness that the defense was challenging the identikit picture and raising a question with respect to the identity of the individual observed by the bank manager driving away from an area near the bank. As a result, the prosecution called Detective Sergeant Taylor and Mrs. Claudette Hales during its case in chief to respond to these contentions.

The opening statement in the United States similarly serves to provide counsel for the prosecution an opportunity to outline the facts he plans to develop at trial in support of his case and to do so in a clear and convincing manner. However, the attorney is limited to a discussion of the facts. Argument in the sense of an inference to be drawn from the facts which a witness could not himself state from the witness stand is considered improper. Thus, the statement made by Crown Prosecutor David Jones in his opening speech that David Fisher "may have made his face to appear darker than it was'' would be objectionable as argumentative if contained in an opening statement in America.

The barrister makes his opening speech standing at his seat. His counterpart in the United States usually stands directly in front of the jury box, peering first at one juror and then another. Taken alone, the location of the advocate in presenting an opening speech or statement is probably insignificant. However, when coupled with the presence of the accused in the dock rather than next to counsel for the defense, with the robes and wigs worn in England, and with the ability of attorneys in most jurisdictions in America, but not in England, to move around the court during questioning on voir dire, during the examination of witnesses, in the handling of exhibits, and during closing argument, the total impact may be significant from the perspective of the accused. Standing in one location in a robe and wig next to an opponent similarly attired leads to a perception of detachment from the cause at hand. Whether this image of detachment of counsel is only apparent or as will be later argued is to some extent real, the appearance of detachment from the matter at hand most certainly harms the accused more than the prosecution in a criminal case.

The opening speech by the barrister for the Crown is followed by the presentation of the prosecution's case in chief. The defendant's opening speech, if permitted, occurs immediately preceding the presentation of evidence by the defense.

THE CASE FOR THE PROSECUTION

The prosecution now presents its evidence in support of the offense charged, including evidence known at this stage of the proceeding to be in the nature of rebuttal to evidence to be adduced by the defendant either during cross-examination of prosecution witnesses or during the defendant's opportunity to present evidence on his own behalf.

After each witness takes the oath, counsel for the prosecution conducts a direct examination. Counsel for the accused may then cross-examine the witness. Redirect examination is permitted where necessary, but recross-examination is not allowed. Witnesses normally stand during their entire examination, although in David Fisher's trial both female witnesses were given permission to testify while seated. Examining counsel also stands while asking questions. If counsel needs documents or other exhibits during the examination, the usher hands the item to counsel or the witness. The barrister remains stationary at all times.

Direct Examination

Conditional witness orders are issued by the court with the consent of the defendant concerning those witnesses whose testimony is not in dispute. Unless the accused has subsequently advised that he desires that the witness made the subject of a conditional witness order be produced at trial, prosecution counsel may publish the statement or deposition of the witness to the jury by reading it aloud, as done in the case of David Fisher with the statement of Mr. Conrad Cross and Police Constable Anthony Buckwell. In contrast, American attorneys on both sides of criminal cases rarely stipulate to former testimony of an available witness being read, preferring to have the witness present for whatever additional impact may be derived from live direct and cross-examination on uncontested matters. Committal proceeding statements and depositions of witnesses are also admissible at trial when offered by the prosecution when the witness is dead, insane, or too ill to travel or when he has been kept from attending by the accused.

All witnesses whose statements were submitted pursuant to a Section 1 committal proceeding or whose depositions resulted from testimony given at a committal proceeding held pursuant to Section 7 of the Magistrates' Court Act 1952 and who were not made the subject of a conditional witness order must be produced by the prosecution at trial. This requirement ensures the presence at trial of witnesses whose statements or depositions may be in part favorable to the accused. If the prosecution desires not to call such a witness, the witness will nevertheless be available to the defense.

The prosecution is not compelled to rely solely upon the evidence tendered at the committal proceeding. However, if the prosecution intends to rely on additional evidence, it must so notify the defense and provide a copy of a witness's statement to the defense and the court in time to permit the defendant to prepare to meet this additional evidence. If notification occurs at trial, the court may grant an adjournment. At the trial of David Fisher, evidence offered in addition to that relied upon at the committal hearing was offered through Mrs. Claudette Hales. A copy of her statement to the police was handed to defense counsel immediately prior to her being called to testify. However, the nature of her testimony did not rquire the defense to seek an adjournment to meet it.

Witness background information is not included in the statement taken from witnesses. Thus, the type of background information that usually introduces the testimony of witnesses in the United States contained in the following illustration is absent in England.

Q. Please state your full name.

A. Sharon Jones.

Q. How old are you, Ms. Jones?

A. I am 23.

Q. What city do you live in?

A. I live in Chicago.

Q. How long have you lived in Chicago?

A. About five years.

Q. Where are you from originally?

A. I was raised in Rockford and lived there until I finished high school.

Q. Did you ever attend any schools after high school?

A. Yes, I went to college at University of Illinois at the Chicago campus.

Q. Did you graduate?

A. Yes, I did.

Q. What field of study did you receive your degree in?

A. I received a bachelor of arts degree with a specialty in education.

Q. What did you do after graduating from college?

A. For the last year I have been working as a 7th grade teacher in the Chicago Public School System.

Q. Which school do you teach at?

A. I teach at Hawthorne School on the south side of Chicago.

Q. Are you single or married?

A. I am single.

Q. Have you ever been married?

A. No.[2]

Counsel for the Crown must normally examine witnesses called to give oral testimony by using nonleading questions, that is, questions which do not themselves suggest the answer desired. As is true in the United States, there are important exceptions to the rule barring the use of leading questions on direct examination. The most important exceptions for our purposes involve the use of leading questions with respect to preliminary, inconsequential, or undisputed matters and where necessary to develop a witness's testimony. The fact that witnesses called by a party in England, unlike America, have not been seen by counsel and had their testimony gone over in advance results in the use of leading questions to focus the witness's attention on particular matters under consideration more often than usually required in the United States. Only the skill of counsel, developed over many years of experience in examining a witness with only the witness's statement before him, keeps the need to resort to leading questions at the minimum level evidenced in the trial of David Fisher.

Exhibits are handled in a very relaxed manner. Items of evidence are often admitted upon agreement. This occurred with the two sets of photographs of the scene of the robbery, the plan of the area, the identikit picture made from the description given by Yvonne Gardener, and the photographs of David Fisher taken upon his arrest. The two statements signed by David Fisher, Exhibits 6 and 10, were identified by the appropriate police officer and treated as admitted into evidence. Neither was formally offered by counsel or ruled admissible by the court. In fact, counsel for the Crown at the commencement of his opening speech handed to the jury, without objection, several copies of a packet of exhibits containing photographs of the bank, the plan of the area, and the two statements signed by David Fisher, Exhibits 6 and 10. Lack of formal introduction applied as well to items of evidence taken from the accused at the airport and those found in his room. To illustrate, DC Pyke's testimony with respect to authentication and admission into evidence of the anorak worn by Fisher during the robbery was as follows:

A. Detective Constable Butler went on to say, "Did you wear any of this clothing when you committed the robbery?" He replied, "I think I had that anorak on, yes I did."

Q. Would you look at Exhibit 7. Is that the anorak he indicated?

A. Yes, that is it.

Notice that DC Pyke was not asked how he recognized Exhibit 7 as the anorak indicated. He probably would have replied to such a question in the United States that he had annexed a label to the anorak at the time it was seized. Alternative foundations would involve either establishing something unique about the anorak which he recalls or establishing a chain of custody of the anorak. In addition, testimony that the anorak is in the same condition now as it was then would most likely have been offered in the United States.

The law of evidence in England appears shallow in comparison to that applied in the United States. When considering, for example, questions of judicial notice, presumptions, the hearsay rule and its exceptions, the concept of res gestae, and the examination of a party of its own witness, the law of evidence in England seems nearly to have stood still during this century. Developments in the United States have been either totally ignored or rejected out of hand by English courts and commentators. Why English courts and commentators look with care at practices and procedures relating to the common law trial everywhere but America can only be the subject of speculation. Fortunately, save one instance, differences in the law of evidence need not be explored in order to appreciate the trial of David Fisher. The instance relates to the examination of a witness called by a party who fails to testify as expected. The English call this failing to come up to proof, referring to his written statement given before trial to one side or the other.

In England, the voucher rule is still applied. The voucher rule provides that a party may not impeach a witness whom he had called. Pursuant to the voucher rule, when a witness called by a party testifies in a manner contrary to his prior oral or written statement, counsel may not refer the witness to the prior inconsistent statement, except in the very unusual case of a witness who can be shown to be "hostile" in the sense of showing antipathy to the party calling him. Accordingly, in England, if the witness says something quite different from what is contained in counsel's proof of evidence, he must accept the answer given and may not formally impeach the witness with his oral or written inconsistent statement or otherwise refer the witness to what he had previously said by means of a leading question.[3]

With respect to refreshing the recollection of a witness, it is to be expected that some witnesses in England, as elsewhere, will have difficulty at trial recalling events occurring many months earlier. In such cases it is considered proper for the witness to review, in advance of trial, a copy of any statement given to the police or the solicitor representing the accused to refresh his recollection of the details of the event. If the witness did not retain a copy of his statement, the police, defense solicitor, or legal executive may provide the witness with a copy and review the statement with the witness. When the police show the witness his statement before trial, it is proper etiquette, but is not required as a matter of law, that the defense be advised concerning what has taken place. In practice, the police often show witnesses their statements without causing the defense to be so advised. Many counsel for the defense, whether advised or not, simply assume that prosecution witnesses have seen their past statements before testifying.

When refreshing the recollection of a witness in court, counsel may not employ leading questions containing a statement of the matter sought. Documents may be used to refresh recollection only if made at the same time as the occurrence of the events to which the witness is being asked to testify, provided in addition that the document was read over and accepted as accurate by the witness while the facts were still fresh in his memory. Thus, unlike the practice in the United States, any document capable of refreshing recollection may not be employed. Only those documents meeting the requirements of the American hearsay exception for past recollection recorded, referred to as recorded recollection in Rule 803(5) of the Federal Rules of Evidence, may be used in England to refresh recollection. Since most occurrence witness statements taken by the police fail to meet the contemporaneous making requirement, failure of a witness to recall at trial may result in the loss of the witness's testimony, raising the possibility of dismissal on the ground that a prima facie case can no longer be proved.

The rules relating to refreshing recollection in court from a contemporaneous document operate to the advantage of the police as witnesses at trial. In practice, police officers invariably contemporaneously record in a notebook the details of their investigation, including notes of any interrogation of the defendant and statements given by a witness. Trial judges give permission to police officers to refer to their notes when they give evidence. As seen from the testimony of the police officers in the trial of David Fisher, their direct examination consists mainly of reading a notebook into the record in reply to nonleading questions from counsel inquiring as to what happened next. Since the police officer's own witness statement submitted at the committal proceeding tracks the officer's notes, defense counsel may read along with the testimony.

With respect to objections to evidence, defense counsel usually indicates to prosecuting counsel in advance of trial the existence of items of evidence referred to in the witness's statements or depositions which he feels are inadmissible. Prosecuting counsel may accept that it is inadmissible, in which case he simply agrees that it should be excluded and, through the Crown Court assistant and the police, warns the witness that the particular part of his original statement should not be mentioned in court. If, however, counsel does not agree, the question of admissibility becomes an issue for the trial judge to decide. Prosecuting counsel will omit all reference to the evidence under objection in his opening speech. When the relevant witness is about to be called, he will often indicate to the judge that both counsel wish to seek his "guidance" on a point of law, and the judge will ask the jury to retire. When the objection can be indicated by reference to the deposition, or written statement, the judge merely hears counsel's argument and gives his ruling. When, however, the matter in dispute is not apparent from the depositions, as when objection is taken to a confession on the ground that it was obtained by threats or inducements and is thus involuntary, all relevant witnesses, including the accused, are examined regarding the matter in issue before the judge decides whether to admit the evidence in question.

Objections to evidence occur much less frequently in England than in the United States. Several reasons may account for this phenomenon. First, defense counsel, armed with the committal statements, knows what evidence is to be forthcoming and therefore does not have to object to prevent the introduction of potentially objectionable unknown evidence. Second, the procedure for obtaining agreement among counsel in advance of trial with respect to evidence asserted by defense counsel to be objectionable, coupled with an attitude of counsel to consider openly and fairly such contentions in the interest of reaching a fair disposition rather than merely assuming an arguable position before the court, leads to a significant reduction in objections. Finally, error may be considered on appeal in England even if no objection was made at trial. Counsel can thus avoid highlighting by objection the damaging effect of inadmissible or arguably inadmissible evidence being presented before the jury, secure in the knowledge that error in admission may nevertheless be raised on appeal.

In the presentation of the prosecution's case in England, in nearly two-thirds of all cases tried at the Crown Court counsel will offer into evidence one or more damaging verbal or written statements or confessions of the accused (see Table 2). Although comparable figures for the United States are not

TABLE 2
Damaging Statements of Defendants Offered at Crown Court Trials in Birmingham and London, 1975-1976

Type of Statement by Defendant	Birmingham Not Guilty Pleas		London Not Guilty Pleas	
	No.	*%*	*No.*	*%*
No statement of any kind	17	3.5	22	8.1
Full written confession only	5	1.0	2	0.7
Full written and full verbal confession	62	12.8	25	9.2
Full written confession and other verbal statement	17	3.5	5	1.9
Full verbal confession only	39	8.0	48	17.7
Written statement not a confession, but full verbal confession	20	4.1	1	0.4
Written statement not a confession	93	19.2	9	3.3
Damaging verbal statement only	96	19.8	72	26.6
Verbal denial only	124	25.6	78	28.8
Other kind of statement	12	2.5	9	3.3
No information or not codable	15		0	
Total	500	100.0	271	100.0

Source: M. McConville and J. Baldwin, *Courts, Prosecution, and Conviction* 112 (Oxford University Press, 1981). Reprinted by permission of Oxford University Press.

available, it is extremely unlikely that, given the system of warnings and rights mandated by *Miranda v. Arizona*,[4] prosecutors in the United States are as frequently so blessed.[5] Moreover, verbal statements admissible in England, such as, "I don't care what you think, that's my story. I still stick to that excuse," "You must be joking if you think I'm going to make a statement. You're not going to prove anything against me. I'm not daft, you know," and "I've been expecting you. I'm saying nothing. You go ahead and charge me. You'll never prove it," would be inadmissible in the United States on the ground that whatever admission may be inferred is clearly overshadowed by the need to permit an accused to assert his constitutional right to remain silent freely and without fear of admission against him.

Cross-Examination

During the cross-examination of prosecution witnesses the defense may, among other things, attempt to elicit evidence favorable to the accused and to discredit the testimony of the witness by various means. These methods include showing of partiality and impeachment by means of inconsistent statements. Leading questions are permitted. Depositions and witness statements are of great assistance to defense counsel in conducting cross-examination.

The most interesting aspect of English cross-examination, in contrast to that in the United States, is the requirement that any evidence to be later introduced disputing the direct testimony of the witness, whether in the form of self-contradiction, the contrary testimony of another witness, or an exhibit, must be "put" to the witness on cross-examination so that he may have an opportunity to deny the content or explain the contradiction. The requirement of challenge applies as well to prosecution counsel "putting" to a defense witness on cross-examination conflicting evidence previously introduced during the prosecution's case in chief.[6] Failure to challenge a witness may constitute acceptance of the witness's testimony on the point. Evidence offered later to contradict may be asserted to be barred on this ground; evidence previously offered may be stricken. Where such an objection is raised, counsel may request the court for leave to recall the witness for further cross-examination. Leave to recall will rarely be granted when the objection that a particular matter should have been aired during cross-examination arises when counsel attacks the witness's testimony for the first time in his closing speech.

Questions on cross-examination challenging the testimony of a witness frequently begin with phrases such as, "I put it to you that," "What really happened was that," or "I suggest that." The phrase "I have been instructed by my client that," although employed, is considered poor form by skillful counsel. Such questions would generally be considered objectionable as argumentative in the United States, because counsel is not by these questions attempting to elicit information but is instead presenting to the witness the opposite of what the witness has already stated for the purpose of advising the jury of counsel's client's disagreement. In America, such an expression of disagreement is argument properly delivered only during summation to the jury.

Another important variation in practice brought about by a combination of factors, including the lack of witness preparation in England as practiced in America and the requirement of challenge to provide any opportunity to deny or explain, is that witnesses on cross-examination are not expected, nor do they usually in practice, merely to answer questions yes or no. When confronted on cross-examination, the witness answers responsively, but naturally, whether that answer be yes or no, coupled with an explanation, or merely a statement. No objection lies to require the witness giving a responsive answer to reply merely yes or no. The witness may give an explanation or qualification at that time. Moreover, counsel in England are more willing to venture forth and ask the "why" or "how come" questions on cross-examination than their American counterparts, being apparently less concerned with the impact of a possible unfavorable answer on the jury.

On a broader front, whether brought about as a result of the rule requiring challenge, the absence of interviews with prosecution witnesses, preparation by counsel usually commencing the night before trial, the relationship of imputation upon the character of prosecution witnesses to impeachment by prior convictions to be discussed later,[7] or a combination of such factors, cross-examination in England appears to be much more a case of merely forcing the witness to dispute the truth of the opponent's position than it is in the United States. One has the sense that counsel for both sides in England resort to impeachment to show partiality, or lack of personal knowledge, less frequently and with less vigor in comparison with cross-examination of similarly situated witnesses in the United States. One wonders whether a combination of the provision of witness statements to the defense, the requirement of challenge, and the sporting theory surrounding imputation by prior conviction have not made it too easy for barristers to avoid undertaking more searching cross-examination.

Reexamination

With respect to new facts emerging on cross-examination and matters affecting credibility where the witness was not provided with or, if provided, did not avail himself of the opportunity on cross-examination to tender an explanation or qualification, counsel may on reexamination, referred to as redirect examination in the United States, elicit such testimony. Counsel cannot question the witness on a matter which was not raised on cross-examination, nor can he refer to a previous statement of the witness which is consistent with the evidence in chief unless it has been made admissible by the cross-examination. Recross-examination as practiced in the United States is not permitted in England.

Examination by the Judge

The trial judge in England shares with his American counterpart the rarely exercised right to call witnesses on his own and the more frequently exercised discretion to permit the recall of witnesses as required in the interests of justice. Judges in England seem to undertake a more active role than judges in the United States regarding both the questioning of witnesses and the prevention of improper questions being asked by counsel. Many questions are asked by the court to clarify the witness's testimony, probably as a result of the necessity for clear testimony so that it can be correctly stated in the court's summation to the jury. Since the court is provided prior to trial with what is called a "bundle," consisting of papers submitted at the committal proceeding, copies of other relevant exhibits, and the social inquiry report which has annexed to it the defendant's record of prior convictions, hesitation to inquire of the witness brought about by the belief common in the United States that counsel, having lived with the matter since its inception, knows more about the case than the court, simply does not apply to the English judge. Finally, given the power of the court to summarize the evidence and to comment on credibility during summation to the jury and the strongly felt obligation to ensure that the jury receives the evidence in a comprehensible manner, the English trial judge will quickly intervene if he feels counsel is attempting to introduce evidence which serves solely to deflect the jury's attention away from the matters truly before them. In America, attempts by defense counsel to introduce such red herrings are more frequently left to be sorted out by opposing counsel during closing argument and ultimately by the jury unguided by judicial comment.

SUBMISSION OF NO CASE TO ANSWER

At the conclusion of the case for the prosecution, counsel for the accused may submit that there is no case for the accused to answer. Counsel may address the court upon his submission, and the court will hear counsel for the prosecution in reply. Counsel for the defense may invite the trial judge to direct the jury that as a matter of law they should acquit the defendant. Such a direction will be given only where either the prosecution has failed to produce any evidence to establish an essential element of the offense charged or the evidence produced is so weak, or so discredited by cross-examination, that no reasonable jury could convict. If the submission of no case to answer is accepted, the case is concluded. If no submission is made, or if the submission is rejected, the defense is called upon to open its case.

DEFENSE COUNSEL'S OPENING SPEECH

When the accused intends to call witnesses concerning facts, other than giving evidence himself, his counsel may open his case by outlining the facts which he intends to prove. If the defense case includes no witnesses other than the accused himself and witnesses, if any, testifying only as to his character, defense counsel cannot address the jury. There is no obligation to make an opening address. In cases which are not complex, even when an opening speech of defense counsel is permitted, it is frequently waived. Considering the posture of the case, including counsel's obligation to challenge those aspects of the prosecution's evidence which the defense disputes, the basic tenor of the accused's defense is most frequently already before the jury. Moreover, since the accused, if he testifies, must be the first witness for the defense, counsel's opening may merely serve to distract the jury from paying attention to the accused's testimony concerning the same facts immediately thereafter.

The inability of defense counsel to make an opening address to the jury prior to the prosecution's case in chief creates a serious disadvantage to the accused. An opening address before the introduction of any evidence at trial allows the accused not only to outline the evidence he intends to introduce but also to apprise the jury regarding the proper attitude they should take in evaluatng evidence as it is received during the trial. In addition, defense counsel can stress prior to the introduction of any evidence the obligation resting upon the prosecution to prove its case beyond a reasonable doubt. Witness the following illustration of a typical opening statement given on behalf of the defendant in the United States, immediately following the opening statement by the prosecution:

May it please the Court, counsel, ladies and gentlemen of the jury, good morning. My name is Steven Cole and this is my partner, Stanley Hill. We are here on behalf of the defendant, Sylvester Strong.

The purpose of the opening statements, of course, is to give you a preview of what we expect the evidence in the case to show. Immediately after the opening statements, the prosecutors will start with their witnesses. After each witness completes his testimony, we, as defense counsel, will be afforded an opportunity to cross-examine those witnesses. It is important that you recognize that the testimony you hear during the cross-examination is as significant as the direct examinations, that is, the information elicited through direct examination.

I ask you to listen very carefully to these witnesses. Observe their demeanor. Make a determination as to their truthfulness and their credibility. Draw upon your own life experiences as you hear this testimony to determine what is fact and what is fiction.

Only after the prosecutors have presented their case will Sylvester Strong have an opportunity to present his case. We ask that each of you keep an open mind about who is right here until you have heard all the evidence, ours as well as theirs. However, before I talk to you about what we believe the evidence will show, I want to make one fact perfectly clear to each of you. We do not contest the fact that Sylvester Strong did in fact shoot and kill the deceased, Shelley Williams, on March 25, 1976, on Bloomingdale Avenue in Chicago. That fact, however, is not the issue in the case.

The only issue in this case is whether or not Sylvester Strong was defending himself when the shooting happened. In other words, ladies and gentlemen, was Sylvester Strong justified in defending himself under the facts and circumstances that unfolded during the afternoon of March 25th? Please remember that we, as the defense, don't have to prove anything. It's the prosecution that has to prove, beyond a reasonable doubt, that Sylvester Strong was not justified in defending himself. The evidence will show that Sylvester Strong was in fact justified in doing what he did and thus is not guilty of any crime.

What really happened before and during the incident? * * *

In short, ladies and gentlemen, we expect the evidence to show that under these circumstances Sylvester did nothing more than what any other reasonable person would have done under those circumstances. He simply defended himself from an armed mob. Therefore, he is simply not guilty of murder or any other crime.

I ask you, ladies and gentlemen, at this time to withhold any thoughts you may have about this case. Please withhold your judgment until you have heard all of the evidence from all of the witnesses, and I am confident that upon hearing all of the evidence you are going to render a verdict in this case that will be fair. We believe that the prosecution will not be able to prove, beyond a reasonable doubt, that Sylvester was not justified in defending himself. We expect that after you deliberate and carefully weigh the evidence in this case you will return the only possible verdict, a verdict of not guilty. I thank you.[8]

THE CASE FOR THE DEFENSE

The defendant is not obliged to give evidence at his trial. He may remain silent[9] or make an unsworn statement from the dock. Because an unsworn statement is not subject to cross-examination by counsel for the prosecution, it is strictly speaking not part of the evidence in the case. If the defendant desires to make an unsworn statement to the jury from the dock, he may do so at the conclusion of his case in chief, after lay witnesses whom he has called have given their evidence on oath. Normally, the defendant will choose to give evidence under oath because such evidence, subject to cross-examination by the prosecution, will inevitably carry greater weight with the jury. If the accused gives evidence, he must be the first defense witness to testify.

Witnesses called by the defense are examined, cross-examined, and reexamined and generally speaking are subject to the same rules governing witness examination applicable to witnesses called by the prosecution. With respect to the conduct of cross-examination, counsel for the Crown is not favored with witness statements similar to those provided to defense counsel prior to the committal proceeding or those provided later in connection with any further evidence to be offered by the prosecution. Counsel for the Crown frequently, however, has the benefit of the Notice of Alibi and statements made by the accused to the police. In addition, counsel will have had the benefit of hearing the defendant's contentions laid bare in questions put to prosecution witnesses challenging their testimony.

The accused in England who chooses to testify stands in the same position as other witnesses, with an extremely important exception relating to evidence of bad character, including reference to prior convictions of the accused. The question of the proper procedure for impeaching the accused with prior bad acts, reputation testimony for untruthfulness, and most, importantly, the establishment of prior convictions as bearing upon credibility has remained an extremely controversial subject in the United States for a long time. The solution adopted in England in 1898 represents a compromise, effected in a manner totally different from any of the approaches followed in America.[10]

Under Section 1(F) of the Criminal Evidence Act 1898, the danger of unfair prejudice from having misdeeds of the defendant exposed to the jury under the rubric of evaluating credibility is resolved in a manner that neither wholly prohibits nor always permits such impeachment. Section 1(F) principally provides the accused with a shield which is only discarded if he gives evidence of his good character or casts imputations on the prosecutor or on a witness for the prosecution. If the shield is discarded, the accused subjects himself to cross-examination on his criminal record and past misdeeds. Section 1(F) states:

> A person charged and called as a witness in pursuance of this Act shall not be asked, and if asked shall not be required to answer, any question tending to show that he has committed or been convicted of or been charged with any offence other than that wherewith he is then charged, or is of bad character, unless—
>
> (i) the proof that he has committed or been convicted of such other offence is admissible evidence to show that he is guilty of the offence wherewith he is then charged; or
>
> (ii) he has personally or by his advocate asked questions of the witnesses for the prosecution with a view to establish his own good character, or has given evidence of his good character, or the nature or conduct of the defence is such as to involve imputations on the character of the prosecutor or the witnesses for the prosecution; or
>
> (iii) he has given evidence against any other person charged in the same proceedings.

Exception (i), covering those instances where the prosecution may offer proof that the defendant has committed, or been convicted, of another offense to establish his guilt of the offense charged, has raised many of the same questions raised in interpreting Rule 404(b) of the Federal Rules of Evidence.[11] By virtue of exception (ii), if the accused asserts his good record or disposition in his own evidence in chief, tries to elicit such assertions from the prosecution witnesses on cross-examination, or calls other witnesses to testify to his good reputation and, possibly, their good opinion of him, he thereby waives the protections of the statute. In England, unlike the United States, it is proper for a defendant who has never been in trouble with the law to testify to such fact before the jury. Exception (iii), concerning the giving of evidence against any other person charged, is, for current purposes, self-explanatory.

Of most concern in applying Section 1(F) is the provision of exception (ii), which states that the defendant waives the bar to admissibility of evidence of his bad character when the nature or conduct of the defense involves imputations on the character of the prosecutor or the witnesses for the prosecution. This exception rests on the premise that, when the accused invites the jury to disbelieve a prosecution witness because of that witness's unreliability based upon notions of character, it is only proper to allow the jury to judge whether the accused is a fit person to make such an invitation. Those who assert that this exception is in reality an application of a sporting theory of justice appear to be closer to the truth. What conduct constitutes an imputation of character leading to an inference of unreliability has created disagreement and, by English standards, considerable litigation.

In the leading case of *Selvey v. Director of Public Prosecutions*,[12] Lord Dilhorne, speaking in the House of Lords, stated the following as established propositions:

1. The words of the statute must be given their ordinary natural meaning;
2. The section permits cross-examination of the accused as to character both when imputation on the character of the prosecutor and his witnesses are cast to show their unreliability as witnesses independently of the evidence given by them and also when the casting of imputations is necessary to enable the accused to establish his defence;
3. In rape cases the accused can allege consent without placing himself in peril of cross-examination;
4. If what is said amounts in reality to no more than a denial of the charge, expressed, it may be, in emphatic language, it should not be regarded as coming within the section.[13]

Under *Selvey*, any assertion by the accused that the police fabricated his purported confession, referred to in England as being "verballed," or planted evidence on his person, would clearly constitute an imputation of character. Cross-examination of a government witness to show partiality through corruption, bias, interest, or prejudice would involve a similar imputation.

Fortunately, the court has discretion to prohibit cross-examination as to prior convictions even though it becomes permitted as a matter of law under Section 1(F)(ii) by virtue of actions of the accused. The House of Lords went on in *Selvey* to provide that the prosecution must indicate to defense counsel when it appears that defense counsel is proceeding too far in the direction of imputation and the prosecution intends to assert its right to attack the character of the accused. The court at this point takes appropriate action to advise the defense of its assessment of the situation. In practice, the court generally exercises its discretion to permit the accused to impute the character of the prosecution's witness when necessary to the presentation of the defense beyond what constitutes a mere denial, without becoming subject to attack on the basis of character, including the use of prior convictions. This attitude, taken together with the overall reluctance of defense counsel, for whatever reason, to undertake an exploration of partiality on cross-examination of prosecution witnesses, permits the accused to testify in almost every case without subjecting himself to cross-examination directed toward his character for truthfulness.

PROSECUTION EVIDENCE IN REBUTTAL

When the defense introduces evidence of some matter which the prosecution could not reasonably foresee, even after challenge on cross-examination, the judge has the discretion to allow the prosecution to call further evidence.

However, judges sparingly exercise this power to admit additional evidence after the close of the case for the prosecution. Only when the evidence offered by the defense is highly probative of a critical fact in the litigation and the introduction of such evidence by the defense could not reasonably have been foreseen, will the court exercise discretion in favor of permitting the prosecution to offer evidence in rebuttal. One example of admissible rebuttal evidence involves the prosecution offering evidence of bad character, following an assertion of good character by the accused for the first time during his direct examination.

CLOSING SPEECHES OF COUNSEL

When prosecution and defense have finished calling their evidence, each side has a right to address the jury. Counsel aims in his closing speech to sum up the evidence in favor of his client's case thoroughly, succinctly, and persuasively. The prosecution speaks first, followed by counsel for the accused. Unlike in the United States, the prosecutor may not reply.

Counsel for the prosecution must not mention certain matters—the failure of the accused or his spouse to give evidence, the failure to call any other evidence, or give any indication that the prosecutor or a witness would be adversely affected by an acquittal. Counsel for the accused acts purely as an advocate and may urge for an acquittal and comment not only on the evidence but on any matter in the case which seems proper. Obviously, however, he must not assert as fact anything not adduced in evidence. It is improper for either counsel to refer to the consequences of conviction, for the jury considers only guilt or innocence; punishment and personal losses are not relevant.

Closing argument in the United States tends to be more assertive and emotional than in England, both for the prosecution and for the defense. While good prosecution advocacy is most often understated, prosecutors in the United States are well known for their vigorous speeches demanding convictions in the interests of society. Good advocacy on behalf of the accused more frequently requires the defense lawyer to demonstrate his sincere conviction in the innocence of his client, without directly saying so, through an emotional appeal. Counsel for both sides in England usually approach the closing speech in a more intellectual and analytical fashion.

For the prosecution, the closing argument provides an opportunity to recap arguments made in his opening speech and to highlight evidence establishing the guilt of the accused. Crown counsel rarely reviews the evidence in detail and makes little reference to the law. He leaves presentation of a full summary of the evidence and instructions to the jury as to the law to the judge's summation. Defense counsel also usually refrains from a complete review of the facts and detailed references to the law. He stresses those facts favorable to his client, almost assuming, without so stating, a burden of proving a defense. While counsel makes reference in passing to the fact that the accused need not prove his innocence and that the jury may convict only if they are satisfied they are sure of his guilt, defense counsel's thrust in his closing speech does not stress the burden of proof and the presence of reasonable doubt to the same degree stressed by defense counsel in America. The attitude of defense counsel during the closing speech, as it is throughout the trial, is usually more detached, less concerned, more businesslike than in the United States. To illustrate, compare the closing speech in *Regina v. David Fisher*[14] with the following closing argument of defense counsel in a murder case tried in the United States.

May it please the Court, Mr. Berry, Mr. Sklarsky, Mr. Cole, ladies and gentlemen of the jury, good morning.

Before I make any comment to you about the evidence in this case, Sylvester Strong, Mr. Cole, and myself would like to thank you for being attentive jurors in this case. We realize you have made a sacrifice in your businesses, you have left your homes and loved ones, and you left your other obligations, but we realize the reason you are doing this is not only because it's your recognition of civic duty, but because you want to make sure that justice is properly administered in our courtroom. Because of this, ladies and gentlemen, we would like to thank you for serving as jurors in this case.

Now it is my turn to discuss with you what we thought the evidence showed in this case. It's important that you all understand at this point that I am not here to appeal to your emotions, I am not here to appeal to your sympathies, I want to let you know, ladies and gentlemen, what I think the reasonable doubts are in this case by reviewing the evidence with you. If there are any conflicts between your recollection of the evidence and mine, I ask you to be governed solely by your own recollection of the facts. If during the course of my final remarks I misquote any testimony, I can assure you that I did not do so intentionally.

Folks, at the beginning of this case, when his Honor, Judge Cousins, was questioning you with respect to your qualifications to serve as jurors, he asked you whether or not you would follow the law, whether or not you would be fair, and whether or not you would hold the prosecutors to their burden of proving Sylvester Strong guilty beyond a reasonable doubt. There was a lot of talk about that and each of you indicated and promised that you would hold the prosecutors to their burden. His Honor, Judge Cousins, when you were being selected as jurors, also asked you whether or not you would presume Sylvester innocent throughout this entire trial and through your deliberations and presume him so unless the State was able to prove him guilty beyond a reasonable doubt. All of you indicated that you presumed him innocent. Additionally, ladies and gentlemen, you were asked to use your common sense and experiences in life in evaluating the testimony of the witnesses. Based upon your responses: "Yes, I can follow the law," "Yes, I will hold the prosecutors to their burden of proof beyond a reasonable doubt," "Yes, I will presume the defendant innocent unless he is proven guilty beyond a reasonable doubt," you were selected as jurors in this case. We are calling upon you now, ladies and gentlemen, to abide by those promises that you made.

Let's now look at the evidence and see why the prosecutors failed to prove Sylvester Strong guilty beyond a reasonable doubt. As Mr. Cole told you at the beginning of this case, we do not contest the fact that Shelley Williams was shot and killed, an unfortunate thing that has happened, and nothing that I can say, nothing that anyone in this courtroom can do can change this. The fact, however, is not the issue in this case. The issue here is: was Sylvester Strong justified in defending himself under the circumstances that existed on that day? Our answer, ladies and gentlemen, is that the evidence indeed shows that the State failed to prove Sylvester Strong guilty beyond a reasonable doubt, because they did not prove, beyond a reasonable doubt, that when he shot Shelley Williams he did not reasonably believe that it was a necessity to defend himself against death or great bodily harm.

Now why do I say this? Ladies and gentlemen, basically it comes down to whose account of the incident you believe. Do you believe the version provided by Rosie Garrett, Willie Williams, Clarence Williams, or Arthur Anderson on that stand or do you believe the defendant, Sylvester Strong, and Ada May Howard? We have diametrically opposed versions in this case as to what happened.

The four occurrence witnesses—we call them occurrence witnesses because they are supposed to have been on the scene and observed the occurrence—were Rosie Garrett, Willie Williams, Clarence Williams, and Arthur Anderson. They would each have you believe that before March 25th, the date of the shooting, there had been absolutely no threats, no threatening gestures made by members of the Williams family directed to members of Sylvester's family.

Rosie Garrett, the first occurrence witness, testified that on March 25, at the corner of Bloomingdale and Winnebago, she observed her son Shelley talking with Sylvester Strong. She claimed that the only thing that happened before the shooting was that Shelley asked her if Sylvester was the person who cursed her. She said Shelley got out of the car and told Sylvester, "I want you to apologize," so Sylvester apologized. Shelley then said, "No, don't apologize to me, apologize to my mother." As Sylvester was turning to apologize to his mother, according to Rosie Garrett's testimony, that is when George Howard came running down the street and shot in the air. She then claims that Sylvester ran over to George Howard, grabbed the gun, saying, "You are not trying to hit him" and started shooting. Rosie Garrett claims that just before the shooting there was no fighting, no cursing, no argument, everything was peaceful, low tones of voice, not yelling loud, just a quiet, peaceful conversation.

Clarence Williams also got on the stand. He said the same thing, nothing happening, no arguments—in fact, he couldn't hear what was being said because the tape deck in the car was playing. He also claims that, for no apparent reason, George Howard ran down the street firing the gun. He claims that Sylvester then, again for no apparent reason, grabbed the gun and started shooting. And he claims that only after the shooting stopped did anybody on the street lay a hand on Sylvester Strong, and that was when Clarence caught him down here by the end of the street with the car and kicked him in the face.

Now, ladies and gentlemen, if you believe the version of what occurred on the day of March 25 given by Rosie Garrett, given by Willie Williams, given by Clarence Williams, given by Arthur Anderson, you would have to believe the following: That when George Howard ran down the street and fired the shots, he was firing them because he was berserk, because there was absolutely no reason at all to fire.

Their witnesses would have you believe there was only peaceful conversation, no fighting, no hitting, not a darn thing happening to Sylvester when, for no apparent reason George Howard went berserk, and then Sylvester went berserk as well. We then got two berserk individuals in the street, just shooting up everybody for no reason at all. If you believe that, I say convict the man of murder. This simply defies common sense, and everybody in this courtroom knows it.

Let's look at some of the other things, ladies and gentlemen: You remember when we went through the addresses of all of the individuals? Did you notice how they all just could incidentally happen to be from outside of this neighborhood? Doesn't it seem just a little suspicious that all these friends of Shelley Williams decided to be on Bloomingdale at the same time? Incidentally, they just happened to catch Sylvester out there in the street around the time Ada May said Shelley Williams would come over there to finish the mess that occurred the night before. Don't these coincidences alone create a reasonable doubt in your mind about whether their witnesses are telling the truth?

When you get in the jury room, ladies and gentlemen, take a look at the photographs of this street. The officer said that the distance between where the shots were fired, and where he saw Sylvester being beaten, was only around 100 feet. Other testimony showed there was nothing wrong with his legs and feet. The testimony also was that Clarence got into the car, drove down the street, and cut Sylvester off. If that's all true, then why couldn't he get more than a hundred feet away? There had to be something wrong with him or he would have gotten much further. Doesn't this prove that Sylvester was attacked before the shots were fired? Isn't the fact that he managed to get only one hundred feet explained only by the fact that he was already injured, and couldn't run very well?

The issue in this case is why Sylvester Strong shot that gun. That is the only issue; and the only one that can tell you the reason for the shooting—why he shot—is this man, Sylvester Strong. He is the only one that can tell you what was going through his mind. The issue, stated in legal terms, is whether or not he reasonably believed under the circumstances that existed at the time of the shooting, he would sustain great bodily harm or death to himself if he didn't defend himself. Shelley Williams can't testify to that. Clarence Williams can't testify to that, and Arthur Anderson can't testify to that. Only Sylvester can, and you heard him tell you what he felt when he fired those shots.

How many shots did he fire? He testified that he just kept on shooting. *Why did you shoot? Because they were trying to kill me. When did you shoot? When they were coming at me, trying to get me.* The only person who could testify as to his intent is Sylvester himself.

I have only a few moments left, so we must go on. The prosecutor talked a lot about the entrance of the bullets, and said that two of the bullets entered Shelley Williams' back. He wants you to believe that Sylvester Strong should be convicted simply because two shots entered Williams' back. Well, it's not as simple as that.

Just for a moment, put anyone else in that same situation. A mob has surrounded you. They are armed with bats and two-by-fours. You instinctively fire your gun. Do you stop to see whether or not the first shot hits anyone? Do you stop to see if anyone is turning while you shoot? *Of course not!* You would fire that gun as fast and as often as you could. Isn't that exactly what a reasonable person would have done under these circumstances? Well, that is exactly what happened, and only what happened, here. The question is whether or not, when the first shot was fired, Sylvester Strong reasonably believed that he was justified in defending himself. If so, it does not make any difference where that first shot or, for that matter, any other shots actually struck.

I believe Judge Cousins will instruct you that a person is justified in using deadly force when that person reasonably believes that such force is necessary to prevent imminent death or great bodily harm to himself. Isn't that what really happened here? Isn't that what Sylvester Strong must have been thinking when he fired that gun? Under these circumstances, surrounded by an angry mob, isn't what Sylvester Strong did exactly what any other reasonable person would have done if faced with the same situation? *Of course it is!* Because what he did was reasonable, Sylvester is simply not guilty of any crime.

The Court will also instruct you that the prosecution has the burden of proof in this case, and that this burden of proof never shifts to the defendant. Although we presented evidence in this case, we are not required to prove anything. We do not have to prove that Sylvester Strong was justified in defending himself as he did. It is the *prosecution* that is required to *disprove* this proposition, and they have to *disprove* it beyond a reasonable doubt.

Who among you can't say that you have a reasonable doubt whether or not Sylvester reasonably defended himself here? Of course you have doubts! You have got to have doubts about that. If nothing else, the evidence you heard here is filled with doubt.

This case will be over soon. I have tried my best to show you what really happened on Bloomingdale Avenue during the afternoon of March 25, 1976. I have tried my best, but my job is done. This case now rests in your hands. When this case is over you, I, and probably some others, will from time to time think back and reflect on this case. It may be in the morning during a spare moment. This case may suddenly come back to you at night when you are trying to fall asleep. Wherever you think of this case, you are probably going to ask one thing: Did I do this defendant, Sylvester Strong, justice? If you have doubts about this case, have them now. For him there is no tomorrow, no second chance. Ask yourself those hard questions now, because for him tomorrow is too late. If during your deliberations you keep that in mind, we are sure that you will return a verdict of not guilty.

Now, ladies and gentlemen, I only have this one chance to talk with you. When I am finished, the prosecutor will have a second chance to get up and make what is known as a rebuttal argument. I don't have a chance to talk to you after him and rebut anything he might tell you. I am confident, however, that since you heard the evidence, you will be able to come up with an answer for anything he might tell you. When he gets up, ladies and gentlemen, ask him to explain to you how it was so unreasonable for Sylvester to defend himself under these circumstances. Have him explain to you why, when surrounded by an armed, angry mob, Sylvester was not entitled to protect himself and save his own life. Have him tell you what would have been more reasonable here. If you have a doubt as to what the right thing to do would have been, then you can't say that what Sylvester did was not reasonable.

Ladies and gentlemen of the jury, I say again that the prosecution has not proved beyond a reasonable doubt that when Sylvester fired that first shot, he did not reasonably believe it was necessary to do so to defend himself. The prosecution has utterly failed to prove that issue beyond a reasonable doubt. Because of their failure, we ask you to return the only verdict this evidence demands. Let him go free. Let him return to his job, his family, and his friends. Find him not guilty.[15]

THE JUDGE'S SUMMATION

After the closing speeches for the prosecution and the defense, the trial judge in England sums up to the jury. There are no precise rules about summing up, and different judges have different methods. Usually the judge begins by explaining to the jury that they are the judges of the facts and that, no matter what he may say about the witnesses, the defendant, or the way in which either the prosecution or the defense has been presented, they remain the judges of the facts and it is for them to decide whether they believe the witnesses. He usually stresses more than once in the course of his summing up that the burden lies on the prosecution to prove the guilt of the defendant beyond a reasonable doubt and that if at the end of the case, after considering the evidence of both the prosecution and the defense, they do not feel sure of the guilt of the defendant, they must acquit. The judge summarizes the evidence introduced on each side and analyzes it as he goes along. The judge has a duty to summarize the relevant evidence for each party, directing the jury to disregard worthless evidence and extraneous matters that may have been inserted into the trial and to remind them of evidence which they may otherwise forget or overlook. The judge may comment on the demeanor of the witnesses, suggest the weight which the jury may give to vital items of evidence and draw the attention of the jury to inconsistencies and omissions.

The judge in his discretion may also comment on the fact that the defendant has not elected to give evidence, although he must stress the fact that the accused is under no legal obligation to give evidence. Most often no comment concerning the accused's failure to testify is made. None was made by the trial judge in his summation in the trial of David Fisher. If the judge is of a mind to so comment to the jury, the comment by the judge on the accused's failure to testify should follow the statement by Lord Parker, C.J., in *Regina v. Bathurst*,[16] that

> the accused is not bound to give evidence, that he can sit back and see if the prosecution have proved their case, and that, while the jury have been deprived of the opportunity of hearing his story tested in cross-examination, the one thing they must not do is assume that he is guilty because he has not gone into the witness box.[17]

Whether the court may comment on the accused's failure to speak to the police or others prior to trial as bearing on the weight of testimony given at trial is the subject of considerable dispute. The comment, when made, draws the jury's attention to the fact that it is "unfortunate that the defense was not set up at an earlier date so as to afford the opportunity of it being tested."[18] The court rarely includes in its summation comment with respect to pre-trial silence. Comment is especially rare where such silence arose in connection with the propounding of questions to the accused by someone in authority.

The judge must direct the jury on the law and its application to each of the charges before the court. If the jury is not so directed, any conviction on a count in the indictment upon which there has been no direction will be quashed. A particularly important part of the judge's duty in summing up on the law is to direct the jury about any legal rules relating to the evidence. To illustrate, the judge must warn the jury about the danger of convicting the defendant on the uncorroborated evidence of an accomplice and must tell them what, in law, amounts to corroboration.

The judge will conclude his summing up by telling the jury that they must endeavor to reach a unanimous verdict and that circumstances have not yet arisen under which he could accept a majority verdict.

If defense counsel considers an error has occurred in the summation, he will usually only merely note this for reference at a later stage when he has to consider grounds of appeal. Failure to object to an improper instruction does not waive the right to raise the matter on appeal.[19] Defense counsel does not consider it his role to draw the attention of the judge to the error that has occurred. An obvious exception exists when defense counsel believes that a corrected instruction would very substantially increase the likelihood of an acquittal. On the other hand, if prosecuting counsel listening to the summation appreciates that there has been some misdirection of law or fact, then he will usually raise the matter with the judge and so obtain any correction necessary before the judge retires.

THE VERDICT

After the judge has finished summing up, the jury retires to consider their verdict. They retire under the supervision of a jury bailiff and choose a foreman to speak for them. Four types of verdicts may, given the facts of the particular case, be open to the jury. First, there is the general verdict, one of guilty or not guilty on the whole indictment. Second, if there is more than one count, a verdict is taken on each count separately. The jury may, thus, find the accused guilty on one or more counts of the indictment and not guilty on others. Third, the jury may find the accused not guilty of the crime charged but guilty of some other crime upon which it is open to them to bring in a verdict of guilty. Thus, on a charge of murder, it may be proper for them to bring in a verdict of not guilty of murder but guilty of manslaughter or infanticide. Fourth, the jury may bring in a special verdict, which is a finding upon certain facts, leaving it to the judge to apply the law to these facts.

Under Section 13 of the Criminal Justice Act 1967, the verdict of the jury need not be unanimous. If, after two hours in a case where there are not less than eleven jurors ten of them agree, or in a case where there are ten jurors nine of them agree, the judge may accept a majority verdict. If, even after allowing for this provision, a jury cannot agree upon its verdict, it will be discharged and a new jury called to try the case. If at the second trial the jury still disagrees, although it is theoretically possible for the prosecution to try the case for the third time, the prosecution usually offers no evidence at the third trial, thus ensuring that the defendant is acquitted.

When a verdict is returned, the foreman announces it in open court. The judge may direct the jury to reconsider it, but ultimately the jury may insist upon having its verdict recorded, despite the unwillingness of the judge.

The verdict of a jury is complete once it is announced, and the Court of Appeal will not consider evidence showing what has occurred in the jury room or that some jurors were not in agreement with the verdict announced. The rationale is to secure a finality to the proceedings and to remove jurors after a case is concluded from threats or pressure to say they were not in agreement with the verdict.

SENTENCE

After a verdict of guilty has been accepted and recorded, evidence is presented by the prosecution relating to the accused's character to assist the court in determining the appropriate sentence. The evidence is presented immediately following the verdict. The jury remains in the jury box until sentence is imposed.

Evidence of previous convictions and the general character of the accused, referred to as "the antecedents," is presented through the testimony of a police officer. The prosecution attempts to confine such evidence to facts admitted by the defense or capable of convincing proof.

The prosecution prepares an Antecedent Report containing a factual statement of the previous convictions, particulars of age, education, and employment, the date of arrest, whether the prisoner has been on bail, and, if previously convicted, the date of his last discharge from prison. It may also contain a short and concise statement of the prisoner's domestic and family circumstances, his general reputation, and associates. If the prosecution asserts that the accused associates with bad characters, the officer giving evidence must be able to speak of this from his own knowledge. This Antecedent Report may be given to counsel for the prosecution either with his Brief or at the outset of the trial. In the case of David Fisher, the report, prepared on May 7, 1980, was furnished to Crown counsel with his Brief in advance of trial. The court also received a copy at that time. A copy of the Antecedent Report was provided to counsel for the accused in connection with the July bail hearing. If the accused denies any or all of the convictions recorded, the police officer must be able to prove them. It may be necessary to call other persons to prove convictions which are denied, when the police officer present lacks personal knowledge. A copy of the Antecedent Report is annexed as Appendix V.

The accused or his counsel then addresses the court both on the circumstances surrounding the commission of the crime itself and on the background and character of the accused. This is referred to as a plea in mitigation of sentence.

Before the court proceeds to sentence, the defendant may ask that other offenses for which he has not yet been tried should be taken into consideration, referred to as TICs, and a comprehensive sentence passed to cover both the substantive offenses of which he has been found guilty and also the others which he wishes considered. This practice is very convenient because it enables outstanding offenses to be cleared and allows the accused after he has served his sentence to start with a clean sheet instead of being charged and tried again. The court is not bound to take such offenses into consideration and may decline to do so when they are of an entirely different nature from the specific offense for which the accused is before the court. Under no circumstances may a judge impose a sentence which is in excess of that which could be passed in respect of the charges of which the defendant has been found guilty.

The court may decide to remand the convicted person in custody for a medical or social inquiry report before deciding on the sentence. In the Fisher case, a social inquiry report dated May 15, 1980, was provided to the court prior to trial. A copy of the social inquiry report is annexed as Appendix VIII.

David Fisher was sentenced on the robbery charge to five years' imprisonment and for possession of a firearm while committing the offense of robbery to three years' imprisonment, the two sentences to run concurrently.

As part of the sentencing process, trial court judges occasionally make strong comments concerning the character of the defendant, such as, "I am satisfied that you are a dangerous and evil man," and "You are a stupid, weak, and contemptible man."[20] They have also been known to compliment or castigate the jury on its verdict. Neither type of judicial comment occurred in the case of David Fisher.

APPEAL

In England, applications for leave to appeal, or appeals of right from a verdict of guilty rendered by a jury are few. Judges grant leave to appeal in only a fraction of the cases. The fact that, of the small number of appeals actually heard, a much smaller number actually result in the quashing of a conviction or a new trial adds a finality to the verdict unknown in the United States.

A defendant like David Fisher convicted at the Crown Court may appeal against his conviction to the Criminal Division of the Court of Appeal. The appeal would be as of right on a question of law alone. Issues which involve questions of fact alone, or which involve questions of mixed fact and law, such as whether a statement was voluntary, will be heard on appeal only if the defendant obtains either a certificate from the trial judge that the case is fit for appeal or leave from the Court of Appeal. The only grounds assertable on an appeal as of right or upon leave against the conviction are that (1) under all the circumstances of the case, the conviction is unsafe or unsatisfactory; (2) a wrong decision was made on a question of law; or (3) there was a material irregularity in the course of the trial.

If the court finds an appeal meritorious on grounds not involving the introduction of newly discovered evidence, it may quash the defendant's conviction and set the defendant free. A new trial may not be ordered. However, the Court of Appeal is not bound to quash the appellant's conviction, even if it holds that a defect has occurred in the trial. The Court of Appeal may dismiss an appeal when, although there has been a wrong decision on a point of law or an irregularity in the trial, the court considers that no miscarriage of justice has actually occurred. Thus, for example, where an item of evidence has been wrongly admitted, the court will apply the proviso contained in Section 2(1) of the Criminal Appeal Act 1968 and dismiss the appeal if the judges feel the jury would inevitably have convicted the defendant even if that improper evidence had not been given. In addition, the court may substitute a conviction for some other offense of which the jury could have found the appellant guilty, if the court is of the opinion that the jury must have been satisfied of facts which would prove him guilty of this other offense. A court might exercise this power when, for example, the evidence does not justify a conviction for the completed offense but amply justifies a conviction for attempt.

When new evidence has become available since the trial, whether documents, expert testimony, or occurrence witness testimony as to facts, the Court of Appeal may receive such evidence if it appears to the court that it is likely to be credible and would have been admissible at the trial if then available. The court must also be satisfied that there is a reasonable explanation for the failure to adduce such evidence in the court below. If the court feels that the new evidence could have caused the jury to reach a different verdict, they may either quash the conviction or order a new trial.

Further appeal lies to the House of Lords at the instance of either side in the exceptional cases where the Court of Appeal certifies that the case involves a point of law of general public importance and either the Court of Appeal or the House of Lords grants leave. A flow chart of appeals for all criminal courts is shown in Figure 4. It is interesting to note that the same High Court judges who preside at the Crown Court also comprise the Court of Appeal, Criminal Division, and the Divisional Court of the Queen's Bench Division. The effect this has on the frequency of appeals being upheld is self-evident.

Figure 4
Flow Chart of Appeals for All Criminal Courts

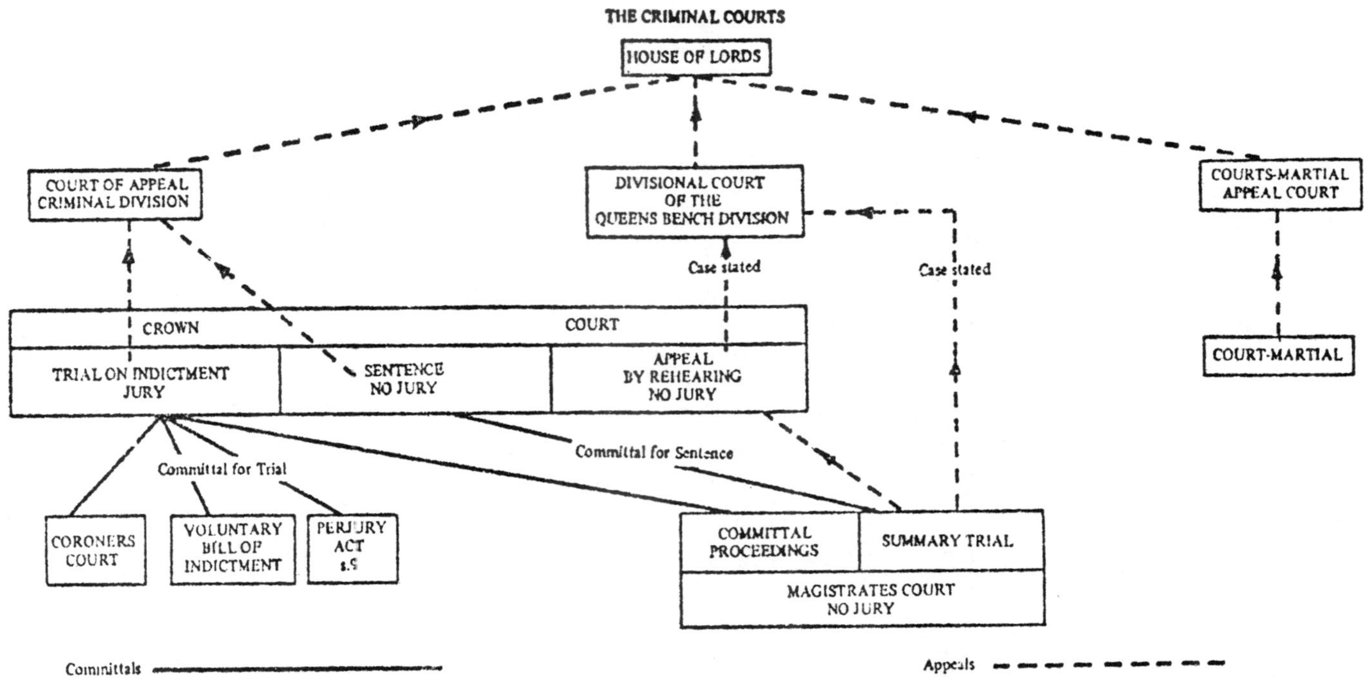

Source: R. Cross and P. A. Jones, *An Introduction to Criminal Law* 410 (1972). Reprinted by permission of Butterworth & Co. Ltd.

NOTES

1. Mauet, *Fundamentals of Trial Techniques* 44-45 (1980).
2. Id. at 112-13.
3. The voucher rule was not incorporated into the Federal Rules of Evidence.

Rule 607

WHO MAY IMPEACH

> The credibility of a witness may be attacked by any party, including the party calling him.

The Advisory Committee's Note to Rule 607 of the Federal Rules of Evidence states that the "traditional rule against impeaching one's own witness is abandoned as based on false premises." Even in those jurisdictions in the United States still applying the voucher rule, a party calling a witness is usually permitted to impeach the witness by means of a prior inconsistent statement where surprise and affirmative damage are present. See, generally, Graham, Examination of a Party's Own Witness Under the Federal Rules of Evidence; A Promise Unfulfilled, 54 Tex.L.Rev. 917, 977-82, 989-90 (1976).

4. The American studies on *Miranda* are described in detail in Baldwin and McConville, Confessions in Crown Court Trials 13-14 (1980).

Much of the research pointing to a minimum effect of the *Miranda* decision was done in the mid- and late 1960s. It is suggested, however, that over time the impact of *Miranda* on confessions in America may have been much greater than originally observed. The growth of public defenders, coupled with a more knowledgeable criminal defendant population, makes the area ripe for renewed investigation.

5. "It is interesting that the two relevant English studies . . . suggest higher proportions of defendants making such admissions than have been reported by researchers in America." Id. at 3.

6. There is no comparable requirement in the United States. The closest common law analogy is the requirement that a witness be confronted on cross-examination with his alleged prior inconsistent statement, thereby providing an opportunity to admit or deny its making. Explanation by the witness of the apparent inconsistency may occur on cross-examination or on redirect. Compare Rule 613(b) of the Federal Rules of Evidence removing the requirement that the opportunity to admit or deny be specifically provided on cross-examination rather than at any time in the litigation.

7. See pages 244-46 infra.

8. Mauet, *Fundamentals of Trial Techniques* 76-78 (1980).

9. The right of the court to comment in charging to the jury on the accused remaining silent is discussed on page 94 infra.

10. Rule 609(a) of the Federal Rules of Evidence provides as follows:

IMPEACHMENT BY EVIDENCE OF CONVICTION OF CRIME

> (a) General Rule. For the purpose of attacking the credibility of a witness, evidence that he has been convicted of a crime shall be admitted if elicited from him or established by public record during cross-examination but only if the crime (1) was punishable by death or imprisonment in excess of one year under the law order which he was convicted, and the court determines that the probative value of admitting this evidence outweighs its prejudical effect to the defendant, or (2) involved dishonesty or false statement, regardless of the punishment.

In some American jurisdictions any crime defined as a felony may automatically be employed to impeach any witness including the defendant. Variations upon these foregoing two approaches are employed in many other jurisdictions.

11. Rule 404(b) of the Federal Rules of Evidence provides as follows:

> Evidence of other crimes, wrongs, or acts is not admissible to prove the character of a person in order to show that he acted in conformity therewith. It may, however, be admissible for other purposes, such as proof of motive, opportunity, intent, preparation, plan, knowledge, identity, or absence of mistake or accident.

12. [1968] 2 ALL. E.R. 497.

13. Id. at 508.

14. See pages 177-85 infra.

15. Mauet, *Fundamentals of Trial Techniques* 331-39 (1980).

16. [1968] 1 ALL. E.R. 1175.

17. Id. at 1178-79.

18. Regina v. Littleboy [1934] ALL. E.R. Rep. 434, 435.

19. In the United States, absent plain error, error in instructing the jury must be properly preserved to be considered an appeal. See Rule 30 of the Federal Rules of Criminal Procedure:

> INSTRUCTIONS
>
> At the close of the evidence or at such earlier time during the trial as the court reasonably directs, any party may file written requests that the court instruct the jury on the law as set forth in the requests. At the same time copies of such requests shall be furnished to adverse parties. The court shall inform counsel of its proposed action upon the requests prior to their arguments to the jury, but the court shall instruct the jury after the arguments are completed. No party may assign as error any portion of the charge or omission therefrom unless he objects thereto before the jury retires to consider its verdict, stating distinctly the matter to which he objects and the grounds of his objection. Opportunity shall be given to make the objection out of the hearing of the jury and, on request of any party, out of the presence of the jury.

20. Birmingham *Evening Mail*, June 5, 1981, at 1.

7 THE TRIAL TRANSCRIPT

The transcript of the trial is presented without edit. In approaching the transcript, it is important to recall that the testimony of David Fisher which follows his sentencing is a simulation presented for the sake of completeness. David Fisher was portrayed by Coleman Treacy. Copies of several exhibits referred to in the course of the trial of concern to the reader have previously been set forth. They are Exhibits 6 and 10, the two signed statements of David Fisher, at pages 10 and 12, Exhibit 11, the identikit picture of the robber made from the description of Yvonne Gardener, at page 6, and Exhibit 12, the photograph taken of David Fisher at the time of his arrest, at page 8.

BIRMINGHAM CROWN COURT.

THE VICTORIA LAW COURTS,
BIRMINGHAM, 4.

9th to 11th February, 1981.

Before :-

HIS HONOUR JUDGE RUSH.

R E G I N A

- v -

DAVID FISHER.

(Transcript of the Shorthand Notes of Marten, Meredith & Co.Ltd., 36-38, Whitefriars Street, London, EC4Y.8BJ. Official Court Reporters).

MR. D. JONES appeared for the prosecution.

MR. B. R. ESCOTT COX, Q.C., and MR. C. TREACY appeared for the defence.

I N D E X.

I N D E X (Continued).

9th February, 1981.

THE CLERK: Are you David Fisher?

THE ACCUSED: Yes.

THE CLERK: David Fisher, on Count 1 of this indictment you are charged with robbery that on the 25th day of February 1980 you robbed Yvonne Gardener of £3,800. David Fisher, do you plead guilty or not guilty?

THE ACCUSED: Not guilty.

THE CLERK: On the second count you are charged with possessing a firearm whilst committing an offence, that on the 25th day of February 1980 at the time of robbing Yvonne Gardener of £3,800 cash, you had in your possession an imitation firearm, namely, a .38 'Chief' blank firing gun. David Fisher, do you plead guilty or not guilty?

THE ACCUSED: Not guilty.

THE CLERK: Members of the Jury, as I call your name will you please answer and step into the jury box which is on my left in the order in which your names are called.

Betty Joan Yates.	Answer:	Yes.
Charles Frederick Spooner.	"	Yes.
Jean Ann Norton.	"	Yes.
Margaret Rose Taylor.	"	Yes.
Roy James Wild.	"	Yes.
Michael Rodney Brookes.	"	Yes.
Margaret Elizabeth Pullin.	"	Yes.
Sylvia Salmon.	"	Yes.
Sonia Scott.	"	Yes.
Angela Hodgson.	"	Yes.
Hilda Gonzales.	"	Yes.
Lily May Harris.	"	Yes.

Will you stand please. David Fisher, the names you are about to hear called are the names of the jurors who are to try you. If you wish to object to them or to any of them the time to do so is when they come to the Book to be sworn and before they are sworn, and your objection shall be heard.

Members of the Jury, you are about to be sworn. When I call your name will you please stand, take the Testament in your right hand, raise it up and read the Oath from the card which is now in front of you. You may then sit down.

Betty Joan Yates..

BETTY JOAN YATES: I swear by Almighty God that I will faithfully try the several issues joined between our Sovereign Lady, the

Queen, and the defendant, and give a true verdict according to the evidence.

Charles Frederick Spooner. (Sworn as above).
Jean Ann Norton. "
Margaret Rose Taylor. "
Roy James Wild. "
Michael Rodney Brookes. "
Margaret Elizabeth Pullin. "
Sylvia Salmon. "
Sonia Scott. "
Angela Hodgson. "
Hilda Gonzales. "
Lily May Harris. "

THE CLERK: Members of the Jury, on this indictment the defendant, David Fisher, is charged on Count 1 with robbery, that on the 25th day of February 1980 he robbed Yvonne Gardener of £3,800. On Count 2 the defendant is charged with possessing a firearm whilst committing an offence, that on the 25th day of February 1980, at the time of robbing Yvonne Gardener of £3,800 cash, he had in his possession an imitation firearm, namely, a .38 'Chief' blank firing gun. To this indictment he has pleaded not guilty, and it is your charge to say, having heard the evidence, whether he be guilty or not.

May I discharge the Jury in waiting your Honour?

JUDGE RUSH: Yes. Sit down Mr. Fisher.

The jurors in waiting whose names have not been called, you are free to leave the Court now and you will be given further instructions outside. Thank you for your attendance.

Would any of you like to take your coats off, Members of the Jury?

JURY MEMBERS: Yes please. (Those members desiring to take off their coat did so and handed it to the usher).

JUDGE RUSH: Yes Mr. Jones.

MR. JONES: Your Honour, Members of the Jury, in this case I appear for the prosecution, and the defendant, Mr. Fisher, is represented by my learned friends Mr. Escott Cox who sits nearer to me and Mr. Colman Treacy who sits nearer to you.

To begin with I will besiege you with some documents and various exhibits. The first are photographs of the scene of a bank robbery. (To the usher) One between two. (To the Jury). You need not look at these documents yet, Members of the Jury; you will see them in due course.

Members of the Jury, there should be six copies of each set. They are not the same set of photographs. Members of the Jury you will ultimately have two sets of photographs for each pair, a plan and two statements, Exhibits 6 and 10. (Photographs handed to Members of the Jury).

Let us check Members of the Jury. First of all there are two sets of photographs; one of the interior of a bank and one of the exterior.

JUDGE RUSH: Mr. Jones, to complete your problems, may I have a volume please?

MR. ESCOTT COX: If your honour is going to have them, perhaps I might ask for them as well.

JUDGE RUSH: Yes. (Sets of documents handed to the learned Judge and to Mr. Escott Cox).

MR. JONES: Two sets of photographs, one plan and two statements, Exhibit 6 and Exhibit 10. The exhibit number is written in the top right hand corner.

Now let us hope there is less difficulty with these next exhibits which I am going to give you Members of the Jury. There should be two sets of photographs, one plan, and two sets of statements, Exhibit 6 and Exhibit 10, the exhibit numbers written in the top right hand corner. If you have got those Members of the Jury, then we can start.

Members of the Jury we can begin now. The last photographs that I have handed to you -- one is an identity kit photograph made up from an identity kit, and the other is the defendant, and they are, believe it or not Members of the Jury, photographs of the same person; at least the same person in the eyes of the bank clerk, Miss Yvonne Gardener. She was at the time staring down the barrel of this gun; it was being pointed at her by a raider, and needless to say you may think most of her concentration would be on the gun rather than the raider in particular. But nevertheless there was nothing wrong with the lighting in the bank, and it was her impression that the man holding the gun was either Asian or a very light skinned West Indian. One cannot alter the toning in a photofit picture but on her account she was under the impression that the man who was holding up the bank, the man who was pointing this gun at her, the man indeed who cocked the gun at her, was either Asian or very light skinned West Indian. She thought he was about 25, about 5-feet 10-inches with dark brown eyes and a long wide mouth. That was the impression of Miss Gardener who was being held up at gun point, indeed the gun had been cocked and money demanded from her, and she was under the impression that that was the person who was holding the gun.

The raider wore a woollen hat and that is why you have got that funny part on the Identikit; that is sort of drawn in by the officer doing the Identikit. He has not got a head shaped like that Members of the Jury, and that woollen hat covered the ears and the hair, so those features were not visible in any event to Miss Gardener.

He made no other attempt to disguise his appearance; there was no mask for instance. You may think it might be, if you are going to hold up a bank, a preliminary precaution if robbing a bank to make some sort of attempt to disguise your appearance -- unless of course he was already disguised. We will never know for the raider was not caught, but it is possible Members of the Jury he may have made his face up to appear darker than he was but we do not know -- that is unless Mr. Fisher tells us, because the prosecution say it was Mr. Fisher who conducted that raid that day, and he admitted he had raided the bank and got away with £3,800.

He had gone into the bank and the day was the 25th February. It was a Monday; there were no customers and it was 3 o'clock in the afternoon. Mr. Fisher went into that bank; he went up to Miss Gardener and she said, "Can I help you?", and then he produced this gun. He pointed it at her, cocked it, and simply said, "Money, money". Not surprisingly Miss Gardener's attention was directed to the gun, and not surprisingly she could give a very accurate description of the gun that was pointed at her. The gun she said was a revolver; that it was very small; that it was about 5-inches in total length; that it had a very very short barrel, and that it was black in colour. Well, that was the description she gave on the day. It is a matter for you, Members of the Jury, whether you think that is an accurate description, but the one thing you may think your attention would be riveted on would be a cocked gun that is pointing at you. Indeed, when the gun was subsequently recovered from the defendant's place of abode, from his lodgings, that gun was shown to Miss Gardener and she said it was identical to the gun that held her up.

Well Members of the Jury, the gun being pointed, money being demanded, Miss Gardener handed over some £3,800, most of it being in £5 notes in bundles of 500 at a time, £5 notes and £10 notes, although there were some £1 notes among them but there were few £1 notes.

The man took out a polythene bag from his coat or anorak, and that polythene bag, according to Miss Gardener, had either a red emblem or red letters on it, and the prosecution say the bag was in fact one of those polythene bags you can see set out on the table there. It is in fact a 'Lucky 7' plastic bag. He took out that bag and he placed the money in the bag and ran out of the bank.

Now coming towards the bank at the time was the bank manager, Mr. Witham. He had gone to see to his car and put some money in a meter and he, as he was returning to the bank and was about 20-odd yards from the bank, saw a man run past him. He was not suspicious at the time, and quite frankly he did not pay any particular attention to the man.

At that stage there was absolutely nothing to be suspicious about, but he did not pay any particular attention although the impression that he got of the man running past him was that the man was dark skinned, possibly coloured -- possibly coloured. But he was paying more attention to some telephone engineers who were working nearby than the person who ran past him. It was a fleeting glimpse in circumstances where he was not on any ground suspicious. It was later when he got towards the bank that he heard the klaxon going, because there is an alarm button that can be pressed at the bank. Poor Miss Gardener, not surprisingly, was so frightened at the gun being pointed at her and being cocked that she was just too frightened to press the alarm on while the raider was standing a few feet away from her, and you may think that is not a cowardly but a sensible thing to have done, and it was only when the raider went out of the bank that she pressed the alarm and the klaxon went off. And indeed even then Mr. Witham, the bank manager, did not associate the alarm with the person who had run past him, and it was only after when he, having spoken to his staff, went out and had a look around to see if there was anything suspicious, that he saw a car and took the number, but that car, Members of the Jury, which was driving off, has nothing to do with the raid at all. Enquiries have been made and that has been checked out, and it has nothing to do with the matter at all. But that was the only time Mr. Withers was suspicious of anything.

Members of the Jury, the klaxon had gone off, the bank had been robbed and £3,800 had gone. Needless to say the police were called, and of course statements were taken. Miss Gardener gave her description of the man who was the robber and indeed on that same day -- your honour I say that because it is a matter of agreement between defence counsel and the prosecution -- on that same day that photofit picture was compiled by Miss Gardener. Now you may think that was not awfully helpful to the police in the light of the person who was subsequently arrested, and indeed as a result of that photofit Members of the Jury, the very last person the police would be looking for as being responsible for this robbery was firstly a white person -- they certainly were not looking for a white person; it was one raider remember, not a group of people -- so it would not be a white person, and although it may be someone who was leaving the country, it certainly would not be someone who was flying into the country who the police would be looking for, and so quite frankly the trail went cold. Nobody was responsible, and it would have remained, perhaps, completely unsolved but for the defendant, a white person, flying into this country from Ireland on the 19th March. He flew into Birmingham Airport from Ireland, and as he was going through clearance he was found to be in possession of a very large quantity of money. This is the money that was in his possession. It amounts -- I forget the coppers Members of the Jury; that does not matter -- but there is £1,358 there, most of which you will see is in £10 notes. £1,358. And because that was found the Airport police were summoned in the form of Police Constable Abolins and Detective Constable Sutcliffe, and of course they knew nothing about the robbery; their duties are simply in relation to crime at the airport, so they were totally ignorant of any details about any robbery in Birmingham or elsewhere. But they of course wanted to know why the defendant was carrying so much money, and indeed not only was he carrying all this money but he was also in possession of a lot of items which were apparently new items. They were still in their boxes; such things as the gold watch, two gold rings, a thing called a watchamacallit although I do not suppose much of the case will turn on that, and some after-shave -- various items which appeared new; the holdall, etcetera.

So the officers interviewed the defendant simply with a view to ascertaining where the money had come from, how he came to be in possession of that much money. It was at 11.25 that he was seen, asked how he had come to be in possession of it and he said, "I'm not going to tell you." He was asked where it had come from and his first explanation was, "I won it gambling, here and there", and he was not any more specific than that. He was told that he was being arrested because it was suspected that the money was stolen.

At 12.15 he was interviewed by the airport police, by Police Constable Abolins and Detective Constable Sutcliffe, and they said, "Well you have given this explanation that you won the money gambling; where did you win it gambling?", and he said, "I won it in Birmingham." He said, "I won it from different blokes in pubs playing cards." Well you may think he has had a rather lucky streak and rather good card schools he was in in Birmingham to have won all that amount of money, and indeed that was the officer's reaction. He said, "Well I've never seen pub card schools with that sort of money. Are you serious that you won it all at cards?", and the defendant said, "Yes". He said -- not surprisingly -- "I can't remember the names of the people or the pubs at the moment where the money was won." He said he wanted a solicitor, and the police said, "Yes, certainly, but in the meantime" the officer said, "I shall go and search your room ..." -- because by this stage they had established his address -- "... and make enquiries at various addresses found in your possession". So although they said he could have a solicitor, the officer equally told the defendant what they would be doing in the interim period, and that clearly caused concern to the defendant because he said, "I suppose you are going to turn over all my friends and make life difficult for them as well.", and the officer simply said, "Look, I'm going to do my duty and that is to find out how you, a man out of work, is in possession of such a large amount of money." The defendant said, "Don't do anything yet, let me think for a bit", and the officer said, "Take as long as you like", and clearly you may think the explanation so far given as to the £1,358 being won in card schools in pubs was a fatuous explanation and one that the defendant himself knew would not possibly stand up.

After he had thought for about five minutes he said, "O.K., I will make your job easy for you, I'll tell you", and not surprisingly, the officers who knew absolutely nothing about the items were interested. The officer said, "What are you going to tell me now?", and he said, "How I got the money." The officer said, "Yes, how did you get it?", and he said, "It was a bank job", so the officer said, "Yes, where, what did you do?", and the defendant said, "It was the Midlands Bank at Hockley, I held it up." Now that was the first knowledge the officers had of the case; they were not the investigating officers at all in that bank robbery, and of course the people who were the investigating officers on that bank robbery were looking for a coloured man. So the officer said, "I don't know any details about this matter at all. Rather than telling me verbally do you wish to make a written statement about the matter." As I was saying, the airport officer was in complete ignorance about the matter. The defendant said he would, and he then made Exhibit No.6, a statement, and that is the statement Members of the Jury which you have before you.

The statement commences with a caption which is simply the equivalent of a caution, and he is told that he need not say anything unless he wishes to do so. "I David Fisher wish to make a statement. I want someone to write down what I say. I have been told I need not say anything unless I wish to do so and that whatever I do say may be given in evidence", and he signed that. Obviously those are not his words; that is simply a caution saying that he need not say anything unless he wishes to do so, but the body of the statement Members of the Jury, these are the defendant's words and of course it was all news to the officers taking the statement. He said, "I had been out drinking at a pub in the town. I'd got no money, I hadn't paid any rent at the hostel because I'd blown it on beer. I'd got a starting pistol on me. I bought it from Bates's in the town. I was three parts drunk. First of all I looked in the Midland Bank in Hockley opposite Cannings. There was a young girl talking to another bloke, a cashier like, but there was no customers. I walked in, pointed the pistol at the girl and said, 'Give us the money.' She just handed over some money to me. I just ran round a few corners. I tried a telephone box to get a taxi but it was broke. I managed to get a taxi later and went to the hostel and then went and got something to eat. I stayed in and around Birmingham for a week or so and then last Tuesday I went across to Ireland and I have been there ever since. Just spending the money like a fool. I'm not absolutely positive but I think there was £4,300 ..." . Now of course the bank cashier knew that there was £3,800 that had gone. " ...I had in tenners and fivers apart from three brand new £1 notes. I know I've been stupid, what more can I say. I'm sorry." Then there is the subscription Members of the Jury, and that is dictated to him, indicating that he can alter it if he wishes, the statement, so again those are not his own words but they are part of the rules for taking a statement, but they are in his hand. "I have read the above statement and I have been told that I can correct, alter or add anything I wish. This statement is true. I have made it of my own free will", and he has signed that matter as well. Then the statement is witnessed by the two officers, Sutcliffe and Abolins who took it down between 12.55 and 1.15 p.m. on that day, the 19th March, when the defendant had flown in to the airport.

Members of the Jury, after that statement was taken of course there were a few queries left over for the officers, and the officer said, "Now just to clear up a few points, I take it all the money that you have in your possession is from the robbery?". He said, "Yes, I spent over £1,000 in Ireland in a week just on booze. I must be bloody barmy." "Where is the gun now?", as of course there was no knowledge by the police as to whether this was a real gun, imitation gun or what have you, and the main concern in such matters is to recover the gun. The gun in fact, Members of the Jury, is not a real gun; it is a starting pistol. It cannot discharge bullets as such, but of course if you are standing there looking at the other end of it, you are not going to enquire whether it fires bullets or not are you? It is in fact a starting pistol and it has chambers in it, Members of the Jury; it opens that way and it fires blank ammunition which is loaded in there. (Counsel demonstrated to the Jury). So the officers enquired where the gun was, and he said, "It's in my room at Warwick Road". So the officers went round to Warwick Road, and indeed the airport police said, "I will inform the Officers who are dealing with this case, of your arrest, and you will no doubt be taken to another police station later today and charged", and later one police officer from the airport, Police Constable Abolins, went to Warwick Road, No.155 where the defendant was staying, and from his room he obtained this gun and this ammunition Members of the Jury. I say 'ammunition'; it is blank ammunition but the gun was in fact loaded, and in the gun there were six live blanks and two used starting blanks, and there was also this box of ammunition with the gun as well.

Now as a result of those enquiries made by the officers at the airport, the officers who were investigating the case, that is Detective Constable Butler and Detective Constable Pyke, were informed of what had happened at the airport, and so they then come on to the scene. They visited the defendant's lodgings as well that afternoon and took possession of virtually all his property, a lot of property, so that they could find out and question the defendant about it, and indeed Detective Constables Pyke and Butler saw the defendant at Steelhouse Lane Police Station on the afternoon of the 19th March at 4.20 in the afternoon.

Now they had got the statement and they had read the statement that the defendant had made at the airport in the police station, and the officer said to him, "We have read your statement and there are a few things I want to make clear", and you have got that statement and the officer was referring to the statement. "You say in your statement, 'I'd got a starting pistol on me. I bought it from Bates's in town'", and he then said, "Is that the shop near to the Post and Mail building?". The defendant said, "Yes. I bought it the same day as I robbed the bank. I can't remember how much it cost." Indeed Members of the Jury, when that first statement was produced no gun had been recovered, they did not know where it was from at all, all that information coming from the defendant in the first statement, and now the officers were engaged in tidying up the whole matter. So they established that it was bought from Bates's near the Post and Mail Building just round the corner from here.

The officer again referred to the statement and said, "In your statement you say, 'I just ran round a few corners'. Which way did you run after robbing the bank?". He said, "Down a street, I think it's called Well Street", and here we can refer to the plan Members of the Jury. If one holds it this way (counsel indicated on plan) with Well Street and Great King Street at the top right hand corner, the bank is at the bottom left hand corner, the bank is in Great Hampton Street, and he described running down a street which he thought was called Well Street, and indeed there is a Well Street that goes along there, and he described his route, and the route he described was turning left at Well Street and he did not know the name of the road but the officer said, "I think that is Stainsby Avenue". He then described going through some flats and by a garage, and there Members of the Jury he described the 'phone box, going up to the 'phone box which was out of order. So he came down Well Street, Stainsby Avenue, through the flats and the 'phone box, passing the garage which is here on the right in Well Street.

The officer said, "What have you done with the cash you stole?", and he said, "I've spent a lot on booze and hotel bills. God I've had a lot to drink. I went to Ireland for St. Patricks Day ..." -- that I think is the 17th March Members of the Jury, and my learned friend Mr. Colman Treacy will no doubt be able to confirm that, and he said, "... but I didn't have a drink on the day as I was in such a bad state. I couldn't even get out of bed." The Officer said, "Well you had with you at the airport a lot of new property. Did you buy any of it with the stolen money?", and of course they were referring to those items there Members of the Jury, and then the defendant ran through a list of the items, where he had purchased them and for how much etcetera. He said the 2 rings -- and you can see the little boxes there -- they were £68 each; the watch was £53. There is a doll -- I think that is called the watchamacallit Members of the Jury -- "I got that at the gift shop at Dublin airport." The aftershave was bought in Galway; the holdall was bought in Woolworths in Galway, and he said "The air tickets to Dublin and back I purchased with the money. The suit ..." -- and there is a suit in there Members of the Jury which you will be able to see if you want to, "... the suit I had from Fosters in Newtown. It cost £39. The jacket was from the same place" -- because there is a jacket in there as well -- "and the radio (that is in the orange box), that was from a shop up Newtown." The officer said, "Did you wear any of this clothing when you committed the robbery?", and he said, "I think I had that anorak on." Now the anorak is a blue one, and again you will not be surprised that Miss Gardener did not think it was a blue one; she thought it was a dark khaki one worn by the raider. He said, "I wore also that red woollen hat", and surprise, surprise, Miss Gardener thought it was a green one Members of the Jury. But those are the items that the defendant pointed out that he had worn on the day of the robbery. At least he had a woollen hat on which he agrees about, but he says it was a red one and Miss Gardener says it was a green one. Well Members of the Jury, those are the items he pointed out.

The officer went on to say, "The cashier says that you put the money in a plastic bag. Where is that now?". "I used one of them two bags", and then he pointed out the plastic bag with the 'Lucky 7' motif on. It looks as though Miss Gardener was closer to the mark on that one at least.

He was then asked if he wanted to make a further statement and he said he did, and that is the other statement which you have Members of the Jury, Exhibit No.10. Has everyone got Exhibit No.10?

MEMBER OF THE JURY: No.

MR. JONES: There is a spare. (Same handed to the Jury).

That statement Members of the Jury, which has the same caption because it is a standard caption saying he need not say anything, is signed. The body of the statement says, "I've been spending like mad since I had the money from the Bank. I've spent a lot on booze and hotel bills. I bought the airline ticket to Dublin and back. Also train tickets and taxis. I bought the 2 rings you showed me with part of the money. I think they were £68 each. The watch was £53, the radio about £8. The doll was £9.99, the aftershave £4.95. The fawn jacket was £10.99 I think. The brown suit was £39 I think it was, and also the brown bag I bought. Also I bought the watchamacallit ..." -- the watchamacallit is that yellow looking ape, and indeed is called "a watchamacallit" in the box. "... the watchamacallit was a couple of quid. These were all bought with the stolen money. The starting pistol you showed me is the one I used. The lucky seven bags you've got, it was one of them I put the money in. I was wearing the woollen hat you found." He signed that, and again with the usual subscription which he has written out at the officer's dictation about this statement being true and being made at his own free will.

So there Members of the Jury, firstly there are the

admissions to the officers who know nothing about the case, and then there are the admissions to the officers who were investigating the case who up until the 19th March had, thanks to Miss Gardener, been looking for a coloured man as being responsible for this offence. So, as I said in opening, the person shown in that photograph, which is a photograph of the defendant on the day of his arrest -- and of course the defendant sits in the dock there Members of the Jury, -- that is in fact the same person as that on the Identikit in the eyes of Miss Gardener. It seems highly improbable, but strangely enough she is not quite so wild is she. Remember there are no ears or hair shown because there was a hat worn, but if you look at the shape of the eyebrows, they are thick eyebrows and the shape is the same as the defendant. The nose is similar. The shape of the face, particularly the jawbone, is in fact the same. The lips are the same, because the important thing to Miss Gardener was that although she thought the man was Asian or very light skinned, he had not got the thick Negroid type lips which are often the situation; they were thin lips and it was a wide mouth, and indeed the shape of the lips and that of the defendant you may think are the same.

Members of the Jury, of course the prosecution do not say, ah Miss Gardener, that is the identification and therefore you can rely on that. Of course not, but Members of the Jury when you are assessing the whole of this matter these are the features to bear in mind. She did say it was a coloured man, Asiatic or very light skinned, but Members of the Jury, bear in mind also the defence; there was not anything wrong wit the lighting in the bank. If you want to look at the photographs -- and perhaps we will look at the photographs now . The photograph showing the interior of the bank, that is the first photograph, and you can see there is a lot of strip lighting around, and 'B' is the position from which Miss Gardener was looking when the raider came. Because of the light from outside there is a slightly darker impression, but Members of the Jury basically that is the lighting in the bank so there is nothing wrong with that light.

Members of the Jury those are the facts. Let me give you two warnings. The prosecution bring the case and it is for the prosecution to prove it and to prove it so that you are sure and secondly, what I have told you in opening are the facts as seen by the prosecution, but it is on the evidence you base your verdict and not upon what I have told you. What I have told you I hope is a useful guide so that you can see where the evidence fits into the overall story, but it is on the evidence you will base your verdict, and that evidence I will now call before you.

Your honour, my learned friends have indicated to me that the plan and the two sets of photographs are agreed. For the sake of completeness the photographs of the exterior of the bank were taken, for what it is worth, on the 26th March, and the photographs of the interior of the bank were taken on the 25th February, the day of the robbery.

MR. ESCOTT COX: Yes, I agree your honour.

JUDGE RUSH: Thank you.

MR. JONES: I will now call Miss Gardener. Yvonne Gardener please.

MR. ESCOTT COX: David can we agree the dates of this?

MR. JONES: Yes. Your honour, the prosecution admit that both the photograph of the photofit and that of the defendant, the photofit picture was compiled on the day of the robbery, the 25th February, and the photograph of the defendant was on the day of his arrest, th 19th March.

JUDGE RUSH: Thank you. Very well.

MISS YVONNE CAROL GARDENER.

Examined by Mr. Jones.

THE CLERK: Will you repeat the oath after me please. I swear by Almighty God ....

THE WITNESS: I swear by Almighty God ....

THE CLERK: ... that the evidence I shall give ....

THE WITNESS: ... that the evidence I shall give ....

THE CLERK: ... shall be the truth ....

THE WITNESS: .... shall be the truth ....

THE CLERK: ... the whole truth ....

THE WITNESS: ... the whole truth ....

THE CLERK: ... and nothing but the truth.

THE WITNESS: .... and nothing but the truth.

MR. JONES: Is your full name Yvonne Carol Gardener, Miss Gardener?

A. Yes.

Q. You prefer to sit down rather than stand do you?

A. Yes I would. (The witness sat down).

Q. Do you work at the Midland Bank, Great Hampton Street in Birmingham?

A. No, I don't any more.

Q. In February of last year were you working at the Midland Bank?

MISS Y.C.GARDENER,
Examined.

A. Yes.

Q. And I think you were working there in the capacity of a bank clerk?

A. Yes.

Q. At 3 o'clock on Monday the 25th February were you working as normal behind the counter?

A. Yes I was.

Q. Were you on your own or were others with you?

A. I was by myself.

Q. Did you see someone come into the bank?

A. Yes.

Q. How would you describe the person who came into the bank?

A. He was about 5-foot 10-inches, very dark complexion.

JUDGE RUSH: Wait a moment. 5-feet 10-inches about. Yes.

A. Yes, dark complexion.

MR. ESCOTT COX: Your honour she said "very dark" the first time.

THE WITNESS: Very dark, yes.

JUDGE RUSH: Very dark complexion. Yes.

THE WITNESS: He was wearing a green woolly hat and a green anorak. He had got a sort of flatish nose from what I can remember.

JUDGE RUSH: A flatish nose from what you can remember?

A. Yes.

MR. JONES: What about race?

A. I would have said he was Asian perhaps.

Q. What was then the colour of his skin?

A. It was dar k; dark complexion.

Q. White people can have a dark complexion, and dark people can have a light complexion. What was the overall picture that you formed?

A. At the time I thought that he was Asian.

MISS Y.C.GARDENER,
Examined.

JUDGE RUSH: Yes.

MR. JONES: Miss Gardener we will come back to the description later, but what did the man say or do?

A. He was standing by the enquiry counter for a while. Then after he had been standing there for a while I asked him if I could help him, and he came over to me and took a gun out of his pocket with his right hand, and a plastic bag out of his other pocket with his left hand, and pointed the gun towards the till and said "Money".

Q. He had the gun in his right hand, took the plastic bag out of his pocket with his left hand, pointed the gun at you and said "Money". The gun -- can you describe the gun?

A. Yes, it was a small one about that long. (Witness indicated).

Q. You indicate, for the sake of the shorthand note, about 5 or 6-inches in length?

A. Yes, about five to six inches. It was all black, and that is all I can remember about it.

Q. What about the size of the barrel?

A. That was only small; about 3-inches.

Q. You indicate about .....?

A. 2 to 3-inches.

Q. Did you hear anything?

A. Yes, he clicked it.

Q. Will you look please at Exhibit No.4. (Exhibit 4 handed to the witness). Is that gun familiar?

A. Yes, that looks like the one I saw.

Q. This gun can be cocked. What do you say about that noise?

A. Yes, that is the noise I heard.

Q. What did you do when the man said that to you?

A. I was a bit taken by surprise and I said, "Money", and he said "Money" too, and pointed to the drawers again.

Q. What state were you in?

A. I was very surprised.

Q. I do not want to know the details of this at all, but have you an alarm bell and buttons in the bank?

MISS Y.C.GARDENER,
Examined.

A. Yes.

Q. Did you press any?

A. No, not until after he had gone.

Q. Why was that?

A. Because it is a loud alarm and you can hear it.

Q. So if you had pressed the alarm the noise would have gone off while the man was still there?

A. Yes.

Q. Now you did not press the alarm and the man indicated you should hand over the money?

A. Yes.

Q. How much money did you take out?

A. £3,800.

Q. How did you know that?

A. It had been a very quiet day that day and I had cashed up my till, and I took the money I had in one particular drawer, so I knew exactly how much there was in there.

Q. What were the denominations of the notes you handed over?

A. There were some £10, £5 and £1 notes.

Q. Were they all old notes or new ones?

A. The £1 notes were new ones. The others were old.

Q. Now when you handed over the money what did the man do?

A. He put it into his bag and ran out.

Q. After he had run out of the bank, what did you then do?

A. I sounded the alarm and told the other members of the staff about it.

Q. I do not want to know what was said but did you subsequently speak to Mr. Witham about the matter?

A. No, Mr. Witham was out at the time.

Q. When he came in did you speak to Mr. Witham?

A. Yes.

Q. On the day, the 25th February, did you speak to the police?

MISS Y.C.GARDENER,
Examined.

A. Yes.

Q. And indeed did you make a statement about this matter?

A. Yes.

Q. And in that statement did you describe the man who had held up the bank?

A. Yes.

Q. When you made that statement was his description still fresh in your memory?

A. Yes.

Q. Your honour, I do not know whether my learned friend has any objection. I wonder if the witness may be referred to her statement to refresh her memory from that?

JUDGE RUSH: Mr. Escott Cox have you any objection?

MR. ESCOTT COX: No.

JUDGE RUSH: Yes.

MR. JONES: I am grateful to my learned friend. Perhaps a typewritten copy would be easier.

JUDGE RUSH: Yes. (A copy of the statement handed to the witness).

MR. JONES: Before you actually look at that Miss Gardener, you describe the man as Asiatic?

A. Yes.

Q. What was there about his looks that gave the impression he was Asiatic as opposed to Negroid?

A. He was not very dark. It was a pale dark complexion.

Q. He was a pale dark?

A. Yes.

Q. That is so far as the colour of his skin is it?

A. Yes.

Q. Please look at the description you gave. That is your statement is it?

A. Yes.

Q. And it is the last but one paragraph, the penultimate paragraph.

MISS Y. C. GARDENER,
Examined.

A. Yes.

Q. How did you describe him on that day? You can read it out.

A. I described him as about 25 years old, 5' 10".

Q. If you could go very slowly. 25 years old?

A. Yes, 5' 10" tall, he was either Asian or a very light skinned West Indian. He had a dark green woollen hat over his head, covering his hair and his ears. He had dark brown eyes, a long wide mouth, but not thick lips. He was wearing a dark khaki jacket, plain in style, and I think I could recognise him again.

Q. I think on that same day you went to Police Headquarters and made a photofit description?

A. Yes.

Q. Will you look please at that photograph, which will be Exhibit 11. Now that is the photofit picture. What do you say about that photofit and the likeness to the man you saw in the bank?

A. That is not how I remember him now.

Q. What is different about the photofit to the man you saw?

A. I think his complexion was a lot lighter than that and his face was a lot smaller that sort of way.

Q. You indicate that his face was not as long?

A. Yes.

Q. And his complexion was a lot lighter?

A. Yes.

Q. Miss Gardener will you look please at Exhibit No.8 which is a woollen hat, a red woollen hat. Do you recognise that woollen hat at all?

A. No.

Q. Forget the colour; is the shape of the hat and the type in any way familiar?

A. Yes. Yes, I described the hat as it was in that sort of style.

Q. The hat was in that sort of style, and it was woollen was it?

A. Yes.

MISS Y.C.GARDENER,
Examined.

Q. And that sort of shape but not the same colour?

A. No.

Q. Will you look please at Exhibit No.9, the two plastic bags. Are they in any way familiar?

A. I did not get much chance to really look at the bags, but they were white and they seemed to have red on the sides.

Q. I see. The blue anorak, Exhibit No.7; does that in any way look familiar?

A. No. It is the same sort of style but I remember it being green and different material really.

Q. The same sort of style but you remember it being green?

A. Yes, and sort of cotton sort of thing. Like the sort an Army combat jacket is made out of.

Q. I see. Dull as opposed to shiny, is that it?

A. Yes.

Cross-examined by Mr.Escott Cox.

MR. ESCOTT COX: Miss Gardener I did not quite catch what you said at the beginning of your evidence when you were asked about your job; your voice fell away. Are you still working for the bank but at a different branch?

A. No, I am at a different job now.

Q. Yes alright. Let us go back to the days when you worked for the Midland Bank. Had you worked very long at that particular branch?

A. No. About a month.

Q. Where had you been before that?

A. I had been working in Erdington.

Q. At another branch?

A. At another branch, yes.

Q. On the counter at times?

A. Yes.

Q. Whatever members of the public may or may not think of people who serve behind the counter at banks, it is quite a difficult and responsible job is it not?

A. Yes.

MISS Y.C.GARDENER,
Cross-examined.

Q. For which you have to have ... and please, I do not want to know ... but presumably you have to have a certain level of education for a job of that sort?

A. Yes.

Q. And then bank training, is that right?

A. Yes.

Q. And of course you have got the responsibility, when you are actually working at the counter, of dealing with quite large sums of cash, both those being paid into the bank by bank customers ... do you agree with that?

A. Yes.

Q. And also of course paying out possibly quite large sums of money to bank customers?

A. Yes.

Q. You also have to deal at the counter with a good many other banking affairs, to do with the movement of credit and cash to filling in documents, getting signatures and so on, do you not?

A. Yes.

Q. Let me ask you about recognition first of all. One of your skills, certainly to be cultivated as somebody who is working at the counter, is recognition of customers because you get to know regular customers don't you?

A. Yes.

Q. This is for many reasons. Obviously one is it creates good customer relations with the bank if you know the customer. That is right, is it not?

A. Yes.

Q. It also speeds up transactions if you know a customer is a good and regular customer. You do not have to make enquiries before you hand over money in payment for a cheque. You agree with that?

A. Yes.

Q. So recognition of customers and sizing up customers generally is quite an important part of the job. You would agree with that?

A. Yes.

Q. And on this particular day when you were held up -- and

MISS Y.C.GARDENER,
Cross-examined.

please, there is no dispute that somebody held you up; you realise that, -- when you were held up it had been rather a quiet afternoon, had it, in February of last year?

A. Yes.

Q. Monday the 25th. And then this particular man who held you up came into the banking hall, and as we can see from the photographs ... I am sorry, you have not got a copy of these photographs. We are having to share them round -- possibly an economy drive, I don't know. (Photographs handed to the witness). That is very much the overall picture of the banking hall?

A. Yes.

Q. It is not a huge area but it is spacious and it is extremely well lit?

A. Yes.

Q. Members of the Jury, I am looking at photograph A of Exhibit 3.

MR. JONES: Exhibit 3?

MR. ESCOTT COX: Of Exhibit 3, yes. (To the witness). For example when the police photographer came down and took that photograph he would have been standing quite a few paces away from the counter, and yet looking at the photograph one has no difficulty at all in distinguishing the features of the young man on our left of that group as we look at that. You would agree with that?

A. Yes.

Q. That gives some indication of how well lit the bank is?

A. Yes.

Q. I suppose those are bank employees are they?

A. Yes.

Q. They were your working colleagues?

A. Yes.

Q. Of course you recognise them because you knew them as people you worked with. I am not making any false point about that; all I am pointing out is that one can distinguish a person's features in this banking hall at a good number of paces?

A. Yes.

Q. And we have overhead fluorescent light in this Court. Is that the sort of light in that banking hall?

MISS Y.C.GARDENER,
Cross-examined.

A. Yes.

Q. You would not have more difficulty in recognising somebody's features in that banking hall -- and when I say 'recognising', taking in somebody's features -- than you would have, if I may respectfully say so, any lady or gentleman on the Jury. You would agree with that?

A. Yes.

Q. When this man who eventually held you up first came in he attracted your attention by behaving in a rather odd way, did he not?

A. Yes.

Q. And you must have had a good look at him then?

A. Yes. Well that particular day we had had quite a few people coming in doing exactly the same thing, so I didn't take all that much notice.

Q. Coming in and standing where there was nobody to serve them and going out again?

A. Well they would come in and stand for a while. You can see there is a bell at the enquiry place, and a lot of people come in and stand there for a while before they realise there is a bell to press.

Q. I see. In fact you were on your own behind that counter, weren't you?

A. Yes.

Q. There was no-one else there at all?

A. No.

Q. But whether you paid particular attention you could see him and see him perfectly well, and he stood there -- I think you have already said but if not I will remind you -- for about a minute, did he not?

A. Yes.

Q. Quite a long time?

A. Yes.

Q. And there was no question of you being attacked at that stage?

A. No.

Q. And the man then came over when you said, "Can I help you?". I suppose you called down to him and he came over and stood

MISS Y.C.GARDENER,
Cross-examined.

in front of you?

A. Yes.

Q. And at that stage you would have a very good look at him would you not?

A. Yes.

Q. There is no question you didn't really look at his face or features because your eyes were riveted on something else. You looked at him properly and full in the face?

A. Yes I did to begin with.

Q. Then of course you were getting money out of the drawer so you would not be looking at him then, but you did look at the gun?

A. Yes.

Q. Did you look a lot at the gun?

A. Not really.

Q. It has been suggested already to this Jury you did not get a good look at the man's face because -- and I quote the exact words --"your attention was riveted on the gun". That is not true at all that your attention was riveted on the gun?

A. No.

Q. Now the man was standing in front of you. Of course you were getting money out and so on for perhaps what -- another half a minute after he came to your counter? How long did it take you to get this money out physically and hand it over?

A. About half a minute.

Q. Yes. I was only guessing but I would not have thought it would take you much longer. Alright. You have only spoken so far at the bank of him producing a plastic bag, is that right?

A. I could not really tell.

Q. You didn't know whether it was one or more than one?

A. No.

Q. But whatever sort of bag he produced, did it strike you as being a very ordinary sort of supermarket, large shopping type of bag with some red on it?

A. Yes.

MISS Y.C.GARDENER,
Cross-examined.

Q. The sort of thing we might find in literally tens of thousands everywhere?

A. Yes.

Q. Then he went out of the bank taking the money with him amd you raised the alarm?

A. Yes.

Q. Can you remember the manager, Mr. Witham, coming in very shortly after that?

A. Yes.

Q. And I think he went out again to try and look for the man in the area?

A. Yes.

Q. And it was at that stage that obviously -- I do not necessarily mean immediately but I expect there was very little delay in calling the police?

A. Yes, they were called immediately.

Q. And the man wasn't found in the area as we all know, the man who had held you up and gone away. And the police came to the bank I suppose and started making enquiries?

A. Yes.

Q. And a lot of those enquiries would be centred on you because you were the actual person who was held up, and I don't suppose any of your colleagues who were working inside the bank ever saw this man at all if you were on your own behind the counter. Is that right?

A. Yes.

Q. Now I expect this was done -- and if not you tell me and put the story right, -- but I expect when the detectives first arrived they asked you to give some preliminary description of what the man looked like on an informal basis?

A. Yes.

Q. And eventually you made the statement of which you have seen a typed copy?

A. Yes.

Q. Where was that done?

A. At the police station.

MISS Y.C.GARDENER,
Cross-examined.

Q. Was it perhaps quite a little bit later in the day you went up there?

A. I went straight up from the bank about half past three, and then went straight to do a photofit picture, and then it was after that so it was about an hour and a half later.

Q. Your thoughts were quite collected at the time you saw the police were they?

A. Yes.

Q. And it was perfectly clear to you I expect that you were the only person at that stage who could give the police any lead. You are an intelligent girl; you did realise that what you were telling them about the raider was of great importance to them?

A. Yes.

Q. So I daresay you would take very great care to get it as accurate as possible to help them?

A. Yes.

Q. And we have had your description. What I am interested in is this. You see there is no qualification of the description there. You described him as 25 years old, 5-feet 10-inches tall and either Asian or very light skinned West Indian?

A. Yes.

Q. So you were describing him either as an Asian or possibly as somebody of negroid features?

A. I would not have described him as negroid.

Q. What is a very light skinned West Indian if it is not negroid?

A. I know. I was getting very confused by that time when I was trying to describe his complexion.

Q. What was confusing you? Here you had been held up in the bank by a man; you have agreed when you went to the police station your thoughts were all collected, and here you were giving your description upon which the police were going to start their enquiries, so obviously your description would need to be given with great care and accuracy, would it not?

A. Yes.

Q. What was confusing to you at that stage?

A. I considered him to be Asian. The police asked me whether Asian or West Indian, and at the time I wasn't really sure what colour West Indian was. I looked through some pictures of people and I pointed out to him what sort of complexion

MISS Y.C.GARDENER,
Cross-examined.

I thought he was.

Q. Forgive me. For somebody who has worked in a bank in Erdington and worked in a bank in Hockley, you are not really saying you don't know what West Indian features or what West Indians look like, are you?

A. No.

Q. What was confusing about it then? You must, in and around the bank and in the streets of Birmingham have seen thousands of West Indians, haven't you?

A. Yes.

Q. What was confusing about it then?

A. I was confused at the time.

Q. But what was the confusion? That is what I don't understand.

A. I said I considered him to be Asian at the time. It was just the different options put to me at the time.

Q. Which you agreed with?

A. No, I didn't agree. I said it could have been, I can't remember.

Q. It could have been. Is what the statement should read, "He was either Asian or he could have been a light skinned West Indian, but I do not think so." Would that have been a fairer, more accurate way of putting your statement down?

A. Yes, I think so.

Q. No, not I don't think so. I want to be sure if I can. If your statement had read, "I describe him as about 25 years old, 5-feet 10-inches tall. He was Asian or he might have been a very light skinned West Indian but I don't think so", would that have been an absolutely fair description of your state of mind?

A. Yes.

Q. One thing that is sure is that you were not in any doubt whatever, and are not even now in any doubt whatever as to the other descriptions that you gave, -- that he had a dark green woollen hat over his head and he was wearing a khaki jacket?

MR. JONES: I am sorry your honour. I hesitate to interrupt but my learned ....

MR. ESCOTT COX: I will rephrase the question. Is that or is that not fair, that he was wearing a dark green woollen hat and a khaki jacket?

MISS Y.C.GARDENER,
Cross-examined.

A. It was a dark green woollen hat and a plain green jacket.

Q. Khaki-ish?

A. Yes.

JUDGE RUSH: Anorak type?

A. Yes.

MR. ESCOTT COX: You then went and saw an expert policeman, expert in making photofit pictures?

A. Yes.

Q. And as a result of that this photofit -- of course the original is quite a lot bigger but that is just the photograph of it -- came into existence?

A. Yes.

Q. Now I do not understand what you are saying about that. You knew when you made that photofit with the help of the officer that it would be in all probability used by police officers in their enquiries into this case to try and catch the man who was responsible. Do you agree with that?

A. Yes.

Q. And did it, at the time you made it, represent how you thought the man who had held you up looked?

A. Yes I think so.

Q. If it hadn't, would you not have said to the officer, "There is no point in looking for a man who looks like that; he didn't look like that"?

A. Yes.

Q. So at the time you made it you really believed that is what the man looked like?

A. Yes.

Q. And your impression of him, as to what he really looked like, would have been much better then than at any time subsequently, memory failing. Would you not agree?

A. Yes.

Q. Then why have you given evidence qualifying the photofit and saying, "Well I don't think he did look like that" if that is what you believed he looked like at the time, and as your memory was better then than now, surely it is the best image we can have from you isn't it?

MISS Y.C.GARDENER,
Cross-examined.

A. Yes.

Q. Of course I daresay that since this all happened you have been told that the police have arrested and charged a white man for this offence, have you not?

A. Yes.

Q. And I expect they have been back to you and asked you about it have they?

A. Yes, well ....

Q. I do not want to know what was said but just the fact that somebody came and discussed this with you after the accused was arrested?

A. Yes.

Q. Possibly showing you a photograph of the accused?

A. No.

Q. They also came back to you and showed you a number of things, as my learned friend Mr. David Jones for the prosecution has indicated in this case, -- clothing and the gun?

A. Yes.

Q. I do not particularly want to go into any of those matters. (To the learned judge). Would your honour bear with me for a moment? (Mr. Escott Cox had a short discussion with Mr. Treacy). (Mr. Escott Cox had a short discussion with Mr. Jones). (To the witness). How much money went do you say?

A. £3,800.

Q. Of which £300 was in £1 notes, and all the rest was in £10 notes and fivers. I think you have already told us that, have you not?

A. Yes.

Q. Yes I thought you had. Miss Gardener I do not want to have a complete utter air of unreality about this case. Since you came into this courtroom I think all of us have noticed, very naturally -- and not a word of criticism; we would be surprised if you hadn't, -- you have been glancing over to the dock and taking a look at the accused, obviously comparing him in your mind with that. (Photograph handed to the witness). Was it the accused's features as you saw him sit in the dock which caused you, in answer to questions from counsel for the prosecution, to qualify that description?

A. No, I cannot see him.

Q. Can you see him at all?

MISS Y.C.GARDENER,
Cross-examined.

A. I can see him now.

Q. I think you would agree he doesn't actually look anything like that photofit picture at all?

A. No.

Q. I think it is a question I have to ask you or put to you. That is not the man who came into the bank, is it, on this day?

A. Yes, I think it is.

Q. Why do you say that when you agree that he looks nothing like the photofit picture?

A. Well, when making up the photofit picture it is very difficult looking at all the different eyes and mouths and nose. He looks more like the man I remember than the photofit picture.

Q. There are a great many photofit features and I am calling for it and we are going to have a photofit kit here in Court, which would probably be a fairer way to cross-examine you about it, but there are a great many features where you can have an individual impression or the face as a whole. You have already agreed the photofit picture does not really look like the accused. Did you say to the officer when he made up the picture, "That doesn't really look like the man who attacked me in the bank"?

A. No.

Q. Why not?

A. At the time it seems to be a likeness.

Q. And your memory would be better then that it is now?

A. Yes.

Q. Let us face it, you have not set eyes on the accused if he was the man who held you up, since the 25th February last year?

A. Yes.

Q. If you have ever seen him before. You agree with me?

A. Yes.

Q. Yes, alright.

Re-examined by Mr. Jones.

MR. JONES: Miss Gardener you said to my learned friend, "I think it is the same man who came into the bank. He looks more like the man I remember than the photofit picture". Now clearly

MISS Y.C.GARDENER,
Re-examined.

with my large bulk in the way you could not see when I was asking you questions. What is it that makes you say that about the defendant?

A. Well from here, his eyes. I recognise his eyes as being how I described them anyway.

JUDGE RUSH: What about his eyebrows, one way or the other?

A. Yes I'd say.

MR. JONES: We know from your statement and indeed your evidence today that you described the man as having a long wide mouth and not thick lips. What do you say about the defendant's lips?

A. I can't see him.

MR. ESCOTT COX: He can stand up. I have no objection. (The accused stood up).

THE WITNESS: I cannot really say.. I cannot really remember his mouth now.

MR. JONES: You cannot remember his mouth now so you cannot really say. The overall shape of the face?

A. Yes, that is the same as I remember.

Q. The nose?

A. I remember that being sort of wider.

Q. You remember the nose being wider. At one stage Miss Gardener you said of the photofit picture a much lighter complexion and shorter face?

A. Yes.

Q. When you were doing the photofit picture how was it done. Were there various shades of face put to you or was that not possible?

A. No, it started off a really dark face, and then it was made lighter with pencils.

Q. So there is a face pattern and that is tried to make lighter?

A. Yes, I think so.

Q. But the features that were put to you, was anything done about those features such as the eyes, nose and mouth?

A. Yes, they were changed. It started off with a longer face and that was made shorter.

Q. But it is one feature after another that is put there, and

MISS Y.C.GARDENER,
Re-examined.

you say 'Yes' or 'No'?

A. Yes.

Q. Yes, thank you very much. Your honour may this witness be released.

JUDGE RUSH: Yes. Thank you very much for your attendance.

MR. ESCOTT COX: She ought to stay because we may want her for the photofit picture.

JUDGE RUSH: You don't want her released?

MR. ESCOTT COX: No your honour. Once we have the actual photofit kit here I may want to ask some more questions.

MR. JONES: Your honour obviously the photofit picture officer was not called. He is not part of the depositions, but I am hoping he will be here at 2.15 with the actual kit.

JUDGE RUSH: That is in train now, is it?

MR. JONES: I hope so your honour, and I hope it will be possible to get him here.

Norman Barnard Witham please.

MR. NORMAN BARNARD WITHAM, Sworn.

Examined by Mr. Jones.

MR. JONES: Is your full name Norman Barnard Witham, Mr. Witham?

A. That is correct.

Q. And I think you are the bank manager of the Midland Bank at Great Hampton Street in Newtown, Birmingham?

A. That is correct.

Q. At a few minutes to 3 o'clock on Monday, the 25th February, I think you parked your vehicle in the car park at the bank?

A. Yes, that is right.

Q. You had been to Wolverhampton?

A. Yes, that is right.

Q. And did you walk from your car along Wells Street towards the bank?

A. Yes, that is right.

Q. What was the weather like?

MR. N. B. WITHAM,
Examined.

A. Similar to today. Raining, and I had my umbrella up.

Q. A pretty dark miserable day?

A. It was, yes.

Q. When you were walking to the bank did you notice someone. Did someone pass you?

A. There were three bodies that attracted my attention. There were telephone engineers working virtually at the corner of Wells Street and Great Hampton Street; the corner at which the bank is placed. They were working on a telephone box fitment against the wall of the bank, and then a running figure came down the street past these telephone engineers and past me.

Q. At the time when the running figure passed you, were you in any way alarmed or suspicious at that time?

A. No.

Q. Did you pay very much attention to the running figure?

A. To a certain extent yes. I was attracted to his mode of running. Also I suppose there was a certain amount of antagonism towards a running figure anyway, coming towards you. Otherwise nothing in detail, no.

Q. Your umbrella you had got up?

A. Yes.

Q. When he ran past you what was your impression of him, his description?

A. He was wearing as far as I can recollect a green woolly hat which was pulled down pretty well over his head, so I really had no opportunity of looking at his hair style. He was wearing an anerak type of jacket, say a lovatt colour khaki, that sort of green colour. I had the impression that he was wearing soft boots. The thing that I recall about his running is that his feet seemed to go out considerably at an angle. He was cradling his arms as if he was clutching something to him as he ran; he was stooping.

Q. Could you see what it was?

A. No, but it was a sort of stooping running figure.

Q. Did you get any chance to assess his complexion or not?

A. He was either ... I would have thought either a swarthy white person or a light coloured Asian. His nose was longish. He wasn't negroid.

Q. Now after he passed you Mr. Witham, did something else attract your attention?

MR. N. B. WITHAM,
Examined.

A. Yes, the alarm went in the bank.

Q. Could that be heard from outside?

A. Yes.

Q. I think for the sake of completeness you did say there were three things?

A. Well three bodies; three people.

Q. How many engineers were there?

A. There were two engineers.

Q. So there were two engineers and the running figure?

A. Yes.

Q. Then you heard the bank warning klaxon given?

A. Yes.

Q. What did you do then?

A. I continued into the bank. I didn't relate that to the running figure at that time.

Q. I don't want to know what was said but did you speak to your staff?

A. I did.

Q. And as a result were the police called?

A. Yes.

Q. And I think you left the bank and walked back along Wells Street to see if you could see anything?

A. That is correct.

Cross-examined by Mr. Escott Cox.

MR. ESCOTT COX: What did you see Mr. Witham when you walked back along Wells Street?

A. I didn't see the running figure I was looking for. As you come down Wells Street there is a cross-roads first of all, so I went down to that cross-roads to look around.

Q. Is this the cross-roads with Barr Street?

A. Yes.

Q. We have got a plan. You know the area so well I don't suppose you need one?

MR. N. B. WITHAM,
Cross-examined.

A. No, I am quite happy without. I realised that if that running figure was the person who had raided the bank in no way was I ever going to catch up with him with the time that had elapsed and the speed at which he was running, so the purpose of my going out was to see if I could see somebody in the distance, in whatever direction they might have run in, so I went down to the cross-roads with Barr Street. There was no sign of a running figure there. I presumed therefore he had gone straight across the cross-roads, so I went down to parallel to Barr Street.

Q. Is that Stainsby Avenue?

A. There is a piece of open land there which was elevated, so I went on to that to see if I could get a view of the surrounding area, but I saw nothing but the movement of cars which I think drew my attention.

Q. Would you be good enough to have a look at the plan and help me, Exhibit 1 -- not to question anything you have said, of course not. We see how the bank is laid out with Great Hampton Street running up and down the left-hand side of the plan, and Well Street running along horizontally. The first cross-road you come to is Barr Street and the next one is Stainsby Avenue, and right opposite the end of Stainsby Avenue there is a large building apparently called the Language Centre, is that right. Did you recognise that?

A. I didn't recognise that as such.

Q. Or is it open?

A. The piece of land immediate opposite the end of Wells Street is open land. To the right of that building which is shown there is a dotted rectangle there with a smaller rectangle with two parallel lines in it. That in fact is open land and that is the open land on which I stood to get a view of the area in general because the land falls away towards New John Street.

Q. So that is the road you crossed, Stainsby Avenue, to go and stand on this piece of land?

A. That is right.

Q. What happened then Mr. Witham? You didn't see anything did you at this stage?

A. I reported the certain movement of a car which I gather ....

Q. Nothing you gathered. I am asking you what you saw at the scene?

A. I did not see the running figure. I saw a car which appeared to be starting off and so attracted my attention for that reason particularly.

MR. N. B. WITHAM,
Cross-examined.

Q. Whereabouts was that car?

A. Travelling along Stainsby Avenue towards Great King Street.

Q. Whereabouts was it in relation to Well Street? Was it by Well Street or nearer to Great King Street?

A. When I saw the car it was travelling across that junction basically. It was going along Stainsby Avenue. I got the impression it started off to the right of Wells Street, and passed the end of Wells Street towards Great King Street.

Q. How many people were in the car?

A. Two.

Q. What were they?

A. The driver was a negro. What attracted me to that car was that I got the impression that the passenger was crouching.

Q. Yes. Did you return to the bank after you had seen that?

A. I did.

Q. Now one thing I want particularly to ask you about Mr. Witham. You obviously saw the police that very day and helped them with such description of the man you had seen running near the bank as you were able to give. Please, nobody is criticising you; you had no reason to be suspicious of him at the time.

A. As he ran past me that is true.

Q. So it was not as if you were watching a possible suspect; it was just watching somebody behave in a rather boring way on a not very wide pavement on a wet day, but I think you agree you described him to the police as 5ft. 5ins. to 5ft. 6ins. tall, slim build, wearing a dark green woollen hat pulled down over his ears, the hat close to his head suggesting he had short hair, and a khaki coloured short jacket similar to an anorak or combat type jacket?

A. Yes. I think it would be probably truer to say I had no idea of his hair style in that the woollen cap was pulled down to such an extent.

Q. I think you were careful to say the hat was close to his head suggesting he had short hair, but obviously you were not committing yourself. Is that fair?

A. Yes, that is fair.

Q. And I am putting it verbatim to you from your statement, but by all means refresh your memory if you wish to.

A. Yes.

MR. N. B. WITHAM,
Cross-examined.

Q. So although you were not sure of his facial description you obviously were sure of at any rate some of his clothing -- the hat, the jacket and perhaps a little less sure of the boots, but anyway of his upper body you had a very firm impression in your mind as to what he was wearing?

A. Yes.

Q. Yes, thank you.

<u>Re-examined by Mr. Jones.</u>

MR. JONES: So far as the car that was going away, did you take the number of that car?

A. I did.

Q. Do you remember the number?

A. I don't remember it. I did give it in a statement to the police.

Q. Yes, and that number you passed on to the police did you?

A. Yes I did.

(Mr. Jones and Mr. Escott Cox conferred together).

MR. JONES: Your honour my learned friend most helpfully indicates that the witness may see his statement in order to get the number of the car.

JUDGE RUSH: Yes. (Statement passed to the witness).

MR. JONES: Mr. Witham did you make a note of the number of the car which is contained therein?

A. Yes, it is here. MXC.388H.

Q. MXC.388H. Thank you very much.

JUDGE RUSH: Yes. Mr. Witham you are free to leave. Thank you for your attendance.

A. Thank you your honour. (The witness withdrew).

MR. JONES: Your honour I tender Miss Angela Woodward because I do not see that she gets either case further forward. I do not know if my learned friend requires her. No.

JUDGE RUSH: Very well. We will dispense with her then.

MR. JONES: Mr. Conrad Cross please. Your honour this witness was conditionally bound and his evidence may be read.

JUDGE RUSH: Yes. Members of the Jury you are about to hear the evidence that would have been given by Mr. Cross. It is not challenged and therefore there is no need for him to be here to give evidence, but it is just as important as if he were giving evidence here on oath. Yes.

MR. JONES: Mr. Conrad Cross, who is over 21 years and a Director of George Bate Gunmakers Ltd., 16 Colmore Circus, Birmingham, says:

"I am a Director of George Bate Gunmakers Ltd., in Colmore Circus, Birmingham.

On Friday, 21st March, 1980 I was shown a 38 Chief blank firing gun and I can say that it is identical to those which are sold in my shop. I was also shown green container containing blank cartridges with a price tag of £1.40p. on with our name printed above it, and I can say that these cartridges were bought from our shop premises.

Due to the popularity of this blank firing hand gun I am unable to say when we sold this particular gun as a great number of these guns are sold by us each week.

I could say that there is a strong possibility that the gun was sold by our shop. The gun is valued at £10.26 pence."

JUDGE RUSH: Yes.

MR. JONES: (To Mr. Escott Cox) Do you want the next witness, the firearms constable?

MR. ESCOTT COX: No.

MR. JONES: Your honour, the next witness may also be read, I understand from my learned friend. Police Constable Bucknall.

JUDGE RUSH: Yes, the same applies again Members of the Jury.

MR. JONES: There is one amendment to his statement which I will read in due course, and I have told my learned friend about it. It is not a particularly significant matter.

Paul Anthony Bucknall, Police Constable, West Midlands Police, Lloyd House, Colmore Circus, Queensway, Birmingham, says:

"I am a Police Constable in the West Midlands Police serving in the Explosives and Firearms Department. I have six years experience in the examination of firearms and ammunition.

On Friday 21st March 1980, Detective Constable Pyke, West Midlands Police, handed to me at the Explosives and Firearms Department, Police Headquarters:-

1. One 6 mm Mondial .38 Chiefs blank revolver, Exhibit No.4.

2. Eight 6 mm. blank cartridges." Those are in that polythene phial; you can see them in due course Members of the Jury.

"3. Eighty eight 6 mm. blank cartridges contained in a plastic box.

The gun is a 6 mm Mondial .38 chiefs eight shot revolver of Italian manufacture which was designed to fire 6mm blank cartridges. It bears no serial number. When received by me it was neither cocked nor loaded. It is made of a relatively soft non-ferrous metal alloy and the barrel is partially blocked. A hardened steel plate is cast into the cylinder approximately ¼" from the rear ...." -- your honour it is not 'front'; it is 'rear' -- "... which is done to prevent the cylinder chambers being drilled through. There is no evidence of any attempt having been made to drill through the partial blockages in either the cylinder or barrel. In its present condition it is not capable of discharging a bulleted cartridge, nor in my opinion can it be readily modified to do so. It is not a Section 1 firearm and acquisition and possession does not require the authority of a firearm certificate. As this blank firing gun has the general appearance of a revolver I consider it to be an imitation firearm as defined by Section 57 (4) of the Firearms Act 1968.

There are eight 6mm. blank cartridges of unknown manufacture, two of which have been fired.

There are eighty-eight 6mm. blank cartridges of unknown manufacture contained in the plastic box.

Both the eight 6mm. blank cartridges together with the eighty-eight 6mm. blank cartridges will chamber and are suitable for use in the blank revolver. Acquisition and possession of these blank cartridges does not require the authority of any certificate. These blank cartridges are not ammunition as defined by the Firearms Act."

MR. JONES: Police Constable Abolins, please.

POLICE CONSTABLE DAVID STUART ABOLINS, Sworn.

Examined by Mr. Jones.

MR. JONES: Is your full name David Stuart Abolins, Mr. Abolins?

A. Yes it is your honour.

Q. Are you a Police Constable with the Airport Police Unit at Birmingham Airport Police Station?

A. I was your honour. I have now transferred back to Solihull.

Q. When you were with the Airport Police Unit Mr. Abolins, what were your duties?

A. They were general duties.

Q. Were you attached to general investigation of crime in the city of Birmingham or were you on a more localised sphere?

A. It was more localised, just covering any crime that happened at the Airport.

POL.CON.D.S.ABOLINS,
Examined.

Q. In March of last year I think you were so engaged at Birmingham Airport were you?

A. I was your honour.

Q. And at 11.25 a.m. on Wednesday, the 19th March, as a result of a radio message, did you go to the International Arrivals Lounge at Birmingham Airport?

A. I did your honour.

Q. There did you see the defendant, Mr. Fisher?

A. I did sir.

Q. Did you have a conversation with him?

A. Yes sir.

Q. Did you make a note of that conversation Mr. Abolins?

A. It is made up in my pocket book sir.

Q. When was the note ....?

MR. ESCOTT COX: I have no objection.

JUDGE RUSH: Yes, you can refresh your memory from your notebook then.

A. Thank you sir.

MR. JONES: Mr. Abolins what did you say to the defendant?

A. I said, "I understand that you are in possession of a large amount of money, and you have stated you are unemployed. Would you mind telling me how this money came into your possession?".

Q. Will you look please at Exhibit No.5. Was that the amount of money to which you were referring?

A. If it amounts to £1,358-07p., it is your honour.

Q. That was the money that was taken from Mr. Fisher?

A. Yes.

Q. When you said that to him Mr. Abolins, what was Mr. Fisher's reply?

A. Mr. Fisher replied, "I needn't tell you anything, in fact I'm not going to tell you."

Q. Were you then joined by another officer, Detective Constable Sutcliffe?

A. I was.

POL.CON.D.S.ABOLINS,
Examined.

Q. I think you spoke to Mr. Sutcliffe, and then what was said?

A. Detective Constable Sutcliffe said to Fisher, "I am Detective Constable Sutcliffe. Where has this money come from?".

Q. His reply?

A. "I've won it gambling here and there."

Q. What did Mr. Sutcliffe say?

A. "You are going to have to be more specific than here and there."

Q. What did Mr. Fisher say?

A. "I say I won it gambling, you're going to have to find out anything else."

Q. So did Mr. Sutcliffe continue his questioning?

A. He did sir. He said, "I am arresting you on suspicion of having stolen that money", and he cautioned Fisher.

Q. And what was Mr. Fisher's reply?

A. Fisher replied, "Do what you like."

Q. And Mr. Sutcliffe?

A. He said, "I am taking possession of your money which amounts to £1,358.07p. until we get to the bottom of this matter."

Q. And I think he was then taken to Birmingham Aiport Police Station?

A. He was your honour.

Q. Is that on the same campus as the airport?

A. It is about 300 yards away from the passenger lounge.

Q. All on the same site?

A. It is.

Q. Now at 12.15 p.m. did you interview him again?

A. I did your honour.

Q. What was said then?

A. Detective Constable Sutcliffe said, "Mr. Fisher you know why you have been arrested, don't you?". He replied, "Yes, of course." Detective Constable Sutcliffe said, "Where has that money come from?", and again he cautioned Fisher, to which he replied, "I told you, I am saying I got it gambling."

POL.CON.D.S.ABOLINS, Examined.

Q. Just pause a moment. What is the caution Mr. Abolins?

A. From the amount of time that has gone past, I cannot remember exactly what Detective Constable Sutcliffe said.

Q. But what was the object of the caution?

A. The objection was to tell Mr. Fisher he need not say anything unless he wanted to.

Q. Having cautioned him what was said?

A. Fisher said, "I told you, I am saying I got it gambling."

Q. And Mr. Sutcliffe?

A. "Alright where, here in Birmingham or over in Ireland?", to which Fisher replied, "Here." Detective Constable Sutcliffe said, "Well now if you tell me where you won it, when and from whom, I can check your story from other people can't I?". Fisher replied, "Different blokes in pubs around, I cannot say who." Detective Constable Sutcliffe said, " What were you gambling on, horses, dogs, cards?". Fisher replied, "Just cards." Detective Constable Sutcliffe said, "I have seen a few card schools in pubs but never with the sort of money you are carrying. You have £1,358.07p. in your possession. Are you seriously saying you won all that amount at cards?". His reply was, "Yes, that's what I'm saying."

Q. What did Mr. Sutcliffe say then?

A. He said, "You are going to have to tell me the names of some of the people who you say you won this money from, and the pubs you know." Fisher replied, "I'll have to think about it, I can't remember any names at the moment." Detective Constable Sutcliffe said, "Which area were the pubs in then?", to which Fisher replied, "Oh around the town, you know." Detective Constable Sutcliffe said, "Shall we carry on playing this silly game or do you think you could tell me the truth about all this?". Fisher replied, "I want to see a solicitor, and I'm saying no more to you about anything until you let me see one." Detective Constable Sutcliffe replied, "Yes you will be able to have a solicitor if that is what you want, and in the meantime I shall go and search your room at 155 Warwick Road, and also I have got to make some enquiries at other addresses found in your possession." Fisher replied, "You bastard." Detective Constable Sutcliffe said, "What do you mean by that?". Fisher said, "I suppose you are going to turn over all my friends and make life difficult for them as well." Detective Constable Sutcliffe said, "David, I am going to do what I consider to be my duty and that is to find out how you, a man out of work, is in possession of such a large amount of money." Fisher replied, "You're not going to let go are you?", and Detective Constable Sutcliffe replied, "No not until you tell me the truth." Fisher said, "Don't do anything yet, let me think for a bit." Detective Constable Sutcliffe said, "Take as long as you like."

POL.CON.D.S.ABOLINS,
Examined.

Q. Having told him he could take as long as he liked, what happened then?

A. Fisher I suppose was thinking about it.

Q. For what sort of period of time?

A. It was about 5 minutes later before he spoke again.

Q. So you were just waiting there?

A. Yes.

Q. What did he then say after that period of time?

A. Fisher said, "Oh, I will make your job easy for you, I'll tell you." Detective Constable Sutcliffe said, "What are you going to tell me now?", and Fisher said, "How I got the money." Detective Constable Sutcliffe said, "Yes, how?". Fisher replied, "It was a bank job." Detective Constable Sutcliffe said, "Yes, where, what did you do?". Fisher replied, "The Midlands Bank at Hockley, I held it up."

Q. Now just pausing there for a moment Mr. Abolins, had you any knowledge of a robbery at the Midland Bank?

A. No your honour.

Q. Did you know anything about what he was talking about at this time?

A. No.

Q. He had said, "It was the Midlands Bank at Hockley, I held it up". What did Mr. Sutcliffe say?

A. Detective Constable Sutcliffe said, "I don't know any details about this matter, rather than telling me verbally do you wish to make a written statement? If you do you can write it yourself, or I will write it for you."

Q. What happened then?

A. Fisher was again cautioned by Detective Constable Sutcliffe.

Q. What did Mr. Fisher say?

A. Mr. Fisher said, "Yes I've told you I'll make your job easy for you, you write it."

Q. Was a statement taken down then at Mr. Fisher's dictation?

A. It was.

Q. Would you look please at Exhibit No.6. Is that the statement that the defendant made to Mr. Sutcliffe which Mr. Sutcliffe wrote down?

DET.CON.D.S.ABOLINS,
Examined.

A. It is your honour.

Q. And is that the statement which you have witnessed at the end?

A. It is your honour.

Q. Indicating that the statement was taken down between 12.55 and 1.15 is it?

A. Yes sir.

Q. And there is first of all the caption at the top; that is to tell him he need not say anything. Those are the words of the police are they?

A. Yes sir.

Q. And he signs that, indicating he need not say anything. And then the body of the statement -- whose words are those?

A. Those are Fisher's words written down at his own dictation by Detective Constable Sutcliffe.

Q. And indeed I think any amendment or alteration is initialled by Fisher is it?

A. It is.

Q. Are there a couple of minor alterations, -- on the second line an 'h' is crossed out which he has initialled, and later on, "I tried a telephone box but", and 'but' is crossed out and he has initialled that?

A. Yes.

Q. And he has signed the body of that statement?

A. Yes.

Q. And then there is, "I have read the above statement and I have been told that I can correct, alter or add anything I wish. This statement is true. I have made it of my own free will". Those are words dictated to him are they not?

A. They are sir.

Q. And they are in his hand?

A. Yes sir.

Q. Your honour, the Jury have had copies of that statement. I do not know whether my learned friend wishes me to go through it to check it with the officer. Perhaps as it is a very short statement we can go through it. If you could just check it with me Mr. Abolins, that it is in fact correct as we have got it.

POL.CON.D.S.ABOLINS,
Examined.

JUDGE RUSH: Yes.

MR. JONES: "I had been out drinking at a pub in the town. I'd got no money I hadn't paid any rent ....."

A. "I hadn't paid my rent".

Q. "I hadn't paid my rent at the hostel because I'd blown it on beer. I'd got a starting pistol on me. I bought it from Bates's in the town. I was three parts drunk. First of all I looked in the Midland Bank in Hockley opposite Cannings, there was a young girl talking to another bloke, a cashier like, but there was no customers. I walked in pointed the pistol at the girl, and said, 'Give us the money.' She just handed over some money to me. I just ran round a few corners. I tried a telephone box to get a taxi but it was broke.. I managed to get a taxi later and went to the hostel and then went and got something to eat. I stayed in and around Birmingham for a week or so and then last Tuesday I went across to Ireland, and I have been there ever since. Just spending the money like a fool. I'm not absolutely positive but I think there was £4,300 I had in tenners and fivers apart from three brand new £1 notes. I know I've been stupid, what more can I say. I'm sorry ", and has he signed that?

A. He has your honour.

Q. And then there is the matter we have already heard about and you have witnessed that statement. Now at the conclusion of that statement Mr. Abolins, did Mr. Sutcliffe say something else to the defendant?

A. He did sir.

Q. What did he say?

A. Detective Constable Sutcliffe said, "Now, just to clear up a few points, I take it all the money that you have in your possession is from the robbery." Fisher replied, "Yes, do you know I've spent over £1,000 in Ireland in a week just on booze. I must be bloody barmy." Detective Constable Sutcliffe said, "And where is the gun now?".. Fisher said, "It's in my room at Warwick Road." Detective Constable Sutcliffe said, "I will inform the Officers who are dealing with this case of your arrest, and you will no doubt be taken to another police station later today and charged." Fisher replied, "Yes O.K."

Q. And was he then placed in the cells?

A. He was sir.

Q. Mr. Abolins, later that day did you go to 155 Warwick Road?

A. I did sir.

Q. And did you go to Mr. Fisher's room?

A. I did sir.

POL.CON.D.S.ABOLINS,
Examined.

Q. What did you find in his room?

A. Underneath the bed in a bag or a case I found a .38 Chief starting pistol.

Q. Would you look please at Exhibit No.4. (Exhibit handed to the witness).

A. Well one Chief starting pistol, containing 6 live, 2 used starting blanks in chamber, and one box of 6mm blank cartridges.

Q. So the six blanks that are in that bag were originally in the gun?

A. They were your honour.

Q. And you say 6 of them were live and 2 were used?

A. They were.

Q. And did you then unload the gun?

A. I did your honour.

JUDGE RUSH: How long do you anticipate your cross-examination will be?

MR. ESCOTT COX: Not very long your honour. I make no secret of the fact my principal cross-examination on the police evidence is going to be of the officer who conducted the interview, and not of this officer who was present but principally as a witness.

<u>Cross-examined by Mr. Escott Cox.</u>

MR. ESCOTT COX: What I would like to ask you Mr. Abolins is this. How did you know where to go. Where had the address 155 Warwick Road come from?

A. It had been given by Fisher.

Q. Was that when he was first stopped? Can you remember when it was he gave you his address?

A. I cannot remember, but it was probably when his details were entered on the Person in Custody sheet.

Q. Was it part of your enquiries at the airport when he was initially stopped to find out his identity? You wanted to know his identity.

A. His identity was already known.

Q. You knew his identity?

A. I didn't, but when I got there ....

POL.CON.D.S.ABOLINS,
Cross-examined.

Q. You knew his address?

A. I cannot remember.

Q. Did you not yourself take possession of anything else from 155 Warwick Road except the starting pistol and the ammunition?

A. No your honour.

Q. Right, thank you.

JUDGE RUSH: Yes?

Re-examined by Mr. Jones.

MR. JONES: Mr. Abolins the address. He had presumably gone through clearance had he?

A. At the airport when you come back you have to fill in a card where you have to put on your name and address.

Q. So that card would have been filled in and completed by him before you ever came on the scene?

A. Yes.

Q. And that contained his name and address?

A. Yes.

MR. JONES: (To the learned Judge). I think that would be a convenient time your honour.

JUDGE RUSH: Yes I agree. Are you the officer in the case or not..

A. No sir.

JUDGE RUSH: Would you object to him being released?

MR. ESCOTT COX: No your honour. (The witness withdrew).

JUDGE RUSH: Members of the Jury we will break off now for a luncheon adjournment and we will start again at 2.15. Please remember not to allow anybody to speak to you about this trial throughout the length of it, other than your own number of course, and perhaps you will remember that at night as well. Do not discuss it with anybody else.

MR. ESCOTT COX: Your honour there is a matter I would wish to discuss with your honour.

JUDGE RUSH: Yes of course. Members of the Jury you are free to leave.

(The Jury left the court at 12.54 p.m..)

MR. ESCOTT COX: Your honour it is simply a question of bail. He has been on bail and has always attended, and I do not know what your honour's attitude to bail at the midday adjournment as opposed to the end of the day is, but I have been specifically instructed to apply for bail and I do so.

JUDGE RUSH: Mr. Jones do you object?

MR. JONES: No your honour. He has been on bail throughout.

JUDGE RUSH: David Fisher stand up please. You have been on bail. Your bail will continue throughout the trial and if things change I will let you know, but that means it is important you should answer to your bail. If you do not answer to your bail you will be punished, probably by imprisonment -- I do not know, -- but it is very important to answer to your bail.

USHER: Court rise.

(The Court adjourned from 12.56 p.m., until 2.15 p.m.)

MR. JONES: Your honour, I call Sergeant Garth Taylor. He is the identikit man your honour. As such there is nothing on the depositions; I cannot give your honour a statement.

JUDGE RUSH: I shall listen carefully.

MR. JONES: Yes. Sergeant Taylor please.

DETECTIVE SERGEANT GARTH TAYLOR, Sworn.

MR. JONES: Your full name please?

A. Garth Taylor.

Q. And Mr. Taylor, what is your occupation?

A. I am a Detective Sergeant with the West Midlands Police, and I am attached to the Scenes of Crime Department at Police Headquarters, Lloyd House, Birmingham.

Q. And it is part of your job as scenes of crime expert to build up identikit pictures?

A. That is one of my jobs, yes.

Q. Tell us please how this is done; the first stage and then the second stage, etcetera.

A. The kit comprises of a selection of photographic prints cut into facial areas. There is an area which governs principally the forehead and the hair, one for the chin, one for the eyes, one for the nose and one for the mouth. These are catalogued according to their colour of hair, type of eyes, size, angle that the eyes are in accordance to a horizontal plain, size of

DET.SGT.G.TAYLOR,
Examined.

mouths and so forth so that they can be put into a logical order in a book which lists them numerically, a frame in which the various portions can be placed so that when the composite is put together it can be viewed through a sheet of glass and can be photographed. The witness first of all gives a description to the operator who, from that description and with her or his assistance builds up a face gradually from a selection of photographs of parts of the face included in this catalogue.

Q. So you have batches of photographs from which have been taken various parts of faces?

A. That is correct.

Q. So so far as any particular feature, it is taken from a photograph?

A. It is taken from a photograph, yes.

Q. So therefore you are governed to that extent by what was on that photograph?

A. Oh indeed, yes.

Q. And in particular areas of lighting, light and dark, you have just what the colour was on the photograph?

A. That is correct. The kits are broken up into male, female, a profile kit, a Caucasian kit and an Asian kit which covers African, West Indian and Indian types of features.

Q. So there is basically the sort of white races type of kit?

A. Yes.

Q. And then there is an Asian kit as one of the sub-divisions, a male and female?

A. Yes. Perhaps I could say something here that might give a further explanation. In building these kits it is necessary to match as near as possible the skin tones throughout the whole of the range, so virtually with regard to both white races and coloured races you have only one skin tone in that particular kit because they have to match. You have to be able to put one brow with a different chin, and if the skin tones were all different you would have to have every tone of skin that there is and it would be a rather large kit and would be unmanageable.

Q. Do I understand therefore it says a black or a white kit, and whatever the shades for instance on the white you are just saddled with what are the white features?

A. With what there are, indeed yes.

Q. And what in the black features, varying from dark to white in the same kit?

DET.SGT.G.TAYLOR,
Examined.

A. Yes, you have only got one tone in each kit.. There may be minor printing errors in the manufacturer's production of it, but basically the manufacturers try to get all the same tone throughout the range so there is only one tone in each case.

Q. What can you do if, for instance in the coloured kit, a person says a person is darker or lighter than the one tone which you have got?

A. In the case of a coloured subject there is very little you can do that will produce the correct result. Unfortunately the only way to make an alteration to the tone -- you are faced with two choices. One is to draw on the kit which is done by placing a piece of clear acetate sheet in front of it and drawing on with a Chinagraph pencil which is a wax type crayon. You are unable to introduce shade into this, so if you put a mark on it it is either a black mark or a white mark. The only other alternative if you want to darken or lighten the skin tone is to do this photographically, and if you try to darken or lighten a person's face you will also darken or lighten the hair, and consequently this is not altogether satisfactory.

Q. So getting a portrayal of the face, you can make the whole lot darker or the whole lot lighter by either over-exposure on a photograph or under-exposure?

A. Yes, that is correct.

Q. But equally that will affect the features you have got?

A. It will indeed.

Q. So there is basically one colour if you have a coloured person's kit, and there is one colour if you have a white person's kit?

A. Yes. We try to build up a composite that the witness sees as a type of face according to the shape of the face.. That is the basic idea of the kit rather than to portray somebody who is darker skinned or lighter skinned. The likeness is in the features rather than in the tone.

Q. How many of these photofit pictures do you do Mr. Taylor?

A. In the West Midlands last year there was something like 200 done, and I would say I probably did about 40 of those. I have been doing them for 10 years.

Q. Do you remember much about this particular photofit picture that was done with a Miss Gardener on the 25th February?

A. Yes, I do remember certain things of it, yes.

Q. Yes. Would you tell us please what you remember when Miss Gardener ....

DET.SGT.G.TAYLOR,
Examined.

MR. ESCOTT COX: Could the witness leave the court?

MR. JONES: My learned friend would like Miss Gardener out of court at this stage.

JUDGE RUSH: Yes, I understand that. (Miss Gardener left the court).

THIS WITNESS: The things I remember most of all is that first of all she described the man as a coloured man and that he had a woolly hat. The catalogue of features also contains headgear, spectacles and so forth, but the type of hats that were available in the kit did not show the type of woolly hat that she described to me and I had to draw the hat on a sheet of vinyl over the face. Also the kit didn't contain the exact lips that she described to me and I had to make a Chinagraph pencil alteration to the thickness of the upper lip. She did say that he was a lighter skinned coloured man. She didn't say how light and appeared to be satisfied with the composite that I built up.

MR. JONES: Now is that the composite with hat aside -- I know you had to draw in the hat top.

A. This is the kit, the parts of the kit that were used to make this composite. As you can see, the face here shows hair whereas in fact the finished result had got a woolly hat which came down on to the ears, and the top lip was made thinner, but those are essentially the parts of the kit we used.

Q. That is the kit unaltered; no artistic work .....

A. Yes, no art work.

Q. No alteration to the lips and no headgear on top?

A. No.

Q. Did you photograph the composite after you had altered the lips and put the hat on?

A. I did, yes.

Q. Do you also produce that?

A. I do. This is a print I have made which, if examined closely, one can see where I have made the pencil alterations on top of the original.

MR. JONES: Your honour, I think, so far as the exhibits are concerned .....

JUDGE RUSH: It will be Exhibit 11A perhaps.

MR. JONES: Yes.

THIS WITNESS: This is a photograph print made from the same negatives as the one you have in your hand sir.

DET.SGT.G.TAYLOR,
Examined.

JUDGE RUSH: Yes, Exhibit 11.

MR. JONES: Your honour perhaps the original photofit could be 11A, and the photographic print from it, 11B.

JUDGE RUSH: Yes.

MR. JONES: And the photograph of the defendant, Exhibit 12. (To the witness). Perhaps Mr. Taylor you would be so kind as to let the learned Judge and then my learned friends and then the Jury see those first.

JUDGE RUSH: Let Mr. Escott Cox have them first.

MR. ESCOTT COX: I have seen them your honour.

JUDGE RUSH: Oh you have. Yes, thank you. (Exhibits passed to the learned Judge). Yes, I think the Jury should have a look at them please. (Exhibits passed to the Jury). I think those should go to the Jury as well.

MR. JONES: Your honour I think the Jury already have Exhibit 12.

JUDGE RUSH: Yes. Mr. Jones I think the pistol could be produced as well while we are looking at exhibits.

MR. JONES: Yes. (The pistol handed to the Jury).

Yes, thank you Mr. Taylor.

Cross-examined by Mr. Escott Cox.

MR. ESCOTT COX: Mr. Taylor your job, in so far as it relates to identikit, is obviously a specialist job for which you have special training?

A. It is, yes.

Q. You need not only practical skill in the use of the various component pieces for building up, but you need skill, both taught and acquired, to gain the confidence and the ease of communication with the witness in order to build up a picture, is that fair?

A. That is so, yes.

Q. And obviously it can be, and I would have thought very often is, very important work building up an identikit?

A. It can be, yes.

Q. Because it is going to form possibly the basis of police investigations?

A. Yes.

Q. It must therefore be an important part of your work that the witness is as near to being completely satisfied with the

DET.SGT.G.TAYLOR,
Cross-examined.

identikit in its completed state as it is practicable to be. Is that fair?

A. That is fair.

Q. In the very nature of it of course it could hardly ever be a truly photographic likeness of a suspect?

A. No, it cannot.

Q. But it can often be a very strikingly close resemblance to a suspect?

A. It can.

Q. And you have no recollection I take it from what you have said, that the witness in this case had any serious or any real reservations about the identikit in its completed form?

A. No. What it is my practice to do when I do a photofit -- one has to bear in mind I have never seen the person they are describing, -- with some witnesses you reach a stage where you know any further you go is going to be of little use and you abandon the exercise because of failure on the part of either the kit or the witness to produce the results that the witness desires. In this case there was no indication that this was the case, but I always say to a witness before we use the photofit, are they satisfied that that is the nearest we are going to get to the person that they are describing, and from asking them that question they either unreservedly say yes, or they say yes and they make some comment. In this particular case I don't recall the witness making any comment other than she was satisfied. She certainly made no comment that I thought would affect the use of the photofit.

Q. So she either made no comment beyond saying she was satisfied, or if she did it was of such a minor nature that it didn't cause you to probe any further in investigations. Is that a fai[r] summary?

A. That is a fair summary of it.

Q. Alright. Thank you very much.

MR. JONES: Thank you Mr. Taylor.

JUDGE RUSH: Yes, thank you very much Detective Sergeant.

MR. JONES: Your honour, my learned friend indicates Miss Gardener may now be released.

JUDGE RUSH: Yes thank you. (The witness withdrew).

MR. JONES: I call Detective Constable Sutcliffe.

DETECTIVE CONSTABLE THOMAS SUTCLIFFE, Sworn.

Examined by Mr. Jones.

THIS WITNESS: Thomas Sutcliffe, Detective Constable, your honour.

MR. JONES: Mr. Sutcliffe in March of last year where were you stationed?

A. At Birmingham Airport.

Q. Are you still stationed there now?

A. Yes sir.

Q. As such, what do you investigate?

A. Any crime at the airport or crime relating to the airport sir.

Q. How long had you been on those duties?

A. Since October sir.

Q. At about 11.30 on Wednesday, the 19th March, did you go to the International Arrivals Lounge at Birmingham Airport?

A. Yes sir. May I use my notebook.

Q. Just a second. Did you see the defendant, Mr. Fisher?

A. Yes.

Q. And had he already been detained by Police Constable Abolins?

A. Yes, sir.

Q. Now Mr. Sutcliffe, did you have a conversation with the defendant?

A. Yes.

MR. JONES (to Mr. Cox): May he refer to his notebook?

MR. ESCOTT COX: Yes.

JUDGE RUSH: Very well.

MR. JONES: What was the first thing you were told?

A. I was told by Police Constable Abolins, in Fisher's presence, that he had over £1,300 in cash and that he would give no reasonable explanation for it, and that he was unemployed.

Q. What did you say?

A. I introduced myself to Mr. Fisher and said, "Where has this money come from?". Fisher said, "I have won it gambling here

DET.CON.T.SUTCLIFFE,
Examined.

and there." I said, "You are going to have to be more specific than here and there." Fisher said, "I say I won it gambling, you're going to have to find out anything else." I said, "I am arresting you on suspicion of having stolen that money", and I cautioned him.

Q. What was his reply?

A. He replied, "Do what you like." I then said, "I am taking possession of your money which amounts to £1,358.07p until we get to the bottom of this matter." We then went to the police station.

Q. That is the Birmingham Airport Police Station?

A. Yes sir.

Q. Mr. Sutcliffe, at 12.15, together with Police Constable Abolins did you again see Mr. Fisher?

A. Yes sir.

Q. What was said to him on that occasion?

A. I said, "Mr. Fisher you know why you have been arrested don't you?",and Fisher said, "Yes of course". I said, "Where has that money come from?", and I again cautioned him. Fisher said, "I told you I'm saying I got it gambling." I said, "Alright where; here in Birmingham, or over in Ireland?". Fisher said, "Here." I said, "Well now if you tell me where you won it, when and from whom, I can check your story from other people, can't I?". Fisher said, "Different blokes in pubs around, I can't say who." I said, "What were you gambling on; horses, dogs cards?". Fisher said, "Just cards." I said, "I've seen a few card schools in pubs but never with the sort of money you're carrying. You have £1,358.07p. in your possession; are you seriously saying you won all that amount at cards?". Fisher said, "Yes that's what I'm saying." I said, "You are going to have to tell me the names of some of the people who you say you won this money from and the pubs you know", and Fisher said, "I'll have to think about it. I can't remember any names at the moment." I said, "Which area were the pubs in then?". Fisher said, "Oh around the town you know." I said, "Shall we carry on playing this silly game or do you think you could tell me the truth about all this?". Fisher said, "I want to see a solicitor and I am saying no more to you about anything until you let me see one." I said, "Yes you will be able to have a solicitor if that's what you want, and in the meantime I shall go and search your room at 155 Warwick Road, and also I've got to make some enquiries at other addresses found in your possession." Fisher said, "You bastard." I said, "What do you mean by that?". Fisher said, "I suppose you're going to turn over all my friends and make life difficult for them as well." I said, "David I am going to do what I consider to be my duty and that is to find out how you, a man out of work, is in possession of such a large amount of money." Fisher said, "You're not going to let go

DET.CON.T.SUTCLIFFE,
Examined.

are you." I said, "No, not until you tell me the truth." Fisher said, "Don't do anything yet, let me think for a bit." I said, "Take as long as you like". A short time later ....

Q. What sort of period elapsed?

A. About 5 minutes sir. A short time later Fisher said, "O.K. I'll make your job easy for you, I'll tell you." I said, "What are you going to tell me now?", and Fisher said, "How I got the money." I said, "Yes how?". Fisher said, "It was a bank job." I said, "Yes where, what did you do?". Fisher said, "The Midland Bank at Hockley, I held it up."

Q. Pausing there Mr. Sutcliffe, you have told us your duties were stationed around the airport, and you had been there since the previous October?

A. Yes.

Q. Did you know anything about a bank robbery at Hockley?

A. Not at that time, no sir, although in fairness it would have been circulated and I would have read about it, but I didn't know any of the details.

Q. I see.

A. I said, "I don't know any details about this matter. Rather than telling me verbally do you wish to make a written statement? If you do you can write it yourself or I will write it for you", and I again cautioned him. Fisher said, "Yes I've told you I'll make your job easy for you. You write it."

Q. Will you look please at Exhibit 6. (Same handed to the witness). Was that the statement that he made after caution?

A. Yes sir.

Q. Which he signed?

A. Yes.

Q. Now you have told us you didn't know anything about this robbery?

A. No sir.

Q. Had you at any stage had anything to do with investigations into this robbery or anything of that sor?

A. No sir.

Q. At the conclusion of the statement what did you say to Mr. Fisher?

A. I said, "Now just to clear up a few points, I take it all of the money that you have in your possession is from the

DET.CON.T.SUTCLIFFE,
Examined.

robbery." Fisher said, "Yes, do you know I've spent over £1,000 in Ireland in a week just on booze, I must be bloody barmy." I said, "And where is the gun now?". Fisher said, "It's in my room at Warwick Road." I then said, "I will inform the officers who are dealing with this case of your arrest and you will no doubt be taken to another police station later today and charged."

Q. I think he said, "Yes O.K."?

A. Yes, and he was then placed in a cell.

Q. Mr. Sutcliffe did you then contact the officers at the police station who were making investigations into the robbery?

A. Yes. I rang the wrong station first. I thought it was Thornhill Road whereas it was Steelhouse Lane.

Q. And you then told them ....

A. Yes, and they made enquiries into his arrest.

<u>Cross-examined by Mr. Escott Cox.</u>

MR. ESCOTT COX: You are used to dealing with suspects?

A. Yes.

Q. Is it usual when making enquiries into an offence that you tell the accused the nature of your investigations?

A. I told him what I intended to do.

Q. I am asking as a general principle.

A. There isn't a general principle guiding that, no.

Q. This man was frequently asking to see his solicitors wasn't he?

A. No sir.

Q. Or to see a solicitor?

A. No sir.

Q. And he told you he didn't want to say anything until he had seen a solicitor?

A. He said he didn't want to say anything more until he had seen a solicitor. That is when I said I would leave him and make further enquiries.

Q. You went on questioning him after that didn't you?

A. No sir.

DET. CON. T. SUTCLIFFE,
Cross-examined.

Q. Have a look at your own notes.

A. When he asked to see a solicitor I said he could and I would go and make further enquiries. He then called me a bastard, and I said, "What do you mean by that?".

Q. Go on. You know that later on in the interview you resumed questioning a man who said to you he didn't want to tell you anything until he had seen his solicitor. You asked him how he got the money. You asked him what job it was.

A. I don't think in fact sir that I have asked a question until he has made an admission of the actual offence. The rest in between time were statements I believe.

Q. But I am not concerned with that. The fact is that here is a man who says he doesn't want to speak to you or answer any questions until he has got a solicitor, and you nevertheless in the same interview go on questioning him. That is right isn't it?

A. As I say sir, I don't believe I put another question to him until ....

Q. Nevermind about 'until'.

A. I certainly asked a question after he made an admission of an offence.

Q. Look at your own record. "I'll make your job easy for you, I'll tell you." Question from you, "What are you going to tell me?".

A. Yes, I agree.

Q. He hadn't made any admission then had he?

A. No sir.

Q. Then you go on questioning him about it. Was the point of telling him you not only intended to search his room but to go and make enquiries at other addresses found in his possession to threaten him?

A. No sir.

Q. What was it?

A. That I wanted to make enquiries at other addresses.

Q. Why tell him that?

A. I think I was being fair to him. He was a man I suspected of having committed an offence, and I wasn't to know ....

Q. Why was it fair to him?

DET. CON. T. SUTCLIFFE,
Cross-examined.

A. I told him ....

Q. How is it being fair to him?

A. He was clearly not co-operating, so in consequence I wanted to find out more about him, and I was being fair to tell him.

Q. How is it being fair to a suspect, a man in custody, to tell him the nature of your future investigations?

A. Well I don't think it is unfair sir.

Q. You said you wanted to be fair to him.

A. I believe I was being fair to him.

JUDGE RUSH: Mr. Sutcliffe, it is important you listen to the question first and then answer it.

MR. ESCOTT COX: How is it being fair to a man to tell him the nature of those future investigations?

A. To let him know what I was doing.

Q. Why is that being fair?

A. I believe it is sir.

Q. Well explain it.

A. If I were making enquiries at his home address, his parents' address and other addresses where he may have friends, I think it is fair to let him know I am doing it.

Q. You keep on saying that; we have got the point. I am asking you to explain how, why or in what fashion it is fair to impart that information?

A. It is just my opinion sir. I cannot give you an explanation.

Q. You cannot give an explanation?

A. That is my opinion.

Q. The explanation is it was a threat wasn't it?

A. No sir.

Q. Where had you got the addresses from?

A. From his property sir.

Q. In what form?

A. In the form I believe sir of letters. I don't think there was an address book but I am not sure.

Q. Well a record would be kept of what property he had on him?

A. Yes sir.

Q. Have you got that record here?

A. No sir, unless it may be outside with the officer in charge of the case sir.

Q. The address was one he had given you -- the address at 155 Warwick Road?

A. That was the home address he gave, yes sir.

Q. And I am putting it to you officer that he repeatedly -- not just once as you have said -- repeatedly asked for a solicitor, and you denied him the right to have a solicitor there until he had made a confession to you?

A. No sir.

JUDGE RUSH: Yes.

<u>Re-examined by Mr. Jones.</u>

MR. JONES: Mr. Sutcliffe, the opposite to being fair is unfair. Did you in any way consider you were being unfair to the defendant in asking those questions?

A. No sir.

Q. Thank you Mr. Sutcliffe.

JUDGE RUSH: Yes, thank you. (The witness withdrew).

MR. JONES: Detective Constable Pyke please.

<u>DETECTIVE CONSTABLE JOHN PYKE, Sworn.</u>

<u>Examined by Mr. Jones.</u>

THIS WITNESS: John Pyke, Detective Constable, your honour.

MR. JONES: Mr. Pyke, I think in March last year you were stationed at Steelhouse Lane Police Station?

A. I was sir, yes.

Q. And you are the officer in charge of this investigation?

A. I am sir, yes.

Q. At 4.20 p.m. on Wednesday, 19th March, together with Detective Constable Butler did you see Mr. Fisher in the Detective Inspectors Office at Steelhouse Lane Police Station?

DET. CON. J. PYKE,
Examined.

A. Yes I did sir.

Q. Had you been somewhere before you interviewed him?

A. Yes, I had been to Birmingham Airport.

Q. From the airport had you been somewhere else?

A. I had been to 155 Warwick Road.

Q. At 155 Warwick Road had you obtained possession of anything?

A. Yes sir. Along with a number of items of clothing Detective Constable Butler recovered two plastic bags.

Q. That is Exhibit 9 is it?

A. Yes that is it, from a chest of drawers, and also a hat and an anorak from the wardrobe.

Q. Then having recovered items including those items, Mr. Pyke did you interview Mr. Fisher at Steelhouse Lane?

A. I did sir, yes.

Q. Mr. Pyke did you make a note of the conversation?

A. I did sir.

MR. JONES: Your honour, my learned friend being his usual helpful self, indicates that the officer may refer to his notes.

JUDGE RUSH: Yes very well. The matters were fresh in your mind were they?

A. Yes sir.

Q. It is a matter of refreshing your memory.

A. Yes.

MR. JONES: What did you say?

A. At 4.20 p.m. in company with Detective Constable Butler I said, "David, I have read your statement which you made earlier today. There's a few things which I want to make clear. Now before I say anything further I must tell you that you are not obliged to say anything unless you wish to do so, but what you say will be taken down in writing and given in evidence. Do you understand?", and he replied, "Yes." I then said, "To start off, you say in your statement, 'I'd got a starting pistol on me. I bought it from Bates's in town'". "Which Bates's, the shop near to the Post and Mail Building?". He replied, "Yes." I said, "When did you buy it?". He said, "The same day as I robbed the bank." I said, "How much did it cost?". He replied, "I can't remember." I said, "You go on to say that - 'She just handed over some money to me. I just

DET.CON. J. PYKE,
Examined.

ran round a few corners, I tried a telephone box'. Now tell me when you came out of the bank which way did you run?". "Round the corner ...."

Q. This is what the defendant replied?

A. Yes sir.

Q. "Round the corner ....."?

A. Yes, "Round the corner, down I think it's called Well Street." I said, "Where to then?". He replied, "Past the garage down to the next street and turned left." I said, "I think that street's name is Stainsby Avenue." He replied, "I don't know the name." I said, "Where did you go then?". He replied, "Down across between some flats and then I went to the phone box." Detective Constable Butler said, "What have you done with the cash you stole?". He replied, "I've spent a lot on booze and hotel bills. God I've had a lot to drink. I went to Ireland for St. Patrick's Day but I didn't have a drink on the day as I was in such a bad state. I couldn't even get out of bed." Detective Constable Butler said, "Amongst your property which you had with you at the airport was a lot of new property, did you buy any of it with the stolen money?". He replied, "Yes." Detective Constable Butler said, "What these two rings?".

Q. Were those the rings you referred to? (Indicated to witness).

A. They are sir, yes.

JUDGE RUSH. What is the exhibit number?

MR. JONES: I think these will all have to be new exhibits your honour. They have not been exhibited hitherto. That will be Exhibit 13.

Q. What was his reply?

A. Detective Constable Butler said, "What these two rings?". He replied, "Yes." Detective Constable Butler said, "How much were they?", and he replied, "I think they were £68 each."

Q. What was said next?

A. "What about this watch?".

Q. Now will you look please at what will be Exhibit 14. Was that the watch that was shown to him?

A. That is the one, yes sir.

Q. What was his reply?

A. He replied, "Yes that was with the money." Detective Constable Butler said, "How much did that cost?", and he replied "£53". Detective Constable Butler said, "This doll?".

DET. CON. J. PYKE,
Examined.

Q. Now I cannot see any doll.

A. It is in that bag there sir. (Usher took the doll out of the bag).

Q. Is that the doll, Exhibit 15?

A. Yes. He replied, "Yeh I got that at the gift shop at Dublin airport." Detective Constable Butler said, "This aftershave and other stuff?".

Q. Would you look please at what will now become Exhibit 16?

A. Yes, that is it.

Q. What was said about the aftershave?

A. He replied, "I got that in Galway." Detective Constable Butler said, "With the stolen cash?". He replied, "Yes." "What about this holdall?".

Q. Is that in our exhibits, 17. Is that the holdall?

A. Yes sir.

Q. What did he say in relation to that?

A. "Yeh I bought that in Woolworths in Galway. I also bought the air tickets to Dublin and back."

Q. And are those the air tickets? (Shown to witness).

A. Yes sir.

JUDGE RUSH: May I have a look at those. (Tickets handed to the learned Judge). These tickets have two passengers.......

A. Tickets for one passenger there and back.

Q. Yes I see. Yes?

A. Detective Constable Butler said, "We have brought all your belongings from your room in the hostel. Is there anything amongst this stuff which you have bought with the proceeds of the robbery?". He said, "Yes this suit, I had it from Fosters in Newtown."

MR. JONES: I think that is probably in the bag.

A. Yes, it is in the bag. (The usher took it out of the bag). Yes, that is the one sir.

Q. It has been screwed up in the bag for a little while now. That is the suit?

A. Yes sir. I said, "How much was that?". He replied "£39. I also had that jacket too from the same place ...."

Q. That will be Exhibit 20 your honour.

DET. CON. J. PYKE,
Examined.

A. That is it sir.

Q. "I also had that jacket too from the same place". Yes?

A. "... and I had the radio from a shop up Newtown".

Q. Would you look at that. Did he indicate that radio? It was in the box.

A. Yes sir.

Q. That is Exhibit 21.

A. Yes. Detective Constable Butler went on to say, "Did you wear any of this clothing when you committed the robbery?". He replied, "I think I had that anorak on, yes I did."

Q. Would you look at Exhibit 7.. Is that the anorak he indicated?

A. Yes, that is it.. Detectiv e Constable Butler said, "Anything else?", and he replied, "Yes, I had that hat on." It was the red ... (Hat shown to witness). That is the one, yes sir.

Q. And that is Exhibit No.8. Yes?

A. I then said, "The cashier says that you put the money in a plastic bag. Where is that now?". He replied, "I used one of them two bags."

Q. Would you look at Exhibit 9. Were those the bags to which he was referring?

A. Yes sir.

Q. Mr. Pyke what was said to Mr. Fisher next?

A. Detective Constable Butler said, "Would you like to make a further written statement about what you told us?". He replied, "Yes". Detective Constable Butler said, "Do you want to write it or shall I write it for you?". He replied, "You write it", and Detective Constable Butler went on to take a statement from Fisher.

Q. Would you look please at Exhibit No.10. Is that the statement that Mr. Fisher made?

A. It is sir..

Q. We already know there was the usual caption which he signed, that he need not say anything unless he wished to do so, etc..

A. Yes sir.

Q. How was the body of the statement taken down; whose words were they?

A. They were Fisher's own words.

DET. CON. J. PYKE,
Examined.

Q. And will you follow it please as I read it, Mr. Pyke, so that we can check it for accuracy. (To the Jury). This is Exhibit No.10, Members of the Jury.

"I've been spending like mad since I had the money from the Bank. I've spent a lot on booze and hotel bills. I bought the airline ticket to Dublin and back. Also train tickets and taxis. I bought the 2 rings you showed me with part of the money. I think they were £68 each. The watch was £53, the radio about £8. The doll was £9.99, the aftershave £4.95. The fawn jacket was £10.99 I think. The brown suit was £39 I think it was, and also the brown bag I bought. Also I bought the watchamacallit ..." That I think ought to be Exhibit 22. There is a thing called a watchamacallit is there not?

A. Yes, that is it. (Indicated).

Q. "The watchamacallit was a couple of quid. These were all bought with the stolen money. The starting pistol you showed me is the one I used. The lucky seven bags you've got, it was one of them I put the money in. I was wearing the woollen hat you found." And has he signed that?

A. He has sir.

Q. Then, "I have read the above statement " etc. That was dictated to him and he has written it down?

A. Yes, in his own hand.

Q. As is the signature, and you have indicated that you have witnessed that statement?

A. Yes I have sir.

Q. On that same day you took possession of the money and the gun?

A. I did, yes sir.

Q. Mr. Pyke just one other matter. You are the officer in charge of the case?

A. I am sir, yes.

Q. As such did you make enquiries into a car?

MR. ESCOTT COX: Your honour if my learned friend wants to pursue this it sounds like hearsay, and I shall make some objection.

MR. JONES: I am not going to ask anything that was said at all.

JUDGE RUSH: Is it going to take the case any further Mr. Jones or not if you were allowed to pursue your questions. Is it something absolutely germane to the issue?

MR. JONES: Your honour one wishes to leave no stone unturned.

DET. CON. J. PYKE,
Examined.

JUDGE RUSH: Well I think you have turned it and you can put it back again now and we will leave it there. Also it does not appear on the witness statements in any event, so in theory if one is going to be precise and correct one would have to have notice of additional evidence to consider this matter.

MR. JONES: Maybe the point can be resurrected at a later stage.

JUDGE RUSH: Very well.

Cross-examined by Mr. Escott Cox.

MR. ESCOTT COX: Mr. Pyke did you yourself take part in the search of the defendant's premises?

A. Yes sir, the second search.

Q. Yes, the second search. As the officer in charge of the case you knew -- I don't suggest word for word -- but you had got quite a good detailed knowledge of the description of the man and his clothing made by the complainant and the bank manager?

A. I had sir, yes.

Q. And may we take it that any article of clothing of the defendant's that you thought could in any way assist with the police enquiries was perfectly properly taken possession of at that search?

A. All his property was taken possession of.

Q. That answers my question even more fully. Thank you. Yes, thank you. (To the learned Judge). I think your honour my learned junior is anxious about a matter, but I think the airline tickets in evidence are Exhibit 15?

THE CLERK: Exhibit 18.

JUDGE RUSH: Anything else Mr. Treacy?

MR. TREACY: No thank you your honour.

JUDGE RUSH: Yes, thank you Mr. Pyke. (The witness withdrew).

MR. JONES: Your honour it has gone a little faster than anticipated. I wonder if your honour would be so kind as to grant a short adjournment. There is a matter I would seek to investigate, to see if the person can be brought to Court today.

JUDGE RUSH: What does a short adjournment mean Mr. Jones?

MR. JONES: Ten minutes at the most your honour.

JUDGE RUSH: Very well, that will be granted. We will sit again at half past three. That will give you twenty minutes and will give everybody a break as well.

USER: Court rise.

(The Court adjourned from 3.09 p.m. until 3.31 p.m.)

JUDGE RUSH: Now Mr. Jones, what have you achieved?

MR. JONES: Absolutely nothing at the moment I am afraid your honour. The situation is that the other witness was sitting in the car, and I would like to have that person here because an issue has been raised about that. Itwas not anticipated before today and didn't form part of the depositions that that witness might be needed, but if any suggestion is being made then it is necessary to have the passengers of that car -- or at least one of them -- here. I have caused enquiries to be made your honour, and I do not know the result of those enquiries because it was only at about ten past three that it looked as if the prosecution case had finished.

I am anxious not to waste any time, but equally your honour if the witness is or may be relevant, then it is necessary to call that witness. Under the circumstances the prosecution would rest their case at this stage subject to ability to re-open it, if my learned friend has no objection, when the witness is available which would be, presumably, tomorrow.

JUDGE RUSH: Yes, I hear what you say. Mr. Cox what do you say about this? I am a little bit out of it because I do not know what is going to be suggested.

MR. ESCOTT COX: No your honour. My learned friend is quite right in anticipating a line of argument. Your honour is well aware that at the end of the prosecution case certain far reaching decisions have to be made on behalf of the accused, and I certainly do not want finally to make such a decision until I have heard all the prosecution witnesses.

It would seem, your honour, the ends of justice from both sides would be observed if your honour would be so kind as to adjourn earlier than usual, and let us meet here tomorrow morning and see where we have got to.

JUDGE RUSH: That would be helpful to both defence and prosecution?

MR. ESCOTT COX: Yes, I think it would be best for both.

JUDGE RUSH: Well Members of the Jury, there you have it. I am not sure what it is we might or might not hear, but it is only fair that justice is done to both sides, and I think therefore we will adjourn much earlier than usual. Instead of half past four it is half past three, and we will resume tomorrow at half past ten. I think that is the right strategy and the approach I will adopt.

Please remember what I have said to you this morning about not talking about this case outside your own number. That is very very important. Very well, we will adjourn until half past ten tomorrow morning.

(The Court adjourned at 3.35 p.m. until 10.30 a.m. 10th February, 1981.)

10th February, 1981.

<u>In the absence of the Jury.</u>

MR. JONES: Your honour I do apologise for yet a further delay. The situation is this: the witness is Mrs. Hales. She and her husband own the car that was seen by Mr. Witham and I have a statement from her that in fact details the movements of her that afternoon. I am getting it photo-copied. My learned friend saw it yesterday but obviously you will require one as well your honour. The situation in a nutshell is that she was picked up by her husband from her work and taken home along that route, along I think Barr Street or something of that nature. That is the effect of her evidence your honour.

JUDGE RUSH: Yes.

MR. JONES: They have I understand moved address, and they are now living in Erdington, and it was not possible to trace the Hales' until this morning. A policeman who had nothing to do with the case went to the house. Mr.Hales is at work; Mrs. Hales was there but is two weeks off giving birth to a baby. He told her (and I do not know who the policeman is) to make her own way to Court, and she rang up those instructing me saying that in her condition it was very difficult for her to get to Court.

Your honour it should not have been left in the situation that the lady was to make her own way to Court at all, and for that I apologise and I will have some further enquiries made as to why it was left like that, but your honour, arrangements were made for her to be picked up and hopefully either the car is going out to her at this moment or has already picked her up. The lady is quite willing to come to Court but owing to her advanced pregnancy it is a little difficult for her. I apologise your honour; it should not have happened that she was told to make her own way to Court.

JUDGE RUSH: Yes. Mr. Cox have you got anything to add?

MR. ESCOTT COX: No your honour. It seems proper that the lady should testify or that one of them should, - either the husband or the wife or both, and one must be patient I think.

JUDGE RUSH: Yes. Mr.Jones how long do you give this as a possibility -- half an hour? I am thinking of the Jury. It is nicer if they can have a set time to be free.

MR. JONES: Oh yes your honour. She should be here by 11 o'clock. Your honour I apologise for the delay. On the other hand through my learned friend's expedition the case has gone with remarkable speed, far faster than I anticipated.

JUDGE RUSH: I make no comment about that. Very well then, we won't start before 11 o'clock, and that will give a timetable for the Jury.

USHER: Court rise please.

(The Court adjourned from 10.36 a.m., until 11.09 a.m.)

In the presence of the Jury.

MR. JONES: Your honour I am grateful for the time the Court has allowed, and I think an explanation is probably due to the Jury because we rose early yesterday afternoon to try and get that witness.

JUDGE RUSH: Yes.

MR. JONES: The witness is Mrs. Hales who is now, happily, here your honour. She was travelling in the car that the bank manager, Mr. Witham, saw. The situation was she was not part of the depositions, she was not going to be called until the matter was, quite properly, raised by my learned friend. Therefore attempts were made to trace her but she and her husband had moved their address from Newtown to Erdington, and it was not possible to check the new address until this morning when the Council House opened because it was a council house they had moved to. Your honour a car was sent round at about 10 o'clock, but the lady was told she was to make her own way here. It was by a person who was not an officer in the case. Well the lady is about two weeks off having a baby and she couldn't easily make her own way here and so a car had to be sent and that has caused the delay for which I apologise.

JUDGE RUSH: Mr. Jones I fully understand that, and we are all in the picture now. Very well.

MR. JONES: Mrs. Claudette Hales please.

MRS. CLAUDETTE HALES, Sworn.

Examined by Mr. Jones.

MR. JONES: Your honour may this witness sit down?

JUDGE RUSH: Yes of course.

MR. JONES: Is your full name Claudette Hales, Mrs. Hales?

A. Yes.

Q. Where do you now live?

A. 26, Pastow Road, Pype Hayes.

Q. I think in February of last year you lived at 119 Brooks Tower, Clifford Walk, Newtown?

A. Yes, that is right.

Q. And I think you live with your husband and a daughter?

A. Yes.

MRS. C. HALES,
Examined.

Q. In February of last year did you and your husband own a car?
A. Yes.
Q. What sort of car was it?
A. A Viva.
Q. Do you remember the registration number?
A. MXC.. I cannot remember the number of it, but it was MXC, the prefix was.
Q. On the 25th February last year what did you do; did you go to work?
A. Yes, I went to work then.
Q. It was a Monday.
A. Yes.
Q. Where did you work?
A. At the Birmingham Post & Mail.
Q. What times did you work?
A. 10 to 3.
Q. What was your job?
A. A secretary.
Q. You finished work at 3 o'clock. Had you finished work at 3 o'clock that day?
A. Yes.
Q. How were you going to get back to Newtown?
A. My husband was meeting me outside.
Q. How did your husband get into town?
A. He drove the car.
Q. That is MXC?
A. Yes.
Q. Approximately what time did he pick you up?
A. Dead on 3 o'clock.

MRS. C. HALES,
Examined.

Q. Where did you go after he picked you up?

A. We went up Constitution Hill and then on to the 69 'bus route and by Lucas's.

Q. Did you go along main roads on the route to Newtown or not?

A. No. I don't know what the No.69 'bus route is but it is not a main road. We turned off Constitution Hill and went down some of the side streets.. I don't know the names of them.

Q. What time did you get home?

A. About ten past three.

Q. What did you do at ten past three?

A. I went upstairs and I started to get the dinner ready.

Q. What about your daughter?

A. She finished school at 3.30 so my husband went out at about 3.25 to fetch her.

Q. Mrs. Hales have you still got the car?

A. Yes.

Q. You still have the car. On the 25th February did you make a statement to the police?

A. Yes.

Q. When you made the statement was the number of your car still fresh in your memory?

A. Well I didn't give them the number anyway because I couldn't remember it. I gave them the prefix. They knew what the number was because they had already seen the car outside.

Q. I see.

<u>Cross-examined by Mr. Escott Cox.</u>

MR. ESCOTT COX: Mrs. Hales just a few matters. First of all you are a black lady. Is your husband a black man?

A. Yes.

Q. How old is he?

A. 29.

Q. And that afternoon you did not see him before 3 o'clock when he picked you up at work?

MRS. C. HALES,
Examined.

A. No.

Q. Was he .... so sorry, that is comment. Now the next thing is, was there ever an occasion when you were in the car when he had occasion to stop in a side street somewhere on your way home?

A. No, because it is very quiet at that time so we don't have to stop.

Q. Thank you. Was there ever an occasion when you were in the car that it was accelerating away rather quickly in any of the side streets in a way that would draw somebody's attention?

A. No.

Q. You were in the car. Were you in the front passenger seat and your husband driving?

A. Yes.

Q. Was there ever an occasion going through any side streets on your way home from work when you were crouched down behind the dashboard as far as you remember?

A. No, not as far as I can remember, unless I bent down to pick something up.

Q. Even then you would not be crouched down would you?

A. No.

MR. ESCOTT COX: Would your lordship bear with me for a moment?

JUDGE RUSH: Yes. (Mr.Escott Cox and Mr. Treacy conferred together).

Q. How old is Mr. Hales?

A. 29.

MR. ESCOTT COX: Yes alright, thank you.

Re-examined by Mr. Jones.

MR. JONES: Where is your husband?

A. He is at work at the moment.

Q. Thank you Mrs. Hales.

JUDGE RUSH: Thank you very much for coming along Mrs. Hales.

(The witness withdrew).

MR. JONES: Your honour, that is the case for the prosecution.

MR. ESCOTT COX: Your honour may I just have literally a moment to take instructions?

JUDGE RUSH: Yes of course.

MR. ESCOTT COX: Your honour, I just wanted to confirm that I am calling no evidence.

JUDGE RUSH: Yes, I see.

MR. JONES: Members of the Jury you have heard all the evidence in this case now and what does it amount to. Certainly the police were looking for a coloured person. You will recall the description: very light skinned, Asian or very light skinned West Indian according to Miss Gardener. The last person therefore„ as I say , they were looking for was the defendant when he flew in from Ireland.

From the defendant's possession, an unemployed man, all this new property was found, a large quantity of money, a gun that is identical with the gun that was used in the robbery. A'll those items were found in his possession. It is not in any way suggested that words were put into his mouth. His full statements of admission, firstly to officers who knew nothing about the case at all, going into details of which they knew nothing -- all a complete admission. And then Members of the Jury, when he is seen by other officers to tidy up the house, again the second statement you have got, Exhibit No.10, clearing up what he purchased with what. Where did he get the money; why did he have the gun? All those items again confirmed in exact detail the statements that he made to the police. He mentioned where he purchased the gun. The gun wasn't in the possession of the police and they later pick it up.

It is perfectly true Members of the Jury, that the bank staff get the clothing wrong, but then Members of the Jury, the hat was right and the colour was wrong, and the colour is something we have had difficulty with throughout this case. The anorak is right except that the colour is wrong. So Members of the Jury, there is the description which I am sure my learned friend will address you on at length and properly.

Then again you have got Miss Gardener and her evidence of yesterday when my learned friend said, "Well, he isn't the same man surely, is he?". She said, "I think it is the same man who came in the bank. It looks more like the man I remember than the photofit picture", and remember in the photofit picture on the evidence of Sergeant Taylor you can't actually change the shade of the skin. There is one shade throughout. All one can do is to try and get it either darker or lighter by either over or under exposure, but that alters the features. Her first reaction when she was questioned, and she had not seen the defendant -- I was in her way, and remember she told you she hadn't seen the defendant before or even a photograph

Closing address by prosecuting counsel.

of him -- she said her first reaction as to the photofit picture when it was put to her, "The man I saw was of far lighter skin". I must quote the exact words Members of the Jury -- "Much lighter complexion; he had a shorter face", and of course you will recall the manager who only had a fleeting glimpse of the man said, "a swarthy complexion, possibly Asian but certainly not negroid features."

Members of the Jury that is the case. The photofit picture you may think contains remarkable similarities, just as the remarkable dissimilarity as to the apparent colour, and as I say you do not know, and never will do, whether there was any disguise used by Mr. Fisher. But the colour aside, the jaw bone and the structure of the face, the lips, the nose, the eyebrows and then the eyes as well, there is a certain similarity on the photofit picture, but remember it was the eyes yesterday that Miss Gardener said was the item or the items that really were so similar to the man she had seen in the bank when the defendant was pointed out to her.

Members of the Jury you have it there; the full statements of admission by the defendant containing the details only known to the robber; the money, the large amount of money recovered, plus the gun, plus the bags that were used; a man unemployed and in possession of all that amount of money. The prosecution say there is only one answer to this and that is guilty to both the offences charged. There are two offences Members of the Jury. They go hand in hand. The one is robbery and the second is that he had that firearm at the time he committed the robbery, so the two offences do go together. Members of the Jury, the prosecution say this is quite a straightforward case and the only proper verdict is one of guilty.

JUDGE RUSH: Thank you Mr. Jones. Mr. Cox?

MR. ESCOTT COX: If it please your honour, Members of the Jury, may I set your mind at rest straightaway. I am not going to address you at great length, nor am I going to address you, please, as if you are a bunch of fools; of course you are not. This is a case in which the issues are fairly narrow and I hope I can deal with them shortly and realistically, and I face, I hope completely realistically, that if you take those alleged confessions at their face value the defendant has no answer to this case. It does not mattor about photofits or identification or anything else. I shall deal with those and deal with them in a little detail because there are matters about them which are very important, and I am going to suggest to you will cause you considerable heartburn and difficulty. So will you bear with me for a moment and not think me unrealistic if we put those on one side to be dealt with in a few minutes, and deal with the question of the actual attack on the bank.

Closing address by defence counsel.

The case is in fact really a very different one to the one that my learned friend opened to you at some length indeed yesterday, anticipating all sorts of arguments and anticipating evidence which I am afraid from his point of view just didn't come up. He is in an embarrassing position; one sympathizes with him but we are not here to sympathize with counsel for the prosecution; we are here to do justice. He had to open the case to you where his principal witness had given a detailed description of her attacker and made a photofit picture which was completely different to the man in the dock, and that is a very embarrassing position when you're prosecuting, of course it is, and you try to undermine the various lines of defence by suggesting that the bank clerk wouldn't have had a good opportunity to see him because her attention would have been riveted on the gun, etc. etc. Of course it proved to be completely false. What did emerge -- and of course I daresay most or all of you would have known this without me asking questions but we have to have the evidence -- it isn't any school leaver who is taken by the scruff of the neck and put behind the counter of a bank; it's a very responsible job. You think of the amount of cash they have to handle. There is nothing to stop anybody walking into a bank, and there is a young lady like Miss Gardener behind the counter handing over cash, securities, cheques worth tens, literally hundreds of thousands of pounds, so they must be very responsible people. They themselves handle cash and they have got to give it out to people, so they are intelligent and sensitive people.

Then there is the question of whether they are used to recognising people; whether it is that sort of job. After all some people might be intelligent, sensitive and sensible people and work in an office, but they really have no contact with the public so their opportunities of being used to recognising or not recognising the features of the general public would be very limied. That isn't Miss Gardener's case or any bank clerk's case, because they have all sorts of people coming in, some of whom are regular customers and are much better to recognise and to accept their name, accept their credit and so on,and you will remember her evidence about that.

Thirdly this man didn't go straight to her -- whoever he was. Here he is in this well lit banking hall on a very quiet afternoon and he comes in -- I accept of course she would not be looking at him with riveted attention; there is no need to -- but for about a minute which is a pretty long time he stood by the end of the counter. At that time she didn't know what was going to happen; she wasn't in fear; she wasn't surprised; her emotions would have been absolutely calm. She had a very very good opportunity indeed of seeing that man, and let us face it Members of the Jury, having had that opportunity -- we are not talking about whether she got the colour of the eyes right or wrong, we are talking about whether she described this man as an Asian, something completely and utterly different, or he could have been a pale skinned West Indian although on her evidence (although it is in her statement) she didn't think so.

Closing address by defence counsel.

So I am not trying to be what I think members of the public sometimes think is the sort of typical defence lawyer trying to pick tiny little holes in the evidence of prosecution witnesses. This is something which is absolutely basic and fundamental coming from a witness of considerable quality and calibre.

Her attention wasn't riveted on the gun.. Of course equally it would not have been riveted on the man's face, but you won't forget what she said afterwards -- that she thought she would be able to recognise him again -- so that whatever opportunity she had of seeing that man she was prepared to tell that to the police within a very short time of this event happening.

You won't have forgotten the description that she gave, the question of the clothing, and again something else that has been a great embarrassment to the prosecution is this: the question of clothing. What is the answer to that? It was suggested to you first of all that it was just the girl who had got the clothing wrong, but now we have heard the evidence we know that both the girl and the bank manager give the same description of this attacker of two articles of clothing, the hat and the jacket. Have they both independently made the same mistake about both articles? Does that seem to you in the slightest probable; does it even seem to you possible that they would both mistake a red hat for a green one and that blue anorak for a khaki battle jacket, because that is the evidence, and you will remember that I was careful to ask the bank manager whether he -- although he didn't pay a great deal of attention to the man's features because he had no reason to; he just felt it was somebody being pretty boring running up the road on a damp day and he had got his umbrella up, and one can understand that -- but he did say that he had observed and he was sure that man had on a green hat and a Lovatt khaki battle jacket. And it is no good my learned friend saying they only got the colour of the anorak wrong; that isn't a battle jacket, it doesn't look like a battle jacket, and the witness Miss Gardener herself said, "No, it doesn't even look like the same material." Very important distinctions Members of the Jury; very important distinctions indeed.

Now what is the answer to all that. The answer to all that is that eventually she goes round to the police station and gives a description and you end up with that photofit. Now don't let us be unrealistic or mince our words Members of the Jury; that bears about as much resemblance to the accused as I do to the boxer Mohammed Ali. It just is nothing like the same man. It is all very well for my learned friend to say well she couldn't complain or she couldn't ask for the shades to be lighter. Let me remind you of two things about that. First of all when she started her evidence what did she say.. She said that the man who came in -- she was asked to describe the man by my learned friend Mr. Jones and she said he had a very dark complexion; a very dark complexion. That was the man who came in and held her up -- a very dark complexion. When we had the evidence from the expert who was with her when she made

Closing address by defence counsel.

that up, he said that she expressed satisfaction with the tone, with the shading. She did not say to him either that doesn't look right in the sense that his features are not properly or well represented there, nor did she say to him that looks like the man in the sense of shape and features but of course it is not very helpful because the man I saw was much paler skinned than that. She did not say either of those things; she did not raise either of those as a complaint. You remember the expert saying that he had no recollection of her making any reservations about that, but that she expressed satisfaction with the tone of the skin. You see Members of the Jury, it is all very well but I suppose all human faces have a certain amount in common if you start stretching your imagination. You remember how my learned friend emphasized when opening this case to you how the shape of the face in that photofit is the same as that of the accused, and saying well if you put the colour on one side look at that important feature, the shape of the face. What does his own witness say when shown the photofit picture? "No, the man hadn't got a face that shape. I think his face was shorter in length." So don't be gulled into making these over-easy comparisons, and you will remember she did not accept, when he took her through the face feature by feature, that they all looked like the man as she remembered. I won't go through that in details with you. You will remember that she said there were some, certainly the eyes, but then there were others, particularly the nose, that were not the same -- and the lips and mouth.

Now Members of the Jury so much for that. Is there any other indication that sheds any light on what happened. Now before I venture further into this may I say that the prosecution (and I will have to come back to it I am afraid later) have nailed their flag to one particular mast. They do not say the accused was indirectly involved in this attack on the bank; they don't say he might have driven a getaway car; they don't say he might have helped plan it but didn't actually go himself; they don't say he didn't go himself but may have received or helped the attacker afterwards. None of those things do they suggest against the accused. You are either sure that he is the man who went into the bank or it is not guilty. There is no choice open to you on this case.

Now let us just see what did happen afterwards. The bank manager ran out. We don't know what time with any certainty the attack took place because the clerk put it at around 3 o'clock, and obviously she wasn't looking at her watch and nobody suggests she was. We don't know whether it was 5 or 10 minutes before or 5 or 10 minutes after, but it is a very strange feature of this case, isn't it, that the bank manager went out and he didn't just see a car going by with a coloured man at the wheel and take its number. If he had done that he would have stopped and taken the numbers of goodness knows how many cars. There was something about the car whose number he took which particularly attracted his attention. It wasn't the fact that it was a coloured man at the wheel because he, in his mind, wasn't even sure that the attacker -- and of course he didn't see the man who ran past other than a fleeting glimpse -- might have been coloured. What was it? Here was

Closing address by defence counsel.

the car accelerating away up that street, Stainsby Avenue -- you have got it on the map. And he saw it and it drew his attention particularly because there was the car behaving in that way. That is what he was saying wasn't it? He believed it had started off from just down the road and was accelerating away and there was somebody in it in the passenger seat crouched down so that he couldn't even see and he didn't know whether they were black, white, child, adult, male or female. You have to be crouched down a pretty long way in a Vauxhall Viva for somebody not to see that. And he took the number. Well it is not for me to make accusations about people who are not before the Court and I don't do so, Members of the Jury. We don't even know that we are necessarily talking about the same car and the same circumstances, but it is a very very odd feature, and the one person who could have come to Court with greatest ease -- the prosecution have had after all since half past three yesterday evening to get him here -- not the poor pregnant wife but the man who was driving that car off that afternoon. They have chosen not to do so; they have chosen to call the wife only. You have to decide the case not on what might have been, what evidence could have been available; you have to decide it on the evidence that we present to you. Those are the rules and his honour will, I am sure, confirm that. We don't know what her husband looks like. We know his age and we know he is a black man. If he had been here in Court wearing a woolly hat, who knows? We just do not know. It is a very uncomfortable feature of the case.

Let us leave that aside Members of the Jury, because after this robbery fourteen days exactly passes by, and at the end of those fourteen days you then, for the first time in this case, know something about the accused. We have got to the 11th March, and on the 11th March he flew off to Ireland. He had got a lot of money. It may be stolen money; it may be this stolen money. Do you know? That doesn't prove that he did the job. And how strange if he had in fact, a man out of work living in some sort of hostel, suddenly come into that very large sum of cash of the sort that would make most people's mouths water just to get their hands on spending money. Did he suddenly go mad and start spending it. Why did he wait a fortnight if he was the bank robber before he starts spending the money, going to Ireland and spending thousands of pounds in Ireland. That is what the evidence is, and if you add to what was found on him -- that is to say approximately £1,400, I think £1,438, something of that sort -- a thousand pounds that he alleges he spent in Ireland, you are getting up to a very large percentage of the total sum of money. Why? Does that sound like the robber who has done successful blag or whatever they call it. He keeps quiet for a couple of days, of course he does, but then goes round the clubs and the pubs and showering money about like it was going out of fashion. Very strange isn't it?

Now Members of the Jury, let me grasp the nettle of these statements. He comes back from Ireland, he is seen by the police and it is perfectly clear that he isn't going to tell them any more than he has to. He wants to see a solicitor and in the end the police say two things to him, and you will bear

Closing address by
defence counsel.

these in mind in looking at why would a man just make a confession of a serious crime to the police. What has he to gain from doing so. Nothing. The officer said two things to him, 1) they were going to go and look at the addresses in his .... sorry, is one of the jurors not well?

MEMBER OF THE JURY: No..

MR. ESCOTT COX: One is that they were going to go and search his own address which he had given to them and there he would know that they would find the starting pistol because it was there -- one of many that were sold by that particular shop.. You may not remember that evidence; it was read, and certainly it was far from a rare occurrence for them to sell that particular sort of starting pistol. And secondly that they were going to make enquiries at and around all his friends. What those enquiries might or might not reveal we do not know. It gave him some motivation apparently, on the police's own evidence, to stop asking for a solicitor and to make this statement. This is put before you, Exhibit 6, as a truthful and accurate account of what took place. If any one or more of you have a pencil I should like, as we go through it, that you should mark in it what I suggest to you are really serious discrepancies between the contents of this statement and the truth of what happened in the bank as we know it.. Have you got it Members of the Jury?

"I had been out drinking at a pub in town. I'd got no money I hadn't paid my rent at the hostel because I'd blown it on beer. I'd got a starting pistol on me. I bought it from Bates's in the town". Now here is the first one: "I was three parts drunk". Is there a word in Miss Gardener's evidence to suggest that the man that she dealt with in the bank was under the influence of alcohol at all let alone three parts drunk. Absolutely not.. There is not a suggestion other than he was perfectly steady, cool and calm, the gun pointed steadily at her, cocked back. That is a serious discrepancy.

"First of all I looked in the Midland Bank in Hockley opposite Cannings". Now just listen to this Members of the Jury.. "There was a young girl talking to another bloke, a cashier like, but there was no customers." Now we know from Miss Gardener that when the man went into the bank she was entirely on her own behind that counter; there was no cashier or other counter staff male or female. Why. Why is that in the statement if it is untrue. "I walked in pointed the pistol at the girl, and said, 'Give us the money.' She just handed over some money to me. I just ran round a few corners. I tried a telephone box to get a taxi but it was broke. I managed to get a taxi later and went to the hostel and then went and got something to eat. I stayed in and around Birmingham for a week or so." He didn't Members of the Jury; he stayed for two weeks. Do you think that a man who had actually carried out the robbery wouldn't even know what day it was that he did it? "And then last Tuesday ...", you see

Closing address by defence counsel.

he remembers exactly which day he went to Ireland. It was indeed Tuesday the 11th March that he went to Ireland. "... I went across to Ireland and I have been there ever since. Just spending the money like a fool. I'm not absolutely positive but I think there was £4,300 ...". Now Members of the Jury it was £3,800. How does he come to tell the police that he stole £500 more than the robber actually did if he was the robber. You will know from your experience of the world and from what we all know of what goes on, plenty of people say to the police, "Oh I committed a crime but I didn't steal as much as it is said. I burgled that house but I didn't have lots of cash". Absolutely commonplace. When have you ever heard-- when has anybody ever heard of a criminal admitting stealing more than was gone. It is not merely the error in itself but the nature of the error. If it had been less there would have been other motives, but what possible motives could the real robber who is coming clean with the police --"Yes, I want to get all this off my chest" -- have for exaggerating his part in the offence.

Then Members of the Jury, last but by no means least, "... I had in tenners and fivers apart from three brand new £1 notes." Now in fact, as we know from the bank clerk, there were no less than three hundred new £1 notes. Had somebody told him something about new £1 notes and he had forgotten that it was three hundred. If he had been the man who had gone into the bank and taken the money away in the plastic bag why didn't he say three hundred brand new £1 notes. After all Members of the Jury let us face it, whoever the robber was can you imagine him going through the pickings afterwards, opening the plastic bag and going through and finding that absolute wad -- I don't know how big 300 new £1 notes is but it would be a healthy wad of money wouldn't it, something you would not forget or overlook if you were the robber. So how does it come that this man, who suddenly decided to come clean to the police and tell them all his part in it, makes a statement in which there are I suggest to you five really serious errors. Of course it contains information in it which he could have known from many sources, not least from the robber himself, like which bank it was, that it was a girl who served and other information of that sort. Of course it does. But when my learned friend says to you that it could have been known only to the robber, and here he is making a statement almost literally a month after the robbery, is that right. Of course it is not. Whoever made that statement, my client knew an unhealthy amount about what had gone on; there is no doubt about that is there -- an unhealthy amount about what had gone on but he didn't know the real details, and if he had he would never have made those serious errors.

And you see, Members of the Jury, it didn't stop there because he was then seen by the officers who are in charge of the case, the actual robbery, and he is asked about it and he says he has been spending all this money from the robbery. Well I won't comment one way or the other about that, but let me just remind you of what he said. The officer said to him, "Did you wear any of this clothing when you committed the

Closing address by defence counsel.

robbery?". Answer: "I think I had that anorak ..." -- that is the blue one -- "... on, yes I did." That isn't in a written statement; that is in an interview Members of the Jury. I am reminding you of the oral interview. "I think I had that anorak on, yes I did." Now the one thing we can be absolutely certain of is that the robber did not have that anorak on. Why is this man apparently confessing all to the police and coming clean and making a clean breast of it, telling them that he wore that anorak at the time of the raid when it isn't true. Does that make any sense to you. Is that the sort of confession on which you would rely. And even more striking than that, he was asked "Anything else?". "Yes, I had that hat on." Now whatever else you know about this case you know that the robber did not have that hat on. And when he came to make his second statement he deals with what he had been buying with the money, and he finished that statement by saying, "I was wearing the woollen hat you found." Why tell the police that when it isn't true.

And indeed if he is the robber and living in obviously extremely modest circumstances -- you will remember what the police officer said; they didn't just take a selection, they took everything that was in his room, took all his worldly possessions,-- we know he hadn't got a khaki battle jacket and we know he hadn't got a green woollen hat. Of course he had had time to get rid of them, but if he were going to get rid of them why not get rid of the gun. Why keep the gun. It makes no sense at all if he wanted to be sure that if his room was searched there would be nothing to tie him to the crime. The gun would have been the first thing he would have got rid of. So when you think about it Members of the Jury it is very strange. Those are not even new garments bought with the stolen money. Nobody has ever suggested they are, -- the anorak and the woolly hat. I don't know whether you can buy woolly hats like that but maybe you can. So it would seem that this man living in very modest circumstances did have an anorak and a woollen hat; they were not the ones used by the robber but for some reason he chose to say that they were.

I repeat realistically, as I hope you think I am being, that if you sweep aside those objections to those apparent frank confessions, there is of course abundant material there on which you can find him guilty regardless of any qualms you may have over the identification, but may I most respectfully suggest that you, as I am sure you will want to, be very fair in your approach to the case. Don't approach it perhaps on that basis. Look at this question of identification or non-identification as it is in this case, and I would suggest that that gives you very considerable qualms indeed as to whether this man could possibly have been the man who went into the bank; and bearing those qualms in mind, look at those very serious, very serious errors of details and fact that could not have been made in a confession by the true robber. Life isn't quite as simple as it is sometimes presented to be, and certainly as the prosecution have suggested it to be in this case.

Closing address by defence counsel.

Members of the Jury I don't flinch from saying to you once again, because it is so important, that no matter how unhealthy a contact this man may have had with the real robber, the prosecution choose not to pursue that contact, not to bring allegations about that contact, possession of stolen money or anything of that sort. This is a matter entirely for them. They have chosen to make these two serious allegations, all of which concern him being the actual man who actually went into the bank, and unless you are sure of that then of course it is a verdict of not guilty. It is not for him in any way to prove his innocence; he doesn't have to testify, he doesn't have to answer questions to the police, he doesn't have to give evidence or any of that. He is perfectly entitled -- and indeed what a marvellous safeguard it is for all of us -- to say through me; look, these are very serious allegations; your evidence on them is quite inconclusive, quite inconclusive, and let me come to you ladies and gentlemen of the jury, as I do, and make these submissions to you and please ask you to find him not guilty on both of the counts on which he is charged.

JUDGE RUSH: Thank you Mr. Cox.

Members of the Jury, we will have a short adjournment perhaps for ten minutes.

(The Court adjourned from 11.57 a.m. until 12.13 p.m.)

USHER: Court please rise.

S U M M I N G - U P.

JUDGE RUSH: Members of the Jury, it is my task now to sum up the case to you, and the first matter which I draw to your attention is to point out what our respective functions are in this case. You must take the law relevant to this case from me, just as you have the equally important task of being the judges of the facts, what the facts are in this case as you find them and drawing such inferences from those facts as you think are sensible, and having done that and your task, then applying the law that I will have directed you upon, coming to a verdict of either guilty or not guilty on the particular count that you are considering. And of course Members of the Jury, it is important that you consider the evidence that you have heard in the case. That is how you decide what the facts are, from the evidence you have heard. As I say you are perfectly entitled to draw such inferences as you think are sensible from those facts as you find them, and of course in your task each one of you brings to bear your own knowledge of life and people.

The first matter of law which I draw to your attention I do because it is so very important. The prosecution bring this case against David Fisher. They charge him with two offences, and when you come to consider each of the counts in the indictment it is important that you remember that the burden of proving the case lies fairly and squarely upon the prosecution from beginning to end, and upon the particular count that you are considering the prosecution must make you feel sure of his guilt on that count before it would be your duty in accordance with your oath to return a verdict of guilty. If you aren't sure about the matter then he is entitled to a verdict of not guilty.

Members of the Jury you know here that there are two counts in the indictment, and you will be asked in due course through your spokesman to return a verdict on each of those two counts, and they do require separate consideration by you albeit perhaps in this particular case the verdicts will be similar in each of the two counts, either of guilty or not guilty. That is a matter for you and not for me to say really. You decide what your verdicts are on each of these two counts, and Members of the Jury, having said that one can go to what actually is alleged against Mr. David Fisher in the indictment.

You can see in Count 1 that the statement of offence is one of robbery contrary to an Act of Parliament, and the particulars of the offence, which it is for the prosecution to prove, are that he on that 25th day of February last year, a Monday, at about 3'ish in the afternoon, robbed Yvonne Gardener of £3,800, and Members of the Jury, it is Yvonne Gardener who is put in the indictment as the person who was robbed because she in fact had control of that money at the particular time that the robbery took place, the prosecution say..

So far as robbery is concerned, there is a perfectly straightforward definition of robbery coming within that Act of Parliament, and the statute says this: "A person is guilty of robbery if he steals, and immediately before or at the time of doing so and in order to do so he uses force on any person, or puts or seeks to put any person in fear of being then and there subjected to force." So you can see that robbery really consists of stealing plus the use or threat of use of force, and you must be satisfied that force or the matter that puts the person in fear is done by the person who is said to be the robber with a view to carrying out the theft going on at the particular time.. So Members of the Jury, there you have it so far as the definition is concerned.

So far as theft itself is concerned, there is a definition there, although you may feel yourselves, although not being able to tell me, that you do not need to be told what theft is, but I do have to tell you what it is in law as to the ingredient parts because again the same Act of Parliament says this: "A person is guilty of theft if he dishonestly appropriates property belonging to another with the intention of permanently depriving the other of it", and in this particular case I need say no more about that. You can see therefore why one has robbery on the facts of this case alleged in Count 1.

Members of the Jury, very much tied up with the robbery of course is the separate aspect set out in Count 2 in the indictment -- possessing a firearm whilst committing an offence, and the offence we are concerned with here is one of robbery: that Mr. Fisher on that day in February, at the time of robbing Yvonne Gardener of £3,800 cash had in his possession an imitation firearm, namely a .38 'Chief' blank firing gun.. Of course that would be without lawful object, and Members of the Jury I need say no more about that offence either. It speaks for itself as set out in the statement of the offence and the particulars thereto.

You see Members of the Jury, in this case it may well be that you will find that there was a robbery in Count 1 as set out in the particulars as to Yvonne Gardener being robbed by someone of £3,800 on that 25th day of February last year, and equally it may take you very little time to feel too that not alone was there that robbery but also that the robber had with him or with her a gun in his possession, an imitation firearm, and therefore that robber, if he was a robber, did possess a firearm while committing an offence, namely the offence of robbery. So you may feel that so far your task in this case is not difficult yet, because as I say you may feel here, looki at the matter objectively, that there was the robbery of the £3,800 from Yvonne Gardener, and that the robber did possess a firearm whilst committing that offence,namely Counts 1 and 2 as set out. Someone robbed. Someone, the same person, possessed the firearm, a firing pistol that you see as an exhibit in the case, Exhibit 4..

Your problem in this case I venture to say, and I say it strongly to you, is whether in fact it was David Fisher who was that robber or the person who had the firearm whilst committing that robbery, if you are satisfied that there was a robbery, and that that person did possess a firearm whilst committing that robbery. The question and the crux of this case, was it this defendant or not, or was it somebody else. You must remember as I have said, you must be sure that it was David Fisher and not somebody else before you would return a verdict of guilty. You have got to be sure.

That therefore brings one to what you have got to be sure of in this case, and it is sure that it was David Fisher who was that man at the bank who robbed Yvonne Gardener of £3,800 and had with him at that time the starting pistol.. So identification is the word that should remain absolutely crystal clear in your mind in your deliberations please, because it is so important when one comes to consider identification because the law has realised in common sense, and sometimes in tragedy as well perhaps in result, that you can in fact have a witness who is absolutely honest as the day, one hundred percent honest, and really genuinely believes that what he or she, or who he or she identified was a particular person, but nevertheless that person can be mistaken. As I say, you can have an honest witness and you can in fact make a terrible mistake upon identification, and you can see the injustice that can happen if that does happen. Therefore Members of the Jury you must look very carefully at all the evidence that there is, particularly on this crucial matter of identification and you will consider, for example, how long the identifying witness had to make up -- as it is here -- how long Yvonne Gardener had to make up her mind so far as trying to remember who she saw in the bank, what sort of distance was there between her and him, what was the light like, was there any impediment or obstacle in the way of the observation being made, what are the discrepancies that there may be between how she described a person for example to the police in the early days when matters were fresh in her mind compared to what she says in the witness box, bearing in mind when I say that that everything she says in the witness box about what she told the police is still part of the evidence. Everything she has actually said on oath is evidence in the case, and her evidence did go over a lot of territory and in particular you may feel of crucial importance in this case is that Exhibit 11, what I have called here the "identikit face", against a background too where you will remember the identikit expert, Detective Sergeant Taylor, telling us how those pictures are made up because you may feel, as Mr. Cox has said, one of the salient features in this case is the difference, just looking at that Exhibit 11 identikit face, to the face of the defendant. That has been put quite clearly before you, and it won't come as a surprise to anyone that that point was put so forcibly because there is that matter which I do ask you to bear in mind throughout in this case.

Members of the Jury there are other matters too which you must consider, for example any discrepancy in the description of what the man was wearing to what we actually know it is said that man was wearing at the time. You have had evidence about the clothing, and indeed Mr. Cox in his address to you so recently went through it very carefully with you, and he went further than that in saying: well you have confessions here, yes, and it seems if the man actually did them of course they are confessions to what he is charged with. But, says Mr. Cox, when you look at that first statement that was made, he points out five points -- which I will go through with you in due course -- which he points out as indicating further material which would indicate that it was not Mr. Fisher who was the robber that day at the bank..

So as I have said Members of the Jury, please look with great care at the evidence in the case on identification, and of course Members of the Jury too, take into account the evidence of what the defendant is said to have said to the police. You have heard the police give their evidence. What did you make of, for example, P.C.Abolins and D.C.Sutcliffe in particular who carried out the main part of the interviews in this case. Did they seem to you to be honest witnesses - number one, - and b) if they were honest witnesses were they reliable on the salient matters that they remembered of the interview that they had with David Fisher. That is very important indeed of course, and that is your realm and your realm alone.. So Members of the Jury, that puts the aspect of identification in perspective I trust, and as I say, you have the evidence of clothing, the identikit face, and you have of course also what was said between the defendant and the police -- all matters which you are entitled to look at and consider in this case. As I say it is back to you; you are the judges of the facts and you decide where the truth lies here.

Now one therefore comes to look at the evidence in this case, and in going through the evidence with you I shall not go through each and every word that was said; that is not my function in going through the evidence. My function is to go through the evidence in such a way that one can highlight perhaps matters of particular importance to assist you in your task. It may well be in doing that that I stress a point which you don't think is important. Well then you disregard the stress that I may have put on that point, or indeed that counsel have put on a point for that matter. On the other hand if you think that a matter which is put before you has something worth remembering in your eyes, then you will no doubt take account of it. So too the comments that are made by counsel with the object of assisting you and the comments from me for the same purpose, some may appeal to you and no doubt you will remember those comments in your deliberations. On the other hand if, for example, I say something about a piece of evidence that you don't think is helpful or not objective in some way, then you totally disregard my comment because it comes back again at the end of the day that you, taking the law from me, are the judges of the facts and you apply the law to those facts as you find them on the evidence you have heard in coming to your verdict, either guilty or not guilty on the particular count you are considering.

Yvonne Carol Gardener, a very important witness for the prosecution because really she was the main witness by a long way who saw the robber, if you accept that she was an honest witness, at the bank that day in Great Hampton Street at about 3 o'clock in the afternoon that Monday, the 25th February, the date laid in the indictment, and she was 21 years of age I think, just. There was one man in the bank who came in. We didn't hear anything about her talking before then to any cashier; perhaps you got the impression from her that she was making out that she had been alone in the bank at that time quite clearly. The man who came into the bank was about 5-ft. 10-ins. tall, And then she went on to describe this very important matter of complexion of that man. She told you at one stage in her evidence that that man had a very dark complexion; he wore a dark green woolly hat, green anorak; he had a flatish nose as far as she could remember, "and I would have said he was Asian at the time, not negroid." Then she went on being asked questions about this complexion element, and at one stage she described the colour of the skin as pale dark skin, so what you make of that is for you to decide and one of the things that you will consider here.

She looked at some of the clothing exhibited in this case: Exhibit 8 a hat of the same style as that worn by the man, and Exhibit 9 the bags with the 'Lucky 7' on them in red which looked the same sort of bags that the man had,

SUMMING UP.

but the anorak -- you will remember this -- is the same style but a different colour she thought, and she said to you when she was pressed about this matter, not unnaturally and quite rightly, that so far as the person who came into the bank is concerned and the looks of that person, she thought that that identikit picture is what the man looked like at that time. She went on to say that she thought in fact now it was the defendant "looking at his eyes and the overall shape of his face, and I think the man in the bank's nose was wider than that of the defendant." Well those are only comments made but they were in answer to questions put, and no doubt you can remember those matters.

She can remember certainly Members of the Jury that that man pointed a gun at her, and you may feel that that gun would have been very much a part of what her attention was riveted to at that time. That is a matter for you but it must have been frightening. That man pointing the gun at her said, "Money", and of the gun that he was holding she described it as small, about 5 or 6 inches long; it was all black, had a small barrel 2 or 3 inches long, and he clicked it, and then she looked at Exhibit 4, the starting pistol we have seen. "That looks like it" she said, and also she recognised the clicking noise of that pistol. "I was very surprised and I did not press the alarm because it would have made a noise while he was there, and I handed over to him £3,800 in £10 notes, £5 notes and £1 notes." He put that money, did the man with the gun, into the bag he had with him and he ran out. She described the bag as a plastic bag she thought with red on it, and she then sounded the alarm and the manager Mr. Witham came in very shortly afterwards and went out again to look for that man. "I spoke to the police that day" she said, -- and remember this Members of the Jury which the defence stress to you, -- "I described the man to the police that day when it was fresh in my memory as accurately as I could", and then she went on to refresh her memory as to what she actually did say to the police that day. "I described him as about 25 years old, 5-ft. 10-ins. tall, he was either Asian or a very light skinned West Indian. He had a dark green woollen hat over his head, covering his hair and his ears. He had dark brown eyes, a long wide mouth, but not thick lips, and was wearing a dark khaki jacket, plain in style."

So far as she could remember that was her evidence as to what happened and the description of the man who had that gun and who got the money from her as a result of pointing the gun at her and asking for money. Of course the picture was then extended to you in evidence in the shape of Mr. Witham the bank manager, Norman Barnard Witham. He parked his car and was walking in Well Street towards the bank and it was raining at the time. It was about 3'ish, and he saw a running figure coming towards him and past him, and that man, that running figure, was wearing a green woolly hat and an anorak type jacket or coat -- "khaki like" he described it, -- soft boots, arms were cradling as if clutching something he said, and he described the man's colour. He was either a swarthy white person or a light coloured Asian and the nose was longish, I think was the way he described it, and he was certainly not negroid. He heard the alarm at this bank go off; he went into the bank, spoke to the staff, the police were called, and he went out looking for the man unsuccessfully. He did notice a car you will remember in Stainsby Avenue with two occupants. He noticed the driver was a negro and the other person in the car seemed crouched to him, and he gave the number of that car to the police, which was MXC.388H.

You heard this morning from Mrs. Hales how they, her husband and she, have a Vauxhall and she remembered the MXC part of the registration number. At about 3 o'clock that afternoon, she told you in relation to this car, she was with her husband. She hadn't seen him before that sort of time, 3 o'clock, and she was going to Newtown with him in the car, and they got home in fact at about ten past three. They have still got that car and her husband, right enough, is a black man aged 29. "We didn't have to stop at all or accelerate unusually during that journey, and I was in the front passenger seat" Mrs. Hales told us, "and my husband was driving. I might have bent down in the car to pick something up." So that deals with the car which Mr. Witham told you he took the number of at the time. How much that helps you in fact in the case is a matter for you to decide.

Of course we then had the evidence read to you of Bate the Gunmaker's director, or one of them, Mr. Conrad Cross, and his evidence was to the effect that that Exhibit 4, a firearm, could very easily have come from his shop. They sell them in quantities in fact, and so far as the firearms expert is concerned, that was P.C.Bucknall, that also was read to you. In his opinion this firearm was an imitation type firearm.

You then had another expert, this time in the shape of Detective Sergeant Taylor who did come before you to give evidence on oath, and he told you -- you may feel in an interesting and sensible way -- the way that these pictures are composed in making up an identikit face. He told you too in particular how they have different combinations so far as colouring is concerned and how I think pencil is used for shading as well, and no doubt you will bear that in mind. He does the pictures first, the tone second, and apparently he was trying to fit together so far as shade is concerned or tone, a lighter skinned coloured man, and you have the photographs, Exhibit 11a and 11b and Exhibit 12, quite apart from Exhibit 11 the identikit face, and no doubt you will look at these photographs with care and remember the points put forward by the defence in relation to those matters. He told you too that there was no comment recorded by him that Miss Gardener was not satisfied with the identikit photograph, Exhibit 11, at that time.

Members of the Jury, then we come to the other part of this case, as to the actual questions and answers made between the defendant and the police, and also bringing in there of course the two written statements, Exhibits 6 and 10 that this defendant made, and you may feel when you retire to your room to consider your verdicts in this case that those two written exhibits are extremely important documents in the case for you to consider. I will deal with them in a moment but I will now straightaway deal with the interview ... really it was P.C.Abbolins who started this evidence for the police.

SUMMING UP.

He was working then you remember -- this is on Wednesday the 19th March, and remember the robbery was the 25th February. You have the time schedule space interval before you, and on the 19th March at Birmingham Airport International Arrivals Lounge at 11.25 in the morning of that Wednesday he sees there David Fisher the defendant, and he said to the defendant, "I understand that you are in possession of a large amount of money ..." -- and we know that the amount of money to be precise was £1,358.07p. -- "...and you have stated you are unemployed. Would you mind telling me how this money came into your possession?". Answer: "I needn't tell you anything, in fact I'm not going to tell you." He was quite right; he didn't have to.

Then D.C.Sutcliffe joins them and you saw D.C.Sutcliffe too give his evidence, and it was those two officers who then went on with the interview of Mr. Fisher. He told the officers about the money he had been found with coming across from Ireland, "I've won it gambling, here and there. I say I won it gambling." He won it here in England he indicated. "I say I won it gambling, you're going to have to find out anything else", and he was told that the police were going to take possession of the money pending further enquiries, and he was then taken some 300 yards down from the passenger lounge to the airport police station.

We are now at 12.15 after midday, and the interview continues between the defendant, D.C.Sutcliffe and P.C.Abolins. The defendant is asked again, "Where has that money come from?". Answer: "I told you, I am saying I got it gambling." He was asked who he had been gambling with, and he replied, "Different blokes in pubs around, I cannot say who. It was just at cards." Then D.C.Sutcliffe makes this comment perhaps rather than question: "I have seen a few card schools in pubs but never with the sort of money you are carrying. You have £1,358.07p. in your possession. Are you seriously saying you won all that amount at cards?". Answer: "Yes, that's what I'm saying." "Which area were the pubs in then?". Answer: "Oh, around the town you know." Then D.C.Sutcliffe says this: "Shall we carry on playing this silly game or do you think you could tell me the truth about all this?". Answer from Mr. Fisher: "I want to see a solicitor, and I'm saying no more to you about anything until you let me see one", and then the officer replied, as D.C.Sutcliffe told you, "Yes you will be able to have a solicitor if that is what you want, and in the meantime I shall go and search your room at 155 Warwick Road, and also I have got to make some enquiries at other addresses found in your possession". Then Mr. Fisher makes the comment, according to the police, "You're not going to let go are you?". He said that to D.C.Sutcliffe who replied, "No not until you tell me the truth", and then Mr. Fisher apparently made this comment, "Don't do anything yet, let me think for a bit." He was told, "Take as long as you like", and then some 5 minutes or thereabouts afterwards one comes to a breakthrough, I suppose the prosecution would say, in the interview of this defendant when Mr. Fisher said, after thinking about it for about 5 minutes, "Oh, I will make your job easy for you, I'll tell you." "What are you going to tell me now?". Answer: "How I got the money. It was a bank job. The Midlands Bank at

SUMMING UP.

Hockley, I held it up." Pausing there for a moment Members of the Jury, you may feel it is worthy of your attention that P.C.Abolins told you when he was giving his evidence that until then he didn't have the details of a bank robbery at the Midland Bank, and you remember D.C.Sutcliffe was asked about this. He didn't give quite the same answer; he said, "Well the robbery might have been circulated for general information but that was all". He too, like his fellow officer Abolins, didn't have details of the robbery.

D.C.Sutcliffe said, "I don't know any details about this matter. Rather than telling me verbally do you wish to make a written statement", and then we have the first statement that you see in front of you, Exhibit No.6, and you may feel that it is unnecessary for me to read that out again to you. You have had it read to you more than once and I feel sure that when you retire in due course you will look at that statement very carefully..

The defence make five points on that statement. They are as follows for you to consider. The first point Mr. Cox drew to your attention was the comment from Mr. Fisher, "I was three parts drunk". There is not a word about him being three parts drunk or appearing to be from Miss Gardener say the defence. Why should he say that. You may remember that we are talking about 3 o'clock in the afternoon.. The second point is about a cashier in the bank being mentioned. We know nothing about a cashier at all talking to a young girl. Miss Gardener herself said that she was on her own. Why should he put that in if he had actually carried out the robbery..

"I walked in, pointed the pistol at the girl and said, 'Give us the money'". That is the robbery you see. "She just handed over some money to me. I just ran round a few corners. I tried a telephone box, etcetera.. I stayed in and around Birmingham for a week or so ..." -- this is the third point. We know in fact it was two weeks which is the correct period of time, whereas in that statement he put "a week or so". Then again the fourth point, "I think there was £4,300". It is said who on earth would admit to taking more than he had taken if he had done it, say the defence. I do not know what you make of that; it is a matter for you. Also finishing off with a fifth point, "... I had in tenners and fivers apart from three brand new £1 notes", when it is the fact in the case as I understand it, that there were 300, not 3, brand new £1 notes. "I know I've been stupid, what more can I say. I'm sorry."

Well it will be for you to decide where the actual truth lies about that statement. Of course when he had made that statement it was put to him, "I take it all the money that you have in your possession is from the robbery?". Answer: "Yes. Do you know I've spent over £1,000 in Ireland in a week just on booze. I must be bloody barmy." "Where is the gun now?". Answer: "It's in my room at Warwick Road".

He was told that later he would be charged and that knowledge of the gun would be passed on, and later that day he, P.C.Abolins, went to 155 Warwick Road and from Mr. Fisher's room he did take from underneath the bed Exhibit 5, that .38 'Chief' starting pistol, and also the blank cartridges that we have heard about which you see as part of the exhibit in the case.

You remember that it was D.C.Sutcliffe who was asked about the aspect of a solicitor being asked for by the defendant. He dealt with that. I need say no more really in outline as to those two officers' recollection of their interview with Mr. Fisher. As I say, you have to decide whether one or both of those police officers were honest witnesses, and if honest, reliable about matters which were after all fresh in their mind when they wrote up their notes together which is the normal course, and therefore able to be of use to them in refreshing their memory in their evidence which they gave to you in the witness box.

Now so far as the second written statement is concerned, it is really D.C.Pyke who deals with that matter. He had come from the airport, had D.C.Pyke. He had been to 155 Warwick Road. He told you about the pistol, the anorak, the hat and the plastic bags, the exhibits in the case, and we heard D.C.Butler telling us that several questions were asked about the different items that we have seen in this case and where they came from. D.C.Butler said -- this is to Mr. Fisher of course -- "Amongst your property which you had with you at the airport was a lot of new property; did you buy any of it with the stolen money?". Answer: "Yes". And then, "These two rings?" Exhibit 13. Answer: "Yes". "The watch?" Exhibit 14. Answer: "Yes". He gave the prices he had paid for these items. "This doll?", Exhibit 15. Answer: "Yeh I got that at the gift shop at Dublin airport." "This aftershave and other stuff?", which is Exhibit 16. "I got that in Galway". "With the stolen cash?" Answer: "Yes". "What about this holdall?", Exhibit 17. "Yeh I bought that in Woolworths in Galway. I also bought the air tickets to Dublin and back", Exhibit 18, and I said it was for two people but in fact it is for one person, a ticket each way.

Then D.C.Butler told Mr. Fisher, "We have brought all your belongings from your room in the hostel. Is there anything amongst this stuff which you have bought with the proceeds of the robbery?". Answer: "Yes, this suit I had it from Fosters in Newtown", and that is Exhibit 19. "How much was that?", that is the suit. "£39. Oh I also had that jacket (Exhibit 20) too from the same place and I had the radio (Exhibit 21) from a shop up Newtown." "Did you wear any of this clothing when you committed the robbery?". Answer: "I think I had that anorak on, yes I did". That is Exhibit 7. Question: "Anything else?". Answer: "Yes I had that hat on", Exhibit 8. Question: "The cashier says that you put the money in a plastic bag, where is that now?". Answer: "I used one of them two bags", pointing to Exhibit 9. Then he was asked if he wanted to make a further written statement and he said, "Yes", and it is then written down at Mr. Fisher's dictation and you see that at Exhibit 10. Again it is for you to decide what you make about that statement and how it helps you in your deliberations as to what the true facts in this case really are.

He went on, did D.C.Pyke, to say that the same day he took possession of £1358.07p, Exhibit 5, from D.C.Sutcliffe, and also the firing gun, Exhibit 4. That was kept by the police, and also on that date with D.C.Butler he had recovered from 155 Warwick Road a red woollen hat, Exhibit 8 , and a blue anorak, Exhibit 7, from a wardrobe, and two plastic bags that I have already dealt with from a chest of drawers so far as the plastic bags are concerned.

Members of the Jury, in outline that is the evidence in the case that you have heard, and you know that I am not going to/[go] through Mrs. Hales' evidence again. I dealt with that earlier when dealing with the motor car and the number thereof which was taken by Mr. Witham.. I do not know how much that assists you or not..

As I have said to you Members of the Jury, that is an outline of the evidence in this case. Please remember that it is possible that there are matters that you still have in your mind which you think are important perhaps and which I have not mentioned, and they are important if you think they are

Members of the Jury, when you come to retire to consider your verdict, do, as you consider each count, try to come to a verdict which is in fact the verdict of you all, a unanimous verdict on the particular count that you are considering. It may be that you have heard there are circumstances in which it is possible for me to accept a verdict from you which is not the verdict of you all.. Those circumstances have not arisen and until they do arise, if ever they arise, I need say no more about that. Please as I say, when you retire do your best in your deliberations to come to unanimous verdicts whatever way they may be -- guilty or not guilty on the particular count that you are considering, and I would suggest, with respect, that the first matter that you should deal with when you have retired is to elect one of your number to act as your foreman or forewoman in this case, because it is that person who will speak for you in due course.

You will go to your room very shortly now armed with the indictment -- copies of it -- and the various exhibits, and you will be given refreshment. I don't know what quality it will be, but you will be given some refreshment when you go out.

Mr. Jones, I think there are no exhibits that aren't relevant are there?

MR. JONES: Your honour I don't know to what extent the Jury will need the items that were purchased.

JUDGE RUSH: The rings and the radio and that sort of thing?

MR. JONES: That is right your honour. They can certainly have them if they wish; they have been shown. There is the gun and the money if they want it.

JUDGE RUSH: Yes, and the identikit picture of course.

MR. JONES: Oh I am sure. They already have the small copies of that on them. The large identikit picture your honour has suddenly disappeared.

JUDGE RUSH: I can see it from here.

MR. JONES: No, that is the identikit your honour. The actual picture that was done with the hat and the shading in of the lips, that has disappeared.

JUDGE RUSH: Yes. Is it there do you think, below the jacket?

MR. JONES: It is Exhibit 11b.

JUDGE RUSH: Yes. 11a, 11b and Exhibit 12.

MR. JONES: Yes, here it is.

JUDGE RUSH: It is the same one isn't it?

MR. JONES: Yes, it actually has a little label on.

JUDGE RUSH: Yes. Thank you.

THE CLERK: Jury bailiffs, you shall well and truly keep this jury in some private and convenient place. You shall not suffer any person to speak to them, neither shall you speak to them yourselves concerning this trial without leave of the Court, unless it be to ask them if they are agreed upon a verdict, so help you God.

USHERS: We will.

(The Jury retired to consider their verdict at 1.02 p.m.)

(The Jury bailiffs took exhibits into the Jury room).

MR. JONES: Your honour I think the brown jacket was one of the items purchased. It would only serve to confuse I think if that one went in since we have left all the other items behind.

JUDGE RUSH: Yes, I think that is right.

MR. JONES: The woolly hat I am sure.

JUDGE RUSH: You don't want them to have the watchamacallit?

MR. JONES: I don't want them to have the watchamacallit your honour. And the plastic bag.

JUDGE RUSH: Yes. Mr. Cox, I won't take a verdict in any event until 2.15.

MR. ESCOTT COX: Thank you very much your honour.

JUDGE RUSH: David Fisher will you stand please. The stage has been reached in the trial now that the Jury have gone out and your bail will not be enlarged. You understand the situation.. So you will go downstairs and you will get your lunch there.

USHER: Court please rise.

(The Court adjourned at 1.04 p.m.)

(The Jury returned into Court at 2.19 p.m.)

THE CLERK: Will the foreman please stand. Mr. Foreman will you please answer my first question either "Yes" or "No". Members of the Jury, have you reached a verdict upon which you are all agreed?

THE FOREMAN OF THE JURY: Yes.

THE CLERK: On the first count of this indictment, robbery, do you find the defendant, David Fisher, guilty or not guilty?

THE FOREMAN OF THE JURY: Guilty.

THE CLERK: On the second count of this indictment, possessing a firearm whilst committing an offence, do you find the defendant guilty or not guilty?

THE COREMAN OF THE JURY: Guilty.

THE CLERK: You find the defendant guilty on both counts, and that is the verdict of you all?

THE FOREMAN OF THE JURY: Yes.

ANTECEDENTS - Examined.

MR. JONES: Your honour I will call Mr. Pyke to give the antecedents.

JUDGE RUSH: Yes.

DETECTIVE CONSTABLE JOHN PYKE, Recalled.

Examined by Mr. Jones.

MR. JONES: Mr. Pyke you are already sworn in this case. Do you produce the antecedents of David Fisher?

A. I do sir, yes.

ANTECEDENTS OF THE ACCUSED, FISHER:

Q. Was he born in Birmingham on the 5th January 1947, so he is 34 years of age. I think he is eligible to an extended sentence but the notices have not been served?

A. Yes sir.

Q. Is he a single man and at the time of his arrest was of no fixed address. His parents it seems live on the outskirts of Birmingham and he is an only child?

A. Yes.

Q. Was he educated at a Secondary Modern School until he was 15?

A. Yes.

Q. Since leaving school and interspersed between custodial sentences has he had employments as a shop assistant in his father's ironmongery business, builders' labourer and casual worker?

A. Yes sir.

Q. Does he say that from April 1976 to June 1976 he was self-employed as a cafe proprietor?

A. Yes.

Q. Was he last released from a prison sentence on the 10th December 1979?

A. He was.

Q. Was he unemployed at the time of his arrest and in receipt of Social Security Benefits?

A. Yes.

Q. Was he arrested on the 19th March 1980 and was in custody for some time. When was he released on bail?

MR. TREACY: The 22nd July.

ANTECEDENTS - Examined.

MR. JONES: The 22nd July I understand. Has he previous convictions?

A. Yes.

JUDGE RUSH: I think you can start Mr. Jones in February 1972.

MR. JONES: Yes your honour. (To the witness). There were convictions in the early 1960's onwards with one prison sentence, and then in February 1972 for burglary, taking and driving away and driving whilst disqualified, was he sentenced to 30 months imprisonment?

A. Yes sir.

Q. That at the time being his second prison sentence?

A. Yes sir.

Q. In November 1973 for taking and driving away, going equipped for theft, driving whilst disqualified, dangerous driving, possessing an offensive weapon and assault on the police, was he sentenced to a total of 2 years imprisonment?

A. He was, yes sir.

Q. Then for loitering with intent and going equipped was he fined, and then in August 1976 for robbery, carrying a firearm, burglary, theft and taking a conveyance, was he sentenced to a total of 5 years imprisonment?

A. He was, yes sir.

Q. Have you the details of the offence of robbery and possessing a firearm?

A. Yes. The brief circumstances are that at approximately 6.30 p.m. on I believe it was the 2/7/76, with a male accomplice who Fisher refused to name, drove a vehicle to the Witton area of the city where he entered a bookmaker's office each brandishing one of the stolen guns. The accomplice kept watch. Fisher pointed the gun at the manageress and demanded money. He said that she would come to no harm if the money was handed over and he stole a wallet containing cash. He drove off in a stolen vehicle. £34 was stolen sir, and only £3 was recovered

MR. ESCOTT COX: No questions.

MR. JONES: Thank you Mr. Pyke. (The witness withdrew).

Your honour I ask for the normal order for costs out of central funds.

JUDGE RUSH: Yes. Have you anything to say about the pistol?

MR. JONES: Your honour I would ask for a restitution order for the money and I think the other matter will have to be subject to negotiation, but I ask for an order for forfeiture of the pistol.

PLEA IN MITIGATION.

JUDGE RUSH: Yes very well, and the costs of the prosecution to come out of central funds?

MR. JONES: Yes your honour.

JUDGE RUSH: Yes. Mr. Cox?

MR. ESCOTT COX: Your honour it is clear from looking at this man's antecedents and convictions which my learned friend has been careful not to adduce, that he obviously has a very serious drink problem. He has been before the courts, and one knows it is only on rare, exceptional and extreme occasions that people are arrested for drunkenness and drunk and disorderly. On many occasions since 1966 many of the convictions on this list are for just that offence, either being drunk and incapable or drunk and disorderly. I have not counted them up but I have put crosses by them and there are a great many. As your honour knows very well, when somebody has a drink problem unfortunately mere enforced absence of drink by way of a prison sentence does nothing to cure the basic craving.

Your honour it is perfectly clear that in this case he may have exaggerated to the police in what the jury have obviously accepted as being a true confession that he was three parts drunk, but it seems extremely likely that he had taken a good deal of drink, no doubt partly to get up the courage to commit this offence.

Your honour to what extent does that mitigate it. Not a very great deal but there are other factors which in my submission put this in an entirely different category to the normal armed robbery. The first thing, your honour, is that he had not actually got a real firearm. Whilst it is just as frightening in fact to the victim, the sense of public outrage must be a very great deal reduced if the victim was never in fact in any real danger, and your honour knows this is only a starting pistol quite incapable of inflicting harm other than fear upon anybody.

Your honour it was an incredibly amateur affair. It is astonishing really, and it has been almost a matter of amusement in the course of the case that he went in so blandly and went away so blandly and nobody as it were laying a hand upon him, and that he behaved in such an incredibly childish way thereafter and frittered away such of the money that he did fritter away in the strange way that he did in buying these almost worthless goods, -- the doll and so on and so forth. Nobody could accuse him of playing for high stakes and high living afterwards, and when one knows that his total possessions in life have been seized by the police and most of them brought into this court, if ever somebody has not profited by his few crimes of any sort of serious dishonesty it is surely this man.

Now in terms of fixing the penalty of course one accepts that society must protect itself by some sort of penalty. I ask your honour to take those matters into consideration and

PLEA IN MITIGATION.

say that this is really in quite a different category from the organised crime, whether it is only 2, 3, 4 or 5 men who go with real firearms to commit a robbery. They are playing for high stakes. Whether it is wages or a bank they expect to get away with large sums of money and live well from the proceeds. This is almost pathetic in comparison to that, and it is really within certain limits -- and I accept there must be certain limits -- in a very different category.

Your honour there is one other matter which carries much less weight because of his plea of not guilty, but it is nevertheless something I hope I can properly pray in aid, and it is that he was almost pathetically,-- childishly on the police evidence -- willing to confess his crime to the police, and that is a very strong indication, as your honour knows, of somebody who is not a true hardened professional criminal such as the ones who will insist on saying absolutely nothing to the police and maintaining complete silence.

Your honour, I hope as a result of all that and the fact that he has been at liberty for only such a short time, will enable your honour, whilst doing justice to the public as one appreciates your honour must do, to temper any sentence with a considerable amount of mercy.

JUDGE RUSH: Thank you very much Mr. Cox.

S E N T E N C E.

JUDGE RUSH: Now David Fisher, stand please. I take into account in your case that no physical violence as such was used in this robbery, and I take into account too that it was an imitation firearm that was used and not a live weapon, but you are 34 years of age and you are mature enough to know what you were doing. This robbery was a deliberate and premeditated robbery as shown by the use of the gun, and there is no mitigation to be obtained from your record.

The sentence of the court in this case on Count 1 of robbery is one of 5 years imprisonment, and for possessing the firearm whilst committing that offence, 3 years imprisonment, and those two sentences will run together, concurrently. Let him go down. (The defendant was taken from the dock).

JUDGE RUSH: Members of the Jury, thank you for your attention to this case. You are free to leave the Court when it rises very shortly, and you will be given further directions outside. Thank you very much indeed.

(The Court adjourned).

The following was taken after the close of the Court as a simulation of the defendant's evidence:-

MR. DAVID FISHER, Sworn.

Examined by Mr. Escott Cox.

MR. ESCOTT COX: Mr. Fisher remember to keep your voice up nice and loud so that his honour and the members of the jury can hear. What is your full name?

A. David Fisher.

Q. Mr. Fisher, at the time that you were arrested were you living at 155 Warwick Road, Birmingham?

A. Yes.

Q. Mr. Fisher you know the nature of the allegation against you which is that at about 3 o'clock on the 25th February you went into the Midland Bank in Hockley and held it up. Is that true; did you do that or not?

A. No sir.

Q. Can you now remember with any certainty what you were doing at about 3 o'clock on the 25th February?

A. Well it's hard to say, but I think I was visiting a friend of mine in some flats.

Q. What is the name of that friend, can you remember?

A. Jimmy Jackson.

Q. Do you know where Mr. Jackson is today?

A. Well he's had a bit of trouble with his head and he's in Hollymoor Hospital.

Q. Hollymoor Hospital, being treated for some mental illness as you say he has had some trouble with his head?

A. Well yes, since you put it that way.

Q. Alright. Now at the time of your arrest you were found in possession of a considerable amount of cash. Is it true first of all that you were unemployed at this time?

MR. D. FISHER,
Examined.

A. Yeh, yeh.

Q. Had you got any job at all, regular or otherwise?

A. Well I had done some casual decorating.

Q. Is that where the money had come from or from some other source?

A. Oh no, not from that.

Q. Where did this money come from that the police officers found on you when you returned to Birmingham Airport?

A. Well it's like this. I go drinking, sometimes to the local, the "Golden Arrow"; that's in the Warwick Road ....

Q. Don't run on too much; his honour is trying to take a note.

A. Sorry my lord. Anyway I go drinking, sometimes in the "Golden Arrow", and sometimes down the "Gothic".

Q. Now just pause there for a moment. Whereabouts in the city are those public houses?

A. Well the "Golden Arrow" is in the Warwick Road, Sparkbrook, and the "Gothic" is out Alum Rock way. I met this Paki in the "Gothic" and we got talking and had a few drinks, and he asked me back with him to play cards with some mates of his.

Q. Pause there for a moment. When you say "a Paki", what do you mean literally by that?

A. Well one of them darkies, a Paki, an Asian.

Q. From Pakistan?

A. Yes, yes.

Q. About how old would this man be?

A. About 30.

Q. About 30, yes. Now what happened after he had invited you back?

A. Well I went back and met some of his mates, and we played cards and he seemed to have a lot of money, and the first night we played I won. I'd got some money on me because I'd got my benefit, and I won the first night.

Q. Now just pausing here for a moment, it is clear from what you are saying you were playing cards for money?

A. Yes.

Q. What sort of game or games were you playing?

MR. D. FISHER,
Examined.

A. It's an Indian game called coluckie.
Q. What sort of stakes were you playing for?
A. £10 a game, but you can double up and .....
Q. Yes, alright. So you say on the first night you won. How much did you win on the first night?
A. About a hundred pounds on the first night.
Q. This is a nett profit. Did you lose at all?
A. Nett profit -- I don't understand you.
Q. Did you come away from the game a hundred quid richer than you went into it, or did you win £100 but lose £50?
A. Put it like this; I went there with 50 and came away with 150
Q. Well I think that answers my question. Was that the only time you played cards with him?
A. No, I went back the next night and there were some more people there, a couple of Greek blokes, and they seemed pretty flush and some other friends of his, and I won a lot of money. We played poker and I won six or seven hundred quid.
Q. Was that all on the second night that you won the six or seven hundred, or was that spread over several nights?
A. No, that was the second night.
Q. Did you play cards again or was that the end of it?
A. No.. Well they'd lost a bit and they said they wanted a chance to win their money back and we agreed to meet at the weekend. I went round there the Saturday afternoon and we had quite a long game and I won a lot of money then, over £2,000.
Q. Yes. Now when you say "there", are you able to give his honour the exact address where you went?
A. Well it's a room over a cafe in the Alum Rock Road. I don't know the name of the cafe but I'm sure I could take you there, you know.
Q. Do you know the number?
A. I don't know. I could find it.
Q. As you understood it, what association had the Pakistani gentleman with that cafe or those premises?
A. I think he knew the owner, and the owner just let him use the room above for gambling.

MR. D. FISHER,
Examined.

Q. Right. At any time did he tell you where he had got this money from?

A. Well not at first if you know what I mean but .....

Q. Did you press him about it at all?

A. Well I asked him how he had got quite a lot of money on him and always seemed to have money, and he said well he ran card games, but there was some talk in the cafe about a robbery at a bank and I heard a bit about it then like.

Q. I think you must tell us more than that.

A. Well I don't really want to get anyone else into trouble.

Q. You needn't worry about that. You have not mentioned any names or anything.

A. Well I don't know any names Mr. Cox.

Q. Alright. You just tell us what was said about a robbery at a bank.

A. Well this bloke said he'd been done for robbery before and a lot of the money that I'd won had come from a bank robbery, and I was curious and I got him to tell me about it.

Q. What did he tell you?

A. He said he'd gone to this bank near Canning's in Newtown, and gone in there and there weren't any customers he said, and there was a girl and a bloke behind the counter, and he said he'd gone in and pulled out a starting pistol and got away with several thousand pounds.

Q. Alright, just pause there for a moment. Do you remember if he ever said to you exactly how much it was he got away with?

A. It was over 4,000. 4,200 or 4,300 I think. Yes, 4,300.

Q. Did he ever tell you whether he wore any disguise or anything about his appearance when he went to the bank?

A. I think he told me he wore an anorak and some sort of hat or woolly thing on his head.

Q. Yes. Did you understand then that this money that you had won from him at gambling was the proceeds of that bank robbery?

A. He didn't say so in so many words but I had a pretty good idea.

Q. Did he ever mention to you how he got away from the bank; whether an alarm had been set or any details of that sort?

A. He said he'd run off but he had got out without any bother, and a mate of his was just down the street in a car and he jumped in and they drove off.

MR. D. FISHER,
Examined.

Q. Right. Now whenabouts -- was that before you had won the £2,000 on the third gambling session, or after you had won the £2,000, or during the session. Can you place that conversation in relation to winning the money?

A. It was on the third time, the time I won all the money, the £2,000, and it was during the course of the playing of the cards.

Q. Yes alright. One thing we do know for certain is that you bought an airline ticket on the 11th, on Tuesday the 11th March, and flew over to Dublin from Birmingham on the same day as you bought the ticket.

A. That's right.

Q. That is Exhibit 18. First of all how long before Tuesday the 18th was it that you won this money; can you remember?

A. Tuesday the 11th you mean.

Q. Tuesday the 11th, I am so sorry.

A. About 10 days. About 10 days.

Q. What was it that prompted you to fly off to Dublin?

A. Well I've got friends in Dublin and they'd asked me over for St. Patrick's Day, and I'd won this money and I thought I'd go and make a week or a fortnight of it.

Q. Did you take the money with you?

A. Yes.

Q. It is suggested that you said to the police you'd spent "over £1,000 on booze". Had you spent that sort of money on booze?

A. I spent a lot of money but not £1,000 on booze. I may have said something like that to the police but it's not literally true.

Q. Alright. Now when you came back to this country the police picked you up. Let me ask you first of all, were you aware that the police carry out a security check by way of anti-terrorism on passengers between Dublin and Birmingham?

A. Well you know they're always on the look-out at the airport.

Q. Did you do anything to conceal or disguise the £1,400 you were still carrying on you?

A. No.

Q. When the police did stop you what did you tell them?

A. I told them the truth; I'd won it gambling.

MR. D. FISHER,
Examined.

Q. Did they believe you?

A. No.

Q. And as we know you were arrested and taken to the airport police station which I believe is only what -- some 300 or 400 yards away from where you were arrested, is that right?

A. That is right, yes.

Q. When you were at the airport police station were you questioned by the officers?

A. I was yes.

Q. What did you tell them?

A. I told them I wanted to see my solicitor and I wouldn't answer any questions until they let me see my solicitor.

Q. Was that just once you mentioned that?

A. No, I kept on about it and they just laughed at me. They said I'd have to answer their questions first.

Q. What was their attitude towards you generally?

A. Well they said they didn't want no brief interfering.

Q. Will you please look at Exhibit 6. Have you got a copy in front of you?

A. Yes.

Q. There came a time when you made and signed that document, didn't there?

A. Yes. Well I didn't make it. I signed it.

Q. Well I will deal with how the words came to be on the paper in a moment, but whether they are your words or anybody else's, you acknowledged it by signing it?

A. Well I did sign it.

Q. Why did you sign that?

A. Well it was hopeless. I mean, they wouldn't let me see my brief or anything. They said, you know, I'd got to answer their questions and they said they'd turn over all my mates and make life difficult for people I knew, and I didn't want that to happen so I thought well I'll tell them what they want to know because I knew a bit about it from this Paki, and I thought I'll tell them what they want to know and I can prove my innocence later in court, so I thought it wouldn't do any harm to sign it. I know it sounds stupid now but that is what I thought at the time. I thought they'd keep me there

MR. D. FISHER,
Examined.

for ever and not let me see anyone.

Q. Where did the information come from that is written down in the statement about this bank robbery?

A. Well most of it came from the Paki.

Q. Yes, but when the actual statement came to be written, where was the information coming from?

A. Oh I see. Well I told them of course from what I knew from the Paki but ... yeh, that's right, yeh.

Q. Now I am not going to go through them one at a time but there are a number of things there which are quite different from the prosecution case. For example, the girl says that she was on her own, and in that statement it says that she was talking to another man, and the amount of money that has gone and so on. Were those deliberate mistakes on your part or were you just relating accurately what the Pakistani had told you?

A. Yes.

Q. Please, one or the other. Try and listen. Did you make any deliberate mistakes when you were giving your account of the matter?

A. Not deliberate mistakes, no, no.

Q. Then later, after your premises had been searched .....

A. Well it's more like a room but you know, a hostel.

Q. Yes alright. The police went to where you had been living and they found the starting pistol and a number of items. Is it true or false that the various items they put to you and you agreed that you bought with the money from the bank, do you agree that that took place -- like the radio for example, and the doll?

A. Oh yeh, yeh.

Q. Alright. Now so far as the starting pistol is concerned, two things arise over that. What was it doing in your possession at all; why had you got a starting pistol?

A. Well you see, I've got this girlfriend and she's got a little lad, and well I bought it for him. I thought it'd be a present for his birthday.

Q. Why didn't you give it to him?

A. Well I tried it out and it made such a loud noise I thought it might frighten him. He's only 8 you know, and I thought I'd better not give it him.

Q. And you were shown first of all the anorak, and then the woolly hat, and it is common ground that you told the police that you were wearing those articles when you committed the robbery?

MR. D. FISHER,
Examined.

A. Yes, that's right.

Q. Why did you say that?

Q. Well I said that because I hadn't done the robbery and I thought that would prove I was innocent.

Q. Did you know what it was suggested the real bank robber had been wearing. Did you know what anybody said he had been wearing?

A. No, not then, although I knew that the bloke at the cafe, like, had said he had worn an anorak and had a gun and had something on his head.

Q. Alright, yes. Very well.

<u>Cross-examined by Mr. Jones.</u>

MR. JONES: When was the little lad's birthday?

A. End of March.

Q. And when did you purchase the gun?

A. The first week in March.

Q. Why did you still have it in your possession?

A. Because you see, like I said, I'd won this money and I had bought the gun, and I just tried it you know, and it wasn't suitable really.

Q. Well why not throw it away or try and sell it back to the shop?

A. Well it never crossed my mind to take it back to the shop, and I'd paid good money for it, why should I throw it away.

Q. Why was it necessary to buy blanks for it?

A. So he could fire it.

Q. You didn't think that would make an excessive noise or anything like that; you thought that was a suitable present for a little 8-year old boy?

A. Well he likes the cowboys on the telly and I thought he and his mates could have some fun, and then when I tried it and saw what it was like I thought it wouldn't do.

Q. Where did you try it?

A. Out in the back garden.

Q. I just want to make it quite clear. You did absolutely nothing wrong at all; this is money you had simply won at cards?

A. Yes.

MR. D. FISHER,
Cross-examined.

Q. And you are not alleging that the police did anything improper at all are you?

A. No.

Q. And indeed, what you told them both at the airport police station and at Steelhouse Lane and what you signed in the statement, those were your words?

A. Yeh, yeh those were my words, yes. But they wouldn't let me see a solicitor.

Q. I understand that. Now it was a Pakistani -- I know you don't wish to disclose his name -- it was a Pakistani gentleman who robbed the bank?

A. Well yeh, Asian. He said he robbed a bank.

Q. Yes, quite. And you said, as I understand it, the only time you had met him was on these three occasions, is that right?

A. Yeh.

Q. And you didn't even know his name?

A. Oh, I called him Chief.

Q. But he wasn't a very good card player was he?

A. Well I struck lucky. It wasn't just him. I mean there was these Greek blokes and they're always flush with money.

Q. On these occasions you had won first of all £100, £600 to £700, and then £2,000. You were on a really lucky streak weren't you?

A. Yes, that's right. I mean, the reason I went back was because I thought I could beat them again, and they wanted to win their money back.

Q. Why didn't you go back to them when you were released on bail, because you still hadn't got a job and surely they would be a useful source of money.

A. Oh I see. Well I never thought of that.

Q. You never thought of it. You hadn't got a job?

A. No.

Q. And all the money you had won had been taken from you, and you hadn't got any particular accommodation had you?

A. No.

Q. So money at this stage was important to you?

MR. D. FISHER,
Cross-examined.

A. Yes it was. I was getting my Social.

Q. How much was that?

A. It was £50 a fortnight.

Q. That wasn't very much was it?

A. Well it's enough.

Q. Not to keep you in the manner to which you are accustomed if you can spend up to £1,000 on booze in Ireland?

A. Well that's when you've had a lucky win, isn't it.

Q. Why didn't you try to make some contacts to have another lucky win. Why didn't you go round to the cafe and try to make contact with your Pakistani friend?

A. I didn't want nothing to do with it when I found out, you know, I'd got into all this trouble over it.

Q. But when you were playing cards you knew where his money had allegedly come from?

A. Yes.

Q. And you didn't mind playing him for that money?

A. No.

Q. And the only reason you had got into trouble was because you had told the police all about it?

A. Yes, but I wasn't in trouble when I was playing at cards was I?

Q. No.

A. I told my solicitor about it.

Q. How were you going to get into more trouble by playing cards?

A. Well I thought it best not to get involved and I told my solicitor, Mr. Jonas, about it and, you know, left it up to him after that.

Q. Why didn't you try to contact him?

A. Well I told Mr. Jonas. I mean, that's his job isn't it.

Q. But you could show him where the cafe was.

A. I told him where; I told him where.

Q. Did you take Mr. Jonas to it?

A. No.

MR. D. FISHER,
Cross-examined.

Q. Well if you could tell Mr. Jonas, tell us please.

A. Well you go out the Alum Rock Road, and at the traffic lights with Heathfield Road there's the cafe.

Q. So you can actually pin-point it down to that extent?

A. Well I told Mr. Jonas.

Q. What was your great loyalty towards this Pakistani gentleman whom you had only met on three occasions. Why didn't you want to say anything against him?

A. Well you don't like to get people into trouble.

Q. Oh but Mr. Fisher, here you were in serious trouble on what you told the police. When you were first seen by the police all they wanted to know was where the money had come from.

A. Well I told them.

Q. Why couldn't you tell them the details you have told us?

A. Well like what?

Q. Like you won it playing cards at a cafe on the Heathfield Road and the corner of Alum Rock Road; that you had won it on three separate occasions; that it was an Asian gentleman from whom you had won it. That wouldn't have got anybody into trouble would it?

A. Your honour I tried to tell them I'd won it gambling and they said where, and I said in Birmingham, and I told them I'd won it gambling and they didn't want to know. They just laughed at me, and when I said I wanted a solicitor they said, "You wait. You tell us the truth."

Q. But that is not true is it Mr. Fisher?

A. They just didn't want to know your honour.

Q. Mr. Fisher that is not true is it, because you haven't challenged any of the conversation. Your initial idea was to tell the police you had won it gambling at cards in pubs. Why did you toll them that?

A. Well that's how it started wasn't it.

Q. The truth was you had won it over a cafe. Why did you have to tell them you'd won it in pubs?

A. Well I met this bloke in the "Gothic" like and we had a small game there, but I won the money over the cafe.

Q. Pubs. You said, "Here and there, I can't tell you where." Why couldn't you tell them where. You wouldn't have got anybody into trouble with that explanation would you?

MR. D. FISHER,
Cross-examined.

A. I could tell them.

Q. Why didn't you?

A. They didn't want to know; they didn't believe me.

Q. Talking about the "Gothic", you were actually in Great Hampton Street on the day of the robbery weren't you?

A. I don't think so.

Q. The "Gothic" public house, through your solicitors you served a notice of alibi didn't you?

A. Yeh, that's right.

Q. And tell us please where, according to that notice of alibi, you were shortly before the robbery?

A. Well, the "Gothic" is in Newtown.

Q. The "Gothic" is in Great Hampton Street.

A. Well, if you say so.

Q. No. Your notice of alibi says that.

A. Well let me see that. (Handed to the witness). Yes, that's what it says here. Great Hampton Street. I didn't know it was Great Hampton Street.

Q. And the bank is on the corner of Great Hampton Street and Well Street, so you were not only getting money later on from that bank, from the person who had apparently robbed it, but also at the time you were actually in the vicinity weren't you?

A. Well not at the time the robbery took place, but I was there, you know, that lunch time.

Q. When you were seen by the police ... you accept the police didn't know anything about this robbery until you told them, did they?

A. I don't know about that Mr. Jones.

Q. They were asking you where the money was from, weren't they. They weren't suggesting to you where it was from?

A. Well they asked me where I'd got the money.

Q. Yes. You volunteered it was from the bank in Hockley?

A. Oh I see what you mean. Yeh, yeh.

Q. Why was it necessary for you to do that?

A. Well because they wouldn't believe where I'd got it from.

MR. D. FISHER,
Cross-examined.

Q. But why lie when you could only put yourself into serious trouble?

A. Well it's like this. They said they were going to make things awkward for me and my mates and turn over their place.

Q. What justified your admitting a serious armed robbery when all that would have happened was that your friends would have been inconvenienced?

A. Well I just didn't want any bother for them. I mean you know what it's like when the police go round to your place and turn it all over, and I thought I'd just keep them away and I can prove I'm innocent afterwards because I didn't do it, so it's easy.

Q. No, it isn't that. You were the one who was telling them about the robbery Mr. Fisher.

A. Yes.

Q. They weren't suggesting anything to you?

A. No.

Q. So why, when you had got a perfectly innocent explanation, and when all that would happen was that your friends might be inconvenienced by being asked questions -- none of your friends could put you in any trouble -- why did you admit this serious offence?

A. Well like I'd got a pretty good idea where the money had come from, and I thought the police would probably be able to trace the notes and that, and I thought, you know, I'd tell them that's where it's come from because that's what I knew.

Q. But these were old notes you were winning.

A. Yes, but I hadn't thought about that. You still have markings and that don't you. You have banks and they mark the notes don't they.

Q. If you were winning from the Greeks as well, how on earth did you think the money might be traced back to the bank?

A. Well because most of the money I won was off the Paki wasn't it.

Q. So he really was a bit of a soft touch so far as gambling is concerned, yet you never went back to him?

A. I didn't go back to him. I told you why.

Q. Why couldn't you tell the police it was a Pakistani who robbed the bank?

A. They didn't want to know. I tried to tell them and they just didn't want to know.

MR. D. FISHER,
Cross-examined.

Q. They were interested about your account weren't they?

A. They were only interested in getting me to say where I'd got the money from.

Q. Weren't you a little surprised that this almost complete stranger was telling you about his robbery and the details of the robbery at the bank?

A. Not really. I mean when you meet blokes in pubs and, you know, get to meet them a few times and talk to them, they tell you all sorts of things about themselves.

Q. I see. The detail into which he went; what did he tell you about the robbery. Think please and tell us all the details.

A. Well he told me he had robbed a bank.

Q. What else?

A. He had a gun.

Q. Did he describe the gun?

A. He said it wasn't a real gun.

Q. So you didn't know it was a starting pistol?

A. Well no, I suppose not.

Q. Please don't look at your counsel.

A. Well I suppose not.

Q. So when you accepted that that was a gun that had been used, you had no idea that the one in your possession was exactly the same as the one described by the cashier. You didn't know that much detail so it was pure coincidence?

A. No, no, because in fact now you mention it, I think I'd mentioned the starting pistol I bought for my girlfriend's baby, and I think I did say to him that I'd got one to sell, and he said, "Well I've got one like that, I used it in the robbery." Yes, you've reminded me now, that's right.

Q. How did he know what yours was like?

A. I'd taken it along to the pub with me.

Q. Why?

A. To try and sell it.

Q. But I thought you were winning so much at cards you'd actually purchased it for that purpose?

A. Sorry, you've lost me there.

MR. D. FISHER,
Cross-examined.

Q. No, no, no. Your money for purchasing the gun was from the proceeds of your winnings; not to sell because you were short of money.

A. Yes, but we had three games, hadn't we, and I won the first time and it was then when I went out and bought the starting pistol.

Q. How were you able to describe the route you took from the bank?

A. How do you mean?

Q. You were able to tell the police you went down Well Street, through Stainsby Avenue, through some flats, past a garage to a telephone box, and the telephone box was out of order. Surely your Pakistani friend didn't tell you that, did he?

A. Well I asked him about it. I don't think I told the police the name of the street........

Q. Why on earth did you ask him about that?

A. Well I wanted to know how he had got away.

Q. Well running away would be sufficient. Why was it necessary to go into such detail even to saying that the telephone box was out of order?

A. He didn't go into any telephone box.

Q. So why did you add that?

A. So that I could show that I was innocent then, because he told me he ran down the street and got into a car and went off in the car.

Q. Exactly. According to your evidence, from what you tell us, he goes into great detail about the garage, the route, the flats and the broken telephone box.

A. Well yeh, so I could show I was innocent.

Q. But I thought you didn't deliberately put any mistakes into your statement. That is what you told your learned counsel.

A. Well I didn't understand what he was getting at.

Q. But he repeated the question to you Mr. Fisher, and you said, "No, I didn't put any deliberate mistakes into the statement"?

A. Well now you mention it I must have, because the Paki bloke told me he got into a car and drove off.

Q. You were able to describe that route because you were the one who robbed the bank, weren't you?

A. I was not.

MR. D. FISHER,
Cross - examined.

Q. You were the one who held up that unfortunate cashier?

A. No.

MR. ESCOTT COX: No re-examination your honour. Stand down Mr. Fisher.

That is the case for the defendant your honour.

11th February, 1981.

MR. JONES: Your honour I wonder if I may mention the case of David Fisher which your honour tried yesterday. At the end of the trial I should have asked for a Restitution Order not only in respect of the money but also in respect of the property that the defendant had in his possession which he admitted had been purchased with the proceeds of the robbery, because that is clearly traceable from the stolen money.

JUDGE RUSH: Yes.

MR. JONES: And your honour I would ask for that Order. I think your honour did order forfeiture of the gun in any case.

JUDGE RUSH: Yes I did. I have that in my note here. Very well, I make that Order.

MR. JONES: Thank you your honour, although what the Midland Bank are going to do with a doll that wets and cries real tears I am not sure!

---

8 COMMENTS ON THE ENGLISH CRIMINAL JURY TRIAL

The English approach to criminal justice from arrest of the accused on suspicion through rules governing appeal strongly favors the prosecution. The system may fairly be described as a well-oiled, cost-efficient, prosecution-oriented machine. Speaking generally, solicitors are not permitted to interfere with police interrogation. Failure by the police to obey rules and laws governing interrogation and search and seizure will rarely result in evidence being treated as inadmissible. Police interrogation is extremely effective, resulting in the introduction of a written or oral admission or confession in roughly 64 percent of all contested trials in the Crown Court. The effect that evidence elicited by the police during interrogation from an accused has upon the rate of guilty pleas is self-evident. Not surprisingly, 92 percent of all defendants plead guilty in the Magistrates' Court, while 60 percent of those committed for trial in the Crown Court also plead guilty.

The legal machinery prior to trial, from initial appearance to arraignment, is simple, quick, and cost efficient. The police prepare statements of witnesses and provide them to the defense prior to the uncontested Section 1 committal. The police also freely disclose exhibits to the accused. In turn, the accused provides a Notice of Alibi defense. Only the police see witnesses for the prosecution prior to trial. Legal executives employed by defense solicitors interview the accused and take statements from defense witnesses. Rarely does anyone on the defense side attempt to interview a prosecution witness. Neither the prosecuting solicitor's office nor the defense solicitor employs private investigators.

The image of a well-oiled, cost-efficient, prosecution-oriented machine of justice applies with equal force at trial. Summary trials before magistrates tend to be short and to the point. The result is a 75 percent conviction rate. Considering that as many as 40 percent of the 25 percent of trials resulting in an acquittal stem from the inability of the prosecution, for a combination of reasons,[1] to produce evidence constituting a prima facie case, the percentage of convictions at the Magistrates' Court approaches 85 percent. The structure of the Crown Court trial has been examined in depth. The Crown Court has a 53 percent conviction rate,[2] which rises to over 67 percent after accounting for acquittals ordered by the court and directions by the court to the jury to acquit.[3] A high conviction rate in the Crown Court should be expected with respect to serious crime. Not only does the presence of incriminating statements in 64 percent of all contested cases favor the prosecution, but, when compared with American trials, every English variation except one tends to facilitate a conviction. These variations include:

1. Placement of the accused in the dock.
2. Placement of counsel next to each other.
3. Wigs and robes worn by counsel.
4. Counsel's inabiity to leave his assigned location during trial.
5. Lack of voir dire.
6. Lack of prosecution witness interviewing by the defense.
7. Day-before perusal of the Brief.
8. Lack of meaningful communication between counsel and the defendant.
9. Permitting police officers to read from their notes in open court.
10. Inability of counsel to seriously attack the character of prosecution witnesses without opening the door to use of prior convictions of the accused to impeach.
11. Lack of recross-examination.
12. Placement of defendant's opening speech following the close of the prosecution's case in chief.
13. Summary of evidence and comment upon credibility being included in the court's summation to the jury.
14. Defining reasonable doubt as "satisfied that you are sure."
15. The absence at all stages of the trial of an emphasis upon the presumption of innocence, the burden of proof resting upon the prosecution, and the concept of proof beyond reasonable doubt.
16. The overall detachment exhibited by defense counsel.

The one factor operating in favor of the accused is the prohibition in practice against use of the accused's prior convictions to impeach credibility. As a result, defendants testify in approximately 95 percent of all Crown Court trials. The importance of this factor to the outcome of the trial can be appreciated by considering that the Chicago jury study indicated that, when a defendant's criminal record is known and the prosecution's case has contradictions, the defendant's chances of conviction are 65 percent, as compared to a 38 percent rate when the conviction is not known.[4] Accordingly, assuming cases having contradictions, a fair assumption with respect to most cases actually tried, and a defendant testifying free from impeachment by means of his prior convictions, in England one could expect roughly a 38 percent conviction rate, not the nearly 64 percent conviction rate observed. It is suggested that the sixteen factors listed above account for much of the variation between what would be expected and what is observed.

There are many individual aspects and broad approaches exemplified in the English criminal justice system worthy of in-depth exploration and analysis by those concerned with the continuing breakdown of law and order in the United States. We should commend the emphasis in England on simple, speedy, effective, and cost-efficient procedures and rules capable of being understood and applied by those responsible. Of even more importance is the recognition in England that the criminal justice system, including questions of pre-trial procedure, trial procedure, and evidence, must be considered as an integrated whole and that this integrated criminal justice system must exist separate and distinct from systems designed to govern the trial of civil cases. The importance of separating criminal justice from civil disputes, of considering criminal justice from arrest through appeal as an integrated system, and of having laws, rules, and procedures applicable throughout the criminal justice system that are simple, cost-efficient, and capable of being understood by those charged with their application will be explored in the next chapter, "Tightening the Reins of Justice in America."

There exist four practices in England referred to directly or indirectly earlier that merit special consideration at this time, either because of their inherent interest or because they form a necessary bridge to consideration of reform in America. The first two practices, the lack of discretion to dismiss and the question of "verballing," are both addressed in the 1981 Report of the Royal Commission on Criminal Procedure.

Regarding discretion to dismiss, the system in current operation requires court action to dismiss a prosecution once the accused is charged by the police. Thus, even if both the police and the prosecuting solicitor believe that the evidence that can actually be produced at trial is insufficient for any reason to constitute a prima facie case, only a judge's approval can remove the case from the court's docket. In 1978, 40 percent of the acquittals at the Magistrates' Court resulted from an inability of the prosecution to present a prima facie case. In the same year, judges ordered 19 percent of all acquittals in the Crown Court prior to the jury being sworn on the representation of the prosecution that it would offer no evidence. Another 24 percent of all acquittals at the Crown Court resulted from directions by the judge to the jury to acquit on the grounds that a prima facie case was not established. In some such instances, the evidence gathered by the police never constituted a prima facie case; the police should never have charged the accused. In many others, what once was a prima facie case evaporated, either at or before trial, when a witness became unavailable or failed to testify in a satisfactory manner, referred to as failing to come up to proof. The Report of the Royal Commission recommends that the prosecuting solicitor have the discretion, without obtaining court approval, to proceed with, modify, or withdraw charges levied against an individual by the police pending before either the Magistrates' Court or the Crown Court.

The question of "verballing," or police fabrication of an oral confession or admission of the accused, is intimately tied up with broader issues surrounding the rights given to suspects questioned by the police and the admissibility of evidence acquired in breach of such rights. The recommendations of the Royal Commission on Criminal Procedure are disappointing with respect to the Judges' Rules concerning questions of enforcement of the right to have a solicitor present and admissibility of statements taken in breach of the Judges' Rules. The Royal Commission advocated no significant change in current practice. It recommended neither the appointment of a solicitor for every defendant at the interrogation stage nor exclusion of statements obtained in breach of the Judges' Rules. In fairness to the Royal Commission, as noted in its report, the resource implications inherent in any true scheme of representation and enforcement of rights were such as to be beyond the willingness of the members of the Royal Commission. As everyone knew, the Conservative government which appointed the Royal Commission was committed to reduce public spending, not to increase it.

The report takes a more positive approach with respect to the narrower question of discouraging "verballing" by recommending steps to ensure accuracy of reporting:

> If some sort of contemporaneous record has not been made or if a suspect does not elect to make a written statement under caution, it should become the practice for the interviewing officer at the end of the interview and in the suspect's presence to note down in writing the main relevant points made during the interview. These should be in summary form and should contain not only admissions or damaging statements but also denials; the summary might also include any remarks made to the police officer outside the police station or before caution. The summary should be read over to the suspect, who should be invited to offer corrections and additions to it if he wishes and also to sign it. If there were another independent person present, as, for example, when a juvenile is interviewed, or the suspect's legal adviser is available, as, on our proposals, it is more likely he will be than at present, that person might also be invited to sign it, if he accepts it as a fair and accurate summary. We recognize that if a suspect has chosen not to make a written statement he may very well be disinclined to sign such a summary. Nonetheless we believe that what we propose represents an improvement over the present practice. Under this the suspect neither signs the officer's record of the interview which is made up after the event nor knows, until sometime afterwards, precisely what goes into it; and the note tends to be represented as a verbatim account rather than as what it is, the

officer's recollection of and report on the main relevant points made. Making the summary should generally take no more time than taking a written statement and would replace the time taken on making up the note of the interview after the event. It would have the advantage for both the police and the suspect of being written much closer than at present to the time of the interview and with both parties to the interview present and aware of its content.

While rejecting a proposal on "a cost and benefit basis" to require the tape recording of the entire interrogation of all suspects, the report did make the following recommendation:

It should become general practice for an interview to be concluded (if there is no written statement) with the officer summarising orally the main points made and at the same time recording them in writing; this could and should include any points made outside the police station. We recommend that that process and, where there is one, the taking of a written statement, should be recorded on tape, with the consent and knowledge of the suspect. He should also be invited to offer his comments upon how he has been treated and, if there is a summary, his comments upon it. The offer made to him and his refusal or acceptance should be recorded. All this would be done openly.

It is important to stress that the Report of the Royal Commission on Criminal Procedure, the twelve research studies commissioned by the Royal Commission, the support document entitled "Investigation and Prosecution of Criminal Offences in England and Wales: The Law and Procedure," and the Summary of the Report, for all their difficulties, present truly worthwhile reading to anyone interested in reform of the American criminal justice system.[5] The work of the Royal Commission on Criminal Procedure evidences a comprehensive approach to many of the problems facing the criminal justice system in England. What is important from the perspective of the American reformer with respect to this particular report is not so much its recommendations as the comprehensive, coordinated approach taken to balance the rights of the accused and the needs of society.

The Report of the Royal Commission on Criminal Procedure did not address either of the remaining two practices of special concern relating to the criminal jury trial in England. The reason for this is obvious. In each instance it is perfectly clear that, unlike "verballing" and the discretion to dismiss, the Royal Commission perceived no problem with current practice. The first practice concerns the English approach to the burden of proof required to be satisfied by the prosecution in a criminal case, the concept of guilty beyond a reasonable doubt. The English approach to defining and communicating to the jury the importance of the concept of guilty beyond a reasonable doubt is not only inherently interesting but also serves to illustrate the difference in approach taken in the two countries to the relationship between the concept of a fair trial and rigorous legal analysis.

Cross on Evidence, the leading evidence text, succinctly analyzes the state of affairs in England with respect to defining the burden of proof resting upon the prosecution in a criminal case:

In 1949 Lord Goddard, C.J., said:

"Once a judge begins to use the words 'reasonable doubt' and to try to explain what is a reasonable doubt and what is not, he is much more likely to confuse the jury than if he tells them in plain language, 'It is the duty of the prosecution to satisfy you of the prisoner's guilt.' "

He returned to this theme in *R. v. Summers*, but his words were much stronger as they amount to a prohibition on the use of the phrase "reasonable doubt" by trial judges when summing up in criminal cases: He said:

"If the jury is told that it is their duty to regard the evidence and see that it satisfies them so that they can feel sure when they return a verdict of guilty, that is much better than using the expression 'reasonable doubt' and I hope in future that that will be done."

Lord Goddard subsequently indicated that his objection to the old formula was the difficulty of following explanation of what does, and does not, constitute a reasonable doubt. He thought that no real guidance is afforded by saying it must not be a fanciful doubt, and to say it must be such a doubt as would make jurymen hesitate in their own affairs does not suggest any particular standard because one juryman might hesitate where another would not do so. In another case Lord Goddard said:

"Let us leave out of account, if we can, any expression such as 'giving the prisoner the benefit of the doubt.' It is not a question of giving the benefit of a doubt; if the jury are left with any degree of doubt whether the prisoner is guilty, then the case has not been proved."

An appeal founded on the ground that the trial judge had not told the jury to give the accused the benefit of the doubt was dismissed in *R. v. Blackburn* where a direction which did not more than stress the point that the jury must be satisfied of the accused's guilt was approved. In *R. v. Murtagh and Kennedy*, on the other hand, an appeal was allowed because the summing up had not made it sufficiently clear that the jury must acquit if they were left in doubt concerning the accused's explanation of the facts. In *R. v. Hepworth and Fearnley* an appeal was allowed on the ground that a direction to the effect that the jury must be satisfied of the accused's guilt was inadequate when the charge was one of receiving. The judgment of the Court of Criminal Appeal was delivered by Lord Goddard, C.J.:

"One would be on safe ground if one said in a criminal case to a jury: 'you must be satisfied beyond reasonable doubt,' and one could also say, 'you the jury, must be completely satisfied,' or better still, 'you must feel sure of the prisoner's guilt.' "

In spite of this approval of three different ways of saying the same thing, including the reference to the time-honoured standard of proof beyond reasonable doubt, the Court of Criminal Appeal and the Court of Appeal have had to express their disapproval of the trial judge's summing up concerning the standard of proof in a number of subsequent cases, and similar difficulties have been experienced in other common law jurisdictions.[6]

In the case of David Fisher, the court instructed the jury that they must "feel sure of guilt" to return a verdict of guilty. The term "beyond a reasonable doubt" was not mentioned. In probably a majority of trials, the jury is instructed with a fourth standard emanating from *Regina v. Summers*[7] that they must be "satisfied that they are sure of the defendant's guilt" in order to convict.

The fact that there are four approved instructions to the jury in defining the prosecution's burden of proof, that each of the four is unlikely to have the same effect upon the jury, and that the definition considered "still better" by Lord Goddard of "you must feel sure of the prisoner's guilt" is probably a lower standard in the minds of a jury than what was originally meant by "beyond a reasonable doubt" has gone unnoticed. If one assigned percentages of certainty to the burdens of persuasion as used in America, "more probably true than not true" would be 50+ percent, "clear and convincing" would be around 75 percent, and "beyond a reasonable doubt" would be 90-95 percent. If one attempted to slot "sure" into these percentages, it is very doubtful that such a burden of proof could be said to exceed 75 percent. On another and probably more important level, it simply sounds easier to be convinced that one is sure than to be convinced beyond a reasonable doubt.

What is important is not whether "sure" is in actuality less than "beyond a reasonable doubt," but that it is certainly arguable that it is so. Yet nobody in England seems to care; all four approved instructions are accepted without dispute as equivalent. Why?

One reason is that the type of rigorous analysis of legal concepts applied to the trial of lawsuits in America is not often undertaken in England, and when undertaken is usually not performed well at all. If one looks at the English approach to burden of proof, judicial notice, presumptions, hearsay, and so forth, it becomes obvious that the analytical development of these concepts which has occurred in the United States during this century has not occurred in England. To illustrate, consider the quotation from *Cross on Evidence* relating to differing "degrees of proof":

> It will be submitted that there are no more than two standards of proof recognised by the law, but allowance must be made for the fact that certain occurrences are antecedently more improbable than others. People are less likely to commit murder than to drive recklessly, less likely to be fraudulent than negligent. The consequence is that prosecutors on the more serious criminal charges and plaintiffs in some civil cases have more hurdles to surmount than when they are making less serious allegations. This led DENNING, L. J., to speak of degrees of proof within the same standard:
>
> "It is of course true that by our law a higher standard of proof is required in criminal cases than in civil cases. But this is subject to the qualification that there is no absolute standard in either case. In criminal cases the charge must be proved beyond reasonable doubt, but there may be degrees of proof within that standard. . . . So

also in civil cases the case must be proved by a preponderance of probability, but there may be degrees of probability within that standard. The degree depends on the subject-matter. A civil court, when considering a charge of fraud, will naturally require for itself a higher degree of probability than that which it would require when asking if negligence is established. It does not adopt so high a degree as a criminal court, even when it is considering a charge of a criminal nature; but still it does require a degree of probability which is commensurate with the occasion."

The point was put more succinctly by MORRIS, L. J., when he said:

"Though no court and no jury would give less careful attention to issues lacking gravity than to those marked by it, the very elements of gravity become a part of the whole range of circumstances which have to be weighed in the scale when deciding as to the balance of probabilities."[8]

Ask yourself, are the positions advanced by Morris, Denning, and Cross expressed clearly? Are the positions advanced consistent? If not, which position is most correct? Why is the leading text in England on the subject of evidence only 669 pages, while Wigmore on *Evidence* is ten volumes and major treatises on the Federal Rules of Evidence are five volumes each?

No simple answer explains why the law in England with respect to trial practice lacks the rigorous analysis found in the United States. Probably the most important factor is one of attitude. The English hold themselves out to be fair and capable of fairness. Decisions by reasonable men can accommodate the interests of disputants at the time of the dispute. It thus becomes unnecessary to attempt in advance to account for all contingencies, to identify and precisely articulate concerns, or to require procedures that address the appearance of impropriety rather than its reality. In their place stands the notion that, given basic principles of justice, a fair man can come to a fair result once apprised of the facts. Accordingly, business agreements in England are shorter than in America. Concern is with basic principles, referred to as heads of agreement, not minute details. English solicitors would hardly negotiate with great zeal a clause defining the rights of the parties in case of condemnation to a three-year lease in a new building on Sixth Avenue in New York. New York attorneys would take this seriously, but not the English solicitor, whose attitude would be that fair men could and would resolve the question justly when it arose if it ever arose.

This sense of fairness, based on the interest and capacity of individuals to be fair if given the basic facts, has many implications concerning the jury trial we have been examining. It is directly related to the fourth and last practice of particular concern—the apparent detachment, lack of interest, and lack of aggressiveness displayed by counsel. Because of the nature of the criminal jury trial, this detachment is more significant when displayed by counsel for the accused. Undoubtedly in comparison with American defense attorneys, the jury does not feel the presence of the defense barrister in the trial. How the concept of fairness interacts in the criminal justice system with the structure of the trial, the concept of a divided profession, and the absence of rigorous legal analysis to create this appearance of detachment is extremely difficult to pinpoint. All that can reasonably be attempted is to describe the resultant interplay of these relevant considerations, as exhibited by the barrister in the criminal jury trial.

The English criminal jury trial to a marvelous extent keeps its eye on the ball—the guilt or innocence of the accused. The trial unfolds as a search for truth in the same sense that a parent faced with two screaming children goes about determining who started the fight. The parent asks one child what happened and then asks the other for his version of the event. In the process of recitation, each child interrupts the other asserting that what is being said is untrue, the equivalent of challenging the witness on cross-examination. The barrister may be viewed as one assisting each child in presenting his version of the events. The parent, like the jury, having heard both sides tell their story, decides who is right.

In representing his client, the barrister rarely acquires the role of the aggressive advocate assumed most frequently by defense counsel in the United States. Generally speaking, the barrister representing the accused in England, unlike the defense attorney representing the defendant in America, does not proceed upon the notion that his function is to obtain an acquittal by enforcing each and every rule applicable to the trial in the hope that the prosecution will falter. Nor does the defense barrister consider it proper to interject irrelevant matters into the case to confuse the jury, to require witnesses testifying as to uncontested matters to appear in court, to object to break the flow of damaging testimony, to turn the trial into an accusation against the complainant or the police where not called for clearly by the evidence, or to ask the jury to try the prosecutor, the judge, or society rather than the accused. Moreover, the defense barrister does not consider it his function to attempt to convince the trier of fact that the accused must be innocent by selling himself and his relationship with the accused to the jury, to consciously build into the trial error to be argued on appeal, or to seek with great intensity a hung jury on the theory that a hung jury is, in most instances, the functional equivalent of an acquittal.

In its place, the defense barrister adopts the overall stance that, notwithstanding the prosecutor's burden of proof, the accused should normally put forth his contentions as to the relevant matters of the case, leaving it for the jury to determine whether they are "satisfied that they are sure" of his guilt after hearing both versions of the relevant events. Accordingly, the accused testifies in roughly 95 percent of the jury trials in the Crown Court. As evidenced by the trial of David Fisher, the burden of proof is mentioned, but not stressed. The absence of voir dire and the timing of the opening speech by defense counsel reduces the opportunity to stress reasonable doubt before the jury. Fisher's counsel in his closing speech merely mentioned the burden of proof; he did not elaborate on it or make it the theme of his closing speech, as defense attorneys commonly do in trials in the United States.

The barrister thus seeks to have the case decided on the contested facts very much as does the parent of the two fighting children. The barrister asks the jury to act like the parent of the fighting children and inflict punishment only if it is sure which version of the story is true. The barrister seeks a fair determination, not an unjust victory. It is thus to be expected that, in comparison to the American defense attorney, the barrister appears detached and uncommitted to the cause of his client.

Incidents associated with the divided profession serve to reinforce both the appearance and actuality of counsel's detachment. Barristers usually prepare the case solely during the evening before trial. Each reads his Brief, consisting mostly of witness statements submitted at the Section 1 committal. Neither speaks to any witness other than experts prior to trial, except that the defense barrister normally confirms the accused's position with respect to disputed facts during a conference with him immediately before trial. Counsel often resolve matters concerning admissibility of evidence prior to trial. The Briefs tell counsel little about the background of the witnesses or the witnesses' ability to acquire the personal knowledge stated and even less about other possible avenues of impeachment. Almost never will the barrister have himself visited the scene of the crime. Combined with the rules relating to challenge and imputations of character, cross-examination of prosecution witnesses often amounts to little more than defense counsel putting the accused's story to the witness to be denied. Cross-examination of defense witnesses often amounts to little more than prosecution counsel putting the Crown's contentions to the witness to be denied.

The structure of the trial itself adds greatly to the impression of detachment. The opposing barristers are located next to each other wearing identical wigs and robes. Because the accused sits in the dock at the rear of the courtroom, the jury never sees him communicate directly with his counsel. There is no voir dire, and thus no opportunity for defense counsel to ingratiate himself and his client with the jury. Defense counsel's opening speech, if permitted, takes place after the close of the prosecution's case in chief and after defense counsel has already been obliged to put the accused's case to prosecution witnesses. Immediately following defense counsel's closing speech, the court in its summation summarizes the evidence and may comment on the credibility of witnesses. Any attempt by counsel in his closing speech to distract the jury from the matter truly at hand or to improperly characterize the evidence will be dealt with harshly by the judge in his summing up.

Contrast the image of the barrister with that often exhibited by defense attorneys in the United States—the defense attorney who puts the state to its proof on all issues, never stipulating to anything or agreeing that witness statements dealing with uncontested matters may be read; the defense attorney who stresses the presumption of innocence and the burden of persuasion on the prosecution to establish each and every element of the offense beyond a reasonable doubt during voir dire, opening, and closing and who insists on such concepts being fully explored once again in the court's instructions on the law; the defense attorney who objects to anything objectionable, and to many questions and exhibits that are not: the defense attorney who frequently attempts to interject extraneous matters in the hope of creating a reasonable doubt in the minds of the jury; the defense attorney who, at all stages of the trial, sells himself and his apparent but often unreal belief in the innocence of his client to the jury; the defense attorney who seeks an acquittal, not a fair determination of guilt or innocence.

An interesting question arises as to why, in England, barristers representing the accused do not become more aggressive in their examination and speeches and more demanding of change in the structure of the trial itself. If securing a high acquittal rate were paramount to the defense barrister, more aggressive advocacy would be observed, and demands for changes in trial practice such as permitting voir dire examination, permitting the accused to sit near counsel, and permitting the defense to make an earlier opening speech would have been heard. It is clear, however, that securing acquittals is not the principal objective of the defense barrister. Nor is the objective to any great extent one of putting on a good show in defeat, as it is for many privately retained defense counsel in the United States.

What is the objective of defense counsel if it is not simply winning or putting on a good show? Is it merely a search for the truth for the sake of truth? It is suggested that it is too idealistic and unreal to ascribe the restraint and detachment exhibited by defense barristers solely to a search for justice. If not solely truth, what else? It has been said that barristers try their cases to obtain the approval of the presiding judge. This claim is difficult to evaluate. On the one hand, the barristers observed and consulted in Birmingham expressed no greater respect for members of the judiciary or ambition to join their ranks than attorneys of similar age and experience in the United States. On the other hand, the power of the English trial judge to influence the outcome of the trial through various means, including the questioning of witnesses as well as the tone and content of his summing up, clearly makes it disadvantageous to have the judge take a personal dislike to a barrister. The difficulty in securing reversals on appeal on the basis of errors committed by the court further inhibits counsel taking any action likely to irritate the trial judge. The fact that the same trial judge sits in civil cases in bench-only trials adds to the chilling effect. Finally, social pressure is placed upon counsel to conform by virtue of the judiciary being senior members of the Inns of Court. Thus, on balance, it is probably fair to say that the desire of the court to have the trial proceed in the customary civilized manner results in counsel exercising more restraint than otherwise might prevail.

Other factors are also at work. The division of the bar leading to barristers preparing cases for trial in civil or criminal cases, motions, and pleas in mitigation each night for the next day requires that all court proceedings be conducted in a steady, low-key manner. Barristers for the most part work alone; the hordes of young associates available to the litigating partner in large American law firms are not available to the barrister. Any preparation in criminal cases must be done either by the barrister, by the Crown Court assistant, or by the legal executive. Moreover, lawyers, like everyone else, cannot maintain a fever pitch day after day, year after year. For the barrister to appear in court as often as he does necessitates accommodations between counsel. Evidence must be capable of being offered with a minimum of foundation, and cross-examination must be simple and straightforward. Counsel for the prosecution frequently has little time for anything but to become sufficiently familiar with the facts to make an opening statement and lead the witnesses through their statements. Counsel for the defense has little time to do anything but prepare to put the accused's version of the facts to prosecution witnesses on cross-examination and to prepare a well-reasoned closing speech. Neither counsel has time to develop a profile of ideal jurors, to explore the factual basis of potential areas of cross-examination not obvious from the witness's statement, or to research the law in support of an objection to the admissibility of evidence. Each counsel is assisted by the conciliatory attitude toward resolving questions of admissibility and the almost casual handling of exhibits. Each counsel is assisted by conditional witness orders, which permit the reading of uncontested evidence in the form of a witness statement to the jury.

Moreover, there is job satisfaction in being a barrister for the accused. Many defendants are acquitted. Not as many receive acquittals as might be anticipated with more aggressive representation, but there are many acquittals nonetheless. In addition, unlike many defense attorneys in the United States, the English barrister understands the importance of his plea in mitigation in connection with sentencing. Barristers and solicitors alike consider it a personal triumph when they are able to secure a fair, if not favorable, sentence for their client considering all of the surrounding circumstances.

In searching for reasons underlying the restraint and detachment exhibited by defense barristers, it is extremely important to realize that tomorrow is a new day, and that today's defense barrister will be tomorrow's prosecutor. With the exception of a few barristers, principally in London, who represent only the prosecution, and even fewer who only appear for the defense, barristers appear for both the prosecution and the defense. These same barristers also appear in civil matters for both the plaintiff and the defendant. Unlike the criminal defense attorney in America, who either wins representing the accused or not at all, the barrister in England knows that tomorrow he will be presenting the prosecution's case opposed by another barrister acting in the same way as he did today. Each barrister knows that only if each barrister acts in accordance with expected tradition, taking into consideration the plight of a brother at the bar, will each be able to carry on in the manner to which each is accustomed. Finally, the fact that the relatively few barristers in England are grouped together in chambers, where an officer's club attitude prevails, certainly serves to restrain counsel from taking any action in court that will embarrass a fellow barrister and thereby raise the level of hostility among barristers.

NOTES

1. For discussion of the reasons for dismissal, see page 230 infra.
2. Nearly 11 percent of all convictions in the Crown Court are by majority verdict.
3. For discussion of the reasons for ordered and directed acquittals, see page 230 infra.
4. Kalven and Zeisel, *The American Jury* 160 (Chicago: University of Chicago Press, 1966).
5. Careful consideration should be given to the commission of research studies aimed at specific areas where additional descriptive or empirical information would be of assistance to any group charged with the formulation of proposals to reform the criminal justice system in America.
6. At 112-13 (1979) (footnotes omitted).
7. [1952] 1 ALL E.R. 1059.
8. At 111 (1970) (footnotes omitted).

9 TIGHTENING THE REINS OF JUSTICE IN AMERICA

THE PROBLEM

In the United States during the last twenty years, in every contested election from councilmen to president of the United States, the public has been subjected to campaign promises that, if elected, the candidate will do something about rising crime in our streets. Today we still hear politicians, from councilmen to the president, vigorously asserting the need to curb crime in the streets. Today's politicians have been joined by many members of the judiciary, the most outspoken of whom is Chief Justice Burger. Yet speeches by judges and politicians, whether before the League of Women Voters, a labor union national meeting, the National Chamber of Commerce, or the American Bar Association, do nothing to actually control crime.

This is not to say that elected officials have not taken action. More policemen have been hired, and training has been improved. More judges have been appointed and courtrooms built to try offenders caught by the police. More prosecutors and public defenders have been hired. More prisons have been built. Job training programs have been expanded both in prison and in the community. Recreation areas have been built in slum neighborhoods. The number of social workers and welfare programs has increased dramatically. Yet the crime rate has continued to rise.

At all levels of government, legislative bodies have revised the substantive criminal law. Changes in the definition of crimes and the alternative permissible penalties have undoubtedly been enacted to demonstrate concern, for all politicians must know after many years of such manipulation that their actions have little or no effect on crime. Congress also acted in another way—a way with which it is all too familiar. It decided to attack the problem of crime by spending large amounts of money. Of course, it also had to set up a huge bureaucracy to administer the spending of such a large sum. The project, the Law Enforcement Assistance Administration (LEAA), lacked direction and purpose. After many years, Congress finally recognized LEAA as a waste of the taxpayer's money and abandoned it.

If the rise in crime in the streets is to be curtailed, elected officials and members of the judiciary must expand their horizons. Not only must we continue efforts already made to improve law enforcement and our prison system, but attention must be focused on the process of adjudication itself. Elected officials and members of the judiciary must begin to focus their attention on developing a criminal justice system like that of the English: a criminal justice system that effectively convicts the guilty; is simple, speedy, and cost efficient; encourages the jury to decide guilt based upon the evidence and not the advocacy of counsel; is simple enough to be understood by law enforcement personnel, attorneys, and judges; does not greatly encourage law enforcement personnel to lie in order to obtain the conviction of a guilty person, as does our present approach; and is intellectually honest in the sense of not saying that it is doing one thing while really doing another.

The overall objective is to create a criminal justice system that by its actions conveys to the villains of society the idea that, once they are caught by the police, they will be convicted and punished. The message must be one of sure and swift justice. The criminal justice system must become more of an effective arm of society and less an arena for advocates to show themselves to be as smart, aggressive, and knowledgeable as their opponents. The criminal justice system must be less a training ground for young attorneys and less a battlefield over everything. The criminal justice system must become more like the English search for truth through the fair presentation of evidence to a jury charged with the responsibility of deciding what happened and less of a game among lawyers enforcing every supposed advantage to the hilt, contesting everything, and distracting the attention of the trier of fact from the matter at hand.

Obtaining the objectives sought requires the implementation of new procedures, procedures which strike at the heart of three separate but related attitudes assumed by many involved in the operation of the criminal justice system. These three attitudes may be described generally as (1) the protection of freedom through overly complex analysis of procedural rights and differentiation of situations, (2) the belief that the more aggressive, more vigorous the advocacy on both sides the more likely a just verdict, and (3) the employment of intellectual dishonesty in the search for justice.

Overly Complex Legal Analysis

The concept of reliance on overly complex analysis of procedural rights and differentiation of situations for the protection of freedom is introduced to the future attorney at law school and reinforced in practice by judicial decision. The law school student is exposed to a learning situation that stresses the ability to spot legal questions, detail relevant policy considerations, and differentiate between situations. The object is to foster the ability of the student to analyze a problem thoroughly. If, for the sake of illustration, a problem area could be said to have a maximum of ten levels of abstraction, the student capable of developing the issues presented to the highest level of abstraction will often receive the highest grade on the essay examination. Reward is thus given to those most capable of extremely complex legal analysis. Professors exhibit cleverness in class by altering the facts of cases under consideration to add yet another level of complexity. The underlying notion is that, as one develops the analysis to the highest level of abstraction, each of the cases considered is more likely to be decided in a just fashion. The student thus begins to understand that the more each problem can be divided into its component parts and each part given proper consideration, the more correct the result. The theory continues that once the analysis is taken to level ten, all one has to do is plug the relevant facts into the computer programmed with the analysis and out comes the correct result. If you then put all these computer programs together, as NASA does with the space program, the result is a system of law that is just and fair.

This process of multilevel analysis based on the notion that maximization of justice with respect to a part means maximization of justice with respect to the whole, is applied throughout the criminal justice system. The body of applicable law grows each year. As relevant legal analysis in each particular area moves up the ladder of analysis toward level ten, the law becomes more and more complex. However, instead of becoming more just, the result is an increased disregard for the law by the police followed by confusion in ascertaining and applying the law on the part of counsel, court, and jury at trial.

The process of multilevel analysis based on differentiation of situations, when carried beyond rigorous analysis to extreme complexity falters in the criminal justice system for a simple reason: the men and women who must apply the extremely complex analytical framework developed are people, not computers. People administering the criminal justice system cannot be programmed to decide questions arising in the day-to-day administration of the criminal law in the same manner as a computer is programmed to take a spacecraft to the moon. Matters relating to criminal justice, which for current purposes includes trial practice, often have to be decided forthwith, whether by the policemen in the field or the judge in court. While extreme complexity may be fine for the tax lawyer in his office, it is not fine for the criminal justice system, where the luxury of unlimited time is not present.

Distortions in the criminal justice system introduced by reliance upon extremely complex legal analysis surface for several often interrelated reasons. Occasionally, the human mind simply cannot store for ready recall, without the benefit of an opportunity to conduct exhaustive research, each and every program developed at the highest levels of legal abstraction. Sometimes a particular human mind when presented with even a single program is not able to appreciate and apply the approach detailed properly.

Rules of law which are analytically too complex to be administered in a proper fashion by those charged with their administration, either because they have no time to research the question or because the analysis extends beyond their capacity to understand, should be made more understandable, even if the simplified rule of law does not mandate the most analytically correct solution in all cases. It is much better to have a rule of law that can be understood and applied uniformly in all cases, thus obtaining the correct result in the vast majority of cases, than to have a set of rules which, while analytically correct in all cases, cannot be readily applied in many cases, for whatever reason, by those called upon to administer them. Ours is a criminal justice system that has to function with human beings. Having a system designed for computers alone is nothing more than a travesty of justice.

Sometimes a rule of law developed by extremely complex analysis cannot be applied, not because the particular person asked to apply the rule is incapable, either because of lack of time or intelligence, but rather because the rule simply is not capable of rational application. A good illustration is Rule 609(a)(1) of the Federal Rules of Evidence which provides that, for the purpose of attacking the credibility of a witness, evidence that he has been convicted of a crime shall be admitted if elicited from him or established by public record during cross-examination, but only if the crime was punishable by death or imprisonment in excess of one year under the law under which he was convicted and the court determines that the probative value of admitting this evidence outweighs its prejudicial effect to the defendant. Employment of a prior conviction to impeach is premised upon the assumption that a person with a criminal record has a bad general character, evidenced by his willingness to disobey the law, and that his bad general character will lead him to disregard his oath to testify truthfully. According to Justice Holmes:

> When it is proved that a witness has been convicted of a crime the only ground for disbelieving him which such proof affords is the general readiness to do evil which the conviction may be supposed to show. It is from that general disposition alone that the jury is asked to infer a readiness to lie in a particular case, and thence that he has lied in fact. The evidence has no tendency to prove that he was mistaken, but only that he has perjured himself, and it reaches that conclusion solely through the general proposition that he is a bad character and unworthy of credit.[1]

Evidence of the prior conviction is admissible under Rule 609 only to impeach the witness's character for truthfulness and not as evidence bearing on the witness's character for being law abiding. Exclusion of evidence of the defendant's prior crimes in relation to the pertinent character trait of being law abiding is a specific instance of the broader prohibition against the prosecution offering evidence of the accused's character for the purpose of proving that he acted in conformity therewith on a particular occasion. The U.S. Supreme Court has stated succinctly the rationale for exclusion of evidence of prior convictions to prove character:

> The inquiry is not rejected because character is irrelevant; on the contrary, it is said to weigh too much with the jury and to so overpersuade them as to prejudge one with a bad general record and deny him a fair opportunity to defend against a particular charge.[2]

Nevertheless, a criminal defendant faces a serious dilemma whenever a prior conviction may be employed for the purpose of impeachment. If he testifies and is impeached with the prior conviction, he risks conviction upon the current charge simply because the jury thinks he is a bad man. This bad man inference takes two forms. First, the trier of fact may infer that, since he previously committed a crime, he must have also committed the crime for which he is on trial. The more similar the prior offense to the crime charged, the stronger the natural, but impermissible, inference of guilt likely to be drawn by the jury. Second, the trier of fact may reason that, since the defendant has been convicted of an offense, he probably has committed other offenses for which he has never been apprehended. Based on this reasoning, the trier of fact will more readily convict him for the offense at hand, being less concerned with convicting a "truly innocent man." Although the jury is instructed to consider the evidence of a prior conviction solely in determining the credibility of the defendant as a witness and not as evidence of guilt of the crime for which the defendant is on trial, it is rarely seriously asserted that the trier of fact is fully capable, much less interested, in making such a distinction. On the other hand, if the defendant chooses to remain silent, the jury may conclude that he is guilty despite instructions that no inference may be drawn against him by reason of his failure to testify.

In reaching a determination under Rule 609(a)(1) whether the probative value of admitting the evidence of a defendant's prior conviction as to his credibility outweighs the prejudice likely to result to the defendant if the jury draws the bad man inference, the court must consider the following factors: (1) the nature of the prior crime; (2) the length of the defendant's criminal record; (3) the defendant's age and circumstances; (4) the likelihood that the defendant would not testify; (5) the nearness or remoteness of the prior crime; (6) the defendant's subsequent career; (7) the similarity of the prior crime to the one charged; (8) the centrality of the issue of credibility; and (9) the need for the defendant's testimony. To this one might add a tenth: the facts surrounding the conviction, including whether the defendant pled guilty or was convicted after trial and whether the defendant testified at the prior trial.[3]

It is suggested that the process of balancing the various factors in a rational manner is extremely difficult at best, if not in fact an impossibility.

Difficulties associated with identifying, evaluating, and balancing up to ten factors in determining whether the probative value of a prior conviction as it bears on the defendant's credibility outweighs its prejudical effect to the defendant is further complicated by the fact that several of the factors relevant to assessing probative value themselves, such as centrality of the issue of credibility and need for the defendant's testimony, pull in opposite directions.

In practice, the question of admissibility of the prior conviction is usually decided upon a motion in limine before trial. The details of the prior conviction are presented to the court. The defense attorney asserts that the defendant will be unduly prejudiced and denied a fair trial if the prior conviction is employed to impeach. The prosecution retorts that it would be misleading to permit the accused to appear as a witness of blameless life. The court then decides. An evidentiary hearing to explore each of the nine or ten factors is rarely held. Even if a hearing were held, it would strain reason to expect that different human beings would approach the process of identifying, evaluating, and balancing up to ten elusive factors in a consistent manner. The court's decision at trial is as likely to be influenced by its assessment of the likely guilt or innocence of the accused and its perception and evaluation of the prosecutor's need to impeach the accused to obtain a conviction as any of the ten factors listed above. When all is said and done, the court relies more on its assessment of what is fair to society and the accused, considered in light of its knowledge that, in spite of a limiting instruction, the jury will consider any prior conviction as giving rise to the prohibited bad man inference. If it was really anticipated that the court would do anything else, one would expect that the court would place heavy emphasis upon whether, with respect to the prior conviction, the accused pleaded guilty or was convicted after testifying at his trial. Yet while this factor is more probative of whether the defendant will testify falsely on the witness stand than any of the factors the court is required to consider, whether the accused testified and was disbelieved at a prior trial is, in fact, rarely considered by the court in determining the probative value of the prior conviction on the defendant's credibility. In many respects, Rule 609(a)(1) thus represents the worst aspects of pick-an-answer jurisprudence. Provided a specific finding is made on the record that the court has considered the appropriate factors and concludes that the probative value of the prior convicton outweighs its prejudicial effect to the defendant, it is extremely unlikely that the court's decision will be reversed on appeal.

Finally, overly complex legal analysis and differentiation of situations leads to instances where the law is perceived by those charged with its enforcement as unclear, confused, and, most importantly, arbitrary. Much of the law of search and seizure falls in this category. The leading treatise on search and seizure is three volumes, totaling approximately 2,300 pages.[4] The annual supplements run nearly 200 pages. The sheer number of cases each year brings the level of analysis closer to level ten, thereby making it more and more impossible for the policeman charged with acting in accordance with the law to know how he should act in any given situation. Maybe a computer could be programmed to respond as specified in the three-volume treatise; a policeman, however, is not a computer. Moreover, the law itself has developed fine distinctions which, even when understandable and understood by the policeman on the scene, often appear to him to make little sense. Laws which make little sense to the policeman are easily disregarded.

To illustrate, in England the police have a common law right to search the premises of the arrested person without obtaining a warrant, even if the arrest took place elsewhere. In the United States for many years it was perfectly proper for the police to search the premises where an arrest occurred without regard to the practicality of obtaining a search warrant. This is no longer the case. As delineated by the Supreme Court in *Chimel v. California*,[5] a search incident to an arrest is permitted only under limited circumstances:

> When an arrest is made, it is reasonable for the arresting officer to search the person arrested in order to remove any weapons that the latter might seek to use in order to resist arrest or effect his escape. * * * In addition, it is entirely reasonable for the arresting officer to search for and seize any evidence on the arrestee's person in order to prevent its concealment or destruction. And the area into which an arrestee might reach in order to grab a weapon or evidentiary items must, of course, be governed by a like rule. A gun on a table or in a drawer in front of one who is arrested can be as dangerous to the arresting officer as one concealed in the clothing of the peson arrested. There is ample justification, therefore, for a search of the arrestee's person and the area "within his immediate control"—construing that phrase to mean the area from within which he might gain possession of a weapon or destructible evidence.[6]

The police may make a broader search of the place of arrest only under the authority of a search warrant.

A policeman who makes a legal arrest of an individual on a premises may very well have difficulty appreciating the sense of any rule of law prohibiting the immediate search of the premises. Many policemen simply proceed to search, willing to "alter" the location of evidence found to fit within what they consider an arbitrary and ridiculous law. Courts faced with deciding admissibility themselves occasionally stretch the concept of "immediate control" to permit introduction of seized evidence. For example, in *United States v. Wysocki*,[7] a search into a box inside a closet was upheld, although the arrestee was seated in a chair with one of the two officers immediately behind him.

With respect to the search of an automobile, as a result of the Supreme Court's decisions in *New York v. Belton*[8] and *United States v. Ross*,[9] when a policeman has made a lawful custodial arrest of the occupant of an automobile he may, without a search warrant as a contemporaneous incident of the arrest, search the passenger compartment of that automobile and examine the contents of any "containers" found in the compartment. A "container" denotes any object capable of holding another object and thus includes closed or open glove compartments, consoles, or other receptacles located anywhere within the passenger compartment, as well as luggage, boxes, bags, clothing, and the like. However, the policeman may not solely by reason of having made a lawful custodial arrest search the trunk of the automobile. The policeman may search the trunk of the car and the contents of any container found in the trunk without first obtaining a search warrant only if the policeman has probable cause to believe that the vehicle contains contraband. Justice Brennan, dissenting in *Belton*, asks some interesting questions:

While the "interior/trunk" distinction may provide a workable guide in certain routine cases—for example, where the officer arrests the driver of a car and then immediately searches the seats and floor—in the long run, I suspect it will create far more problems than it solves. The Court's new approach leaves open too many questions and, more important, it provides the police and the courts with two few tools with which to find the answers.

Thus, although the Court concludes that a warrantless search of a car may take place even though the suspect was arrested outside the car, it does not indicate how long after the suspect's arrest that search may validly be conducted. Would a warrantless search incident to arrest be valid if conducted five minutes after the suspect left his car? Thirty minutes? Three hours? Does it matter whether the suspect is standing in close proximity to the car when the search is conducted? Does it matter whether the police formed probable cause to arrest before or after the suspect left his car? And *why* is the rule announced today necessarily limited to searches of cars? What if a suspect is seen walking out of a house where the police, peering in from outside, had formed probable cause to believe a crime was being committed? Could the police then arrest that suspect and enter the house to conduct a search incident to arrest? Even assuming today's rule is limited to searches of the "interior" of cars—an assumption not demanded by logic—what is meant by "interior"? Does it include locked glove compartments, the interior of door panels, or the area under the floorboards? Are special rules necessary for stationwagons and hatchbacks, where the luggage compartments may be reached through the interior, or taxicabs, where a glass panel might separate the driver's compartment from the rest of the car? Are the only containers that may be searched those that are large enough to be "capable of holding another object"? Or does the new rule apply to any container even if it "could hold neither a weapon nor evidence of the criminal conduct for which the suspect was arrested"?[10]

It is suggested that legislatures and courts should come to the realization that extremely complex legal analysis applied throughout the criminal justice system, from arrest to appeal, often results in a denial of justice. A system of justice that is too complex, for any reason, to be applied by those charged with its application, when application is demanded, leads to injustice. What the system needs instead are rules capable of being applied by the human beings charged with administering them. The proper procedure to be followed to obtain such a system is first to analyze problems to the highest level of abstraction possible. Having explored all theoretical possibilities that can be foreseen, the next step is to formulate rules at a level of abstraction and complexity that can be understood and applied without inordinate delay and expense by those charged with administration of the rule. In many cases, the level of abstraction will be lower than that reached through complex legal analysis. The net result is rules that can be applied and thus will be applied uniformly by those charged with their application. The price of having a functional criminal justice system will be that in a particular given instance a decision might be contrary to that if complex legal analysis were taken to the extreme. However, this does not mean that the result of the trial will be incorrect or that the accused will not receive a fair trial. The level of abstraction ultimately chosen must be high enough, whatever the cost, to prevent such a result. This principle may be referred to in the 95 percent rule, or the rule of least damaging alternative.

The law of search and seizure is significant in another respect as well. While simplification will help to some degree to curtail problems associated with search and seizure, a more fundamental change is also required. Simply put, if society really wants to do something more about punishing the guilty, it must come to grips with the fact of life that the police must be given more freedom to act. Why should the police need to obtain a warrant to search the premises of persons legally arrested at their residences? Why shouldn't the police be able to search the trunk of an automobile of a person arrested for a nontraffic offense? The police have these rights in England, yet the Englishman does not consider himself less free than the American. To the contrary, the average Englishman considers himself more free, in the sense that he feels safer in his home and on the street than an American because the police are given more power to apprehend criminals. If the American legal system does not begin to simplify its procedures and in the process also make the pendulum of justice swing more in favor of the prosecution, little will occur to improve society's response to crime. If society wants to achieve speedy, effective, and cost-efficient justice, rules of law governing the conduct of the police must be brought into line.

Overly Aggressive Advocacy

Not only is simplification and ready understandability required with respect to rules applicable to the criminal justice system, we must curtail distortions to the truth-seeking process masquerading under the rubric of the adversary process. If the English barrister may be fairly criticized for being too detached, attorneys involved in the criminal process in the United States may frequently be described as overcommitted to winning. The road to winning is advocacy, not advocacy in the sense of fairly presenting the facts and suggesting inferences fairly drawn from such facts, but rather advocacy in the sense of contesting everything and interjecting into the trial whatever will tend to persuade the trier of fact to return the desired verdict. The only limit on advocacy is what the court will allow and the jury accept. Our system mistakenly believes that unbridled advocacy on both sides brings out the truth. The truth is that responsible advocacy brings out the truth; overly aggressive advocacy seeks to distort the truth by confusing and distracting the trier of fact in its search for the truth. A great deal of overly aggressive advocacy is systemic: it occurs in every case from pre-trial, through voir dire, to appeal. Systemic overly aggressive advocacy often causes delays, increases costs, distracts and confuses the trier of fact, and distorts the truth-seeking process, sometimes leading to the conviction of the innocent or the acquittal of the guilty.

With respect to pre-trial procedures, up until the last thirty years the objective of counsel for both sides was to keep from the opponent as much information as possible. The prosecution believed that if the accused could discover in advance of trial the content of the evidence against him, the defendant would be inclined to fabricate, suppress, and tamper with the evidence. The defendant in his turn simply said to the state that it had the burden of proof, go prove the crime. The result was trial by surprise, neither side knowing very much in advance concerning the testimony likely to be offered by the other. This absence of disclosure was maintained by also providing for secrecy with respect to testimony given before a grand jury and by the extensive use of hearsay at preliminary hearings.

Today in most jurisdictions the accused is entitled to full discovery. For example, Illinois Supreme Court Rule 412(a) provides:

> (a) Except as is otherwise provided in these rules as to matters not subject to disclosure and protective orders, the State shall, upon written motion of defense counsel, disclose to defense counsel the following material and information within its possession or control:
>
> (i) the names and last known addresses of persons whom the State intends to call as witnesses, together with their relevant written or recorded statements, memoranda containing substantially verbatim reports of their oral statements, and a list of memoranda reporting or summarizing their oral statements. Upon written motion of defense counsel memoranda reporting or summarizing oral statements shall be examined by the court in camera and if found to be substantially verbatim reports or oral statements shall be disclosed to defense counsel;
>
> (ii) any written or recorded statements and the substance of any oral statements made by the accused or by a codefendant and a list of witnesses to the making and acknowledgment of such statements;
>
> (iii) a transcript of those portions of grand jury minutes containing testimony of the accused and relevant testimony of persons whom the prosecuting attorney intends to call as witnesses at the hearing or trial;
>
> (iv) any reports or statements of experts, made in connection with the par-

ticular case, including results of physical or mental examinations and of scientific tests, experiments, or comparisons;

(v) any books, papers, documents, photographs, or tangible objects which the prosecuting attorney intends to use in the hearing or trial or which were obtained from or belong to the accused; and

(vi) any record of prior criminal convictions, which may be used for impeachment, of persons whom the State intends to call as witnesses at the hearing or trial.* * *

Illinois Supreme Court Rule 413 provides for similar disclosure by the accused:

(c) Medical and scientific reports. Subject to constitutional limitations, the trial court shall, on written motion, require that the State be informed of, and permitted to inspect and copy or photograph, any reports or results, or testimony relative thereto, of physical or mental examinations or of scientific tests, experiments or comparisons, or any other reports or statements of experts which defense counsel has in his possession or control, except that those portions of reports containing statements made by the defendant may be withheld if defense counsel does not intend to use any of the material contained in the report at a hearing or trial.

(d) Defenses. Subject to constitutional limitations and within a reasonable time after the filing of a written motion by the State, defense counsel shall inform the State of any defenses which he intends to make at a hearing or trial and shall furnish the State with the following material and information within his possession or control:

(i) The names and last known addresses of persons he intends to call as witnesses together with their relevant written or recorded statements, including memoranda reporting or summarizing their oral statements, and record of prior criminal convictions known to him; and

(ii) any books, papers, documents, photographs, or tangible objects he intends to use as evidence or for impeachment at a hearing or trial;

(iii) and if the defendant intends to prove an alibi, specific information as to the place where he maintains he was at the time of the alleged offense.

(e) Additional disclosure. Upon a showing of materiality, and if the request is reasonable, the court in its discretion may require disclosure to the State of relevant material and information not covered by this rule.

Notice that what is called full discovery in the United States usually extends only to written and recorded statements and to verbatim accounts of oral statements. If the policeman, investigator, or prosecuting attorney chooses not to make a verbatim account of an oral statement, preferring summary notes instead, the accused is denied access to the oral statement. Unlike in the committal proceeding in England, the prosecution has no obligation to obtain and disclose to the accused written statements from all prosecution witnesses. Careful consideration to requiring the preparation of written statements from all witnesses to be called by the prosecution at trial is worthwhile. Adoption of such a procedure would truly make disclosure "full."

What is called full discovery in America is not provided in all jurisdictions. For example, the United States government in criminal prosecutions still relies heavily upon the aspect of surprise under 18 U.S.C. § 3500, known as the Jencks Act.

> (a) In any criminal prosecution brought by the United States, no statement or report in the possession of the United States which was made by a Government witness or prospective Government witness (other than the defendant) shall be the subject of subpoena, discovery, or inspection until said witness has testified on direct examination in the trial of the case.
>
> (b) After a witness called by the United States has testified on direct examination, the court shall, on motion of the defendant, order the United States to produce any statement (as hereinafter defined) of the witness in the possession of the United States which relates to the subject matter as to which the witness has testified. If the entire contents of any such statement relate to the subject matter of the testimony of the witness, the court shall order it to be delivered directly to the defendant for his examination and use.
>
> * * * * *
>
> (e) The term "statement," as used in subsection (b), (c), and (d) of this section in relation to any witness called by the United States, means—
>
> (1) a written statement made by said witness and signed or otherwise adopted or approved by him;
>
> (2) a stenographic, mechanical, electrical, or other recording, or a transcription thereof, which is a substantially verbatim recital of an oral statement made by said witness and recorded contemporaneously with the making of such oral statement, or
>
> (3) a statement, however taken or recorded, or a transcription thereof, if any, made by said witness to a grand jury.

Notice that under the Jencks Act verbatim accounts of government witnesses' oral statements not adopted or approved by them are not even discoverable after the witness testifies.

The Jencks Act is an expression of overly aggressive advocacy. It proceeds on the assumption that a trial is to be conducted like a war, each side trying to surprise each other at every turn, each side afraid that knowledge of the other's plans would lead to alternative planning, which in the case of the accused would be fabrication, suppression, and tampering. While in individual cases such may occasionally occur, it has been shown that the interests of justice are best served by full discovery. To borrow from previous discussion, full discovery is the 95 percent rule, the least damaging alternative.

The adversary system, as practiced all too frequently in the criminal courts, also exhibits a tendency to distort, distract, confuse, and waste time with the initial stage of the trial itself—voir dire. Jury selection is not only an opportunity to select an unbiased panel to hear the dispute, it is counsel's first opportunity to influence the jury. Trial lawyers, when given the opportunity to personally address the jury, take full advantage of the chance to create a good impression and lay a foundation for their theory of the case. One jury selection manual for criminal defense lawyers lists the following twelve purposes of voir dire:

1. To move the jury as a group.
2. To discover prejudice.
3. To eliminate extreme positions.
4. To discover "friendly" jurors.
5. To exercise "educated" peremptories.
6. To cause jurors to face their own prejudices.
7. To teach jurors important facts in the case.
8. To expose jurors to damaging facts in the case.
9. To teach jurors the law of the case.
10. To develop personal relationships between lawyer and juror.
11. To expose opposing counsel.
12. To prepare for summation.[11]

Nine of the purposes have nothing to do with the stated objective of voir dire examination but are intended to influence the behavior of the potential jurors who remain on the jury. These nine purposes, classified more generally as ingratiation and indoctrination, have no legitimate function in the trial of the accused. The trier of fact is sworn to decide the case by applying the facts as he finds them from the evidence to the law as given by the court, not to find facts in favor of the attorney who appeals most to the jury. Not only are indoctrination and ingratiation improper on voir dire, they are extremely time consuming. The average English criminal jury trials takes 8.5 hours; selecting a jury alone in the United States frequently takes half that long and sometimes much longer.

Consideration should be given to mandating, rather than simply providing as an alternative, that the court conduct all questioning of prospective jurors. The attorney's participation should be limited to the submission in writing of suggested questions to be asked by the court. The merits of court conducted voir dire are clear. Our criminal system should proceed forthwith with this practice.

Whatever the problems with pre-trial and voir dire, systemic overly aggressive advocacy really comes to the forefront with respect to the presentation of evidence at trial. The criminal jury trial in the United States is best viewed as a play, with the attorney for each side acting as the producer, director, and supporting actor, if not the star. The attorney decides which witnesses he calls, and in what order. The attorney goes over the order in which direct testimony will be elicited with the witness at rehearsal, known as witness preparation. Specific answers of the witness are discussed. The lawyer frequently makes suggestions to improve the impact of the witness's answers. Nonleading questions can safely be asked at trial since both counsel and witness know the next line in the script. Responses to anticipated cross-examination and possible redirect examination are explored. Little time bombs are often discussed to be exploded by the witness if opposing counsel ventures into the mined area on cross-examination. Specific directions, such as those which follow, on how to approach answering questions on both direct and cross-examination are provided:

Prepare the witness for his courtroom testimony. Explain that following these rules will favorably affect the way the court and jury will evaluate and weigh the witness and his testimony:

a. Listen carefully to every question. Answer only that question. Do not ramble on or volunteer information. Look at the jury when answering questions. Speak clearly and loudly so that the last juror can easily hear you. Don't look at the judge or lawyer for help on difficult questions.
b. If you do not understand a question, say so and the lawyer will rephrase it. If you can't remember an answer to a question, say, "I can't recall" or "I can't remember." (You will be allowed to review any of your statements to jog your memory.) If you can only approximate dates, times, and distances, give only your best approximation. If you cannot answer a question "yes" or "no," say so and explain your answer. However, give positive, clear, and direct answers to every question whenever possible. Answer the questions with the words you normally use and feel comfortable with. Don't use someone else's vocabulary, "police talk," or other stilted speech.
c. Be serious and polite at all times. Do not exaggerate or understate the facts. Don't give cute or clever answers. Never argue with the lawyers or the judge. Never lose your temper. The lawyer on cross-examination may attempt to confuse you, have you argue with him, or have you lose your temper. Resist these temptations.
d. You will be allowed to testify only to what you personally saw, heard, and did. You generally cannot testify to what others know, or to conclusions, opinions, and speculations.
e. If an objection is made by either side to any question or answer, stop. Wait for the judge to rule. If he overrules the objections, answer the question. If he sustains the objection, simply wait for the next question. Never try to squeeze an answer in when an objection has been made.
f. Explain the purposes of direct, cross, redirect, and recross and the forms of questions employed in each type of examination.
g. Explain trick questions that the other side may ask, such as: "Have you talked to anyone about this case," "What did your lawyer tell you to say in court," and "Are you getting paid to testify." Explain how such questions can be accurately and fairly answered.
h. Above all, always tell the complete truth according to your best recollection of the facts and events involved.[12]

In addition, witnesses are often advised on what clothes to wear and as to other aspects of grooming. Finally, the attorney also explains the arrangement of the courtroom (the stage) and describes the participants (the actors).

The net result is a carefully rehearsed play. With all the kinks having been removed at New Haven (pre-trial), it is now ready for Broadway (trial). Contrast the play that unfolds at trial in the United States with the criminal jury trial in England, where witnesses other than the defendant are not interviewed by counsel, much less thoroughly prepared in every aspect. What the jury sees in the United States may be significantly influenced by the attorney-director; what the jury sees in England is relatively speaking spontaneous and unrehearsed. What tends to undermine the search for justice is not the fact that counsel in the United States has fully prepared his witness to testify. Preparation alone fosters clarity and understanding. What tends to undermine the search for justice is the natural tendency of overly aggressive advocates bent on winning to attempt consciously, or unconsciously, to overtly direct witnesses to alter their testimony, or, more often, to subtly influence witnesses to color their testimony, to present more persuasively what the attorney feels will be a winning case.

Overly aggressive advocacy leading to distortion, distraction, and confusion is a substantial problem with respect to cross-examination as well. While cross-examination is commonly thought of as destructive, with examining counsel attempting to affect the trier of fact's assessment of the weight to be accorded the testimony of the witness given during direct examination, cross-examination entails much more. Counsel on cross-examination may (1) attempt to elicit disputed facts from the witness favorable to his case, (2) have the witness repeat those facts testified to on direct examination favorable to the cross-examiner, (3) have the witness testify to nondisputed facts essential to presentation of his theory of the case, (4) attempt to have the witness qualify or modify his testimony with respect to unfavorable versions of disputed facts given on direct examination, (5) establish that the witness's testimony is not harmful to the advocate's case on the critical points under dispute, and/or (6) ask questions to the witness designed primarily to keep the cross-examiner's theory of the case before the trier of fact. It is, however, with respect to cross-examination designed to affect the jury's assessment of the credibility of the witness where overly aggressive advocacy is most prevalent.

Credibility depends upon the ability and willingness of the witness to tell the truth. His ability to tell the truth about an event of which he purports to possess personal knowledge is the product in turn of his physical and mental capacity, the extent of actual employment of such capacity to perceive, record, and recollect in the matter at hand, and his ability to narrate. Impeachment of a witness may be directed to one or more such component of credibility. Thus, the objective sought in any given situation may be to draw into question the accuracy of the witness's perception, recordation, recollection, narration, and/or sincerity.

Counsel may often discredit a witness simply with a leading question. For example, a witness may be asked if it wasn't nighttime when the event occurred, or whether he was over 400 feet away at the time. Where the attack is upon sincerity, since a simple leading question will tend to be argumentative, attorneys must resort to a specific mode of impeachment, such as prior conviction or prior inconsistent statement. Of course, with respect to certain modes of impeachment, particularly contradiction and prior inconsistent statements, the attack also extends to personal knowledge. To illustrate, if the witness denies being 400 feet away, asserting instead that he was only 20 feet from the event, a prior inconsistent statement that he was 400 feet away constitutes an attack not only upon sincerity but also upon perception, recordation, and recollection. The modes of impeachment potentially permissible depending upon the circumstances are (1) reputation for truth and veracity, (2) prior acts of misconduct, (3) prior convictions, (4) partiality, that is, interest, bias, corruption, or coercion, (5) contradiction by other evidence, including conduct of the witness himself, and (6) self-contradiction with one's own prior inconsistent statement. Impeachment by reference to matters of religion is rarely, if ever, now allowed. In assessing the credibility of a witness, the trier of fact looks not only to the content of the witness's testimony on direct examination and his answers to questions asked on cross-examination, but also to the demeanor of the witness throughout.

Counsel conducts cross-examination to discredit by using leading questions to control the witness. The objective is to ask short precise questions that can be answered yes or no. If the witness attempts to elaborate, a motion will be made to strike the witness's testimony and the jury instructed to disregard the answer. The original question is asked once more. Through this process the attorney obtains control of the witness, permitting only yes or no answers to his leading questions. Counsel on cross-examination also attempts to elicit only that information necessary for his closing argument, avoiding the question referred to as the one question too many, which permits the witness to explain. To illustrate, lawyers tell a story of a witness who testifies on direct that A bit B's ear off. On cross-examination, counsel establishes that the witness was 100 feet away from A and B during their fight, it was midnight, there were no lights and no moon, and moreover there was a row of large trees between the witness and the fighters. The one question too many which counsel should not ask is, "How come you say that A bit B's ear off?" to which comes the answer, "I saw him spit it out." Query: If the witness has an explanation, shouldn't the jury searching for the truth be provided the explanation? Why should the jury have to wait for redirect examination, where such an explanation would clearly be forthcoming? In contrast, in England witnesses are not required to answer yes or no. In fact, it is expected that they will answer responsively in a full manner, providing any qualification or explanation that is appropriate.

The distorting effect of witness control rests not in areas where an explanation will obviously be elicited during redirect examination, but rather where the particular point made on cross-examination is less central to the litigation, or where the witness's explanation is less telling. Under such circumstances, counsel may be reluctant to explore the matter on redirect. Since redirect examination will by necessity have to refocus the jury on the particular difficulty before offering an explanation, thereby reinforcing the impeachment, counsel often refrains from seeking the explanation. The jury is thus deprived of the explanation. This situation frequently arises with respect to prior inconsistent statements, where the cross-examiner merely confronts the witness with the content of the alleged inconsistent statement and inquires whether the witness made the statement. Counsel most often demands a mere yes or no answer, occasionally adding the aside to the effect that if the witness thinks he has an explanation it can be elicited by his counsel during redirect.

A great deal of discrediting cross-examination concerns questions exploring personal knowledge, questions developing partiality in the sense of interest, bias, corruption, or coercion, and questions attempting to establish inconsistent statements. With respect to prior inconsistent statement impeachment, in some cases counsel employs a prior statement which, if inconsistent at all, requires a magnifying glass to discover, while assuming an attitude of having destroyed the witness. In other cases, while an inconsistency does exist, counsel does not really believe that the fact he is attempting to discredit, such as that the witness was sixty feet instead of fifty feet from the scene of the fight, is of any real importance. In such cases the object, especially of defense counsel, is to cast doubt. The more inconsistencies, the more partiality, the more questions he raises concerning personal knowledge, the less weight the jury may give to the witness's testimony and the greater the likelihood of their concluding that the prosecution has failed to prove the guilt of the accused beyond a reasonable doubt. It is commonly asserted that cross-examination, bit by bit, makes mountains out of molehills. Another way to characterize this activity is that counsel is groping around in the dirt, hoping some of the dust will settle on the witness. Occasionally, defense counsel becomes desperate enough to proceed beyond groping and to adopt a course of cross-examination designed to inject issues other than the guilt or innocence of the accused into the case or to attempt to unjustly shift guilt to someone other than the defendant. Attempts by defense counsel to "try" the police, the court, and society at large have increased dramatically in the last twenty years.[13]

In some situations, truly discrediting cross-examination, cross-examination designed to make mountains out of molehills, or cross-examination designed to inject false issues or try someone other than the accused is not reasonably available to counsel. In such circumstances, counsel may conduct an "apparent" cross-examination, for example, by examining the witness as to the following collateral points:

1. Who asked him to be a witness?
2. Was he subpoenaed?
3. Who has he talked to about the case?
4. Discussed testimony with lawyer?
5. Attend any meetings with other witnesses present?
6. Read other materials to prepare his testimony?
7. Make any notes on the incident?
8. Read depositions and prior statements?
9. Any financial or business interest in outcome of case?
10. Any personal interest in outcome of case?
11. Know any of the parties or witnesses?
12. Compensation as a witness?[14]

As the author who suggested this list goes on to state, "None of these topics directly attempts to attack the testimony. However, pursuing the appropriate ones can plant a seed of doubt in the jury's mind so that it will at least think about the testimony rather than blindly accept it."[15]

Not letting witnesses explain, making mountains out of molehills, trying someone other than the accused, and conducting apparent cross-examinations are certainly not calculated to advance the jury's search for truth. While English barristers may be accused of being less than forceful in exploring those avenues of impeachment which truly exist, they are loath to undertake solely the appearance of discrediting cross-examination for the sake of confusing and deceiving the jury. Moreover, the English trial judge would not permit such cross-examination if it was attempted. The American trial judge, on the other hand, when faced with an objection by opposing counsel, for example, that the prior statement is not inconsistent is very likely to merely reply that the weight accorded to the impeachment is a matter for the jury to decide.

Overly aggressive advocacy also occurs on the part of counsel opposing cross-examination. When the witness is floundering during the conduct of cross-examination, the witness's own counsel often exhibits a tendency to interrupt the examination with an objection. In some cases, he designs the objection to give the witness time to gain composure and to break the flow of the cross-examiner's questioning. In others, the objection has even more sinister motives: to warn or coach the witness to give a better or safer answer. Objection for such purposes is improper. Mauet describes such objections as coming in three basic forms:

First, lawyers will constantly interject "if he knows" objections after a proper question has been posed. Invariably the witness will then answer the question: "I don't know." This kind of interjection is improper and is an obvious attempt to coach the witness in answering the question. You should object forcefully if your opponent constantly resorts to such tactics and, if necessary, ask the court to direct your opponent to desist. Regardless of what the court does, the jury will quickly realize what the lawyer is doing.

Another tactic is the "clarification" request. When the witness has given an answer on cross that the lawyer does not like, he will interrupt your examination and say, "Your Honor, could the witness tell what he means by the term 'transfer'? I'm not sure that was clear to the jury," or some similar interjection. The effect, of course, is to interrupt the flow of your cross-examination and, at the same time, cue the witness that the last answer wasn't very good. When this happens, you should again object to the lawyer's conduct and point out that these "clarifications" can properly be made during the redirect examination.

Probably the most common problem the cross-examiner faces is the lawyer who constantly makes speeches in conjunction with the objections. (E.g., "Objection, your Honor, I don't see how the witness can possibly answer the question in light of the other evidence which has clearly shown that . . .") Objections, of course, should only state the legal basis for the objection. Any argument should be out of the jury's hearing. The lawyer who constantly objects is trying to disrupt your examination and make periodic summations to the jury. Pointing this out to the judge promptly and forcefully will usually cure the problem.[16]

Concern with opposing counsel improperly presenting evidence to the jury by making speeches in conjunction with objections, by including inadmissible evidence in questions to witnesses, or by preparing witnesses to respond to questions in a certain way has led many attorneys to file motions in limine prior to trial for an order prohibiting such activity. The recent growth of motions in limine adds further delay and cost to an already overburdened system. However, considering the proclivities of some attorneys, resort to motions in limine provides opposing counsel the best opportunity to ensure a fair trial to his client, whether the defendant or the governmental unit bringing the charge.

The situation with respect to the case presented by the defense is difficult to evaluate. All defense attorneys know that it is improper to insinuate in any way to the accused that he should testify in an untruthful manner. However, we know that a significant proportion of personal injury plaintiff's attorneys do convey to their clients the facts which must be established to prove liability in a manner obvious enough to be picked up on by the less than honest claimant. It is beyond reason to conclude anything other than that the desire to win exhibited by many defense attorneys throughout the trial does lead some to convey similar signals to the accused during the pre-trial process. The approach may be subtle, but the message is loud and clear. The pressure to assist clients may be greater for the privately retained counsel, who derives his livelihood directly from defendants, than for public defenders paid from government funds. The

English barrister, by not personally meeting the accused prior to the day of trial, is substantially insulated from any such possibility.

When it comes to closing argument in America, either attorney may object that his opponent misstates evidence. The court often responds to the objection with the statement that it is the jury's recollection of the evidence which governs. If opposing counsel begins to stretch his interpretation of the evidence in response, the overall distortion that results is obvious. Defense counsel in his closing will often attempt to take matters that are irrelevant, or, if not irrelevant, inconsequential, and attempt to argue that a reasonable doubt exists. The jury usually sees through most, but not necessarily all, of these arguments. Since the court, even when permitted, will rarely comment to the jury concerning its evaluation of such an argument, defense counsel with little else to put forth has nothing to lose. While undoubtedly good advocacy, in the sense that it may constitute the argument most likely to result in an acquittal, this intentional distortion, distraction, and confusion of the jury is inconsistent with a search for justice. In the unlikely event an English barrister would be prone to make such argument, he is restrained by his knowledge that the court will make short shrift of the contention in its summation to the jury.

In the trial of criminal cases in America, counsel for both sides exhibit from jury selection to jury instruction, an attitude of mortal combat. Every rule of evidence is enforced to the hilt. Counsel exploit every tactical advantage, whether real or imaginary. The approach taken with exhibits best illustrates this attitude. In England, as we have seen, exhibits are casually handled. If there is no real dispute as to authenticity, the exhibit is simply employed at trial when needed. A witness eventually identifies the exhibit; it is not ritualistically offered or received in evidence. In the United States, exhibits are major bones of contention. Pictures of the victim and real evidence such as guns are the subject of endless dispute. In order to introduce an exhibit, testimony must be introduced from a witness with personal knowledge identifying the item and stating where relevancy requires that the item is in substantially the same condition now as it was at the relevant time. Counsel in the United States rarely act like their English counterparts and stipulate to admissibility. Defense counsel rarely agrees that statements of witnesses establishing a foundation may be read to the jury, as done in the trial of David Fisher with the statements of Conrad Cross and PC Buckwall concerning the starting pistol. In the United States, conditional witness orders are not employed—the defense demands the presentation of all witnesses, under the theory that even though there is no real dispute concerning the foundation, or even the admissibility of the exhibit itself, there is always the possibility that the witness will be unavailable for trial or otherwise fail to come up to proof. Since under such circumstances the exhibit would be inadmissible, defense counsel insists on production of all witnesses. Where the name of the game is reasonable doubt and winning, such an approach is eminently sensible. Where the approach is one of having a fair determination of the guilt or innocence of the accused based upon the contested facts, such an attitude is inappropriate and will not be countenanced.

The reluctance to stipulate to the admissibility of exhibits is not one-sided. The prosecution often takes great relish in laying a foundation and offering into evidence pictures, guns, and particularly narcotics. Laying a foundation for an exhibit gives counsel the opportunity to display his own proficiency before the jury, a display of proficiency he hopes will impress the jury with the overall merits of his case. In the process of laying the foundation, the exhibit itself remains the focus of attention, adding emphasis and thereby creating a tactical advantage for the prosecution. Thus, it is not surprising to see the prosecuting attorney spending an hour of court time laying a chain of custody foundation for narcotics and qualifying an expert witness to express an opinion that the content of the exhibit is heroin when the accused's defense is that the heroin belonged to someone else or was planted on him by the police. Such a waste of time would not occur in England, where narcotics would be handled much the same as all of the exhibits were handled in the trial of David Fisher.

After the prosecution has laid a proper foundation through live testimony, the jury may awake to find counsel objecting to the introduction of the picture, gun, or other exhibit on the ground that the probative value of the items is substantially outweighed by the danger of unfair prejudice. In the process, defense counsel will all too often take the opportunity to make a speech for the benefit of the jury, complaining that the prosecution is attempting to unfairly prejudice the defendant and that such action should not be countenanced. If the defense attorney argues that the item of evidence is unnecessary on the ground that the fact for which offered is not being disputed or even further that such fact is agreed, the prosecution will counter that the jury is entitled to see the exhibit for the "moral weight" of the evidence. While it is doubtful whether anyone, much less everyone concerned, has any idea what is meant by the "moral weight" of the evidence, the result of such a retort is usually for the court to admit the item into evidence over defense objection.

Constitutional entitlement of the indigent defendant to a lawyer at public expense has changed the face of criminal practice while adding to the problem of overly aggressive advocacy. In the last decade the number of public defenders rose from less than 3,500 in 1971 to over 8,000 in 1978.[17] More courts, more judges, more supporting staff, and more prosecuting attorneys have also been added as needed. Today in large cities, small cities, and rural areas alike, most criminal trials are conducted by two attorneys paid for by public funds. In many large cities, attorneys from the prosecutor's office and public defender's office are assigned to particular courtrooms, appearing against each other each day before the same judge. Each lawyer's office is the courtroom; only the name of the accused changes.

The growth of the public defender has exacerbated the problem of overly aggressive advocacy. The trial is no longer between a prosecutor and one of many attorneys representing defendants. The trial is now part of the holy war between the army of prosecutors and the army of public defenders. Each has its chain of command, each has its special divisions, each has its internal promotion procedure, and each has its own war college. Like the army, both are staffed predominantly by young soldiers trying to cement a place in the organization for themselves through success. Like the army, both are staffed by soldiers who are using their temporary service to learn a skill, which in the case of young lawyers is usually designed to give them the experience and credentials to handle a job outside the service with a private law firm doing civil litigation, most often concentrating on personal injury. Like the army, few of the most intelligent young men and women enlist; the class of new recruits consists predominantly of those graduating in the middle or lower segment of their law school class. What these recruits may lack in technical skill or raw legal ability, they make up for by being much better than average natural advocates and by possessing a true competitive attitude. However, unlike in the army, the generals of the holy war are usually themselves young. Upward mobility is rapid. Most district attorneys, public defenders, and their chief assistants leave for private civil practice, the judiciary, or an elected office after comparatively few years of service, thus perpetuating the cycle.

Young, unsure prosecutors and public defenders pursue victory—victory which not only establishes manhood but ensures promotion in the ranks. The cost of this overly aggressive advocacy is born entirely by the state. Both the prosecutor and the public defender get paid the same each month no matter how long each trial lasts. Economic factors which apply to attorneys in civil matters retained by the hour or on a contingent fee basis fail to operate to the same extent in criminal matters when both attorneys receive salaries. If extensive pre-trial motion practice, fewer plea bargains, and longer trials cause delays in the disposition of cases pending against other defendants, the state must build more courts, pay more judges, hire more prosecutors, and, of course, hire more public defenders.

The depth of antagonism between prosecuting attorneys and public defenders should not be underestimated. Each motion, plea negotiation, and trial is a single battle in a never-ending war. Not too long ago, I attended a meeting of representatives of prosecutors and public defenders to discuss the combining of their separate training programs in trial advocacy for attorneys with two or three years' experience. Members of both sides expressed the view that a joint training program would make it impossible for each to educate its own with respect to those trial tactics giving its side an advantage without disclosing such tactics to the opponent. A comment by a neutral party that there are no trial tactics unknown to the other side fell on deaf ears. No further meetings were held. On another occasion, a trial court judge told me of an experience in his courtroom with a young public defender representing an accused. The attorney was doing an extremely poor job. When the court called the attorney to the bench to inquire about a particular matter, the attorney advised the court that, in his opinion, the only chance the accused had was to raise the question of ineffective assistance of counsel on appeal and that he was going to give the defendant that chance.

Intellectual Dishonesty

Intellectual dishonesty refers to establishing a rule of law requiring that something be done, with full knowledge that the realities of life, for one reason or another, result in the rule of law being disobeyed. A few illustrations have previously been mentioned. Policemen asked to apply on the street the law of search and seizure as contained in a three-volume treatise in many cases cannot, and in others simply choose not to, do so. In some situations, the policeman does what he thinks best, leaving it to the court to sort out the legality of his action. In other situations, the rule of law may make so little sense to the policeman that he is willing to consciously fabricate evidence to convict the guilty. How often has a policeman stated that an item was in plain view when it was not? Is it logical to believe that so many packages containing narcotics fall out of defendant's pockets as they get out of cars? Judges are not stupid. They know that the policeman is fabricating, yet they do not wish to exclude the evidence and let a guilty person go free. Maybe there is something wrong with a set of rules that both the police and the court disregard. Maybe such rules should be changed.

Another area previously discussed is discretionary balancing of factors by the court to determine whether a prior conviction punishable by imprisonment in excess of one year or death may be used to impeach a defendant under Rule 609(a)(1) of the Federal Rules of Evidence. It is suggested in fact that it is impossible for the court to reach a rational, consistent, and predictable result employing the balancing of nine or ten factors. Hard decisions, such as whether to permit prior conviction impeachment, are not properly resolved by simply making the matter totally discretionary. The area of prior conviction impeachment, however, illustrates more than difficulties associated with balancing nine or ten factors. Prior conviction impeachment clearly represents an area of blatant intellectual dishonesty. Consider the following comments.

> The idea that a prior conviction provides a motive for perjury misconstrues the theory of impeachment. The reason for exposing the defendant's prior record is to attack his character, to call into question his reliability for truth-telling by showing his prior, relevant antisocial conduct. One need not look for prior convictions to find motivation to falsify, for certainly that motive inheres in any case, whether or not the defendant has a prior record. What greater incentive is there than the avoidance of conviction? We can expect jurors to be naturally wary of the defendant's testimony, even though they may be unaware of his past conduct.[18]

Although prior conviction evidence should be used only for evaluating the defendant's credibility, available empirical studies seem to indicate that jurors may often be unable to divorce completely this evidence from the material issues. The resulting mental confusion may lead the jury to consider the prior conviction evidence improperly, either as conclusive of defendant's general criminal tendencies or as indicative of guilt in the particular circumstances on trial. Moreover, the actual effect of the standard limiting instruction, by which the Court instructs the jury to limit its consideration of the prior conviction evidence to credibility purposes only, has long been viewed with skepticism: "Thus, with a wave of the evidentiary wand, what previously was too prejudicial to be heard by the jury becomes reliable, valid evidence." Hence a growing number of judges and commentators articulate a concern for the probative value of prior conviction evidence, especially when juxtaposed against its prejudicial effects on the jury. The evidence may not always reflect directly upon credibility, and the jury may not always have the mental discipline to consider it only for impeachment purposes.[19]

We accept much self-deception on this. We say that the evidence of the prior conviction is admissible only to impeach the defendant's testimony, and not as evidence of the prior crimes themselves. Juries are solemnly instructed to this effect. Is there anyone who doubts what the effect of this evidence in fact is on the jury? If we know so clearly what we are actually doing, why do we pretend that we are not doing what we clearly are doing?[20]

These areas of intellectual dishonesty are not alone. Policemen generally, and FBI agents in particular, have been known to destroy their notes of witness's interviews, thereby precluding disclosure to the criminal defendant. In many more instances notes are simply not taken in verbatim form to accomplish the same objective. Hearsay testimony is presented at the preliminary hearing to avoid subjecting a witness to cross-examination, or the preliminary hearing is bypassed altogether in favor of the grand jury. Prosecution witnesses are impeached by the prosecution under Rule 607 of the Federal Rules of Evidence with a prior inconsistent statement for the sole purpose of publishing the statement to the jury. Ineffectual limiting instructions are given to jurors that they should consider a prior inconsistent statement as bearing solely upon the credibility of the witness but not for the truth of the matter asserted. The same holds true with admissibility of confessions taken in violation of *Miranda* and illegally seized evidence admitted solely to impeach. Juries are also instructed with respect to presumptions in criminal cases in a manner which is impossible for anyone to understand. Criminal presumptions illustrate only one type of jury instruction which, while technically correct, is clearly incomprehensible to the lay juror. On a broader front, it is in fact extremely questionable whether many pattern jury instructions, devoid of references to the facts of the particular case, have a high level of understandability as presented at trial to the jury. Finally, while the judge may instruct the jury that the law does not require a defendant to prove his innocence, or produce any evidence at all, and no inference whatever may be drawn from the election of the defendant not to testify, these instructions defy logic, and juries tend to act in logical ways. The list could be extended.

Intellectual dishonesty resulting in the disregard of the rule of law should never be consciously sought or passively maintained. If a rule of law is disregarded for any reason, it should be reexamined with a view toward either its enforcement or its abandonment. The damage caused to the criminal justice system from what may appear an expedient position of saying one thing with full knowledge that the contrary occurs is never justified. Disrespect for the law breeds more disrespect for the law.

A SUGGESTED APPROACH

In searching to improve the criminal justice system in the United States, potential reformers may learn much from the English. While particular practices and procedures deserve careful attention, the most important thing to be absorbed from the English approach to criminal justice is the necessity of viewing the criminal justice system, from arrest through appeal, as an integrated whole, separate and distinct from civil litigation. Only if courts and legislatures in the United States become committed to this attitude will meaningful reform occur.

The criminal justice system in America, from arrest through appeal, is rarely examined and studied as an integrated whole, but rather as a series of distinct parts. Some of the parts are considered uniquely criminal, others coextensive with civil cases, while still others are considered constitutional in dimension. Although reformers study each part to a very great degree, they often fail to appreciate the interrelationship among the parts and the fact that the whole is in fact both more and less than the sum of its parts. The absolute necessity to treat *all* parts of criminal justice as an integrated whole, separate and distinct from civil litigation, has gone virtually unnoticed.

Consider the approach taken by law schools in designing courses. The traditional law school curriculum teaches substantive criminal law the first semester of the first year, followed by criminal procedure in the second semester. The course in criminal procedure concentrates predominately on the constitutional dimensions of criminal procedure. The second-year course in evidence deals with the law of evidence in both civil and criminal cases. Trial advocacy programs, now coming into vogue, instruct students with respect to the techniques of trial practice applicable to both civil and criminal trials. Similarly, moot court programs deal with both civil and criminal appeals. While courses dealing with appellate advocacy, evidence, and trial practice highlight differences in rules applicable to civil and criminal cases, students receive the idea that the trial of a criminal and civil case is basically the same. This is not to be faulted. What is to be faulted is that the student is never forced to look at the relationship between substantive criminal law, criminal procedure, especially nonconstitutional criminal procedure, evidence, trial practice, and appeal as an integrated package in the context of the criminal justice system.

Separation by courts and legislatures of rules of law governing the criminal justice system from rules of law governing the disposition of civil disputes would not only signal the beginning of a truly integrated approach, separation would also serve to highlight the inherent difference between the criminal justice system and practice and procedure composing the pre-trial and trial of civil cases. A great deal of the difference has to date been lost among the many similarities. As these differences are isolated and explored, the merit of differing responses will emerge.

A clear illustration of difficulties caused by the lack of an integrated approach is the question of whether testimony given by a witness at a preliminary hearing is admissible if the witness is unavailable at trial. Fed. R. Crim. Proc. 5.1(a) specifies the procedure to be followed at a preliminary hearing in the federal court:

> If from the evidence it appears that there is probable cause to believe that an offense has been committed and that the defendant committed it, the federal magistrate shall forthwith hold him to answer in district court. The finding of probable cause may be based upon hearsay evidence in whole or in part. The defendant may cross-examine witnesses against him and may introduce evidence in his behalf.

With respect to the admissibility of testimony at trial of an unavailable witness given at a preliminary hearing, Rule 804(b)(1) of the Federal Rules of Evidence provides:

> (b) Hearsay Exceptions. The following are not excluded by the hearsay rule if the declarant is unavailable as a witness:
>
> (1) Former Testimony. Testimony given as a witness at another hearing of the same or a different proceeding, or in a deposition taken in compliance with law in the course of the same or another proceeding, if the party against whom the testimony is now offered, or, in a civil action or proceeding, a predecessor in interest, had an opportunity and similar motive to develop the testimony by direct, cross, or redirect examination.

Under Rule 804(b)(1), testimony given by the witness at the preliminary hearing may be offered by the prosecution against the same criminal defendant if the witness becomes unavailable, provided further that the defendant had an opportunity and similar motive to conduct meaningful cross-examination of the witness at the preliminary hearing. The question, of course, is that, given the circumstances surrounding the preliminary hearing, when can it be said that the defendant had the required motive and had in fact been afforded such an opportunity? Analysis is complicated by the nature of the preliminary hearing itself, tactical questions faced by counsel, as well as whether discovery to a meaningful extent is available prior to the preliminary hearing. Recall that pursuant to 28 U.S.C. § 3500, the Jencks Act, the defendant may discover written, recorded, or adopted statements only after the witness has testified at trial. Moreover, a preliminary hearing ordinarily involves a much less searching exploration of the merits of a case than a trial, simply because the function is the more limited one of determining whether probable cause exists to hold the accused for trial. Adversary safeguards are not constitutionally demanded; hearsay testimony is permitted. Defense counsel faced with the testimony of a witness realizes that to the extent his interrogation attempts to discredit the witness by attacking, for example, powers of observation or showing bias, the effort is extremely unlikely to affect the result. Counsel tactically might prefer to spring such matters for the first time at trial. Whether determination of the adequacy of opportunity to conduct meaningful cross-examination focuses on the practical realities facing defense counsel, or upon the scope and nature of the opportunity for cross-examination permitted by the court, is yet undecided. In *Ohio v. Roberts*,[21] the Supreme Court, in discussing admissibility in terms of the confrontation clause, stated that it need not decide whether mere opportunity to cross-examine rendered the prior testimony admissible.

The interplay of a statute, two procedural rules, and a Supreme Court decision raising constitutional questions thus fails to come to grips fully with the question. Given the separate consideration that continues to be given to each of the various aspects of the problem, it is unlikely that a practical resolution will be forthcoming. On the contrary, what can be anticipated is more overly complex legal analysis and differentiation of each part leading to more and more confusion with respect to the problem as a whole.

Consideration of the criminal justice system as a separate integrated whole is an achievable goal. Ironically, the person most able to achieve the objective, Chief Justice Burger, has spoken out most frequently over the years for the need to curtail the rise of crime. Separation and integration can be achieved through the mechanism of the advisory committee structure and the promulgation of rules of procedure. The Supreme Court, subject to congressional approval, has the power to prescribe rules of pleading, practice, and procedure with respect to any and all aspects of the criminal trial process. Thus, under the auspices of the Supreme Court and its standing rules committee, an advisory committee structure could be established with the task of proposing an integrated set of rules designed to achieve the simple, speedy, cost-efficient, and, most importantly, effective criminal justice system needed to tighten the reins of justice.

The work of advisory committees since their inception has been admirable. They have promulgated forward-looking, simple, clear, and concise rules. The amendment process to the Federal Rules of Civil, Criminal, and Appellate Procedure has kept pace with developments. Unfortunately the Advisory Committee to the Federal Rules of Evidence has been disbanded. The result was predictable. Efforts to enact proposed evidence rules deleted by Congress during adoption have been abandoned.

Problems introduced into the rules during congressional enactment have gone unattended. Difficulties that have surfaced since adoption in 1975 have not been addressed. Moreover, in the absence of an advisory committee, Congress added a new rule, Rule 412, entitled "Rape Cases: Relevance of Victim's Past Behavior." As Congress displayed earlier in amending Rule 301 dealing with presumptions prior to enactment in 1975, the drafting of Rule 412 is a shambles. It is not merely inconsistent in style and approach with the other rules, it was drafted in the manner of the Internal Revenue Code. Without the appointment of a new advisory committee dealing with evidence, not only will current difficulties present in the rules of evidence not be resolved, Congress is sure to add to the confusion in the future.

Whether there should be one or more advisory committees to deal with the criminal justice system is a minor matter. What is important is that the scope of the charge to the advisory committee or committees be as broad as possible. Separate rules are clearly needed for criminal evidence and trial practice, criminal procedure, and appellate criminal procedure. Codification of rules dealing with search and seizure and questions raised by *Miranda* are also needed. The objective is to achieve an integrated, simplified, cost-efficient, intellectually honest, effective, yet fair approach to the prosecution of a criminal case from arrest through appeal.

The promulgation of rules by the Supreme Court is suggested as the vehicle for change for several reasons. Not only has the advisory committee structure proven extremely capable of approaching difficult problems in the past, but the enactment of rules of procedure by the federal government has always been followed by considerable action by the states. Since 1975, over twenty states have adopted the Federal Rules of Evidence in slightly modified form. There is no reason to believe future rules drafted by the advisory committee would be less enthusiastically received. Moreover, since rules dealing solely with criminal cases would avoid the natural resistance to change traditionally exhibited by those attorneys involved only in civil litigation, state enactment modeled on the federal rules would possibly be even more widespread. For example, it is certainly likely that a set of rules simplifying the law of search and seizure, while broadening the authority of the police, would be more than welcomed by the states. The importance of enhanced likelihood of adoption fostered by having separate rules dealing with the criminal justice system should not be underestimated. Conversely, attempts at reform of the criminal process not adopted at the federal level have been dismal failures. Inertia is too great a force to be overcome by model code proposals. Action alone leads to action, and action today in the area of criminal justice means the promulgation of separate and integrated rules governing the criminal justice system by the Supreme Court and the approval into law by Congress.[22]

In summary, separation of the criminal justice system from civil litigation would permit the development of an integrated approach through rules drafted by an advisory committee appointed by the Supreme Court. Rules governing the operation of the criminal justice system would be drafted in such a manner as to avoid the pitfalls of overly complex analysis. In addition, such rules would curtail the problems of distortion, distraction, and confusion of factual issues for the jury to decide, caused by overly aggressive advocacy. Needless incurrence of costs through waste of time would also be reduced. Finally, a separate, integrated criminal justice system would provide the opportunity to eliminate intellectually dishonest rules of procedure in favor of an intellectually honest approach to the fair determination of guilt or innocence of the accused.

A PROPOSAL

A broad outline of a proposal designed to reduce overly complex analysis, curtail overly aggressive advocacy, and eliminate intellectually dishonest rules of procedure is set forth below. The proposal illustrates a separate, integrated approach to the criminal justice system; the merits of any particular segment of the proposal or the integrated proposal as a whole is clearly secondary. This proposal, like any bold and adventurous proposal, will clearly meet opposition from both prosecution and defense attorneys, who will argue that the approach provided for a particular segment is unfair, unconstitutional, or both. Many of such arguments will be a natural extension of reliance on overly complex legal analysis and, once again, a failure to see that the whole is both more and less than the sum of its parts. The proper test to be applied in judging this or any other proposal put forth is, first, whether the proposal for reform *when considered as an integrated whole* is a workable, intellectually honest, cost-conscious criminal justice system which suffers from neither overly complex legal analysis nor overly aggressive advocacy and, second, and most important, whether such a criminal justice system is likely to lead to a fair determination of guilt or innocence of the accused. If the proposed reform to the current system taken as an integrated whole satisfies these criteria, those who would argue that an individual aspect is unfair, favors one side, or is unconstitutional under current doctrines fail to appreciate the workings of an integrated criminal justice system. Only if reformers are willing to boldly alter existing procedures, and in the process make constitutional what is now unconstitutional, and vice-versa, will meaningful reform be possible.

The proposal which is here put forth draws very heavily upon both current English procedure and recommendations for change put forth in England by both the Royal Commission in 1981 and the Criminal Law Revision Committee in 1972. Many aspects are consistent with proposals that have surfaced in the United States over the years. The critical components of the proposal are:

1. To encourage the defendant to testify at trial by prohibiting impeachment by prior conviction, by prior act of misconduct, and by reputation or opinion

testimony with respect to the accused's character for untruthfulness unless the defendant first opens the door;

2. To encourage the defendant to testify at trial by permitting comment by counsel and/or the court concerning proper inferences to be drawn from such failure;
3. To provide full discovery to the accused at the earliest possible stage of the proceeding, either prior to or at a preliminary hearing;
4. To encourage discovery by the prosecution and the early disposition of matters through plea negotiation by (a) giving the accused an opportunity to testify at the preliminary hearing and (b) conditioned upon the prosecution presenting a prima facie case at the preliminary hearing, providing for disclosure to the jury and comment by counsel and/or the court at trial if the accused fails to testify at the preliminary hearing; and
5. To encourage the court to control overly aggressive advocacy by either counsel by providing for full discovery, by mandatory admission at trial of witness statements concerning either undisputed or inconsequential matters, and by requiring the court to summarize and comment upon the evidence in its instructions to the jury.

The concept of the preliminary hearing provides the focal point of the proposal for reform. Under current procedure, a probable cause determination at a preliminary hearing or other proceeding must be made as a condition to any significant pre-trial restraint of liberty. An adversary determination of probable cause is not now constitutionally required;[23] hearsay testimony is properly considered.[24] Even in those states which determine probable cause employing an adversary preliminary hearing, procedures vary greatly. The same is true even within a given state. For example, in Cook County, Illinois, with respect to certain serious offenses, a full-scale adversary hearing is held as soon as possible following the accused's arrest, most often the next day. Hearsay testimony is not accepted. In other matters in Cook County and elsewhere in the state, preliminary hearings are held many days later, with hearsay regularly if not exclusively received.

At the preliminary hearing envisaged by the proposal, evidence submitted by the prosecution would be either through witness testimony subject to full cross-examination, thereby preserving their testimony for trial in case of unavailability, or through the submission of witness statements taken under oath by the police, the prosecuting attorney, or investigators employed by the prosecuting attorney's office. Rules governing whether any, and if so which, witnesses for the prosecution the defense could require to be produced for live testimony at the preliminary hearing would have to be developed. It is anticipated, for example, that the complainant would be required to appear in person, while the laboratory technician normally would not.

The prosecution would bear the burden of presenting a prima facie case. If such a prima facie case is presented, the defendant would have the opportunity to testify to his version of relevant events subject to cross-examination by the prosecution. The defendant would not normally call other witnesses, but could if he believed that such evidence might cause the state's prima facie case to evaporate. If the defendant refused to testify at the preliminary hearing, whatever inference naturally flowing from such refusal would be presented to the jury, argued by counsel, and referred to by the court in commenting upon the case to the jury.

It is anticipated that full disclosure at the preliminary hearing stage, coupled with the substantial pressure placed upon the accused to testify at the preliminary hearing, will greatly encourage many defendants to plead,[25] or at least attempt to negotiate a plea bargain at that time. Knowledge that absent unusual circumstances, penalties upon a plea taken at this stage of the proceedings would be less than that received upon a plea before or at trial would provide additional incentive.[26]

The proposed preliminary hearing places the court in a meaningful position to exercise increased control over proceedings leading up to and at trial. Armed with copies of witness statements, transcripts of the testimony of prosecution witnesses, and the transcript of the testimony of the accused, the court can seek agreement among counsel and enter an order, over objection if necessary, concerning which prosecution witnesses are to be produced at trial. If, for example, the defendant claims solely that the substance found in an apartment belonged to someone else, the defendant would not be able to require, nor would the prosecution be permitted to call, live witnesses to go through a chain of custody and chemical analysis of the substance. Short-form witness statements establishing a foundation and identifying the substance would be read to the jury at trial. Armed with knowledge of the prosecution's prima facie case and the accused's testimony, the court would also be in a better position to control counsel at trial to curtail the introduction of extraneous matters designed to confuse the jury and to distract their attention from the crucial issues. In addition, the court could intervene to stop the making of mountains out of molehills, whether by impeaching a witness with marginally inconsistent statements or by not permitting a witness on cross-examination to explain his answer.

The obligation placed today upon the court is in practice one of solely protecting the rights of the accused in the holy war of advocacy. If defense counsel does not know how to properly impeach a witness with a prior inconsistent statement, most judges will come to the defense attorney's assistance, if for no other reason than to prevent a reversal on appeal on the grounds of ineffective assistance of counsel. With respect to the questioning of witnesses, judges tend to allow great leeway, especially on cross-examination. The justification for such leeway has to a great extent been that counsel is more familiar with the case than the court, and thus the court must provide counsel leeway within which to try his case. Since under the proposal the court would be aware of the respective positions of both sides prior to trial, the court would be in a position to actively intervene when necessary to keep the trial on track. Tightening the reins on counsel will force them to concentrate upon the crucial contested issues and thereby assist the jury in reaching a correct result.

Forewarning concerning the respective position of both sides would also better prepare the judge to conduct the entire voir dire examination himself, permitting counsel only to submit questions for his consideration. In criminal matters, a properly developed jury questionnaire will give counsel most of what is important in discerning challenges for cause or in exercising peremptory challenges. Court questioning of the panel provides sufficient additional follow-up information. Ingratiation and indoctrination are not the proper purpose of jury selection. Attempts by counsel to ingratiate and indoctrinate waste time, adding considerable expense to the cost of the trial. The time has long since past when society should pay the salary of two attorneys who take turns smiling at number seven juror in the second row while inquiring what magazines she reads or whether she is a vegetarian.

Overly aggressive advocacy on closing argument and misstatement of facts by counsel will naturally dissipate in the face of the court's summation and comments on the evidence. Proposed Rule 105 to the Federal Rules of Evidence stated as follows:

> After the close of the evidence and arguments of counsel, the judge may fairly and impartially sum up the evidence and comment to the jury upon the weight of the evidence and the credibility of the witnesses, if he also instructs the jury that they are to determine for themselves the weight of the evidence and the credit to be given to the witnesses and that they are not bound by the judge's summation or comment.

Proposed Rule 105 dealing with the discretionary authority of the trial judge to sum up and comment to the jury upon the weight of the evidence and credibility of the witnesses was not enacted by Congress. The report of the House Committee of the Judiciary states that deletion reflects no conclusion as to the merits of Proposed Rule 105. Moreover, the report recognizes that Proposed Rule 105 is consistent with longstanding and current federal practice and that the federal practice taken from the common law of affording the trial judge discretionary authority to comment on and summarize the evidence is left undisturbed. Section 4.7 of the American Bar Association Maximum Standards for Criminal Justice: Trial by Jury, Tentative Draft, 1968, is more specific:

> (a) The court, at the time it instructs the jury, may summarize and comment on the evidence, provided the jury is clearly and unequivocally instructed that it is the exclusive judge of the facts, that it is to determine the weight of the evidence and the credibility of witnesses, and that it is not bound by the comments of the court.
>
> (b) The summary and comment permitted in subsection (a) is governed by the following principles:
>
> (i) The court may analyze the evidence, draw the attention of the jury to

important portions of the evidence, and fairly and accurately summarize the contentions of both the prosecution and the defense.

(ii) The court may not suggest a verdict of guilty or not guilty, nor may the court directly express an opinion on the guilt or innocence of the defendant.

(iii) The court may not present any item of evidence as a proven or undisputed fact unless the matter has been affirmatively conceded or is the subject of judicial notice.

(iv) The court may state the law and comment on matters in evidence bearing on the credibility of any witness, but may not directly express an opinion that certain testimony is worthy or unworthy of belief.

The power to sum up and comment on the evidence is not meaningful unless used. Where used properly, counsel is greatly encouraged to restrict his advocacy to matters relating to the crucial issues for the jury to decide. The court can deal with attempts to distort, distract, or confuse fairly in its charge to the jury.

In addition, the court in its charge to the jury should also be permitted to comment on the accused's failure to testify at trial. Prosecution counsel could do likewise in his closing argument. Comment on failure to testify is justified in light of the elimination of all impeachment by the prosecution of the defendant as a witness through establishment of prior convictions, prior acts of misconduct, or reputation and opinion testimony as to character for untruthfulness.

Anticipation of the court exercising its right to guide the presentation of evidence to a greater extent than is usually now done and to summarize the evidence and comment upon credibility must be accompanied by a more restrained attitude toward the function of appellate review. If each decision of the trial court is to be examined against an overly complex analytical framework, the flexibility necessary to the conduct of a trial will be curtailed. If the trial court is expected to act, it must be given a wide berth within which to do so. Moreover, any error which is injected into the trial by action of the court beyond its wide berth of discretion must be judged by a realistic and unapologetic harmless error test.

The proposals made with respect to impeachment of the defendant by means of a prior conviction highlight the necessity of an integrated approach. Use of a prior conviction to impeach is designed in great measure to put substantial pressure on the defendant with a provable prior conviction to plead guilty. He is placed on the horns of the dilemma. If he testifies, his prior conviction will be disclosed, with the jury drawing the bad man inference in spite of instructions to the contrary. If the defendant does not testify, the jury will draw adverse inferences from such failure, again in spite of instructions to the contrary. The inherent intellectual dishonesty of permitting use of prior convictions, nominally to impeach but in reality for the bad man inference, is intensified, not diminished, by conditioning impeachment as done in Rule 609(a)(1) of the Federal Rules of Evidence upon satisfaction of a discretionary balancing test incapable of being applied in a rational manner. All that has been accomplished by Rule 609(a)(1) is to place inequity arbitrarily upon some but not all defendants with respect to serious convictions less than ten years old.

Elimination of intellectually dishonest impeachment by prior conviction runs the risk that more defendants will choose to go to trial, thereby creating a further backlog of criminal trials. This risk appears to be negligible, for in England, where prior conviction impeachment is for all practical purposes not permitted, over 87 percent of all defendants in the Magistrates' Court and Crown Court plead guilty and do so in the absence of a formalized plea negotiation system.[27] Moreover, other reforms, including effectively requiring the accused to testify at the preliminary hearing and reducing the likelihood that overly aggressive advocacy will distort, distract, and confuse the jury, should discourage more defendants from proceeding to trial than elimination of the intellectually dishonest procedure of prior conviction impeachment would encourage. Finally, if a slight increase in the number of defendants seeking a jury trial did arise, it is a small price to pay for an intellectually honest and fair determination of guilt or innocence.

Having eliminated impeachment by prior conviction and its companions, prior bad acts and reputation and opinion testimony with respect to character for untruthfulness, it becomes possible to effectively mandate that the accused testify both at trial and at the preliminary hearing, by permitting comment to the jury by court and counsel on his failure. In turn, effectively mandating that the defendant testify at the preliminary hearing requires that the prosecution first produce a prima facie case. These rearrangements of current procedure in turn carry with them the additional benefit of full disclosure of the prosecution's case and sufficient disclosure of the accused's defense to permit the court to conduct voir dire, to effectively control both counsel at trial, and to begin to form a framework for its summation and comment on evidence to the jury.

Each aspect of the proposals thus draws upon the other in a major reform of the criminal justice system. Full discovery is provided. Defendants are encouraged to plead at an early stage of proceedings. Time is saved during voir dire and at trial. Unnecessary witnesses are avoided by reliance on the witness statements. Overly aggressive advocacy is curtailed throughout. Coupled with rules resulting from reexamination of the law of search and seizure and *Miranda*, examination for the first time of rules addressing questions falling within the field of trial advocacy, and continued improvement and refinement of rules of pre-trial criminal procedure, evidence, and appeal, the net result is a criminal justice system that effectively convicts the guilty, encourages guilty pleas, reduces trial time, saves considerable sums of money, is intellectually honest, and is fairer to the accused by providing that the determination of guilt be made by the jury better able to focus its attention upon crucial factual areas in dispute.

NOTES

1. Gertz v. Fitchburg, R.R. Co., 137 Mass. 77, 78 (1884).
2. Michelson v. United States, 335 U.S. 469, 475-76 (1948).
3. Gordon v. United States, 383 F.2d 936 (D.C. Cir. 1967).
4. LaFave, *Search and Seizure* (1978).
5. Chimel v. California, 395 U.S. 752 (1969).
6. Id. at 762-63.
7. 357 F.2d 1155 (5th Cir. 1972).
8. 453 U.S. 454 (1981).
9. ____U.S.____, 102 S.Ct. 2157 (1982).
10. 453 U.S. at 469-70.
11. *The Voir Dire Examination, Juror Challenges and Advisory Advocacy* 16-17 (1978).
12. Mauet, *Fundamentals of Trial Techniques* 13-14 (19080).
13. See People v. Hanks, 17 Ill. App. 3d 633, 638, 307 N.E.2d 638 (1974):

> Although on cross-examination the range of evidence for the purpose of discrediting is very liberal, an undue latitude in the cross-examination of witnesses in criminal cases as to their character, reputation, and past activities when not relevant or material injects issues other than the guilt of the defendant and tends to shift unjustly that guilt to persons other than the defendant. . . . The courts must ever be alert to the injection of extraneous and prejudicial issues into the trial under the guise of due process or fair trial and never condone this as sound or accepted defense tactics. The statement of Justice Schaefer of the Illinois Supreme Court may be appropriate under the circumstances: "There has been an increasing tendency in criminal cases to try some person other than the defendant, and some issues other than his guilt." (People ex rel. Sears v. Romiti (1971), 50 Ill.2d 51, 55, 277 N.E. 2d 705, 707, cert. denied, Hanrahan v. Sears, 406 U.S. 921, 92 S. Ct. 1778, 32 L. Ed. 2d 121.)

14. Mauet, *Fundamentals of Trial Techniques* 286 (1980).
15. Ibid.
16. Id. at 287.
17. U.S. Department of Justice, Bureau of Justice Statistics, *Sourcebook of Criminal Judicial Statistics* (1980).
18. Brown v. United States, 370 F. 2d 242, 244 (D.C. Cir. 1966).
19. United States v. Garber, 471 F. 2d 212, 215 (5th Cir. 1972).
20. Griswold, "The Long View," 51 *A.B.A.J.* 1017, 1021 (1965).
21. 448 U.S. 56 (1980).
22. While it can be argued with much force that the need for reform, as well as the particular reforms suggested, are more applicable to state than federal prosecutions, the fact remains that the only way significant reform will occur in the states is if the federal government acts first. Any set of rules drafted would have to take account of the nature of the various criminal matters coming before the federal courts. Even if rules of general reform could be applied in only a small percentage of federal cases, the impact in state court proceedings would clearly make the effort worthwhile.
23. Gerstein v. Pugh, 420 U.S. 103 (1975).
24. Rule 5.1 of the Federal Rules of Criminal Procedure ("The finding of prob-

able cause may be based upon hearsay evidence in whole or in part'').

25. A complicating but not insurmountable factor in federal criminal cases with respect to enhancing the function of the preliminary hearing is the provision of the Fifth Amendment that no person shall be held to answer for an infamous crime, ''unless on a presentation or indictment of a Grand Jury.''

26. The notion of assessing costs against a criminal defendant who pleads guilty at a later date or is convicted at trial is also worthy of consideration.

27. With respect to plea bargaining in England, see generally Baldwin and McConville, *Negotiated Justice* (London: Martin Robertson, 1977).

10 CONCLUSION

The criminal justice systems in the United States and England have taken different roads over the last two hundred years. The English system has developed into a highly efficient yet fundamentally fair prosecutorial machine. The message sent to those committing offenses by the criminal justice system in England is one of high probability of conviction following arrest. Technical rules of procedure will not render inadmissible evidence gathered against him, nor will defense counsel's activities prevent a conviction by distracting the jury from properly approaching the task they are empaneled to perform.

The situation in the United States is quite different. The American system has over the recent years become marked by complexity caused by extremely intricate legal analysis and confusion caused by overly aggressive advocacy. The result is an unduly complex legal structure that in many respects is too complex to be applied by those charged with the task of its administration. The result is that a guilty person is set free in the mistaken belief that society's freedom requires prohibiting the police from searching the residence of an accused properly arrested on the premises. The result is an overly aggressive advocacy system which distorts the jury's search for truth with rules prohibiting a witness from explaining his answer to a question asked on cross-examination and distracts the jury from its search for the truth by permitting defense attorneys to inject extraneous issues in the case in the hope of confusing the jury. The result is a criminal justice system which is extremely time consuming and expensive. The result is a criminal justice system where neither side stipulates to anything and witnesses must be called to establish undisputed points. The result is an intellectually dishonest criminal justice system where juries are told to do one thing with full knowledge that they are incapable, even if willing, of being able to do so.

The underlying notion of the English criminal justice system from the point of charge through appeal is one of professionalism. Solicitors, barristers, and judges all desire that the guilty person be convicted and the innocent be acquitted. The English criminal justice system encourages those who are guilty to plead and those who profess innocence to present their version of the relevant events before the jury. In comparison, guilty defendants in the United States are often encouraged to put the prosecution to its proof, in the hope that a witness will become unavailable before trial or that some critical item of evidence will be suppressed for violation of a technical rule of procedure. The English simply do not consider pre-trial and trial of a criminal offense a competitive game where the rules permit, if not encourage, defense counsel to put the prosecution through all of its paces with full knowledge that, if the ball is dropped, an acquittal may follow.

Analysis of the English criminal jury trial has developed the importance of the role played by a divided profession in maintaining the English attitude toward a search for fundamental fairness and, in particular, the importance the fact that barristers try cases for both the prosecution and defense plays in maintenance of a professional attitude. We have also seen that several less desirable consequences, such as weak preparation and investigation and an overly detached approach by counsel, appear to be necessary byproducts of maintaining a divided profession. We have also noted that, while an intellectually honest approach characterizes the trial itself, the English approach to the law of search and seizure and enforcement of the Judges' Rules do not share such characteristics.

It is obvious that for societal and logistical reasons the divided profession itself does not provide a meaningful avenue of exploration for practical reform of the American criminal justice system. Meaningful avenues of exploration for practical reform do, however, arise from the overall attitude displayed by the English criminal jury system—simple rules of practice and procedure designed to focus the jury's attention on the real factual issues to be decided in the case. Full discovery is followed by a trial, where the accused is permitted to testify free from impeachment by a prior conviction. Exhibits are admitted on stipulation, and witness statements concerning relevant but undisputed matters are simply read to the jury. Barristers do not attempt to create mountains out of molehills or otherwise distort the search for truth. The trial is neither a holy war nor a coming of manhood, but rather a search for the truth. Any accidental straying by a witness or counsel is quickly corrected by the court on its own initiative. The trial concludes with the judge charging the jury, summarizing and commenting upon the evidence as to the crucial factual questions to be decided by the jury, and instructing the jury as to the law. The approach throughout the trial is simple and straightforward, intellectually honest, cost efficient, and, most important from the perspective of the reformer, integrated. The message conveyed to the accused throughout the criminal justice system of the value placed upon maintenance of law and order is clear and unmistakable.

Those interested in tightening the reins of justice in the United States can draw heavily upon the English experience, not only in terms of particular procedural rules but in terms of the attitude displayed by those called upon to operate the criminal justice system. The goal is an integrated criminal justice system incorporating reasonable legal rules applied by professional advocates focusing upon the task assigned to the jury of deciding whether the accused has been proved to be guilty beyond a reasonable doubt by resolving the factual issues crucial to the determination. The means to reform are the promulgation of integrated sets of rules dealing with search and seizure, *Miranda*, pre-trial procedure, trial advocacy, evidence, and appeal drafted by an advisory committee appointed by the Supreme Court.

The law governing the trial of criminal cases in the United States has grown over the last twenty years like government regulations governing airlines. However, unlike government regulations governing airlines, when it is perceived that overly complex regulation of the criminal justice system is undesirable, nothing is done to correct it. In other areas of the law of procedure, when similar situations were perceived action was taken. When code pleading grew overly complex and confused, notice pleading and pre-trial discovery were introduced. When pre-trial criminal discovery experienced similar difficulties, new rules were introduced. In both areas the new approach was innovative, comprehensive, and, of course, integrated. In both areas the new approach took the form of rules drafted by an advisory committee appointed by the Supreme Court.

Procedural rules drafted by an advisory committee representing an integrated approach to the law governing arrest through appeal will without doubt make constitutional what has been unconstitutional, and unconstitutional what is now constitutional. This is to be commended, not feared. Our current system of determining the rights of the accused on a case-by-case basis, and with it procedural rules for criminal trials, has proven a failure. We have clearly lost sight of the forest for the trees. Constitutional rights of the accused have been added piecemeal. When problems are perceived in the application of the new-found right, exceptions are grafted onto the rule and new interpretations are pronounced. Rights once created are eroded. However, rights once created never seem to be removed. Nevertheless, nothing prevents the Supreme Court from once again reinterpreting applicable constitutional provisions in a manner consistent with rules governing the criminal justice system themselves promulgated by the Supreme Court. If in the process what is now unconstitutional becomes constitutional, so be it. Only if the Supreme Court is willing to undertake the project of looking at the criminal justice system in an innovative, comprehensive, and integrated fashion will meaningful reform result. The Supreme Court helped get us into the straitjacket now crushing the criminal justice system—it is now time for the Supreme Court to take the lead in getting us out.

Procedural reform alone, of course, will not solve the rising crime rate. It can, however, have an impact on crime by conveying to those who break the law that an entirely new attitude is being taken. The message must be loud and clear that the reins of justice are tightened. No longer will technicalities result in dismissal of the charge. No longer will the trial be treated as a game between young lawyers finding their way in the world. When the message conveyed to the defendant by his defense attorney is the same conveyed to the accused in England by his solicitor, barrister, and ultimately the court, that the only applicable ground for acquittal is that guilt has not been established beyond a reasonable doubt and that everyone involved in the criminal justice system, including the public defender appointed to represent him, has only that objective in mind, the legal system will have accomplished what it can and must accomplish in a free democratic society.

APPENDIX I

JUDGES' RULES AND ADMINISTRATIVE DIRECTIONS TO THE POLICE

HOME OFFICE CIRCULAR NO. 89/1978:

Judges' Rules and Administrative Directions to the Police

The Chief Officer of Police

Sir,

I am directed by the Secretary of State to say that he is anxious to ensure that the Judges' Rules and the related Administrative Directions to the police are known by all police officers and readily available to all members of the legal profession and others who may be concerned with them. He has accordingly decided, with the agreement of the Lord Chief Justice, to re-issue the Rules and Directions taking account of related Home Office circulars issued since new Rules were made in 1964.

2. The Rules which are reproduced in Appendix A to this circular are identical to those issued under cover of Home Office circular No. 31/1964. The Judges have made it clear that the Rules are concerned with the admissibility in evidence against a person of answers, oral or written, given by that person to questions asked by police officers and of statements made by that person. In giving evidence as to the circumstances in which any statement was made or taken down in writing, officers must be absolutely frank in describing to the court exactly what occurred, and it will then be for the Judge to decide whether or not the statement tendered should be admitted in evidence. The Rules should constantly be borne in mind, as should the general principles which the Judges have set out before the Rules. But in addition to complying with the Rules, interrogating officers should always try to be fair to

From the Royal Commission on Criminal Procedure, *The Investigation and Prosecution of Criminal Offenses in England and Wales: The Law and Procedure*, Command 8092-1, January 1981 at 151-165.

the person who is being questioned, and scrupulously avoid any method which could be regarded as in any way unfair or oppressive.

3. Appendix B contains the Administrative Directions to the Police, which have been revised to take account of relevant Home Office circulars issued since 1964. Attention is drawn to the following points at which the Directions differ from those issued in 1964:

(i) Home Office letter of May 31, 1968 on interviewing, fingerprinting and photographing children and young persons made it clear that the advice contained in the first sentence of paragraph 4 of the Directions should be taken as relating to all persons under 17 years of age. Paragraph 4 of the Directions has been amended accordingly.

(ii) Home Office circular No. 66/1976 clarified the second paragraph of Administrative Direction 7(*a*), by pointing out, for the avoidance of doubt, that the sending of telegrams and letters by persons in police custody should be subject to the same proviso as telephone communications with the person's solicitors and friends (covered by the first paragraph of Direction 7 (*a*)). Administrative Direction 7 (*a*) has now been recast accordingly.

(iii) Home Office circular No. 109/1976 gave guidance on the need for special care in the interrogation of mentally handicapped persons. A new paragraph, 4A, now incorporates that guidance. The reference to a "social worker" as an example of the sort of person who might be asked to be present should not be narrowly interpreted—any person with a professional interest in the mentally handicapped would be suitable. Chief officers of police may find that if the Director of Social Services is approached locally it may be possible to make suitable arrangements in advance.

In addition, the heading but not the sense of Administrative Direction 5 has been altered.

4. Home Office circular No. 148/1977 set out arrangements for obtaining the services of competent interpreters in cases where police enquiries involve the questioning of a deaf person. For convenience, the substance of this circular is set out in Appendix C attached.

5. Section 62 of the Criminal Law Act provides that where any person has been arrested and is being held in custody in a police station or other premises, he shall be entitled to have intimation of his arrest and of the place where he is being held sent to one person reasonably named by him without delay or, where some delay is necessary in the interest of the investigation or prevention of crime or the apprehension of offenders, with no more delay than is so necessary. Guidance to the police on section 62 is contained in Home Office circular No. 74/1978. Paragraph 1 of that circular makes it clear that the provision in section 62 in no way detracts from the Judges' Rules and Administrative Directions.

I am, Sir,

Your obedient Servant,

R. T. ARMSTRONG.

Appendix A

JUDGES' RULES

Note

The origin of the Judges' Rules is probably to be found in a letter dated October 26, 1906, which the then Lord Chief Justice, Lord Alverstone, wrote to the Chief Constable of Birmingham in answer to a request for advice in consequence of the fact that on the same Circuit one Judge had censured a member of his force for having cautioned a prisoner, whilst another Judge had censured a constable for having omitted to do so. The first four of the pre-1964 Rules were formulated and approved by the Judges of the King's Bench Division in 1912; the remaining five in 1918. They were much criticised, *inter alia* for lack of clarity and of efficacy for the protection of persons who were questioned by police officers; on the other hand it was maintained that their application unduly hampered the detection and punishment of crime. A Committee of Judges devoted considerable time and attention to producing, after consideration of representative views, a new set of Rules which was approved by a meeting of all the Queen's Bench Judges and issued in 1964.

The Judges control the conduct of trials and the admission of evidence against persons on trial before them; they do not control or in any way initiate or supervise police activities or conduct. As stated in paragraph (*e*) of the introduction to the present Rules, it is the law that answers and statements made are only admissible in evidence if they have been voluntary in the sense that they have not been obtained by fear of prejudice or hope of advantage, exercised or held out by a person in authority, or by oppression. The Rules do not purport to envisage or deal with the many varieties of conduct which might render answers and statements involuntary and therefore inadmissible. The Rules merely deal with particular aspects of the matter. Other matters such as affording reasonably comfortable conditions, adequate breaks for rest and refreshment, special procedures in the case of persons unfamiliar with the English language or of immature age or feeble understanding, are proper subjects for administrative directions to the police.

PREAMBLE

These Rules do not affect the principles

(a) That citizens have a duty to help a police officer to discover and apprehend offenders;

(b) That police officers, otherwise than by arrest, cannot compel any person against his will to come to or remain in any police station;

(c) That every person at any stage of an investigation should be able to communicate and to consult privately with a solicitor. This is so even if he is in custody provided that in such a case no unreasonable delay or hindrance is caused to the processes of investigation or the administration of justice by his doing so;

(d) That when a police officer who is making enquiries of any person about an offence has enough evidence to prefer a charge against that

person for the offence, he should without delay cause that person to be charged or informed that he may be prosecuted for the offence;

(e) That it is a fundamental condition of the admissibility in evidence against any person, equally of any oral answer given by that person to a question put by a police officer and of any statement made by that person, that it shall have been voluntary, in the sense that it has not been obtained from him by fear of prejudice or hope of advantage, exercised or held out by a person in authority, or by oppression.

The principle set out in paragraph (*e*) above is overriding and applicable in all cases. Within that principle the following Rules are put forward as a guide to police officers conducting investigations. Non-conformity with these Rules may render answers and statements liable to be excluded from evidence in subsequent criminal proceedings.

RULES

I. When a police officer is trying to discover whether, or by whom, an offence has been committed he is entitled to question any person, whether suspected or not, from whom he thinks that useful information may be obtained. This is so whether or not the person in question has been taken into custody so long as he has not been charged with the offence or informed that he may be prosecuted for it.

II. As soon as a police officer has evidence which would afford reasonable grounds for suspecting that a person has committed an offence, he shall caution that person or cause him to be cautioned before putting to him any questions, or further questions, relating to that offence.

The caution shall be in the following terms:

"You are not obliged to say anything unless you wish to do so but what you say may be put into writing and given in evidence."

When after being cautioned a person is being questioned, or elects to make a statement, a record shall be kept of the time and place at which any such questioning or statement began and ended and of the persons present.

III.*(a)* Where a person is charged with or informed that he may be prosecuted for an offence he shall be cautioned in the following terms:

"Do you wish to say anything? You are not obliged to say anything unless you wish to do so but whatever you say will be taken down in writing and may be given in evidence."

(b) It is only in exceptional cases that questions relating to the offence should be put to the accused person after he has been charged or informed that he may be prosecuted. Such questions may be put where they are necessary for the purpose of preventing or minimising harm or loss to some other person or the public or for clearing up an ambiguity in a previous answer or statement.

Before any such questions are put the accused should be cautioned in these terms:

"I wish to put some questions to you about the offence with which you have been charged (*or* about the offence for which you may be prosecuted). You are not obliged to answer any of these questions, but if you do the questions and answers will be taken down in writing and may be given in evidence."

Any questions put and answers given relating to the offence must be contemporaneously recorded in full and the record signed by that person or if he refuses by the interrogating officer.

(c) When such a person is being questioned, or elects to make a statement, a record shall be kept of the time and place at which any questioning or statement began and ended and of the persons present.

IV. All written statements made after caution shall be taken in the following manner:

(a) If a person says that he wants to make a statement he shall be told that it is intended to make a written record of what he said. He shall always be asked whether he wishes to write down himself what he wants to say; if he says that he cannot write or that he would like someone to write it for him, a police officer may offer to write the statement for him. If he accepts the offer the police officer shall, before starting, ask the person making the statement to sign, or make his mark to, the following:

"I,.., wish to make a statement. I want someone to write down what I say. I have been told that I need not say anything unless I wish to do so and that whatever I say may be given in evidence."

(b) Any person writing his own statement shall be allowed to do so without any prompting as distinct from indicating to him what matters are material.

(c) The person making the statement, if he is going to write it himself, shall be asked to write out and sign before writing what he wants to say, the following:

"I make this statement of my own free will. I have been told that I need not say anything unless I wish to do so and that whatever I say may be given in evidence."

(d) Whenever a police officer writes the statement, he shall take down the exact words spoken by the person making the statement, without putting any questions other than such as may be needed to make the statement coherent, intelligible and relevant to the material matters; he shall not prompt him.

(e) When the writing of a statement by a police officer is finished the person making it shall be asked to read it and to make any corrections, alterations or additions he wishes. When he has finished reading it he shall be asked to write and sign or make his mark on the following Certificate at the end of the statement:

"I have read the above statement and I have been told that I can correct, alter or add anything I wish. This statement is true. I have made it of my own free will."

(f) If the person who has made a statement refuses to read it or to write

the above mentioned Certificate at the end of it or to sign it, the senior police officer present shall record on the statement itself and in the presence of the person making it, what has happened. If the person making the statement cannot read, or refuses to read it, the officer who has taken it down shall read it over to him and ask him whether he would like to correct, alter or add anything and to put his signature or make his mark at the end. The police officer shall then certify on the statement itself what he has done.

V. If at any time after a person has been charged with, or has been informed that he may be prosecuted for an offence a police officer wishes to bring to the notice of that person any written statement made by another person who in respect of the same offence has also been charged or informed that he may be prosecuted, he shall hand to that person a true copy of such written statement, but nothing shall be said or done to invite any reply or comment. If that person says that he would like to make a statement in reply, or starts to say something, he shall at once be cautioned or further cautioned as prescribed by Rule III(*a*).

VI. Persons other than police officers charged with the duty of investigating offences or charging offenders shall, so far as may be practicable, comply with these Rules.

Appendix B

ADMINISTRATIVE DIRECTIONS ON INTERROGATION AND THE TAKING OF STATEMENTS

1. *Procedure generally*

(a) When possible statements of persons under caution should be written on the forms provided for the purpose. Police officers' notebooks should be used for taking statements only when no forms are available.

(b) When a person is being questioned or elects to make a statement, a record should be kept of the time or times at which during the questioning or making of a statement there were intervals or refreshment was taken. The nature of the refreshment should be noted. In no circumstances should alcoholic drink be given.

(c) In writing down a statement, the words used should not be translated into "official" vocabulary; this may give a misleading impression of the genuineness of the statement.

(d) Care should be taken to avoid any suggestion that the person's answers can only be used in evidence against him, as this may prevent an innocent person making a statement which might help clear him of the charge.

2. *Record of interrogation*

Rule II and Rule III(*c*) demand that a record should be kept of the following matters:

(a) when, after being cautioned in accordance with Rule II, the person is being questioned or elects to make a statement—of the time and place at which any such questioning began and ended and of the persons present;

(b) when, after being cautioned in accordance with Rule III(*a*) or (*b*) a person is being questioned or elects to make a statement—of the time and place at which any questioning and statement began and ended and of the persons present.

In addition to the records required by these Rules full records of the following matters should additionally be kept:

(a) of the time or times at which cautions were taken, and

(b) of the time when a charge was made and/or the person was arrested, and

(c) of the matters referred to in paragraph 1(*b*) above.

If two or more police officers are present when the questions are being put or the statement made, the records made should be countersigned by the other officers present.

3. *Comfort and refreshment*

Reasonable arrangements should be made for the comfort and refreshment of persons being questioned. Whenever practicable both the person being questioned or making a statement and the officers asking the questions or taking the statement should be seated.

4. *Interrogation of children and young persons*

As far as practicable children and young persons under the age of 17 years (whether suspected of crime or not) should only be interviewed in the presence of a parent or guardian, or in their absence, some person who is not a police officer and is of the same sex as the child. A child or young person should not be arrested, nor even interviewed, at school if such action can possibly be avoided. Where it is found essential to conduct the interview at school, this should be done only with the consent, and in the presence, of the head teacher, or his nominee.

4A. *Interrogation of mentally handicapped persons*

(a) If it appears to a police officer that a person (whether a witness or a suspect) whom he intends to interview has a mental handicap which raises a doubt as to whether the person can understand the questions put to him, or which makes the person likely to be especially open to suggestion, the officer should take particular care in putting questions and accepting the reliability of answers. As far as practicable, and where recognised as such by the police, a mentally handicapped adult (whether suspected of crime or not) should be interviewed only in the presence of a parent or other person in whose care, custody or control he is, or of some person who is not a police officer (for example a social worker).

(b) So far as mentally handicapped children and young persons are concerned, the conditions of interview and arrest by the police are governed by Administrative Direction 4 above.

(c) Any document arising from an interview with a mentally handicapped person of any age should be signed not only by the person who made the statement, but also by the parent or other person who was present during the interview. Since the reliability of any admission by a mentally handicapped person may even then be challenged, care will still be necessary to verify the facts admitted and to obtain corroboration where possible.

5. *Statements in languages other than English*

In the case of a person making a statement in a language other than English:

(a) The interpreter should take down the statement in the language in which it is made.

(b) An official English translation should be made in due course and be proved as an exhibit with the original statement.

(c) The person making the statement should sign that at (*a*).

Apart from the question of apparent unfairness, to obtain the signature of a suspect to an English translation of what he said in another language can have little or no value as evidence if the suspect disputes the accuracy of this record of this statement.

6. *Supply to accused persons of written statement of charges*

(a) The following procedure should be adopted whenever a charge is preferred against a person arrested without warrant for any offence:

As soon as a charge has been accepted by the appropriate police officer the accused person should be given a written notice containing a copy of the entry in the charge sheet or book giving particulars of the offence with which he is charged. So far as possible the particulars of the charge should be stated in simple language so that the accused person may understand it, but they should also show clearly the precise offence in law with which he is charged. Where the offence charged is a statutory one, it should be sufficient for the latter purpose to quote the section of the statute which created the offence.

The written notice should include some statement on the lines of the caution given orally to the accused person in accordance with the Judges' Rules after a charge has been preferred. It is suggested that the form of notice should begin with the following words:

"You are charged with the offence(s) shown below. You are not obliged to say anything unless you wish to do so, but whatever you say will be taken down in writing and may be given in evidence."

(b) Once the accused person has appeared before the court it is not necessary to serve him with a written notice of any further charges which may be preferred. If, however, the police decide, before he has appeared before a court, to modify the charge or to prefer further charges, it is desirable that the person concerned should be formally charged with the further offence and given a written copy of the charge as soon as it is possible to do so having regard to the particular circumstances of the case. If the accused person has then been released on bail, it may not always be practicable or reasonable to prefer the new charge at once, and in cases where he is due to surrender to his bail within forty-eight hours or in other cases of difficulty it will be sufficient for him to be formally charged with the further offence and served with a written notice of the charge after he has surrendered to his bail and before he appears before the court.

7. *Facilities for defence*

(a) A person in custody should be supplied on request with writing materials.

Provided that no hindrance is reasonably likely to be caused to the processes of investigation or the administration of justice:

(i) he should be allowed to speak on the telephone to his solicitor or to his friends;

(ii) his letters should be sent by post or otherwise with the least possible delay;

(iii) telegrams should be sent at once, at his own expense.

(b) Persons in custody should not only be informed orally of the rights and facilities available to them, but in addition notices describing them should be displayed at convenient and conspicuous places at police stations and the attention of persons in custody should be drawn to these notices.

Appendix C

POLICE ENQUIRIES INVOLVING DEAF PERSONS

When, in the course of police inquiries, it becomes necessary to ask questions of a deaf person, there is sometimes difficulty in arranging for the proceedings to be interpreted with sufficient clarity, especially when such persons have no useful hearing and can only communicate manually by means of finger-spelling and signing. In these circumstances the services of competent interpreters for the deaf may be required. It has been agreed with the Association of Directors of Social Services and the Royal National Institute for the Deaf that Directors of Social Services will, on request, designate points of contact (which may, depending on local circumstances, be an office of the local authority or of a voluntary organisation) through which arrangements for securing the services of interpreters can be made. Chief officers of police are therefore requested to get in touch with Directors of Social Services locally so that arrangements for designating a point of contact can be made.

In cases of difficulty The Royal National Institute for the Deaf, 105 Gower Street, London WC1E 6AH (telephone number 01-387 8033) will be glad to advise.

Origin and history of the Judges' Rules

The implications of the law of evidence and its application by the courts for the investigation of crime were first defined for the police in an authoritative way by Lord Brampton (formerly Mr Justice Hawkins) in a Preface to Vincent's Police Code (1882), where he said of questioning:

> "Much discussion has on various occasions arisen touching the conduct of the police in listening to, and repeating, statements of accused persons. I will try, therefore, to point out what I think is the proper course for a constable to take with regard to such statements.
>
> *Questioning; when Permissible:* When a crime has been committed, and you are engaged in endeavouring to discover the author of it, there is no objection to you making enquiries of, or putting questions to, any person from whom you think you can obtain useful information. It is your duty to discover the criminal if you can, and to do this you must make such enquiries; and if in the course of them you should chance to interrogate and to receive answers from a man who turns out to be the criminal himself, and who inculpates himself by these answers, they are nevertheless admissible in evidence, and may be used against him.
>
> *When not Permissible:* When, however, a constable has a warrant to arrest, or is about to arrest a person on his own authority, or has a person in custody for a crime, it is wrong to question such person touching the crime of which he is accused. Neither judge, magistrate, nor juryman, can interrogate an accused person—unless he tenders himself as a witness—or require him to answer questions tending to incriminate himself. Much less, then, ought a constable to do so, whose duty as regards that person is simply to arrest and detain him in safe custody. On arresting a man a constable ought simply to read his warrant, or tell the accused the nature of the charge upon which he is arrested, leaving it to the person so arrested to say anything or nothing as he pleases. For a constable to press any accused person to say anything with reference to the crime of which he is accused is very wrong. It is well also that it should be generally known that if a statement made by an accused person is made under, or in consequence of, any promise or threat, even though it amounts to an absolute confession, it cannot be used against the person making it. There is, however, no objection to a constable listening to any mere voluntary statement which a prisoner desires to make, and repeating such statement in evidence; nor is there any objection to his repeating in evidence any conversation he may have heard between the prisoner and any other person. But he ought not, by anything he says or does, to invite or encourage an accused person to make any statement without first cautioning him that he is not bound to say anything tending to incriminate himself, and that anything he says may be used against him. Perhaps the best maxim for a constable to bear in mind with respect to an accused

person is, 'Keep your eyes and your ears open, and your mouth shut'. By silent watchfulness you will hear all you ought to hear. Never act unfairly to a prisoner by coaxing him by word or conduct to divulge anything. If you do, you will assuredly be severely handled at the trial, and it is not unlikely your evidence will be disbelieved."

2. This clear and authoritative guidance issued by a judge in a police guide marks an important departure, and may be considered the forerunner of the present Judges' Rules. The origin of those rules as such however lies in a letter which the Chief Constable of Birmingham sent to the Lord Chief Justice in 1906 asking for advice following one case in which a judge disapproved of a caution and another in which a judge criticised its omission. In reply the Lord Chief Justice advised that the approved practice was that whenever a constable determined to made a charge against a man he should caution him before taking a statement from him. The Lord Chief Justice went on to suggest that the words "against you" should be omitted from the usual caution ("You are not obliged to say anything unless you wish to, but anything you say will be written down and may be used in evidence against you,") on the ground that the man might just as well say something in his favour as against him.

3. From this modest beginning the Judges' Rules have grown. Four rules were in existence by 1912. In 1918 there were nine. These rules remained in force until 1964. They were as follows:

> "1. When a police officer is endeavouring to discover the author of a crime, there is no objection to his putting questions in respect thereof to any person or persons, whether suspected or not, from whom he thinks that useful information can be obtained.
>
> 2. Whenever a police officer has made up his mind to charge a person with a crime, he should first caution such person before asking any questions, or any further questions, as the case may be.
>
> 3. Persons in custody should not be questioned without the usual caution being first administered,
>
> 4. If the prisoner wishes to volunteer any statement the usual caution should be administered.
>
> It is desirable that the last two words of the usual caution should be omitted, and that the caution should end with the words 'be given in evidence'.
>
> 5. The caution to be administered to a prisoner, when he is formally charged, should therefore be in the following words: 'Do you wish to say anything in answer to the charge? You are not obliged to say anything unless you wish to do so, but whatever you say will be taken down in writing and may be given in evidence.'
>
> Care should be taken to avoid any suggestions that his answers can only be used in evidence against him, as they may prevent an innocent person making a statement which might assist to clear him of the charge.
>
> 6. A statement made by a prisoner before there is time to caution him is not rendered inadmissible in evidence merely by reason of no caution

having been given, but in such a case he should be cautioned as soon as possible.

7. A prisoner making a voluntary statement must not be cross-examined, and no questions should be put to him about it except for the purpose of removing ambiguity in what he has actually said. For instance, if he has mentioned an hour without saying whether it was morning or evening, or has given a day of the week and day of the month which do not agree, or has not made it clear to what individual or what place he intended to refer in some part of his statement, he may be questioned sufficiently to clear up the point.

8. When two or more persons are charged with the same offence, and statements are taken separately from the persons charged, the police should not read these statements to the other persons charged, but each of such persons should be furnished by the police with a copy of such statements and nothing should be said or done by the police to invite a reply. If the person charged desires to make a statement in reply, the usual caution should be administered.

9. Any statement made in accordance with the above rules should, whenever possible, be taken down in writing and signed by the person making it after it has been read to him and he has been invited to make any corrections he may wish."

4. These rules were confirmed in 1930 when the Home Office issued a circular of guidance to the police (following consultations with the Judges) to deal with some points raised by the Royal Commission on Police Powers and Procedure, which had reported the previous year (Cmd 3297). Subsequently further guidance was issued by the Home Office on the use of interpreters, taking written statements, and administrative matters of that kind.

5. Matters remained in this form until the early 1960s when the Rules and attendant circulars were reviewed. In 1964 the revision was issued to the police under cover of Home Office Circular 31/1964, which was subsequently published.

6. The published document falls into a number of parts. First there is the Home Office circular, which explains the main changes made, and sets out the underlying basis of the rules. Secondly, there is a note which sets out briefly the origin of the Rules, and explains the nature of the rules. In the second part of this preamble there is a statement of certain fundamental principles which are not affected by the rules. Thirdly, there are the Rules proper. These had been revised by a Committee of Judges and approved by a meeting of all the Queen's Bench Judges. And, fourthly, there are some administrative directions drawn up by the Home Office and approved by the judges.

7. These Rules remain in force today. They were supplemented, so far as the police are concerned, by the issue of two Home Office circulars in 1968 and 1976 giving further guidance on particular points of doubt which had arisen in connection with the administrative directions, and in 1976 a circular was also issued on the interrogation of mentally handicapped persons. In June 1978 a revised edition of the Judges' Rules and Administrative Directions incorporating the guidance given in these circulars was published.

APPENDIX II

TEXT OF HOME OFFICE CIRCULAR NO. 74/1978 TO CHIEF OFFICERS OF POLICE CONCERNING SECTION 62 OF THE CRIMINAL LAW ACT 1977, DATED 28 APRIL 1978

The Criminal Law Act 1977 (Commencement No 5) Order 1977 will bring section 62 of the Criminal Law Act 1977 into force on 19 June 1978. Section 62 provides that—

> "Where any person has been arrested and is being held in custody in a police station or other premises, he shall be entitled to have intimation of his arrest and of the place where he is being held sent to one person reasonably named by him, without delay or, where some delay is necessary in the interest of the investigation or prevention of crime or the apprehension of offenders, with no more delay than is so necessary."

This circular, which contains guidance on the implementation of the section, has been drawn up in consultation with the Association of Chief Police Officers and others concerned. There has also been consultation with the Lord Chief Justice. Section 62 in no way detracts from the provisions of the Judges' Rules and the Administrative Directions to the Police. It is recognised that much of what follows already takes place as a standard procedure within police forces.

Information to the arrested person

2. When a person is arrested (with or without warrant) after the section has come into force, and is taken into custody, the terms of the section should be drawn to his attention. This should be done on arrival at the police station by the station officer and/or duty officer receiving the arrested person into custody. It will be for chief officers to decide the precise way in which this should be done. One possibility is for a notice outlining the provisions of section 62 to be displayed in conspicuous places at police stations to which the attention of arrested persons can be drawn. Alternatively, chief officers may wish to arrange to have leaflets available explaining the provisions of section 62 which can be handed to arrested persons. Where, exceptionally, an arrested

From the Royal Commission on Criminal Procedure, *The Investigation and Prosecution of Criminal Offenses in England and Wales: The Law and Procedure*, Command 8092-1, January 1981 at 166-169.

person is held in custody in premises other than a police station, or it is clear that there will be some delay before he is taken to a police station, he should be told of the terms of the section by the senior police officer present. (See also paragraph 22 below.)

Initial steps on receiving a request

3. In some cases it is the responsibility of the police to initiate action to notify a parent, relative or other person of an arrest, even if the arrested person does not himself make a request for this to done. This is especially important in the case of mentally handicapped persons, children and young persons (see also paragraph 16 below) and nationals of certain foreign or Commonwealth states (see also paragraph 19 below). In these cases, and wherever there may be some doubt as to the capacity of the arrested person to understand his entitlement under section 62, the police should follow their normal practice of automatically seeking to notify a responsible person or the appropriate authorities of the arrest of the person concerned. In the majority of cases, however, it will be for the arrested person to decide whether he wishes to make use of the entitlement given to him by section 62. In most cases where he wishes to do so he will no doubt inform the officer who draws his attention to the terms of the section. However, if he makes no immediate request, it will nonetheless remain open to him to do so at any time while he is in custody. Similarly a request within the terms of section 62 which is made *before* the arrested person has been informed formally of his entitlement (for example one made in the police car on the way to the police station) will be a valid request for the purposes of section 62, and should be treated accordingly.

4. If a person in custody asks for a person to be informed of his arrest and of the place where he is being held, the effect of the Act is to require intimation to be sent to the person named without delay unless:

(i) the choice of person is not reasonable, or

(ii) some delay is necessary in the interest of the investigation or prevention of crime or the apprehension of offenders (in which case there is to be no more delay in sending the intimation than is necessary).

Reasonably named person

5. When a request is made the police should therefore first consider whether the person to be notified is a "reasonably named" person. In most cases a person in custody will name a member of his family or a solicitor as the person whom he wishes to be informed of his detention, and such a person should normally be considered "reasonably named". Where some other individual is named, and it is clear that he is known personally to the person in custody (eg a flat-mate or neighbour) he should normally be considered a reasonably named person. So should an individual not personally known to the arrested person if he is likely to take an interest in his welfare (eg a community worker or an official of an organisation likely to take such an interest). If the person names an organisation, but does not know the name of an official within it, the police should take account both of the likelihood of that organisation being concerned with the welfare of the arrested person, and also of the readiness with which they may be able to contact an official at the relevant time. If, however, the person in custody names someone who is not personally

acquainted with him and cannot be expected to take an immediate interest in his welfare (eg famous pop star, football player or Government Minister not being the person's own Member of Parliament) then the arrested person should be informed that that person is not "reasonably named". If the person in custody then names a "reasonably named" person his request should be met without delay, provided that it is otherwise within the terms of the section. If the arrested person nominates a person who is not in the United Kingdom, the Channel Islands or the Isle of Man he should be informed that that person is not "reasonably named".

Use of the proviso

6. When a request is made consideration will also need to be given to the possible application of that part of section 62 which provides that intimation may be delayed in the interest of the investigation or prevention of crime or the apprehension of offenders for so long as this is so necessary (but no longer). It will be for the station officer and/or duty officer, in consultation with the officer in charge of the case, to decide when this qualification applies (see also paragraph 21 below). The qualification will no doubt be particularly relevant where the arrested person is, or may be, associated with others involved in crime, or where the family of the arrested person, or a person living at the same address, may be aware of his criminal activities and there is a risk, for example, that stolen property will be disposed of, or evidence destroyed. In such cases immediate intimation may lead to the escape of other offenders, the destruction of evidence or the commission of other offences. It will therefore be appropriate to delay the intimation until such considerations have ceased to apply. Where the police decide that the qualification is to apply the arrested person should be informed that his request for an intimation to be conveyed is being delayed.

7. The following are some examples of situations when it may be considered necessary to delay an intimation—

(i) The police have arrested one member of a terrorist gang, and consider that immediate intimation of his arrest carries the risk that other members will escape and be able to continue their activities.

(ii) They have arrested a man in the act of conveying stolen goods to a receiver, and wish to conduct a search of the area for the receiver; immediate notification may lead to his escape.

(iii) A person suspected of being a persistent shoplifter is arrested and there is reason to believe that the family, if notified, will move or destroy the proceeds of previous thefts.

(iv) The police have arrested a member of a bank robbery gang and immediate intimation may lead to the destruction of evidence or threats to witnesses.

The Secretary of State recognises however that no list of possible situations in which the qualification may be appropriately exercised can be comprehensive. Equally, however serious the offence under investigation, the qualification set out in the latter part of section 62 should never be applied as a matter of routine, but only after a careful review of the considerations which apply in that particular case.

Conveying an intimation

8. Section 62 entitles the arrested person only to have intimation *sent* to a reasonably named person. Nevertheless the Secretary of State is sure that chief officers will take such steps as are reasonably practicable to ensure that an intimation is received by the person to whom it is addressed within a reasonable period. He recognises however that there will be some cases where there can be no absolute assurance that the intimation has reached the person named.

9. Where the named person can be reached by telephone the intimation should be so conveyed. Alternatively, the arrested person may wish to name someone else with whom a telephone message can be left. In some cases it may be necessary to send a police officer to notify the named person personally; if so, it may be possible to combine this task with the perfomance of other duties in connection with the same, or some other enquiry. In cases where a person is arrested at his home in the presence of his relatives or of someone who is likely to be named as the person to whom intimation is to be conveyed, it is suggested that the arresting officer should wherever practicable inform the latter person of the police station to which the arrested person is being taken. It will then be clear, when the arrested person is informed of his entitlement on arrival at the police station, that the provisions of the section have already been complied with and that no further action by the police is required.

10. The Secretary of State fully recognises the burdens that the police are already carrying in dealing with crime, and in the course of their other duties. He is concerned therefore to ensure that the additional duties placed on the police by section 62 of the Criminal Law Act 1977 are kept to a minimum, commensurate with the proper observance of the section. It is for that reason among others that he suggests that the intimation should wherever possible be conveyed by telephone rather than by a police officer in person. Nevertheless he recognises that in some circumstances the duty of informing a named person will impose considerable extra duties on the police, and that the question of priorities will arise, particularly in busy urban police stations at peak periods.

He recognises that there may be periods when officers engaged on other urgent duties (for example, dealing with a large number of youths arrested during an outbreak of football hooliganism) cannot justifiably be spared to undertake a series of telephone calls or to pay a personal visit to the named person. In such cases, the police will no doubt follow their normal practice of giving priority to those cases where intimation is particularly pressing on humanitarian grounds (eg where the intimation affects the welfare of children). It is, however, important in all cases that a request for intimation should not be lost sight of, and that it should be attended to as soon as the other urgent duties permit. Chief officers will no doubt take steps to ensure that this is clearly understood, and that the importance of conveying an early intimation is appreciated, within their forces.

APPENDIX III

WITNESS STATEMENTS SUBMITTED AT COMMITTAL PROCEEDING

STATEMENT OF WITNESS
(C.J. Act. 1967, ss. 2, 9, M.C. Rules 1968 n58)

Statement of. Allan Parker

Age of Witness (if over 21 enter "over 21") . . . Over 21

Occupation of Witness . . . . Technical Assistant

Address and Telephone Number. . . . . West Midlands Police

Steelhouse Lane Police Station

Birmingham

This statement, consisting of 1 pages each signed by me, is true to the best of my knowledge and belief and I make it knowing that if it is tendered in evidence, I shall be liable to prosecution if I have wilfully stated in it anything which I know to be false or do not believe to be true.

Dated the 14th day of April, 1980.

Signed A. Parker

Signature witnessed by ________________

I am a technician employed as a plan drawer with West Midlands Police. On Monday, 14 April 1980 I prepared a plan to a scale of 1/1250 showing city streets between the junction of Well Street and Great Hampton Street and New John Street West at Great King Street.

STATEMENT OF WITNESS
(C.J. Act, 1967, ss. 2, 9, M.C. Rules, 1968 n58)

Statement of. Anthony Arnold Dewey

Age of Witness (if over 21 enter "over 21") . . . Over 21

Occupation of Witness . . . . Police Photographer

Address and Telephone Number. . . . . West Midlands Police

Lloyd House

Birmingham

This statement, consisting of 1 pages each signed by me, is true to the best of my knowledge and belief and I make it knowing that, if it is tendered in evidence, I shall be liable to prosecution if I have wilfully stated in it anything which I know to be false or do not believe to be true.

Dated the 1st day of April, 1980.

Signed A.A. Dewey

Signature witnessed by ________________

On the 26 of March 1980, I went to Well Street, Hockley. There I took a number of photographs towards Smith Street and across the junction with Smith Street.

From the unretouched negatives in my possession, I produce enlarged photographs.

STATEMENT OF WITNESS
(C.J. Act, 1967, ss. 2, 9, M.C. Rules, 1968, n58)

Statement of. . . . . Anthony Arnold Dewey

Age of Witness (if over 21 enter "over 21") . . . Over 21

Occupation of Witness . . . . Police Photographer

Address and Telephone Number. . . . . West Midlands Police

Lloyd House

Birmingham 236 5000
Ext 2222/2205

This statement consisting of 1 pages each signed by me, is true to the best of my knowledge and belief and I make it knowing that, if it is tendered in evidence, I shall be liable to prosecution if I have wilfully stated in it anything which I know to be false or do not believe to be true.

Dated the 24th day of March, 1980.

Signed A.A. Dewey
Signature witnessed by ________________

On the 25 of February 1980 I photographed the scene of a robbery at the Midland Bank, Great Hampton Street, Hockley.

I later produced an album of enlarged photographic print(s) from the unretouched negatives in my possession.

STATEMENT OF WITNESS
(C.J. Act, 1967, ss. 2, 9, M.C. Rules, 1968, n58)

Statement of. . . . . Yvonne Carol Gardner

Age of Witness (if over 21 enter "over 21") . . . 20 years (6.12.59)

Occupation of Witness . . . . Bank Clerk

Address and Telephone Number. . . . . Midland Bank Ltd.

Great Hampton Street,
Birmingham

Tel. Work: 554.1915

This statement, consisting of 3 pages each signed by me, is true to the best of my knowledge and belief and I make it knowing that, if it is tendered in evidence, I shall be liable to prosecution if I have wilfully stated in it anything which I know to be false or do not believe to be true.

Dated the 25th day of 2, 1980.

Signed Y. C. Gardener
Signature witnessed by C. Higgins
D.C.2283.

I am a Bank Clerk, working for the Midland Bank, Great Hampton Street, Birmingham.

Today at approximately 3 p.m. Monday 25th February 1980, I was working as normally behind the counter. I was on my own at the counter when I saw a coloured man come into the Bank hall. There were no other customers in the Bank at this time.

I was working from the 2nd till along from the manager's office wall. This man stood by the wall near to the 1st till where there was no one serving.

He stood there for about a minute, then I said to him, "Can I help you?" He walked up to the till where I was, he had both of his hands in his pockets at this stage. He then took out his right hand from his pocket and he was holding a small hand gun. It was like a revolver. It was very small, about 5' long in total length.It had a very short barrel, it was black in colour. He pointed the gun at me and said, "Money, money." He pointed the gun to the till where the money was. As he pointed the gun, it clicked. I didn't know whether he had actually pulled the trigger or not.

I took some notes from the 2nd drawer down under the till. I never took any money from the actual till where I serve from. The notes were all bundled up. The five pound notes were in quantities of £500's. The ten pound notes were also in £500's and the one pound notes were in £100's.

Altogether there was £3,800.00. There was £300 in £1 notes, they were all new notes. The rest was used notes. The man took out a polythene bag from his other pocket. It was a white bag with either red letters on it, or a red emblem.

I passed the money to him, under the glass,and he placed it into the bag. He took the money with the same hand he was holding the gun with. After he took the money he just ran out of the Bank. I then pressed the alarm with my foot and told my colleagues what had happened.

I didn't want to press the alarm at the time of handing the money over, because I was too scared in case he may have fired the gun. It happened so quick I wasn't too sure what the best thing was to do.

I describe him as about 25 years old, 5'10" tall, he was either Asian or a very light skinned West Indian. He had a dark green woolen hat over his head, covering his hair and his ears. He had dark brown eyes, a long wide mouth, but not thick lips.

He was wearing a dark khaki jacket, plain in style. I think I could recognise him again.

STATEMENT OF WITNESS
(C.J. Act, 1967, ss. 2, 9, M.C. Rules, 1968, n58)

Statement of. Yvonne Carol Gardener

Age of Witness (if over 21 enter "over 21") . . . 20 years 6.12.59

Occupation of Witness . . . . Bank Clerk

Address and Telephone Number. . . . . Midland Bank Limited

Great Hampton Street

Hockley

This statement, consisting of 1 pages each signed by me, is true to the best of my knowledge and belief and I make it knowing, that if it is tendered in evidence, I shall be liable to prosecution if I have wilfully stated in it anything which I know to be false or do not believe to be true.

Dated the 24th day of March, 1980.

Signed Y. C. Gardener

Signature witnessed by John Pyke DC 7086

Further to my original statement on Monday, 24 March 1980 I was shown a quantity of money. I examined each note but there was no marks on them which I recognise as marks made by me.

But on four bundles of £10 x 10 notes there were four paper clips securing each of the bundles, the clips were in identical places where I put them when I am making notes up into bundles of £100 pounds. I always place the paper clips on the top left hand side of each bundle.

STATEMENT OF WITNESS
(C.J. Act, 1967, ss. 2, 9, M.C. Rules, 1968, n58)

Statement of. Yvonne Carol Gardener

Age of Witness (if over 21 enter "over 21") . . . 20 years

Occupation of Witness . . . . Midland Bank Clerk

Address and Telephone Number. . . . . Midland Bank

Gt. Hampton Street

Newtown

This statement, consisting of 2 pages each signed by me, is true to the best of my knowledge and belief and I make it knowing that, if it is tendered in evidence, I shall be liable to prosecution if I have wilfully stated in it anything which I know to be false or do not believe to be true.

Dated the 2nd day of April 1980.

Signed Y. C. Gardener

Signature witnessed by John Pyke DC 7086

Further to my previous statements on Wednesday, 2 April 1980 I was shown a red woollen hat, a blue anorak type coat and two white plastic bags and also a hand gun.

After examination I can say that I do not recognise the anorak and the hat is not the same colour as the one I remember my attacker wearing. But the plastic bags which are identical I recognise them as being similar to the one which the man had with him on the day of the robbery. The bag I recognise by the red writing on the side even though I don't remember what was written on the bag which the attacker was carrying. The pattern is very similar to that I have been shown.

The hand gun is identical to that which the attacker pointed at me, it is identical in size and the clicking noise which I heard at the time of the robbery, the same noise was obtained when the trigger of the gun was 'cocked'.

STATEMENT OF WITNESS
(C.J. Act, 1967, ss. 2, 9, M.C. Rules, 1968, n58)

Statement of. Norman Barnard Witham

Age of Witness (if over 21 enter "over 21") . . . Over 21 B. 8.3.1933

Occupation of Witness . . . . Bank Manager

Address and Telephone Number. . . . . 64 Gt. Hampton Street,
Newtown, Birmingham.

Home: 427 2330

This statement, consisting of 5 pages each signed by me, is true to the best of my knowledge and belief and I make it knowing that, if it is tendered in evidence, I shall be liable to prosecution if I have wilfully stated in it anything which I know to be false or do not believe to be true.

Dated the 25th day of February, 1980.

Signed Norman Witham

Signature witnessed by M.J. Coall 4891

I am the Manager of the Midland Bank, 64 Gt. Hampton Row, Newtown, Birmingham.

At about a few minutes to 3 o'clock Monday, 25th February, 1980 I parked my vehicle in the car park of my bank, having returned from Wolverhampton. I then had to walk from my car along Wells Street to the bank. It was raining and I was carrying my umbrella. I was walking along Wells Street on the same side of the bank, I was about 20 yards from the front door of the bank. At this stage my attention was centered on the telephone engineers who were working on electrical equipment housed on the outside wall of the bank. As I was watching the engineers I saw a man run past them towards me on the same pavement as myself.

I would describe this man as late teens or early twenties, about 5'5" to 5'6", slim build. He struck me as being dark skinned, possibly coloured. He was wearing a dark green woollen hat pulled down over his ears, the hat was close to his head, suggesting he had short hair. He had a khaki coloured short jacket similar to an anorak or combat type jacket. It had smooth material and possibly two pockets at the hips. He was wearing dark trousers, gave me the impression they were short possibly just above his ankles. They appeared to be trouser material as opposed to jeans or corduroy, the style was parallel, not particularly tight fitting. His shoewear gave me the impression they were dark soft soled boots. As this man ran past me his arms were crossed just below chest level as though he was cradling something.

This man ran past me. I paid no particular attention to him, I carried on towards the bank, as I approached the front door of the bank the 'Klaxon' alarm sounded. This alarm is usually activated to warn of a raid. At this stage I did not associate the alarm with the man I saw running. I then entered the bank and after a brief discussion with staff I discovered that a raid had, in fact, taken place in the bank and the man responsible was the man I saw running past me in Wells Street. I immediately left the bank and walked back along Wells Street towards Barr Street making a search of the area for the man I had seen earlier.

At the junction with Wells Street and Barr Street I looked around but could not see anything. I then continued along Wells Street towards Smith Street. I crossed Smith Street and stood on some raised land to get a general view of the area but again saw nothing untoward. I stood there for about thirty seconds ~~and as I turned round to cross Smith Street to return to the bank my attention was drawn to a mid blue Vauxhall Viva being driven along Smith Street in the direction of Great King Street and was to my left which would be the Great Hampton Row side of the junction of Smith Street and Wells Street.~~

~~As I looked at the car I could see the driver was a light coloured negroid. He appeared to be quite tall, possibly wearing dark overalls. His hair was afro style, about two inches long; he appeared to be in his early twenties. The only other occupant of the car was in the front passenger seat; this person was crouched down level with the dashboard. I could see very~~

~~little detail of the person in the circumstances. This appeared very suspicious and as the car past me, travelling towards Great King Street along Smith Street, I took the registration number mentally from the rear of the vehicle. This registration number was MXC 388H. I got the impression that the car had only just started due to the speed of the car and the sound of the engine. This car travelled along Smith Street and turned right into Gt. King Street where I lost sight of it.~~

I then returned to the bank. I doubt if I would recognise the man who ran past me again.

STATEMENT OF WITNESS
(C.J. Act, 1967, ss. 2, 9, M.C. Rules, 1968, n58)

Statement of. Mr. Norman Barnard Witham

Age of Witness (if over 21 enter "over 21") . . . Over 21

Occupation of Witness . . . . Bank Manager

Address and Telephone Number. . . . . 64 Gt. Hampton Street

Newtown

Birmingham

This statement, consisting of 1 pages each signed by me, is true to the best of my knowledge and belief and I make it knowing that, if it is tendered in evidence, I shall be liable to prosecution if I have wilfully stated in it anything which I know to be false or do not believe to be true.

Dated the 2nd day of April, 1980.

Signed Norman Witham

Signature witnessed by John Pyke DC 7086

Further to my statement dated the 25 February 1980. On Wednesday, 2 April 1980 I was shown a red woollen hat, a blue anorak type jacket and two white plastic bags.

After looking at them I do not recognise them as being worn or carried by the man who ran past me shortly after 3 pm on Monday, 25 February 1980 as I was entering my bank in Great Hampton Street, Newtown.

STATEMENT OF WITNESS
(C.J. Act, 1967, ss. 2, 9, M.C. Rules, 1968, n58)

Statement of. Miss Angela Woodward

Age of Witness (if over 21 enter "over 21") . . . 18 years

Occupation of Witness . . . . Bank Clerk

Address and Telephone Number. . . . . 29 Ashwood Close

Streetly

Sutton Coldfield 353 3612

This statement, consiting of 1 pages each signed by me, is true to the best of my knowledge and belief and I make it knowing that, if it is tendered in evidence, I shall be liable to prosecution if I have wilfully stated in it anything which I know to be false or do not believe to be true.

Dated the 25th day of February, 1980.

Signed A. Woodward

Signature witnessed by John Pyke DC 7086

I am a single girl and I live at the above address with my mother and father. I am employed as a Bank Clerk for the Midland Bank and I work at the Great Hampton Street, Branch in Birmingham.

At about 3 pm Monday, 25 February 1980 I was at work in the Branch working in the typing area which is divided from the counter of the bank by a wooden partition when suddenly Yvonne Gardener who was working on the counter, leaned over the partition and said, "We've been raided, shall I sound the alarm?" I said, "Yes."

I looked into the customer area of the Bank and there was no one there. I hadn't seen who Yvonne had served.

STATEMENT OF WITNESS
(C.J. Act, 1967, ss. 2, 9, M.C. Rules,1968, n58)

Statement of. . . . . Mr. Conrad Cross

Age of Witness (if over 21 enter "over 21") . . . Over 21 years

Occupation of Witness . . . . Director

Address and Telephone Number. . . . . George Bate Gunmakers, Ltd.,

16 Colmore Circus, Birmingham

236 7451

This statement, consisting of 2 pages each signed by me, is true to the best of my knowledge and belief and I make it knowing that, if it is tendered in evidence, I shall be liable to prosecution if I have wilfully stated in it anything which I know to be false or do not believe to be true.

Dated the 21st day of 3, 1980.

Signed Conrad Cross

Signature witnessed by John Pyke DC 7086

I am a Director of George Bate Gunmakers Ltd., in Colmore Circus, Birmingham.

On Friday, 21st March, 1980 I was shown a .38 chief blank firing gun and I can say that it is identical to those which are sold in my shop. I was also shown green container containing blank cartridges with a price tag of £1.40p with our name printed above it, and I can say that these cartridges were bought from our shop premises.

I could say that there is a strong possibility that the gun was sold by our shop. The gun is valued at £10.26 pence.

STATEMENT OF WITNESS
(C.J. Act, 1967, ss. 2, 9, M.C. Rules, 1968, n58)

Statement of. Paul Anthony Bucknall

Age of Witness (if over 21 enter "over 21") . . . Over 21

Occupation of Witness . . . . Police Constable

Address and Telephone Number. . . . . West Midlands Police,
P. O. Box 52, Lloyd House

Colmore Circus Queensway,
Birmingham B4 6NQ

This statement, consisting of 2 pages each signed by me, is true to the best of my knowledge and belief and I make it knowing that, if it is tendered in evidence, I shall be liable to prosecution if I have wilfully stated in it anything which I know to be false or do not believe to be true.

Dated the 25th day of March, 1980.

Signed P.A. Bucknall PC 5269

Signature witnessed by ____________

I am a Police Constable in the West Midlands Police serving in the Explosives and Firearms Department. I have six years experience in the examination of firearms and ammunition.

On Friday 21 March 1980, Detective Constable 7086 Pyke, West Midlands Police, handed to me at the Explosives and Firearms Department, Police Headquarters, Birmingham:

1. One 6mm Mondial .38 Chiefs blank revolver (Exhibit no. 4)
2. Eight 6mm blank cartridges (Exhibit No.)

3. Eighty eight 6mm blank cartridges contained in plastic box (exhibit No.)

1. This is a 6mm Mondial .38 chiefs eight shot revolver of Italian manufacture which was designed to fire 6mm blank cartridges. It bears no serial number. When received by me it was neither cocked nor loaded. It is made of a relatively soft-nonferrous metal alloy and the barrel is partically blocked. A hardened steel plate is cast into the cylinder approximately 1/4" from the front which is done to prevent the cylinder chambers being drilled through. There is no evidence of any attempt having been made to drill through the partial blockages in either the cylinder or barrel. In its present condition it is not capable of discharging a bulleted cartridge, nor in my opinion can it be readily modified to do so. It is not a Section 1 firearm and acquisition and possession does not require the authority of a firearm certificate. As this blank firing gun has the general appearance of a revolver I consider it to be an imitation firearm as defined by Section 57(4) of the Firearms Act 1968.

2. These are eight 6mm blank cartridges of unknown manufacture, two of which have been fired.

3. These are eighty-eight 6mm blank cartridges of unknown manufacture contained in a plastic box. Both the eight 6mm blank cartridges (Exhibit No.) together with the eighty-eight 6mm blank cartridges (Exhibit No.) will chamber and are suitable for use in the blank revolver (Exhibit No. 4). Acquisition and possession of these 6mm blank cartridges does not require the authority of any certificate. These 6mm blank cartridges are not ammunition as defined in Section 57(2) of the Firearms Act 1968.

STATEMENT OF WITNESS
(C.J. Act, 1967, ss. 2, 9, M.C. Rules, 1968, n58)

Statement of. David Stuart Abolins

Age of Witness (if over 21 enter "over 21") . . . Over 21

Occupation of Witness . . . . Police Constable 3398

Address and Telephone Number. . . . . Airport Police Unit

Birmingham Airport Police Station

Birmingham Airport Tel: 021 742 6666

This statement, consisting of 5 pages each signed by me, is true to the best of my knowledge and belief and I make it knowing that, if it is tendered in evidence, I shall be liable to prosecution if I have wilfully stated in it anything which I know to be false or do not believe to be true.

Dated the 3rd day of April, 1980.

Signed D.S. Abolins PC 3398

Signature witnessed by ________________

I am Police Constable 3398 stationed at Birmingham Airport.

At about 11.25 am Wednesday, 19th March 1980, as a result of a radio message I went to the International Arrivals Lounge at Birmingham Airport where I saw David Fisher.

I said to him, "I understand that you are in possession of a large amount of money, and you have stated you are unemployed. Would you mind telling me how this money came into your possession?"

Fisher, said, "I needn't tell you anything in fact I'm not going to tell you."

I was then joined by Detective Constable SUTCLIFFE. I told DC SUTCLIFFE what had happened and he said to FISHER, "I am Detective Constable SUTCLIFFE where has this money come from."

FISHER said, "I've won it gambling here and there."

DC SUTCLIFFE said, "You are going to have to be more specific than here and there."

FISHER said, "I say I won it gambling you're going to have to find out anything else."

DC SUTCLIFFE said, "I am arresting you on suspicion of having stolen that money."

He cautioned FISHER who then said, "Do what you like."

DC SUTCLIFFE said, "I am taking possession of your money which amounts to £1,35807p until we get to the bottom of this matter (TS1 Exhibit No. 5).

FISHER was then taken to Birmingham Airport Police Station. At 12.15 pm in an interview room at the Police Station in company with DC SUTCLIFFE I again saw FISHER. DC SUTCLIFFE said to FISHER, "Mr. FISHER you know why you have been arrested, don't you."

FISHER said, "Yes of course."

DC SUTCLIFFE said, "Where has that money come from," he then cautioned FISHER.

FISHER said, "I told you I am saying I got it gambling."

DC SUTCLIFFE said, "All right where, here in Birmingham or over in Ireland."

FISHER said, "Here."

DC SUTCLIFFE said, "Well now if you tell me where you won it, when and from whom, I can check your story from other people can't I."

FISHER said, "Different blokes in pubs around, I can't say who."

DC SUTCLIFFE said, "What were you gambling on horses, dogs, cards."

FISHER said, "Just cards."

DC SUTCLIFFE said, "I have seen a few card schools in pubs but never with the sort of money you are carrying, you have L1,358.07p in your possession are you seriously saying you won all that amount at cards."

FISHER said, "Yes that's what I' saying."

DC SUTCLIFFE said, "You are going to have to tell me the names of some of the people who you say you won this money from and the pubs you know."

FISHER said, "I'll have to think about it I can't remember any names at the moment."

DC SUTCLIFFE said, "Which area were the pubs in then."

FISHER said, "Oh around the town you know."

DC SUTCLIFFE said, "Shall we carry on playing this silly game or do you think you could tell me the truth about all this."

FISHER said, "I want to see a solicitor and I'm saying no more to you about anything until you let me see one."

DC SUTCLIFFE said, "Yes you will be able to have a solicitor if that is what you want and in the meantime I shall go and search your room at 155 Warwick Road, and also I have got to make some enquiries at other addresses found in your possession."

FISHER said, "You bastard."

DC SUTCLIFFE said, "What do you mean by that."

FISHER said, "I suppose you are going to turn over all my friends and make life difficult for them as well."

DC SUTCLIFFE said, "David I am going to do what I consider to be my duty and that is to find out how you, a man out of work is in possession of such a large amount of money."

FISHER said, "You're not going to let go are you."

DC SUTCLIFFE said, "No not until you tell me the truth."

FISHER said, "Don't do anything yet, let me think for a bit."

DC SUTCLIFFE said, "Take as long as you like." After about five minutes, FISHER said, "O.K. I will make your job easy for you, I'll tell you."

DC SUTCLIFFE said, "What are you going to tell me now."

FISHER said, "How I got the money."

DC SUTCLIFFE said, "Yes, how."

FISHER, said, "It was a bank job."

DC SUTCLIFFE said, "Yes, where, what did you do."

FISHER said, "The Midlands Bank at Hockley, I held it up."

DC SUTCLIFFE said, "I don't know any details about this matter, rather than telling me verbally do you wish to make a written statement. If you do you can write it yourself or I will write it for you." He again cautioned FISHER.

FISHER said, "Yes I've told you I'll make your job easy for you, you write it."

DC SUTCLIFFE then took down a statement at FISHER's dictation which FISHER later signed and captioned. I witnessed the statement (TS2 Exhibit No. 6).

At the conclusion of the statement DC SUTCLIFFE said, "Now just to clear up a few points, I take it all the money that you have in your possession is from the robbery."

FISHER said, "Yes do you know I've spent over £1,000 in Ireland in a week just on booze I must be bloody barmy."

DC SUTCLIFFE said, "And where is the gun now."

FISHER said, "It's in my room at Warwick Road."

DC SUTCLIFFE said, "I will inform the Officers who are dealing with this case, of your arrest and you will no doubt be taken to another Police Station later today and charged."

FISHER said, "Yes O.K."

He was then placed in the cell.

Later that day I went to a house at 155 Warwick Road, and from FISHER's room I got one .38 Chiefs Starting Pistol, containing 6 live, 2 used starting blanks in chamber and one box of 6mm blank cartridges (DSA1 Exhibit No. 4).

STATEMENT OF WITNESS
(C.J. Act, 1967, ss. 2, 9, MC. Rules, 1968, n58)

Statement of. Thomas Sutcliffe

Age of Witness (if over 21 enter "over 21") . . . Over 21

Occupation of Witness . . . . Detective Constable

Address and Telephone Number. . . . . Airport Police Unit

Birmingham Airport Police Station

Birmingham Airport Tel: 021 742 6666

This statement, consisting of 4 pages each signed by me, is true to the best of my knowledge and belief and I make it knowing that, if it is tendered in evidence, I shall be liable to prosecution if I have wilfully stated in it anything which I know to be false or do not believe to be true.

Dated the 3rd day of April, 1980.

Signed Thomas Sutcliffe

Signature witnessed by ________________

At about 11.30 am on Wednesday, 19th March 1980, I went to the International Arrivals Lounge at Birmingham Airport where I saw a man I now know to be David Fisher and had detained by Police Constable 3398 Abolins.

PC ABOLINS told me in FISHER's presence, that FISHER had over £1,300 in cash in his possession, and would not give any reasonable explanation for having this amount of money on him. He also informed me that FISHER was unemployed.

I said to FISHER, "I am Detective Constable SUTCLIFFE where has this money come from."

FISHER said, "I have won it gambling here and there.

I said, "You are going to have to be more specific than here and there."

FISHER said, "I say I won it gambling, you're going to have to find out anything else."

I said, "I am arresting you on suspicion of having stolen that money." I cautioned Fisher who then said, "Do what you like."

I said, "I am taking possession of your money which amounts to £1,358.07p until we get to the bottom of this matter." (TS1 Exhibit No. 5).

FISHER was then taken to Birmingham Airport Police Station.

At 12.15 pm in an interview room at the Police Station accompanied by PC ABOLINS I again saw FISHER.

I said to him, "Mr. FISHER you know why you have been arrested don't you."

FISHER said, "Yes of course."

I said, "Where has that money come from." and cautioned him.

FISHER said, "I told you I'm saying I got it gambling."

I said, "Alright where, here in Birmingham, or over in Ireland."

FISHER said, "here."

I said, "Well now if you tell me where you won it, when and from whom I can check your story from other people, can't I."

FISHER said, "Different blokes in pubs, around I can't say who."

I said, "What were you gambling on, horses, dogs, cards."

FISHER said, "Just cards."

I said, "I've seen a few card schools in pubs but never with the sort of money you're carrying, you have £1,358.07p in your possession and you're seriously saying you won all that amount at cards."

FISHER said, "Yes that's what I'm saying."

I said, "You are going to have to tell me the names of some of the people who you say you won this money from and the pubs you know."

FISHER said, "I'll have to think about it I can't remember any names at the moment."

I said, "Which area were the pubs in then."

Fisher replied, "Oh around the town you know."

I said, "Shall we carry on playing this silly game or do you think you could tell me the truth about all this."

FISHER said, "I want to see a solicitor and I am saying no more to you about anything until you let me see one."

I said, "Yes you will be able to have a solicitor if that's what you want, and in the meantime I shall go and search your room at 155 Warwick Road and also I've got to make some enquiries at other addresses found in your possession."

FISHER said, "You bastard."

I said, "What do you mean by that."

FISHER said, "I suppose your going to turn over all my friends and make life difficult for them as well."

I said, "David I am going to do what I consider to be my duty and that is to find out how you a man out of work is in possession of such a large amount of money."

FISHER said, "You're not going to let go are you."

I said, "No not until you tell me the truth."

FISHER said, "Don't do anything yet let me think for a bit."

I said, "Take as long as you like."

After about five minutes FISHER said, "O.K. I'll make your job easy for you. I'll tell you."

I said, "What are you going to tell me now."

FISHER said, "How I got the money."

I said, "Yes how."

FISHER said, "It was a bank job."

I said, "Yes where, what did you do."

FISHER said, "The Midland Bank at Hockley, I held it up."

I said, "I don't know any details about this matter rather than telling me verbally do you wish to make a written statement if you do you can write it yourself or I will write it for you," and I again cautioned him.

FISHER said, "Yes I've told you I'll make your job easy for you. You write it."

I then took down a statement at his dictation which he later signed and captioned in my presence (TS2 Exhibit No. 6).

At the conclusion of the statement I said to FISHER, "Now just to clear up a few points I take it all of the money that you have in your possession is from the robbery."

FISHER said, "Yes do you know I've spent over £1,000 in Ireland in a week just on booze, I must be bloody barmy."

I said, "And where is the gun now."

FISHER said, "It's in my room at Warwick Road."

I said, "I will inform the Officers who are dealing with this case of your arrest and you will no doubt be taken to another Police Station later today and charged."

FISHER said, "Yes, O.K."

He was then placed in a cell.

STATEMENT OF WITNESS
(C.J. Act, 1967, ss 2, 9 M.C. Rules, 1968 n58)

Statement of. . . . . John Pyke

Age of Witness (if over 21 enter "over 21") . . . Over 21

Occupation of Witness . . . . Detective Constable 7086

Address and Telephone Number. . . . . West Midlands Police

Steelhouse Lane Police Station

Birmingham 021 236 5000

This statement consisting of 3 pages each signed by me, is true to the best of my knowledge and belief and I make it knowing that, if it is tendered in evidence, I shall be liable to prosecution if I have wilfully stated in it anything which I know to be false or do not believe to be true.

Dated the 15th day of April, 1980.

Signed John Pyke DC 7086

Signature witnessed by ________________

At 4.20 pm on Wednesday, 19 March 1980 together with DC 2253 Butler I saw a man I now know to be David FISHER in the Detective Inspectors office at Steelhouse Lane Police Station.

I said, "David, I have read your statement which you made earlier today. There's a few things which I want to make clear. Now before I say anything further I must tell you that you are not obliged to say anything unless you wish to do so but whatever you say will be taken down in writing and given in evidence. Do you understand?" He replied, "Yes." I said, "To start off you say in your statement, 'I'd got a starting pistol on me. I bought it from Bates' in the town'. Dave, which Bates', the shop near to the Post and Mail Building?" FISHER said, "Yes." I said, "When did you buy it?" He said, "The same day as I robbed the bank. I said, "How much did it cost?" He said, "I can't remember." I said, "You go on to say that - 'She just handed over some money to me, I just ran round a few corners, I tried a telephone box'. Now tell me when you came out of the bank which way did you run?" FISHER said, "Round the corner down I think it's called Well Street." I said, "Where to then?" He said, "Past the garage down to the next street and turned left." I said, "I think that street's name is Stainsby Avenue." He said, "I don't know the name." I said, "Where did you go then?" FISHER said, "Down across between some flats and then I went to the phone box." DC Butler said, "What have you done with the cash you stole?" FISHER said, "I've spent a lot on booze and hotel bills, God I've had a lot to drink, I went to Ireland for St. Patrick's Day but I didn't have a drink on the day as I was in such a bad state. I couldn't even get out of bed." DC Butler said, "Amongst your property which you had with you at the airport was a lot of new property, did you buy any of it with the stolen money." FISHER said, "Yes." DC Butler said, "What these two rings?" (Ref. No.) (Ex. No.). FISHER said, "Yes." DC Butler said, "How much were they?" He said, "I think they were £68 each." DC Butler said, "What about this watch?" (Ref. No.)(Ex. No.) FISHER said, "Yes that was with the money." DC Butler said, "How much did that cost?" He said, "£53." DC Butler said, "This doll?" (Ref. No.)(Ex. No.) FISHER said, "Yeh I got that at the gift shop at Dublin airport." DC Butler said, "This aftershave and other stuff" (Ref. No.)(Ex. No.) FISHER said, "I got that in Galway." DC Butler said, "With the stolen cash?" He said, "Yes." DC Butler said, "What about this holdall?" (Ref. No.)(Ex. No.) FISHER replied, "Yeh I bought that in Woolworths in Galway. I also bought the air tickets to Dublin and back." DC Butler said, "We have brought all your belongings from your room in the hostel. Is there anything amongst this stuff which you have brought with the proceeds of the robbery?" FISHER said, "Yes this suit I had it from Fosters in Newtown." (Ref. No.)(Ex. No.) I said, "How much was that?" He said, "£39, Oh I also had that jacket too from the same place and I had the radio from a shop up Newtown." DC Butler said, "Did you wear any of this clothing when you committed the robbery?" FISHER said, "I think I had that anorak on, yes I did." Ref. No.)(Ex. No. 7). DC Butler said, "Anything else?" FISHER said, "Yes I had that hat on." (Ref. No.)(Ex. No. 8). I said, "The cashier says that you put the money in a plastic bag where is that now?" He said, "I used one of them two bags." (Ref. No.) (Ex. No. 9) DC Butler said, "Would you like to make a further written statement about what you told us?" FISHER said, "Yes." DC Butler said, "Do you want to write it or shall I write it for you?" FISHER said, "You write it." DC Butler then took down a written statement under caution which I captioned. DC Butler and myself were later present when he was charged and cautioned to which he made no reply. On the same day I took possession of £1,358.07p (Ref. No.)(Ex. No. 5) from DC Sutcliffe and a .38 'Chief' blank firing gun from PC 3398 Abolins. I later placed the cash in the Detained Property Office at Digbeth and the firearm in the Detained Property Office at the Armory. Also on this date together with DC Butler I recovered from 155 Warwick Road, Olton a red woollen hat (Ref. No.)(Ex. No. 8) and a blue anorak (Ref. No.)(Ex. No. 7) from a wardrobe and two plastic bags (Ref. No.) (Ex. No. 9) from a chest of drawers.

STATEMENT OF WITNESS
(C.J. Act, 1967, ss 2, 9, M.C. Rules, 1968, n58)

Statement of. Christopher Butler

Age of Witness (if over 21 enter "over 21") . . . Over 21

Occupation of Witness . . . . Detective Constable 2253

Address and Telephone Number. . . . . West Midlands Police

Steelhouse Lane Police Station

Birmingham 236 5000

This statement consisting of 3 pages each signed by me, is true to the best of my knowledge and belief and I make it knowing that, if it is tendered in evidence, I shall be liable to prosecution if I have wilfully stated in it anything which I know to be false or do not believe to be true.

Dated the 15th day of 4, 1980.

Signed Christopher Butler

Signature witnessed by ________________

At 4.20 pm on Wednesday, 19 March 1980 together with DC 7086 Pyke I saw a man I now know to be David FISHER in the Detective Inspectors Office at Steelhouse Lane Police Station. DC Pyke said, "David, I have read your statement which you made earlier today. There's a few things which I want to make clear. Now before I say anything further I must tell you that you are not obliged to say anything unless you wish to do so but whatever you say will be taken down in writing and given in evidence. Do you understand?" He replied, "Yes." DC Pyke said, "To start off you say in your statement, 'I'd got a starting pistol on me. I bought it from Bates' in the town.' Dave, which Bates' the shop near to the Post and Mail Building?" FISHER said, "Yes." DC Pyke said, "When did you buy it?" He said, "The same day as I robbed the bank." DC Pyke said, "How much did it cost?" He said, "I can't remember." DC Pyke said, "You go on to say that - 'She just handed over some money to me, I just ran round a few corners, I tried a telephone box.' Now tell me when you came out of the bank which way did you run?" FISHER said, "Round the corner down I think it's called Well Street." DC Pyke said, "Where to then?" He said, "Past the garage down to the next street and turned left." DC Pyke said, "I think that street's name is Stainsby Avenue." He said, "I don't know the name." DC Pyke said, "Where did you go then?" FISHER said, "Down across between some flats and then I went to the phone box." I said, "What have you done with the cash you stole?" FISHER said, "I've spent a lot on booze and hotel bills, God I've had a lot to drink, I went to Ireland for St. Patrick's Day but I didn't have a drink on the day as I was in such a bad state. I couldn't even get out of bed." I said, "Amongst your property which you had with you at the airport was a lot of new property, did you buy any of it with the stolen money?" FISHER said, "Yes." I said, "What these two rings?" (Ref. No.)(Ex. No.) FISHER said, "Yes." I said, "How much were they?" He said, "I think they were £68 each." I said, "What about this watch?" (Ref. No.)(Ex. No.) FISHER said, "Yes that was with the money." I said, "How much did that cost?" He said, "£53." I said, "This doll?" (Ref. No.)(Ex. No.) FISHER said, "Yeh I got that at the gift shop at Dublin Airport." I said, "This aftershave and other stuff?" (Ref. No.)(Ex. No.) FISHER said, "I got that in Galway." I said, "With the stolen cash?" He said, "Yes." I said, "What about this holdall?" (Ref. No.)(Ex. No.) FISHER replied, "Yeh I bought that in Woolworths in Galway. I also bought the air tickets to Dublin and back." I said, "We have brought all your belongings from your room in the hostel. Is there anything amongst this stuff which you have brought with the proceeds of the robbery?" FISHER said, "Yes this suit I had it from Fosters in Newtown." DC Pyke said, "How much was that?" He said, "£39, oh I also had that jacket too from the same place and I had the radio from a shop up Newtown." I said, "Did you wear any of this clothing when you committed the robbery?" FISHER said, "I think I had that anorak on, yes I did." (Ref. No.) (Ex. No. 7) I said, "Anything else?" FISHER said, "Yes I had that hat on." (Ref. No.) (Ex. No. 8) DC Pyke said, "The cashier says that you put the money in a plastic bag where is that now?" He said, "I used one of them two bags." (Ref. No.) (Ex. No. 9) I said, "Would you like to make a further written statement about what you told us?" FISHER said, "Yes." I said, "Do you want to write it or shall I write it for you?" FISHER said, "You write it." I then took down a written statement under caution which DC Pyke captioned. DC Pyke and myself were later present when he was charged and cautioned to which he made no reply. Also on the same date together with DC Pyke I recovered from 155 Warwick Road, Olton, a red woollen hat (Ref. No.)(Ex. No. 8) and a blue anorak (Ref. No.)(Ex. No. 7) from a wardrobe and two plastic bags (Ref. No.) (Ex. No. 9) from a chest of drawers.

APPENDIX IV

POLICE REPORT PREPARED FOR COMMITTAL PROCEEDING

1. The defendant FISHER was arrested on Wednesday, 19th March, 1980 and charged as per the attached schedule. He has remained in custody since his arrest and is presently remanded until Thursday, 24th April, 1980. These papers are submitted with a view to committing FISHER in respect of the offence of robbery. An amended charge has been included and this varies in respect of the property stolen only. Following perusal of these papers you may feel that the Suggested Further Charge should also be preferred.

2. The complainant in this matter, the Midland Bank is a medium size bank occupying a corner position on the A41 at the junction of Gt. Hampton Street and Well Street. It is situated in a mainly manufacturing district on the fringe of Birmingham's Jewellery quarter from where it draws most of its customers. The interior is modern and well lit with security glass and grills at each of its three tills. Plans of the scene and photographs are included in these papers for your information.

3. At about 3 p.m. on Monday, 25th February, 1980 Miss Yvonne Carol GARDENER aged 20 years, a Bank Clerk was alone at the counter serving at the centre till when she saw a man enter the bank and stand at the till next to her. There were not customers present in the Bank. After about a minute Miss GARDENER spoke to the man who then produced a gun from his pocket and said, "Money, Money" and indicated Miss GARDENER'S till. She then took from a drawer a bundle of bank notes later ascertained to be £3,800 and handed them to the man. He then ran out of the bank into Well Street making good his escape. As he did so he passed Mr. Norman Barnard WITHAM the Bank Manager who

was walking along Well Street in the opposite direction.

4. Miss GARDENER and Mr. WITHAM were the only persons traced who saw the robber. Both supplied a description of the suspect and Miss GARDENER prepared a photofit picture. The question of identification in the event of a 'Not Guilty' plea will be important and I will deal with this aspect later.

5. Enquiries were made both locally and of a general nature but no information was forthcoming.

6. However, on Wednesday, 19th March, 1980 David FISHER arrived at Elmdon Airport. Information was passed to Police Constable ABOLINS of Airport Police Unit that FISHER was in possession of a large sum of money and as a result he was interviewed by Police Constable ABOLINS and Detective Constable SUTCLIFFE.

7. FISHER subsequently made a statement under caution in which he admits the offence.

8. As a result of what FISHER said, the gun used in the robbery and certain items of clothing were recovered from FISHER'S room in an exoffenders hostel.

9. FISHER was further interviewed by Detective Constable BUTLER and Detective Constable Pyke and made a further statement under caution. He was later charged.

10. The descriptions supplied by GARDENER and WITHAM it must be said do not accurately describe FISHER, in particular the reference to the robber being negroid or Asian are particularly inaccurate. FISHER is of European appearance albeit of swarthy complexion. There is a discrepancy also in Miss GARDENER'S and Mr. WITHAM'S account of the colour of the clothing worn by FISHER. FISHER indicated the clothing worn during the commission of the offence and this was recovered. No clothing of similar colour to what described was traced to his possession.

11. A statement is included from Mr. CROSS of George Bates, Gunmakers Ltd. and this corroborates as far as possible FISHER'S account of his possession of the gun.

12. The gun was examined by Police Constable Paul BUCKNALL who is able to say that it is an imitation firearm as defined by Section 57(4) of the Firearms Act, 1968, in consequence its possession is not restricted.

13. The vehicle and driver referred to by the witness WITHAM were traced and eliminated.

14. The G.P.O. van and workmen referred to by WITHAM have not been traced.

15. A list of property the proceeds of the cash stolen in the robbery is included. The property together with the recovered cash of L1,358.07p is sought as restitution by the Midland Bank Ltd., and compensation in respect of the outstanding balance.

* * *

APPENDIX V

ANTECEDENT REPORT

WEST MIDLANDS POLICE GM/PF

COURT NO. 80/0.637

WC.209.

CROWN COURT at BIRMINGHAM

ANTECEDENT REPORT David FISHER CRO.No. 8590/66

Date 7th May 1980

David FISHER was born in Birmingham on the 5th January 1947 and is 33 years of age.

He is eligible to an extended sentence. A notice as required by Section 29, Powers of Criminal Courts Act, 1973 has not been given to him. If required, it is intended to prove the convictions and sentences dated (1) 3rd February 1972, (2) 8th November 1973 and (3) 26th August 1976.

He is a single man and at the time of his arrest was of no fixed address. His parents live on the outskirts of Birmingham and he is an only child.

FISHER was educated at a Secondary Modern School until 15 years of age.

He says since leaving school and interspersed between custodial sentences he has had employments as a shop assistant in his fathers ironmongery business, builders labourer and casual worker.

He says that from April 1976 to June 1976 he was self-employed as a cafe proprietor.

FISHER was last released from a prison sentence on the 10th December 1979.

He was unemployed at the time of his arrest and in receipt of Social Security Benefits.

He was arrested on the 19th March 1980 and has since remained in custody.

There are previous convictions recorded against him.

Gordon Mayling
Detective Constable

WEST MIDLANDS POLICE PF

COURT NO. 80/0 637

WC.207.

CROWN COURT at BIRMINGHAM

LIST OF CONVICTIONS OF David FISHER

DATE	COURT	OFFENCE	SENT / ORDER
24.10.63	Birmingham M.C.	Factorybreaking	£10
7.2.66	ditto	Shopbreaking 2 cases	£20 on each
18.4.66	ditto	Drunk	£1
6.5.66	ditto	On enclosed premises	3 mths detention
7.11.67	ditto	Drunk and disorderly Wilful damage	£2 £2 + 25/- comp
26.1.68	ditto	On enclosed premises	3 mths imp susp 2 yrs
1.4.68	ditto	Drunk and disorderly	£5
10.12.68	ditto	Shopbreaking Drunk and disorderly Assault P.C. Breach of suspended sentences of 26.1.68	3 mths imp 1 mth imp conc 3 mths imp conc 3 mths imp consec
29.9.69	ditto	Drunk and disorderly	£2
9.2.70	ditto	Drunk	£3
2.3.70	ditto	Drunk and disorderly	£5
11.6.71	ditto	M/car take & drive away No insurance	£25 L.E. Disq 1 yr £25 L.E.
26.7.71	ditto	Drunk	£5
3.2.72	Birmingham C.C.	Burglary Take & drive away Drive whilst disq	30 mths impt 12 mths imp CONC 12 mths imp conc disq 3 yrs
21.5.73	Birmingham M.C.	Drunk & disorderly	£6
8.11.73	Dudley C.C.	Take & drive away Going equipped for theft Drive whilst disq Dangerous driving Take and drive away Possess offensive weapon Assault on Police	12 mths imp 3 mths imp conc 6 mths imp conc 4 mths imp conc 12 mths imp consec 3 mths imp conc 1 mth imp conc

DATE	COURT	OFFENCE	SENT / ORDER
24.5.76	Birmingham M.C.	Drunk	£5
4.6.76	ditto	Loiter with intent Going equipped	£50 or 60 days + £15 L.A. £100 or 90 days consec L.E
26.8.76	Birmingham C.C.	Take conveyance 2 cases Theft (2 cases) Burglary Robbery Carry firearm (2 TIC)	12 mths impt each case conct 12 mths impt conct each case 3 yrs impt conct 5 yrs impt conct 2 yrs impt Restn order for gun
25.1.80	Birmingham M.C.	Drunk & disorderly	Fd. £20 Adv Fee £5

APPENDIX VI

COMMENTS UPON DEPOSITIONS

Comments upon Depositions of David Fisher 4.7.1980

PARKER

No Comment.

DEWEY

No Comment.

GARDENER

4. My movements at this time are as my Notice of Alibi shows.

There are thousands of bags such as the one I had in my possession. I can't tell whether it was the same type of bag or whatever.

It is quite possible that I did have notes in my possession from the bank.

I know who broke into the bank and I was gambling with him at a later stage.

WITHAM

8. I do drive but I don't own a car. The last time I owned a car was in 1976. I do occasionally hire a car but not at this time.

WOODWARD

Agree.

CROSS

Agree.

BUCKNALL

14. I know nothing about guns.

ABOLINS

16. The plane leaving Dublin was at 9.45. I must have landed about 10.15-10.30 a.m.

I was stopped by Security People and detained. They searched through my luggage twice and the police arrived about 45 minutes later.

I told the Police that I had already explained about the money and they wouldn't believe me.

I gave them my account. They wanted to know how an unemployed man could go to Dublin etc. I told them a friend had given me the money.

Then said "all I say is that I won it gambling, thats it".

Can't remember being arrested. I wasn't cautioned until reaching the station.

I was asking to see a Solicitor as soon as they found the money. They wouldn't let me telephone a Solicitor.

There was actually £1,428.00 approximately. I actually signed for this amount in the Airport.

They took me in the car to the station. It is only a few hundred yards away.

I was placed in a Detention room. He came in gave me a blanket and left me for 20 minutes. They then interviewed me.

Sutcliffe was talking about winning money in pubs but he said it was such a lot of money. I said "I didn't say it was a pub".

He wanted to know, I said "I'm not saying anything else I want to see a Solicitor and make a telephone call".

He said "You've got over £1,400 in your possession.

He asked me about names. I said, "You know the score I'm not saying anything."

He said "No way are you going to make a statement or give me a satisfactory account of how you got the money."

He told his mate to get someone to search 155 Warwick Road and also go around to an address at 13 Haselour Road, Kingshurst. This was the address of a friend's wife.

When I called him a bastard, he laughed and said "we are going to make as much aggravation as possible through other people and let those other people know who has caused this aggravation."

He didn't actually say that he was going to beat me up but it was at the back of my mind.

I was afraid of the aggravation that disturbing my friend's wife and other people would cause.

I also knew from experience that I would have been fitted up if they hadn't have found anything.

I told them I would have to think about it before I made a statement.

They didn't want me to tell the truth, they wanted me to make a statement so I would incriminate myself.

They left me in the room and then looked in after 5-10 minutes.

He said "are you going to make a statement now?" I said "Yes".

I tried to think of what I could tell which would convince them and then to able to prove my innocence later.

I knew about the Midlands Bank at Hockley from the Paki or Asian in the Gothic pub.

I had bought the gun Wednesday or Thursday before from Bates in town. It cost about £10. I knew it was in my room and I knew they would find it.

It was in the wardrobe.

I bought the gun for my girlfriend's lad. It was too loud for him and I never gave it to him.

SUTCLIFFE

As above.

PYKE

25. I was at the Airport at least two hours before being moved to Steelhouse Lane.

I told the officers that I couldn't remember when I bought the gun.

I said I can't remember where I ran to. He said did you do this and that. I said "Yes" etc.

They wanted to know what I had bought. I didn't know what to say.

He said "this looks new, have you bought this". I said "Yes" etc.

I had bought all this stuff, not with the stolen money but money I had won gambling.

The Pakistani told me it was £4,300 stolen from the bank.

APPENDIX VII

PROOFS OF EVIDENCE

DAVID FISHER 4.7.80
7 HASELOUR ROAD,
KINGSHURST,
BIRMINGHAM

At present in H.M. Prison
Winson Green
D.O.B. 5.1.1947
AGED 33

I am a single man born in Birmingham and have always lived here. I do not have any relatives from Ireland at all but used to go around with an Irish girl.

I received a Secondary Modern Education leaving school at 15.

I have had jobs in shops etc. My last job was with my father in a hardware shop in Summer Lane.

I still have connections with my parents but they do not come to visit me at all whilst in prison. I haven't seen them for about 3 1/2 months.

I met Caroline Walker a couple of weeks before my arrest. She is divorced and has 3 children. She comes up to see me twice a week.

She seems quite genuine and has never had anything to do with crime at all.

I was released from my last custodial sentence on December 10th. I served for 3 yrs. 5 months in Longlarton of a 5 year sentence for robbery.

It was a book-makers shop and I stole £34. I was also imprisoned for contravening the firearms act.

I have been arrested quite a few times for drunk and disorderly. I have had drinking problems in the past.

I have various friends in the criminal fraternity. They are mainly people who I have met in prison and have stayed in touch with.

David Fisher 7.8.1980

Jimmy Jackson is in High Croft Hospital he is an alcoholic. He has been in the hospital for three months.

I remember the 25th February 1980 reasonably well.

I was staying at my girlfriend's house and returned to the hostel at 7.00 a.m. I returned there to pick up dirty clothes for my girlfriend to wash for me.

I left the hostel at 9.00-9.30 a.m. and went to Asda in the Bull Ring Shopping Centre and got a couple of tins of food.

I walked around to the Crown Pub in Corporation Street. I saw someone I knew about a party.

I was only there about 10 minutes then caught a Taxi to the Gothic Pub in Hockley arriving there at about 10.50 a.m. I had to wait outside for it to open. I met Jimmy Jackson and Michael McDonough outside. I have known each of them years. We were in the Gothic Pub until 2.40 p.m. I had about 6-7 pints of beer which wouldn't make me drunk.

Jimmy was drunk when he left. Mickey stayed in the pub as far as I know.

I offered Jim a meal from a cafe but he told me he was having something to eat in Lewis'.

I made my way towards the cafe. The time was about 2.45 p.m.

About half way down Constitution Hill I realised that the place was knocked down.

I went back towards the Gothic and went to his flat in Newtown. The time was about 2.50-2.55 p.m.

Jimmy was in the flat at the time. We stayed there until 3.30 p.m.3.45 p.m.

I persuaded him to come with me. We called a Taxi and then went to the hostel. I had to drop some other washing and pay the rent.

David Fisher 11th July 1980

My social life involves drinking regular about five times a week. I use pubs in the City Centre or perhaps the local Golden Arrow, Warwick Road.

When I was released from my last custodial sentence I went to live at a hostel. The hostel was at Olten. There were roughly a dozen ex-offenders there. The rent there was £11.20 and I was getting on reasonably well. I was there when I was arrested.

I worked casually painting and decorating for friends. I was also drawing Social Security of £25.10 per week.

I have also done a little bit of gambling. I gamble mainly on horses but I have also got into card school.

The card schools were mainly held at a Cafe in Alum Rock on the Alum Rock Road. I don't know the name. I only went there three or four times.

I met an Asian fellow in the Gothic pub shortly after I came out. He know of me but I didn't know him. He knew a friend of mine.

He was about 28 years old, smartly dressed reasonably tidy. He was a Pakistani or Indian with short hair. I didn't know his name at all. I addressed him as 'Chief'.

On one occasion he mentioned a card school.

I had £50 plus on me because I had drawed a fortnight money.

He took down to the Cafe introduced me and about six of us played Coluckie. It is an Indian game that I knew.

We were playing £10 per game, but it is possible for one person to put in £30.

I lost the first two games. I was intending to play only with £30 and then finish. I won the third game which was £90. I carried playing and won three hands out of 6 or 7. I cleared £200 that day.

There were two Greeks, one Pakistani and the rest were white.

We were playing upstairs.

I went down there the following Friday and won £400-£500.

The third occasion I played draw poker with two others who had quite a bit of money. It was played with a split deck.

I won almost £2,000 altogether. There was an argument and I had to wait for a taxi to come and take me away.

The owner was taking £10 out of each game as a form of commission. He then supplies sandwiches and drinks.

My friend the Pakistani told me the week before I went to Ireland that he had robbed the bank.

He was one of the main losers in the card games and I wondered if he was upset. He said "How do you fancy doing a robbery." I said "I don't want to know". He started saying it would be worth a bit of money. He wanted me to drive the car for him.

He said "I know you have been done for robbery before I decided to ask you". I asked him "If the money he had lost were proceeds from a robbery and he said yes."

I was going to sell him a starting pistol and he told me that that was the gun he used on the robbery.

He had given it back to me because he decided he didn't want to buy it.

He described the circumstances in a boastful sort of way. He said he had got away down Wells Street and they drove off.

The following Tuesday I went to Ireland with about £2,000 on me. The notes were paperclipped from when I had won the money.

I spent £600-£700 in 8 days in Ireland, on booze, hotels and having a good time. I went to Golway, I haven't got relatives but I do have friends there.

On the 19th March I flew back to Elmdon. I was carrying holdalls and carrier bags. I walked through the 'nothing to declare section.' I was apprehended in the arrivals lounge. I had my embarkation card checked.

As I got to the counter he said "Have you got baggage". I said "Yes". He said "do you mind if I check them". I said "No".

I took the bags to him and two rings were found, various odds and ends.

My pockets were emptied and I showed him my wallet containing about £20. The bulk of the money was inside my inside pocket. I told them I had £20-£30. They seemed satisfied and asked where I had bought the rings from. They checked this out and said "how do you manage to go to Ireland whilst unemployed." I had to fill a form in and put all correct details apart from my parents address being filled in.

After this I started to get annoyed. I said "Are you arresting me for anything. I am going". One of them said "You owe a £5 fine which you haven't paid. They said you will have to wait for the Police to come to pay the fine at the station."

I didn't owe the £5 at all.

Whilst I was waiting my pockets were searched and my money was found.

He said where did you get the money from. I said "You won't believe me. I won it gambling." He said "You're nicked it." I told him there was £1400 there. I said there was £1500 but I used some of it so there should be roughly £1400. He then said to someone "find out if there has been any robberies done." He came back later and shook his head.

The uniformed officer then arrived. They told him about finding the money on me and another one came over to see me.

They took me to the station in the car.

My particulars were taken and I was put into a detention room.

I was then seen as my comments upon Depositions show.

APPENDIX VIII
SOCIAL INQUIRY REPORT

to the
Crown Court, sitting at Birmingham
on May, 1980

1. Name David FISHER Age 33 years

Address c/o 7 Haselour Road, Kingshurst, Birmingham. Date of Birth 5/1/47

P.S.D.

Present Offence Robbery

2. I have been in contact with Mr. Fisher, both as his through and after-care officer since June, 1979, when I visited him in Long Lartin Prison. The information contained in this report is based on records, interviews and personal observations.

3. The address given by Mr. Fisher is that of his girlfriend, whom he knew for approximately two months prior to his arrest. Apparently she is a divorcee with three children and has no connections with the criminal fraternity.

4. Mr. Fisher was adopted at the age of three weeks and obviously has great affection for his adoptive parents. His father was in partnership in a retail iron-mongery business and although there was little profit until about ten years ago, it is now a flourishing enterprise. Mr. Fisher says he thinks his parents were indulgent and perhaps gave him too much affection. I am told they view the life-style he has pursued since the age of sixteen years with self-recrimination. Mr. Fisher absolves his mother and father and accepts complete responsibility for his own actions. Since being discharged from prison in December, 1979, and taking up residence in Dormer House Hostel, he has been a frequent visitor to their home and his parents have given him emotional and financial support during the last few months.

5. At the age of fifteen years Mr. Fisher left his secondary modern school without any formal academic qualifications. He tells me he never liked the academic side and admits to 'playing around', but he did enjoy cricket and football. It seems he became involved with a gang during the last two years and gained a sense of importance from 'smashing things up'. In retrospect he feels this was the beginning of his criminal career.

6. For the first two years after leaving school, Mr. Fisher changed his employment at frequent intervals. He then spent four years as an unskilled worker in a factory. He has also spent several years working with his father at various times, but apart from a brief period as a self-employed driver, has not been in regular employment since 1973. I tried to encourage him to answer

advertisements at the beginning of this year, but in spite of several applications, nothing that Mr. Fisher deemed suitable materialized. It may well have been, however, that there was a lack of confidence in his own ability.

7. There have been no health problems, but Mr. Fisher's list of previous convictions for being drunk and disorderly indicate that alcohol has been a dominant factor in his life. He says he is able to go for periods without drinking, but then a bout could last for several weeks, until he became too physically ill to continue. He is then able to abstain and regain his health, but seems to lack the desire for total sobriety.

8. Whilst Mr. Fisher has a friendly manner and communicates well on a superficial level, he would seem to have difficulty in forming close relationships. He suffers from a low image of himself and it may well be that his drinking bouts initially start as a need to project a more confident veneer.

9. Mr. Fisher is a man who until now has accepted his prison sentences with certain fatalism and records show that he has not evinced any particular interest even in parole. He explains this attitude by saying that in the past, if he could not follow the only lifestyle that would satisfy him, and this could cost up to £100 a day, he felt he was better off in prison. Since meeting his present girlfriend at the beginning of this year, he tells me this attitude has now changed and believes it is possible to have a satisfying relationship as a normal wage earner.

10. I am told by Mr. Fisher that he is pleading not guilty to the offence of entering a Bank, producing a hand gun and demanding money.

11. Although Mr. Fisher had a stable home background, it may be that his parents, in an endeavour to compensate him for being an adopted child, were over indulgent and protective when behavioural difficulties began to emerge during adolescence. He never found satisfying employment and seems to have drifted into criminality as a way of life. Although he does not yet accept that one of his major problem areas is alcohol consumption, he does concede the possibility of a link between this and his record. Prison is not a deterrant and unless there is some change in his personal life that will enhance his confidence, for example the development of the relationship with his present girlfriend, there seems little likelihood of any future motivation for change. In view of the seriousness of the offence, Mr. Fisher realises the inevitability of a prison sentence if there is a finding of guilt.

Probation Officer
J. M. Salmon (Mrs.)

BIBLIOGRAPHY

Abrahams, G. *Police Questioning and the Judges' Rules*. London: Oyez, 1964.

Allen, C. *The Queen's Peace*. London: Stevens and Sons, 1953.

______. "The Report of the Departmental Committee on Proceedings Before Examining Justices." 1958 *Criminal Law Review* 647.

Archbold, *Pleading, Evidence and Practice in Criminal Cases*. Fortieth Edition. London: Sweet and Maxwell, 1979.

Baldwin, J., and McConvile, M. *Confessions in the Crown Court*. Royal Commission on Criminal Procedure, Research Study No. 5. London: H.M.S.O., 1980.

______. *Jury Trials*. London: Oxford University Press, 1979.

______. *Negotiated Justice*. London: Martin Robertson, 1977.

______. "Police Interrogation and the Right to See a Solicitor." 1979 *Criminal Law Review* 145.

Bankowski, Z., and Mungham, G. *Images of Law*. London: Routledge and Kegan Paul, 1976.

Barnard, D. *The Criminal Court in Action*. London: Butterworths, 1979.

Barnes, P. "The Office of the Director of Public Prosecutions." In *The Prosecution Process*. Institute of Judicial Administration, University of Birmingham Monograph, 1975.

Bates, J. V. *The Prosecutor's Handbook*. London: Oyez, 1980.

Bottomley, A. K. *Criminology in Focus*. Oxford: Martin Robertson, 1979.

______. *Decisions in the Penal Process*. London: Martin Robertson, 1973.

Bottoms, A. E., and McClean, J. D. *Defendants in the Criminal Process*. London: Routledge and Kegan Paul, 1976.

Brown, S. "The Role of Counsel for the Crown." In *The Prosecution Process*. Institute of Judicial Administration, University of Birmingham Monograph, 1975.

Burney, E. *Magistrate, Court and Community*. London: Hutchinson, 1979).

Carlen, P. *Magistrates' Justice*. London: Martin Robertson, 1976.

Central Statistics Office. Annual Abstract of Statistics. London: H.M.S.O., 1980.

Chapman, S. G., and St. Johnston, T. E. *The Police Heritage in England and America: A Developmental Survey*. East Lansing: Michigan State University Press, 1962.

Cooke, R. K. "A Police Officer's Notes." 1954 *Criminal Law Review* 833.

Coutts, J. A. *The Accused: A Comparative Study*. London: Stevens and Sons, 1966.

Cox, B. *Civil Liberties in Britain*. Harmondsworth: Penguin, 1975.

Criminal Law Revision Committee. *Evidence (General) 11th Report*. Command 4991. London: H.M.S.O., 1972.

Criminal Statistics: England and Wales 1977. Command 7289. London: H.M.S.O., 1978.

Cross, R. *Cross on Evidence*. Fifth Edition. London: Butterworths, 1979.

______. *The English Sentence System*. Third Edition. London: Butterworths, 1981.

______, and Jones, P. A. *An Introduction to Criminal Law*. London: Butterworths, 1972.

Danks, P.K.L. "The Prosecuting Solicitor." In *The Prosecution Process*. Institute of Judicial Administration, University of Birmingham Monograph, 1975.

Devlin, Lord P. *The Criminal Prosecution in England*. Oxford: Oxford University Press, 1960.

______. *The Judge*. Oxford: Oxford University Press, 1979.

______. *Trial by Jury*. London: Stevens and Sons, 1956.

Director of Public Prosecutions. Written Evidence to the Royal Commission on Criminal Procedure, 1978.

Elkin, W. A. *The English Penal System*. Harmondsworth: Penguin, 1957.

Fellman, D. *The Defendant's Rights*. New York: Rinehart, 1958.

Fitzgerald, P. J. *Criminal Law and Punishment*. Oxford: Clarendon Press, 1962.

Friesen, E. C., and Scott, I. R. *English Criminal Justice*. Birmingham: Institute of Judicial Administration, 1977.

General Council of the Bar. "Evidence in Criminal Cases." Memorandum on the Eleventh Report of the Criminal Law Revision Committee, 1973.

Giles. F. T. *The Magistrates' Courts*. Second Edition. London: Stevens and Sons, 1963.

Grierson, E. *Confessions of a County Magistrate*. London: Golancz, 1972.

Hain, P., Humphrey, D., and Rose, B. *Policing the Police*. London: Calder, 1979.

Hampton, C. *Criminal Procedure*. London: Sweet and Maxwell, 1977.

Heydon, J. D. "Illegally Obtained Evidence." 1973 *Criminal Law Review* 603.

______. "Obtaining Evidence Versus Protecting the Accused: Two Conflicts." 1971 *Criminal Law Review* 13.

Holdaway, S. *The British Police*. London: Arnold, 1979.

Home Office. *The Feasibility of an Experiment in the Tape-recording of Police Interrogations.*, Command 6630. London: H.M.S.O., 1976.

Hopkins, R. R. "The Function of Committal Proceedings." 1976 *Justice of the Peace* 287.

Investigation and Prosecution of Criminal Offences in England and Wales: The Law and Procedure. Command 8092-1. London: H.M.S.O., 1981.

Irving, B. *Police Interrogation: A Case Study of Current Practice*. Royal Commission on Criminal Procedure, Research Study No. 2. London: H.M.S.O., 1980.

Irving, B., and Hilgendorf, L. *Police Interrogation: The Psychological Approach*.

Royal Commission on Criminal Procedure, Research Study No. 1. London: H.M.S.O., 1980.

Israel, J. H., and LaFave, W. R. *Criminal Procedure: Constitutional Limitations.* St. Paul: West, 1980.

Jackson, R. M. *The Machinery of Justice in England.* Sixth Edition. Cambridge: Cambridge University Press, 1972.

James' Committee. *The Distribution of Criminal Business Between the Crown Court and the Magistrates' Court.* Command 6323. London: H.M.S.O., 1975.

Judicial Statistics: England and Wales 1978. Command 7627. London: H.M.S.O., 1979.

Justice. *The Interrogation of Suspects.* London: Justice, 1967.

______. *Memorandum on Eleventh Report of the Criminal Law Revision Committee.* London: Justice, 1972.

______. "Pre-trial Criminal Procedure: Police Powers and the Prosecution Process." Evidence submitted to the Royal Commission on Criminal Procedure, 1979.

______. "The Prosecution Process in England and Wales." 1970 *Criminal Law Review* 668.

Karlen, D. *Anglo-American Criminal Justice.* Oxford: Oxford University Press, 1967.

______. *Appellate Courts in the United States and England.* New York: New York University Press, 1963.

King, M. *Bail or Custody.* London: Cobden Trust, 1971.

LaFave, W. R. *Search and Seizure.* St. Paul: West, 1978.

Legal Action Group. "Legality in the Criminal Process." Evidence submitted to the Royal Commission on Criminal Procedure, 1979.

Leigh, L. H. *Police Powers in England and Wales.* London: Butterworths, 1975.

Mauet, T. A. *Fundamentals of Trial Techniques.* Boston: Little, Brown, 1980.

McConville, M., and Baldwin J. *Courts, Prosecution, and Conviction.* Oxford: Oxford University Press, 1981.

Meador, D. *Criminal Appeals: English Practices and American Reforms.* Charlottesville: University of Virginia Press, 1973.

Megarry, R. E. *Lawyer and Litigant in England.* London: Stevens and Sons, 1962.

Milner, N. A. *The Court and Local Law Enforcement: The Impact of Miranda.* Beverly Hills: Sage, 1971.

Milton, F. *In Some Authority: The English Magistracy.* London: Pall Mall Press, 1959.

Morris, P. *Police Interrogation: Review of Literature.* Royal Commission on Criminal Procedure, Research Study No. 3. London: H.M.S.O., 1980.

Morton, J. "To Combat Verbals." 1975 *New Law Journal* 830.

Napley, D. "The Case for Preliminary Inquiries." 1966 *Criminal Law Review* 490.

Pepinsky, H. E. "A Theory of Police Reaction to Miranda v. Arizona." 1970 *Crime and Delinquency* 379.

President's Commission on Law Enforcement and the Administration of Justice. *Task Force Report: The Courts.* Washington, D.C.: Government Printing Office, 1967.

Prosecuting Solicitors' Society. "Written Evidence to the Royal Commission on

Criminal Procedure: Part II Policy,'' 1979.

Royal Commission Criminal Procedure. Report. Command 8092. London: H.M.S.O., 1981.

Samuels, A. ''Commentary.'' In *The Prosecution Process*. Institute of Judicial Administration, University of Birmingham Monograph, 1975.

Scott, I. R. *The Crown Court*. London: Butterworths, 1972.

Seeburger, R. H., and Wettick, R. S. ''Miranda in Pittsburgh—A Statistical Study.'' 1967 *University of Pittsburgh Law Review* 1.

Softley, P. *Police Interrogation: An Observational Study in Four Police Stations*. Royal Commission on Criminal Procedure, Research Study No. 4. London: H.M.S.O., 1980.

Vennard, J. Contested Trials in Magistrates' Court: The Case for the Prosecution. Royal Commission on Criminal Procedure, Research Study No. 6. London: H.M.S.O., 1980.

Williams, G. ''The Power to Prosecute.'' 1955 *Criminal Law Review* 600.

______. *The Proof of Guilt: A Study of the English Criminal Trial*. Second Edition. London: Stevens and Sons, 1958.

______. ''Proposals to Expedite Criminal Trials.'' 1959 *Criminal Law Review* 82.

______. ''Questioning by the Police: Some Practical Considerations.'' 1960 *Criminal Law Review* 325.

Witt, J. W. ''Non-coercive Interrogation and the Administration of Criminal Justice: The Impact of Miranda on Police Effectuality.'' 1973 *Journal of Criminal Law and Criminology* 320.

Wootton, B. *Crime and the Criminal Law: Reflections of a Magistrate and Social Scientist*. Second Edition. London: Stevens and Sons, 1981.

Younger, E. J. ''The Impact of the Miranda and Dorado Decisions.'' 1966 *Fordham Law Review* 255.

______. ''Results of a Survey Conducted in the District Attorney's Office of Los Angeles County Regarding the Effect of the Miranda Decision upon the Prosecution of Felony Cases.'' 1966 *American Criminal Law Quarterly* 32.

Zander, M. ''Access to a Solicitor in the Police Station.'' 1972 *Criminal Law Review* 342.

INDEX

About the Author

MICHAEL H. GRAHAM brings to his present position as Professor of Law at the University of Illinois College of Law several years of experience as an attorney in New York City. In addition to a J.D. from Columbia University, he holds a Diploma in Criminology from the Institute of Criminology, Cambridge, England. He is the author of *Handbook of Federal Evidence*; *The Federal Rules of Evidence in a Nutshell*; and *Handbook of Illinois Evidence*. Research leading to *Tightening the Reins of Justice in America* was conducted while Graham was in Birmingham, England, as a Hays-Fulbright Research Fellow.